HUMAN RELATIONS

HUMAN RELATIONS

MARIE DALTON, Ed. D.
San Jacinto College
Pasadena, Texas

DAWN G. HOYLE
NASA–Johnson Space Center
Houston, Texas

MARIE W. WATTS
Equal Employment Opportunity Commission
Houston, Texas

GK40AA
PUBLISHED BY
SOUTH-WESTERN PUBLISHING CO.
CINCINNATI, OH   DALLAS, TX

Credits

Acquisitions Editor: Karen Schneiter
Developmental Editor: Penny Shank
Production Editor: Susan Freeman
Designer: Jim DeSollar
Production Artist: Sophia Renieris
Associate Photo Editor/Stylist: Linda Ellis
Photographer: Diana Fleming

Copyright © 1992
by SOUTH-WESTERN PUBLISHING CO.
Cincinnati, Ohio

Library of Congress Cataloging-in-Publication Data

Dalton, Marie.
   Human relations/Marie Dalton, Dawn G. Hoyle, Marie W. Watts.
     p.   cm.
   Includes bibliographical references and index.
   ISBN 0-538-70368-7
   1. Personnel management. 2. Communication in personnel
management. 3. Interpersonal relations. 4. Psychology, Industrial.
I. Hoyle, Dawn G., 1943–   . II. Watts, Marie W., 1950–   .
III. Title.
HF5549.D245 1992
650.1′3—dc20   91-9167
                                      CIP

ISBN: 0-538-70368-7

2 3 4 5 6 D 6 5 4 3 2

Printed in the United States of America

BRIEF CONTENTS

CONTENTS

PREFACE

Human relations is at its most dynamic today with a high level of skill required in many different topics. Examples of these are teamwork, etiquette, communications, goal setting, creativity, motivation, leadership, perception, and decision making. Also required is a concern for legal and ethical issues, wellness, change, substance abuse, and self-growth. Our goal is to help readers become successful in predicting, understanding, and influencing the outcome of their interactions. This book approaches some of the most intriguing and important aspects of human relations as seen in action in organizations and in personal lives and as appropriate for basic study in business or social sciences. It will form a solid foundation for further study in a number of disciplines. Anyone with an interest in relating more effectively to others will find this text interesting and valuable.

KEY FEATURES

Instructors and students will enjoy using this textbook because it has the following features:

1. Uses a direct, nontechnical, and interesting style
2. Emphasizes specific and practical individual action rather than general theory
3. Presents material in an easy-to-understand manner enabling students to more easily make immediate application of information discussed
4. Is written to help develop critical thinking
5. Utilizes an experiential format that actively involves students in the learning process and encourages growth—cases, discussion questions, roleplaying, and instrumented feedback
6. Includes a balanced treatment of traditional and emerging human relations topics
7. Lends itself to a variety of instructional formats and settings—from a 16-week semester to seminar-length classes and from traditional classroom to business/industry training site.

TEXT ORGANIZATION

Part One of this text, Psychology of People, presents the key foundations of the book with four chapters. Chapter 1 contains an introduction that motivates students by making clear why studying human relations is important. This chapter also provides an organizational and historical framework for the study of human relations. Chapter 2 explains how our perception of people, events, and things can determine the nature of our relationships. Chapter 3 is a comprehensive study of communications. It covers various types of communication—verbal, nonverbal, written, and listening—and explores barriers that impede communication between people. Chapter 4, Group Dynamics, stresses the evolving importance of groups at work and explores aspects of group interactions.

Part Two of the text, which includes Chapters 5 through 8, addresses the topic of Putting Human Relations to Work in a personal manner. Chapter 5 identifies organizational structures and discusses the strengths and weaknesses of the most common types of organizations. Chapter 6 is a summary of current and past thinking about why people act as they do. Chapter 7 presents a helpful, how-to oriented approach to setting and achieving objectives. Its discussion of performance appraisal is unique in that it suggests ways that employees can make this a more pleasant, useful, and growthful experience for themselves and their supervisors. With change today so much a part of society and work, no human relations book would be complete without a discussion of change dynamics. Chapter 8 does this and includes a helpful section on coaching and counseling, two additional contemporary topics.

Part Three, consisting of Chapters 9 through 12, targets The Leader and the Group. Chapter 9 covers functions and styles of leadership. Chapter 10 on sources and uses of power challenges readers to develop their own bases of power and shows them how to do this. Chapter 11—Problem Solving, Decision Making, and Creativity—suggests effective ways to solve problems and improve the quality of decisions. It also includes a lively discussion of creativity, its importance to organizational survival, and ways to foster it in ourselves and others. Chapter 12, Teambuilding, discusses the need for team concepts in the work environment and how teams can increase productivity. Several types of teams are discussed as well as how to build an effective team.

Part Four, Chapters 13 through 16, turns to legal and ethical considerations. The contemporary topics of employee rights (Chapter 13), status of unions (Chapter 14), substance abuse (Chapter 15), and guidelines for developing ethical behavior (Chapter 16) are addressed.

Part Five, made up of Chapters 17 through 20, discusses self-growth and the reader's future. Chapter 17 emphasizes the important role that etiquette plays in our success today and presents guidelines regarding the current topics of office politics, networking, mentoring, and office romances. Job-seeking skills are covered in Chapter 18, including how to look for a job, apply for it, and interview for it. The last two chapters are additional strengths of this book. Chapter 19 presents information for developing a personal wellness program, and Chapter 20 summarizes projections for the year 2000 and suggests ways of preparing for it.

Chapter Organization

This book was written to develop critical thinking. To this end each chapter is introduced with objectives that the reader should meet after studying the chapter. Throughout the chapters are activities and experiential exercises. Since human relations means interaction among people, the more participative the class can become, the more students can learn from each activity.

At the end of each chapter are summaries, key terms, review questions, discussion questions, and bibliographies as well as two case studies that can be done during class or as outside assignments. Additionally, some chapters include a suggested reading list. Marginal notes identify important information within the paragraphs. They are ideal for reviewing the chapter or finding necessary material.

Supplementary Materials

Instructor's Manual—includes chapter previews, purpose and perspective, teaching-learning suggestions, possible essay test questions, presentation outlines, definitions of key terms, suggested responses to review questions, answers to discussion questions, answers to case questions, and supplemental exercises. Additionally, because this book covers topics important in employee and supervisory development, suggested seminar outlines are included.

Test Bank—contains approximately 1,000 questions. Each chapter has 25 true-false questions, 15 multiple choice questions, and 10 fill-in-the-blank questions. The test bank is available in both printed and microcomputer (MicroSwat III) versions.

Teaching Masters—to be used with the supplementary activities.

ACKNOWLEDGMENTS

Many people have contributed to the development of this text. For their helpful suggestions as reviewers of the original manuscript, we are especially grateful to the following individuals:

Mildred J. Blowen, Vice President, PTI, Inc., Houston, Texas
Maxine Gross Christenson, Aims Community College, Greeley, Colorado
Lucy Guin, Director of Education for Proprietary Schools, Houston, Texas
Charles R. Holloman, Augusta College, Augusta, Georgia
F. Stuart Keene, President, PTI, Inc., Houston, Texas
Richard C. Kogelman, Delta College, University Center, Michigan
Patricia Laidler, Massasoit Community College, Brockton, Massachusetts
Gloria McDonnell, Kingsborough Community College, Brooklyn, New York
Marilyn Price, Kirkwood Community College, Cedar Rapids, Iowa
Carla Rich, Pensacola Junior College, Pensacola, Florida
Connie Roberts, Central Washington University, Ellensburg, Washington
Beverly Stitt, Southern Illinois University, Carbondale, Illinois
Peter Venuto, Bloomsburg University, Bloomsburg, Pennsylvania

Emily Volavka, Southern Ohio College, Fairfield, Ohio
Darlene Waite, Miami-Jacobs College of Business, Dayton, Ohio
Arlene White, Texas State Technical Institute, Waco, Texas

Finally, and most important, we offer our gratitude to our past and present students who helped clarify our thinking of what a human relations book should be and to future students and faculty who use this book as a reference and learning aid. Have a pleasant journey in getting to know yourselves and others!

Marie Dalton
Dawn Hoyle
Marie Watts

PART ONE

PSYCHOLOGY OF PEOPLE

CHAPTER ONE
INTRODUCTION TO HUMAN RELATIONS

Why are certain people successful? Doris Lee McCoy undertook to answer this question by interviewing more than one thousand of the most successful people today. Among the qualities consistently found in the lives of successful people and reported in her 1988 book, *Megatraits*, was mutually winning relationships. One of the persons interviewed pointed out that self-respect leads to respecting others. Adds the author, "Many of those I interviewed expressed their beliefs that an important element in success is ensuring that both parties benefit from any transaction or relationship, whether business or pleasure . . . where everyone wins." (p. 7)

OBJECTIVES

After studying this chapter, you should be able to:
1. Explain the meaning of human relations.
2. Discuss the importance of human relations.
3. Trace the development of human relations in business.
4. Explain the purpose of organizations, what causes change within organizations, and the role human relations plays in organizations.
5. Identify how you can contribute to the objectives of an organization and how the study of human relations will help you succeed in your career.

WHAT IS HUMAN RELATIONS?

Human rela-
tions, the study
of relationships
among people,
helps us work
effectively with
others.

Human relations is the study of relationships among people. The relationships can develop in an organizational or personal setting and can be formal or informal, close or distant, conflicting or cooperating, and emotional or unemotional. In an organization human relations includes the study of people, their behavior, and their relationships in order to match individuals' goals and objectives with organizational goals and objectives. Relationships on the job may be with subordinates, coworkers, supervisors or other superiors, or clients and customers. At home relationships exist with parents, friends, siblings, children, and spouses. Groups also form relationships. The major reason for studying human relations is to learn to work more effectively with others.

Human relations involves an understanding of the psychology of ourselves and others, the use of effective communication skills, and an appreciation for groups and

FIGURE 1.1   Human relations skills are an important part of work.

their dynamics. Knowledge of motivation and morale, goal setting and job performance, management of change, sources and uses of power, problem solving and decision making, creativity, team building, and legal and ethical considerations are also crucial elements in strong human relations skills.

WHY IS HUMAN RELATIONS IMPORTANT?

Effective use of human relations skills results in greater productivity for the company and greater satisfaction for employees. Companies that attempt to provide fair and just treatment of all employees and to fulfill both personal and organization goals will normally be more successful than organizations that do not. These organizations usually have less conflict, fewer errors in the work product, less illness and absenteeism, lower employee turnover, and higher morale.

Human relations becomes increasingly important as our economy evolves. We are moving from an economy that produces goods to one that provides services and is information-based. This type of economy requires employees to communicate and interact in complex situations, as we will see.

An example of the importance of human relations in complex situations appeared in *The Wall Street Journal* in late 1989. A cereal company president was fired, and a failure of management "chemistry" was cited by the company's chairman and chief executive officer. The *Journal* reported that some employees viewed the president as demanding, abrasive, and often unwilling to listen.

As shown in Figure 1.2, human relations skills will remain consistently important throughout your career. Many individuals lose their jobs or fail to be promoted,

FIGURE 1.2   Human relations skills remain consistently important throughout our careers.

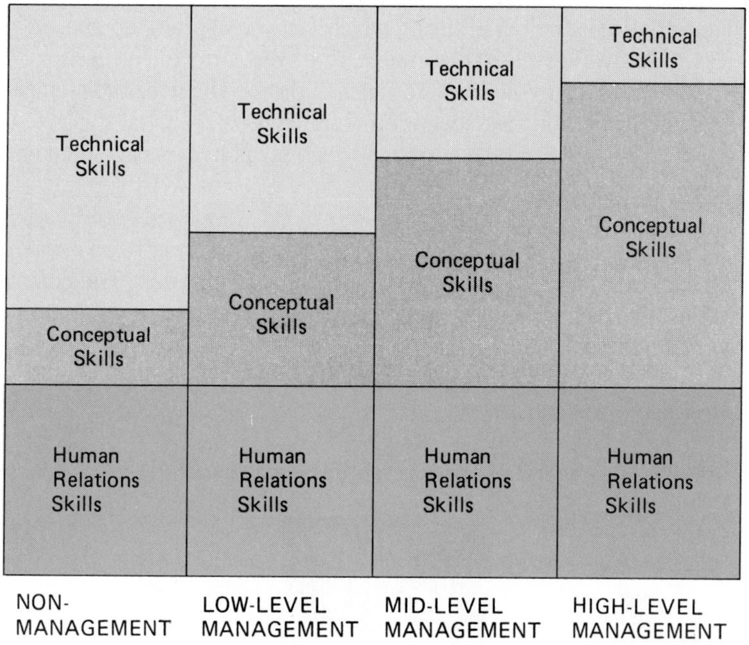

NON-MANAGEMENT	LOW-LEVEL MANAGEMENT	MID-LEVEL MANAGEMENT	HIGH-LEVEL MANAGEMENT

not because they cannot do the job, but because they cannot get along with others. For this reason human relations skills are as important as technical skills. A better quality of work life will result when you, your coworkers, and supervisors use good human relations skills. Practicing the techniques in this book will increase your awareness of your own needs and those of others and the organization in which you work.

Human relations is important to individuals for another reason. The average worker will make three major career changes throughout life. These changes may require different technical skills. However, because few people today work in isolation, all positions require similar human relations skills. Persons with these skills and the necessary technical skills will be in great demand.

HOW DID HUMAN RELATIONS DEVELOP?

To understand how the importance of human relations in organizations was uncovered, we must look at the history of the United States economy and management practices. During the 1700s Americans were primarily farmers and craftspeople who lived in rural areas. People, for the most part, grew their own food and made their own supplies. Craftspeople made goods to supplement what the farmers were unable to produce themselves.

This era, known as the Agricultural Era, came to an end in 1782 with the invention of the steam engine. This machine revolutionized work because it provided a cheap source of power to run factories. During the 1800s the United States shifted into the Industrial Era, during which factories sprang up and towns grew.

As workers began to move from the farm to the factory, factory managers realized that they needed to manage the behavior of their employees to increase productivity. The early twentieth century was the most dynamic period ever in the history of work, and the period in which studies of management and worker relationships began.

The invention of the computer in the 1950s ushered in a new age, called the High Tech or **Information Age.** This age is characterized by increasingly large and complex organizations and better-informed employees. The complexity of organizations and heightened expectations of employees have made human relations skills even more important. This importance will increase as world economies become more global and work forces more interactive. The Information Age will be discussed in Chapters 8 and 20.

> Studies of management-worker relationships began during the Industrial Era.

FIGURE 1.3   The Information Age requires strong human relations skills.

Optel Communications, Inc.

What Studies Came First?

The search for new management techniques began with a base in the social sciences—psychology, sociology, and anthropology. These studies deal with the institutions and functioning of society and the interpersonal relationships of individuals as members of society.

Psychology is the most influential of the disciplines because it focuses on the behavior of individuals. The discipline of industrial psychology looks specifically at such subjects as motivation, leadership, decision making, and uses of power within the organization.

Sociology also plays an important part in the study of managing individuals. It centers on the interaction of two or more individuals and their relationships in group settings. Understanding these relationships is vital because the organization consists of small groups.

Anthropology, which focuses on the origins and development of various cultures, also has contributed to the development of management techniques. It will increase in importance as our work force becomes more multicultural and our economy more global, interacting with nations that do not share our values and practices.

In studying human relations, we are concerned with why individuals and groups behave the way they do. Another area of importance is determining what can be done to improve their interactions.

Armed with knowledge from the three disciplines of psychology, sociology, and anthropology, people began to study how to increase productivity at work. Their studies resulted in different and distinct ways of treating employees. Their efforts have been divided into three schools of management: classical, behavioral, and management science. Figure 1.4 shows these three schools of management theory. Each developed at a different time in American history.

FIGURE 1.4   Schools of management theory.

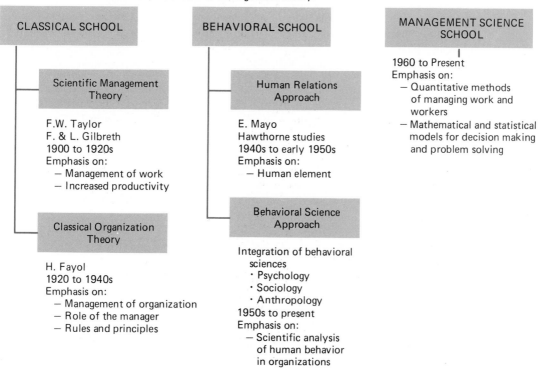

CLASSICAL SCHOOL

Scientific Management Theory

F.W. Taylor
F. & L. Gilbreth
1900 to 1920s
Emphasis on:
— Management of work
— Increased productivity

Classical Organization Theory

H. Fayol
1920 to 1940s
Emphasis on:
— Management of organization
— Role of the manager
— Rules and principles

BEHAVIORAL SCHOOL

Human Relations Approach

E. Mayo
Hawthorne studies
1940s to early 1950s
Emphasis on:
— Human element

Behavioral Science Approach

Integration of behavioral sciences
· Psychology
· Sociology
· Anthropology
1950s to present
Emphasis on:
— Scientific analysis
  of human behavior
  in organizations

MANAGEMENT SCIENCE SCHOOL

1960 to Present
Emphasis on:
— Quantitative methods
  of managing work and
  workers
— Mathematical and statistical
  models for decision making
  and problem solving

The Classical School of Management

The **classical school of management** was the first. It focused on the technical efficiency of work. Often managers tried to increase output of products and services without concern for the workers. Two different branches of the classical school of management evolved. One, **scientific management theory**, focused on the management of work itself; the other, **classical organization theory**, focused on the management of the organization as a whole.

Scientific Management Theory   Scientific management theory was begun in the early 1900s by Frederick W. Taylor. Taylor was a self-taught engineer who began his career as a laborer at the Midvale Steel Company and later became its chief engineer. He believed that tasks could be scientifically analyzed and structured so that they could be performed more efficiently. For instance, he discovered that changing the shape of a shovel resulted in more coal being moved with the same amount of effort. His work earned him the title of "Father of Scientific Management."

Taylor believed that maximum productivity could only be achieved through the cooperation of management and labor and that everyone would share in the increased profits. His work was criticized by those who felt it increased profits without increasing worker wages and benefits and dehumanized the workplace even further.

Frank and Lillian Gilbreth, a husband and wife team, also contributed heavily to scientific management theory. Whereas Taylor attempted to speed up the worker (time), the Gilbreths tried to shorten the work (motion). The combination of these two ideas resulted in the famous "time and motion" studies that became a popular means of improving productivity. The Gilbreths used still and motion photography to identify the distinct steps required to do a task and then deleted the nonessential ones.

Classical Organization Theory   As more studies were done, emphasis shifted from viewing the work itself to viewing the management of the organization as a whole. This view is known as classical organization theory. The first person to gain recognition in this area was French industrialist Henri Fayol, who in 1916 published *General and Industrial Management.*

For the first time management was viewed with a holistic belief that human relations, productivity, and the general administration of the organization could be improved by applying basic principles. Fayol's fourteen basic principles of management define division of work, authority, discipline, chain of command, and other concepts still used in management today.

The Behavioral School of Management

By the late 1920s the **behavioral school of management** had begun as managers continued to look for ways to improve productivity. Many felt that the views of the classical school of management theorists were too authoritarian and task-oriented and were contributing to widespread employee dissatisfaction. Employees were beginning to unionize to protect their rights and stand together to demand a more

Side notes:

Frederick W. Taylor is the "Father of Scientific Management."

Taylor concentrated on speed; the Gilbreths studied motion.

Fayol developed 14 basic principles of management.

humane environment. The Depression, followed by the boom of the post–World War II economy, boosted this concern.

The behavioral school also has two branches: the human relations approach and the behavioral science approach. Each is discussed below.

Human Relations Approach   Changes in corporate America, such as unions demanding employee rights and the growing size of corporations, helped begin the **human relations approach**. An important study done during this period was led by Elton Mayo. His work earned him recognition as the "Father of Human Relations" and led to the development of the human relations approach branch of the behavioral school.

Elton Mayo is the "Father of Human Relations."

Mayo and a group of researchers from Harvard Business School conducted a study of the impact of physical working conditions on worker output. The research was done at Western Electric's Hawthorne plant near Chicago, so the studies later became known as the Hawthorne studies.

A small group of workers was isolated in a separate room of the plant where their day-to-day activities could be monitored by the research team. The workers were interviewed and allowed to say how they felt about their workplace, work conditions, and the job in general. Then for two years their productivity, behavior, and attitudes were observed under a variety of conditions.

The researchers found that regardless of changes—such as heating, humidity, lighting, work hours, rest periods, and supervisory styles—productivity levels increased significantly. Finally, the researchers realized that productivity increased because the workers were receiving attention and felt that someone cared about them.

The Hawthorne effect: the human element is more important to productivity than technical or physical aspects of the job.

The idea that the human element is more important to productivity than the technical or physical aspects of the job became known as the **Hawthorne effect**. Managers began to pay more attention to the emotional needs of workers, making human relations more important to the organization.

Behavioral Science Approach   In the mid- to late 1950s researchers began to use scientific methods, such as controlled experiments, sample surveys, and case studies, to explore efficient management techniques. This approach became known as the **behavioral science approach**. These studies were done on both workers and managers for a total view of human behavior in the workplace. During the behavioral science period, management studies began to combine psychology, sociology, and anthropology to increase understanding of the organizational environment.

The Management Science School of Management

The **management science school** began during World War II. Both the British and U.S. military needed to solve complex problems, such as coordinating massive troop movements and seeing that supplies arrived at appropriate places and in correct quantities. The military enlisted the help of mathematicians, physicists, and other scientists. The results were so successful that the techniques developed were later used by companies to solve complex business problems.

Two statistical
models to help
planning and
control are
PERT and CPM.

The computer increased the use of management sciences and made **statistical models** easier to use. Models are analytical tools that help managers with the planning and controlling of organizational activities. Examples of models developed by this school of management are the **Program Evaluation and Review Technique (PERT)** and the **Critical Path Method (CPM)**.

PERT is frequently used when a major project to be finished by a contract deadline is made up of many separate activities or steps, each of which requires a certain amount of time to complete. Usually one activity must be completed before another can be started. A PERT chart assists in coordinating these activities. PERT charts can be used for projects ranging from planning the company Christmas party to building a new corporate headquarters and moving employees to it. Figure 1.5 shows a PERT chart.

FIGURE 1.5   PERT charts assist managers in coordinating activities.

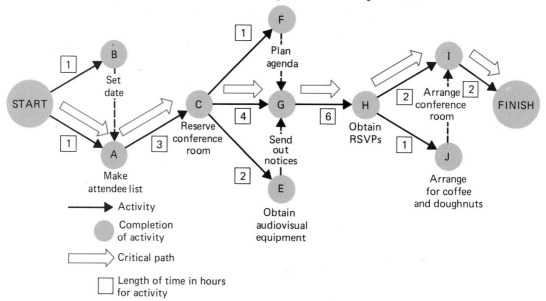

The critical path is the sequence of activities in a PERT chart requiring the longest time for completion. It will show the minimum time needed to complete a project.

Today computer models assist managers in making decisions. For instance, a model can predict how many units the company is likely to sell at a certain price. The computer is not infallible and cannot make decisions. It is merely a tool for managers' use.

Management Techniques Used Today

Today's effective organizations respect the organization principles of the classical school, the importance of the person in the behavioral school, and the models of the management science school. They draw from all three of these schools, choosing the techniques that best fit the situation. Research continues for ways to improve productivity.

WHAT FACTORS INFLUENCE HUMAN RELATIONS IN ORGANIZATIONS?

An important part of using effective human relations at work is knowing how we fit into the overall organization. The quality and type of interaction among individuals and how it changes in organizations is influenced by many factors. They include goals, cultures, conflicts between departments, and outside influences.

Different organizations have different goals and objectives. Even those organizations with similar goals may have different cultures. Within organizations different groups with different purposes may develop conflicts. Also, outside influences can change the nature and purpose of business and influence existing relationships.

Being aware of the goals of your organization and the changes that can occur within it is vital. Such awareness will assist you in using your human relations skills to adapt to changes that are occurring more rapidly than ever before.

Purpose of Organizations

Any organization has specific goals. A primary goal of business is to make a profit. These profits can be earned by providing goods or services. If a profit is not made, the business will fail.

Government and nonprofit organizations do not seek to make a profit, but they still have the goal of providing a service. They must provide a service that the public needs and wants at a price the public can afford. These organizations, like business, labor under budget constraints; what they can spend is limited by taxes collected (in the case of government organizations) or contributions received (in the case of many nonprofit organizations). To function adequately, government and other nonprofit organizations must practice the same management and cost-saving concepts that private enterprise uses.

Being aware of the purpose of your organization can help you understand why certain decisions are made and actions taken. Strong human relations skills can help you function more effectively, adapt, and cope with changes that occur while your organization is trying to meet its goals.

Organizational Culture

Organizational culture: a mix of the beliefs and values of society, workers, and the organization's leaders and founders.

According to Terrence Deal and Allan Kennedy in *Corporate Cultures—The Rites and Rituals of Corporate Life,* organizations, even those in the same industry, are different. Each has its own distinct culture. **Organizational culture** can be defined as a mix of the beliefs and values of society at large, the individuals who work in the organization, and the organization's leaders and founders. The culture determines what goals the organization wants to accomplish and how it will go about accomplishing them.

Some organizations have strong values that are expressed. Some examples of expressed values are:

The Girl Scouts—"Do a good turn daily"

DuPont—"Better things for better living through chemistry"

Caterpillar—"Twenty-four hour parts and service anywhere in the world"

Sears, Roebuck—"Quality at a good price"

Unfortunately, other cultural norms are not openly communicated, but must be learned. Organizations, for instance, may have heroes—people with the beliefs, attitudes, and behavior that the organization wishes to reinforce. These people with the "right stuff" are identified as persons after whom employees should model themselves. Disney Productions, for example, reflected Walt Disney's values.

Behavior standards are not uncommon. These standards may include unwritten rules concerning dress codes, formats for meetings, language standards for interpersonal communication, decision-making styles, and activities in which employees participate off the job.

Other organizations have rituals and rites. For instance, Mary Kay Cosmetics is known for its seminars that founder Mary Kay Ash has described as a combination of the Miss America pageant, the Academy Awards, and an opening on Broadway. The top salespersons are awarded diamonds, Cadillacs, and minks.

The following anecdote illustrates how behavior may vary from one organization to another:

> **Jules started to work for TS, Inc., a chair manufacturing company, and immediately noticed differences between TS, Inc., and his former employer, Recliner Heaven. At TS, Inc., no one takes a lunch break. Employees work through lunch and snack at their desks. Also, relationships are informal. No one knocks before entering an office, and everyone shares ideas and gives advice and suggestions to coworkers. Rank does not entitle anyone to special office furniture or to a corner office with a view. Birthdays are important and the company holds a monthly party complete with cake and ice cream for the birthday persons of the month.**
>
> **Jules has a complete closet of three-piece suits that he wore every day at Recliner Heaven. However, at TS, Inc., employees dress in slacks and sweaters.**

Good human relations skills can help you learn the cultural norms of companies in which you work. Armed with this knowledge, you can cope more effectively with the expectations of the organization.

Special Functions Exist within the Organization

Organizations have formal structures that help them carry out their goals and objectives. Because one person cannot perform all functions of a large organization, duties are delegated to individuals or groups of individuals. Understanding that departments must work together to avoid or reduce conflicting objectives is important.

The basic functions of an organization are marketing and sales, production, finance, human resources, and accounting. In each, knowledge of human relations can reduce problems.

Marketing and Sales   The **marketing and sales** department decides what types of products and services are salable and which sector of the market desires them. The marketing function is also responsible for the selling, advertising, and distribution of products and services to customers. Employees in marketing and sales need effective human relations skills in understanding goals of the organization for which they work, in communicating with clients and customers, and in coordinating their work with others in their organization.

Production   The **production** sector is responsible for actually producing goods or performing services. Raw materials must be purchased and goods manufactured. Many decisions, such as the layout of a factory, must be made by this division.

Teamwork is an element of human relations extremely important to production. People must work together effectively if deadlines are to be met and quality maintained. Other elements of special importance include motivation, morale, goal setting, job performance, problem solving, and decision making.

Finance   The **finance** department helps make decisions about how the business should be financed. Is money borrowed? Will stock be issued? What insurance and how much should be purchased?

Important to employees in finance is an ability to listen and communicate effectively in order to make recommendations and decisions appropriate for the organization.

Human Resources (Personnel)   The responsibility for hiring and training the employees of a company rests with the **human resources** (or personnel) department. This department is also responsible for salary and benefit decisions and monitoring to ensure that the organization abides by various regulations concerning employees. Human relations skills are necessary to handle confidential information and legal and ethical matters.

Accounting   The **accounting** department is in charge of keeping track of money that comes in and leaves the organization. The department produces reports on the financial position of the company and prepares budgets for future spending. An element of human relations particularly important in accounting is communication, both verbal in working with others and written in compiling reports.

Often these parts of an organization will have different goals. For instance, the accounting department may be concerned with seeing that an accurate account of inventory is kept, while the production department is concerned with completing its work on time and cannot see the importance of filling out routine forms accurately. If you are to function effectively at work, you must recognize the needs of others in the organization and respect what they are trying to accomplish as a part of overall organizational goals. The development of sound human relations skills will help you.

Outside Forces at Work

All organizations, profit and nonprofit, are vulnerable to their environments. If they do not adjust to these environments, they will lose jobs or go out of business. Human relations skills can assist the individual in adapting to and understanding these changes. Discussed below are eight environments that may affect a business. TS, Inc., our fictitious chair manufacturing concern owned by Tran and Susan, is used to illustrate their effects.

Economic Environment   Many changes in the economic environment can affect organizations. The price of raw materials may rise dramatically because of a large strike or a natural disaster. A general recession may cause people to postpone luxury spending and save their money for more basic purchases, such as food and shelter. The interest rate may rise, making borrowing money to expand or improve organizations more expensive. Another business may open down the street and sell its product for less or provide better service.

Here is how the economic environment may affect TS, Inc.:

> **TS, Inc., has been selling chairs for $50 each to the Rock Away Store, which, in turn, sells the chair to the consumer for $70. A new chair factory has entered the market and has begun to sell its chairs, which are similar to TS, Inc.'s, for $40. Susan has just been informed by the owner of Rock Away that he will not order as many chairs from her next month because he is unable to sell them. Customers are buying the new chairs, which Rock Away is selling for $60. Susan and Tran must now decide what to do. Will they drop their price? Can they afford to do so and give the raise that they promised their employees? Will they lay off employees because of the reduced demand?**

Legal-Political Environment   An increase in taxes may limit the funds available for salaries and expansion. Road construction in front of a place of business may dampen sales. A change in export regulations may slow foreign sales of some corporations. New environmental regulations may require costly changes in manufacturing processes. These are the types of changes brought about by the legal-political environment. The legal-political environment may affect TS, Inc., in this way:

> **TS, Inc., is monitoring the activities of the Consumer Product Safety Commission. The Commission is investigating the number of deaths that have allegedly been caused by the new, space-age, high-tech "Arwi" chair. The chair, which has special electrical outlets, has been named in a number of electrocutions. New standards have been proposed for these chairs to reduce accidents. TS, Inc., produces these chairs and, if the new standards are adopted, will have to change materials and method of construction to conform to the new regulations.**

Socio-Cultural Environment   Consumer tastes fluctuate in the socio-cultural environment. Items that have been in demand may soon not interest consumers.

Numerous earlier products are no longer popular. The mustache cup, hoop skirt, black-and-white television, and pocket watch are just a few examples.

Here is one way the socio-cultural environment affects TS, Inc.:

> **TS, Inc., found a great deal on red paint and purchased ten thousand gallons of it. However, the sales of red chairs have dramatically decreased. Consumers now want blue chairs. Tran must decide what he is going to do with the red paint.**

Changing Technology   Changing technology may cause a product or service to become obsolete. The automobile, for instance, led to the near extinction of companies that built carriages, shod horses, and produced harnesses and saddles. At the same time it created new industries dedicated to the production of automobiles and automobile accessories, the servicing of the automobile (such as car washes and gasoline stations), and the construction of roads and bridges for automobile travel.

TS, Inc., can be affected by changing technology in this way:

> **A new, space-age material has been developed. It is more durable than plastic, has the look and feel of wood, and is less expensive than either. Tran must now decide whether TS, Inc., will begin to use this new material. The cost to convert the factory will be enormous.**

Unexpected Disasters   Unexpected disasters can change the course of a business. A fire or tornado can disrupt business. Many companies have recently struggled to handle calamities. The explosion in midair of the Challenger spacecraft, the discharge of poisonous gas at the Union Carbide plant in India, various airline crashes, and the Tylenol poisonings are examples of tragedies with which organizations have had to cope.

The following scenario is an example of how TS, Inc., can be affected by unexpected disasters:

> **On February 23, a heavy rain caused the roof of the TS, Inc., warehouse to collapse. The recliners that were scheduled for shipment to Rock Away on the 25th were ruined. Susan now must place an emergency order for new raw materials to replace the shipment and must schedule overtime to construct new recliners as quickly as possible.**

Corporate Mergers and Sales   When corporations are bought or merged, the new management may find that it has too many employees who perform similar work. The result is that some of the work force may be laid off.

Here is what could happen at TS, Inc.:

> **A factory has just opened down the street and has made an offer to purchase TS, Inc. The new factory has a large sales force and will not need those salespersons who work for TS, Inc. The consolidation will cause a loss of jobs.**

Management Changes   Mergers, sales, and growth of organizations bring changes in management. Managers retire or leave the company and new managers take their place. These new persons inevitably bring a change in philosophy and work methods.

TS, Inc., can also be affected by management changes:

> **Susan and Tran have found that the factory is becoming too large to handle and have hired Jose to manage the accounting section. Jose is a fanatic about punctuality. Tran did not mind when employees were ten to fifteen minutes late, but Jose does. He has begun issuing written warnings to tardy employees and has told those who are late that they will be terminated if they do not improve.**

Global Economy   The world now operates in a global economy. This means that no longer does the economy of one nation stand alone; all are closely intertwined. What happens in one economy may have immediate effects on the economy of another country. Additionally, goods may be produced as the output of a combination of economies. Workers in Asia or Mexico may be able to produce certain goods less expensively than United States workers, causing businesses to move their factories outside the United States or to have one or more phases of the work done in different parts of the world.

Here is how TS, Inc., can be affected by the global economy:

> **The purchasing agent for Rock Away Stores has just told Susan that he had a call from a salesman whose company is producing recliners in Mexico. These recliners are available to Rock Away at $100. TS, Inc., charges Rock Away $150 for a similar recliner.**

Another way in which the global economy affects human relations is the increasing need to interact with people of many different nations with a sensitivity to and acceptance of their customs, values, and attitudes. The global economy will be discussed in greater detail in Chapter 20.

WHAT ARE YOUR RESPONSIBILITIES?

Employees should be flexible, retrain, and learn human relations skills.

Employees have a responsibility to assist the organization in accomplishing its purposes and goals. Having the necessary skills, understanding your objectives, accomplishing them as well as possible with the least expense and fuss, and making others' jobs easier by carrying your own weight are how you do that. Human relations skills are essential. An employee who does not assist in helping the organization grow and prosper will not be a valued member of the team.

Contributing to the Organization

You can contribute to your organization by performing your job well. Knowing your job tasks, using effective human relations, and being polite and helpful to customers are of the utmost importance. Ignoring or being rude to a customer may cause the shopper to go down the street to another business to trade. Peters and Waterman in their book, *In Search of Excellence*, point out that one key to business success is

FIGURE 1.6 Environments that can tug on business organizations.

superior customer service. A study for the White House Office of Consumer Affairs found that 96 percent of unhappy customers never complain about discourtesy, but up to 91 percent never return. Additionally, the average unhappy customer will tell at least 9 other people about the discourtesy, and 13 percent will tell more than 20 people.

FIGURE 1.7 One key to business success is superior customer service.

THE WIZARD OF ID   by Brant parker and Johnny hart

By permission of Johnny Hart and NAS, Inc.

Another way in which you can contribute to your organization is through effective communication. Communication with subordinates and supervisors is crucial to your performance. If you do not understand an assignment, you should ask for clarification. If you know that you will not meet a required deadline, let your supervisor know as soon as possible. Doing your work the way the supervisor wants, not the way you think it should be done, is vital. If your supervisor gives you instructions to do the assignment in the manner that you think best, which will probably happen once you have acquired experience and have demonstrated your responsibility, then you may do it your own way. Most organizations have room for honest discussion on the best way to approach a task. However, when the supervisor has made a decision following discussion, employees should comply with these guidelines.

Being Flexible

Flexibility is crucial. Employees should follow orders that their supervisors issue and cooperate if asked to assist other workers or help with tasks not specifically assigned to them. When the time comes for a layoff and choices must be made, which employee will the company lay off—the cooperative, helpful one or the one who is always complaining and refusing to help?

This willingness is particularly important today. A 1989 Report of the President pointed out that the proportion of employment in small-business–dominated industries is increasing while the proportion of employment in large-business–dominated industries is falling. This growth is shown in Figure 1.8. For small businesses to grow, they require the flexibility of a cooperative employee.

FIGURE 1.8 Employment growth in small and large businesses, June 1987 to June 1988.

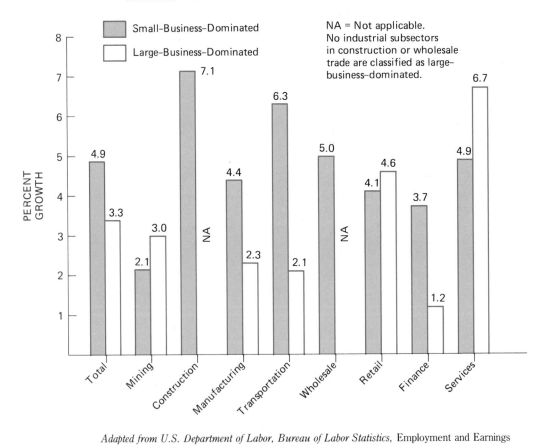

Adapted from U.S. Department of Labor, Bureau of Labor Statistics, Employment and Earnings *(Washington, DC: U.S. Government Printing Office, August 1988).*

We must all be willing to retrain. As technology changes, the work force will be called on to do different jobs. According to *Worklife Visions*, by Jeffrey Hallett, 50 percent of the actual jobs performed in 1987 did not exist in 1967. The rate of change will increase, and by 2007 almost all work will be new. In addition, 33 percent of all jobs in existence in 1987 will be obsolete by 1992. The implication is that employees will need to learn new skills at an increasing rate. Even though technology changes, human relations skills will continue to be vital.

Personal Needs Sometimes Clash with Corporate Needs

Individuals work for different reasons. Money, social relationships, power, prestige, status, and growth are only a few of the motives. Sometimes the needs and styles of the individual and the corporation clash.

As an employee you must understand yourself and your own wants and needs and be aware of the unwritten rules in your organization. Often you must play a role. For instance, you may prefer to wear blue jeans every day, but if the unwritten rule is to wear a nice dress or slacks, then you should adapt to this standard. People unable to meet organizational expectations may not function well or thrive professionally in that particular environment and should probably consider finding a position that is more in line with their values.

Jobs today do not last forever. Technology comes and goes and businesses open and close. However, the skills of human relations can be used in any setting and can prove indispensable in adapting to the changing world.

SUMMARY

Human relations is the study of relationships among people. The major reason for studying human relations is to learn to work more effectively with others.

Organizations value employees with effective human relations skills because these skills can result in greater productivity. For individuals knowledge of human relations is important in increasing their sensitivity to the needs of themselves, others, and the organization. All jobs require some human relations skills. The need for human relations became obvious once workers moved from the farm to the factory, where managers were increasingly concerned about productivity. Today's Information Age, with its large and complex organizations, better-informed employees, and global economies, increases the need for human relations skills.

The study of human relations involves knowledge of psychology, sociology, and anthropology. Various individuals, armed with knowledge from these disciplines, have looked for ways to increase productivity at work. Their efforts are divided into three schools of management: classical, behavioral, and management science. The classical school includes scientific management theory and classical organization theory. The behavioral school of management includes the human relations approach and behavioral science approach. The management science approach contributed statistical models used in planning and control. Today's effective organizations draw from all three schools of management.

Human relations in organizations can be influenced by numerous factors. One such factor is purpose. Awareness of an organization's purpose helps employees understand decisions and actions. Another factor influencing human relations in organizations is organizational culture. Knowledge of and respect for that culture is a part of human relations. A third factor is function within an organization. The basic functions of an organization are marketing and sales, production, finance, human resources, and accounting. Knowledge of human relations is important in all of them. Outside forces can also influence human relations. These forces can include the economic environment, legal-political environment, socio-cultural environment, changing technology, unexpected disasters, corporate mergers and sales, management changes, and the global economy. Strong human relations skills can help individuals adapt to these changes when they occur.

Employees have the responsibility to assist their organization in accomplishing its purpose and goals. They can contribute by having the necessary technical and human relations skills. Communication, flexibility, and constant retraining are important, along with a desire to meet organizational expectations. Developing solid human relations skills will help you adapt to rapidly changing technology and circumstances.

KEY TERMS

human relations
Information Age
psychology
sociology
anthropology
classical school of management
scientific management theory
classical organization theory
behavioral school of management
human relations approach
Hawthorne effect
behavioral science approach
management science school of management
statistical models
Program Evaluation and Review Technique (PERT)
Critical Path Method (CPM)
organizational culture

marketing and sales function
production function
finance function
human resources function
accounting function

REVIEW QUESTIONS

1. Explain the meaning of human relations.
2. Why is human relations important in business? What do you think would happen to a business that did not use effective human relations skills?
3. List the three schools of management and tell what they contributed to the study of organizations.
4. What is the purpose of an organization?
5. What can cause changes in an organization?
6. Explain how you can contribute to an organization.

DISCUSSION QUESTIONS

1. Identify some situations from home and work in which poor human relations skills were used. What happened? How could the situation have been improved?
2. Compare the three behavioral sciences (psychology, anthropology, and sociology). How do they differ? What does each contribute to the study of organizations?
3. Name the three schools of management theory and explain why they evolved?
4. Discuss the job skills needed in the Agricultural Era, the Industrial Era, and the Information Age. How are they different? How are they the same?
5. What changes are taking place in your community that affect local businesses? Identify the environment that causes the change.

TROUBLE IN TOYLAND

Tom is the production supervisor for a small company that manufactures children's board games. He has four employees.

Jane is 18 years old and this is her first job.

Alice is 32 years old and has been with the company three years. She has been absent frequently because of an ill child.

Alberto is 44 years old with ten years of service. Alberto spends quite a bit of time in the restroom.

Fujio is 53 years old and has been with the company two years. He is Tom's most productive worker.

Tom has been having trouble with machine one, and it has been producing dice with incorrect dots on them. In addition, the work space is organized so that the workers have to carry the dice 100 feet from the end of the machine that produces them to the loading docks. They have been carrying the dice in small baskets. They are so busy carrying dice that they forget to tend to the other machines.

In addition, Tom never seems to have the correct amount of raw materials. He always finds that he is missing paint or plastic on the day that he wants to produce the red-and-white dice.

Tom's production has fallen lately. He is producing less, and it is of lower quality.

Estelle, Corporate Vice President of Production, has been told by her boss that she has six months to improve production or the company will be forced to close. Estelle calls Tom into the office and shuts the door.

1. What do you think Estelle will tell Tom?
2. Identify the problems Estelle needs to correct. Which management schools may provide ideas to assist Estelle in solving which problems?
3. Identify the problems Tom needs to correct. Which management schools may provide ideas to assist Tom in solving which problems?

CASE STUDY 1.2

COMPUTER CRISIS

"I'm really upset about the election, Margaret," said John, the president of a computer manufacturing company. "That group elected to Congress is serious about restricting exports to foreign countries. I wonder what that will do to our sales?"

"I know," said Margaret. "I'm even more worried about the less expensive foreign versions of our computers that are coming out. I'm afraid customers will no longer want our model."

"You're right," replied John. "Those worries plus the fact that the technology is changing so fast that our computer will be in a museum in several years are enough to make anybody's hair turn gray!"

1. What environments are affecting the computer company?
2. What changes might the company have to make in order to stay in business?
3. What human relations skills will the managers need to adapt to these changes? The employees?

BIBLIOGRAPHY

Bittel, Lester R., Ronald S. Burke, and Lawrence LaForge. *Business in Action*. New York: McGraw-Hill, 1984.

Bittel, Lester R., and J. E. Ramsey, eds. *Handbook for Professional Managers*. New York: McGraw-Hill, 1985.

Burke, Ronald S., and Lester R. Bittel. *Introduction to Management Practice*. New York: McGraw-Hill, 1981.

Culligan, Matthew J., et al. *Back to Basics Management*. New York: Facts on File, 1983.

Deal, Terrence E., and Allen A. Kennedy. ***Corporate Cultures—The Rites and Rituals of Corporate Life***. Reading, MA: Addison-Wesley Publishing Company, 1982.

Fayol, Henri. ***General and Industrial Management***. Trans. Constance Storrf. London: Sir Isaac Pitman and Sons, Ltd., 1949.

Gibson, Richard. "Personal 'Chemistry' Abruptly Ended Rise of Kellogg President." ***The Wall Street Journal*** 84, no. 104 (November 28, 1989): AI.

Glos, Raymond E., Richard D. Steade, and James R. Lowery. ***Business—Its Nature and Environment***. Cincinnati: South-Western Publishing Co., 1980.

Hallett, Jeffrey. ***Worklife Visions***. Alexandria, VA: American Society for Personnel Administrators, 1987.

McCoy, Doris Lee. ***Megatraits—12 Traits of Successful People***. Plano, TX: Wordware Publishing, Inc., 1988.

Mayo, Elton. ***The Human Problems of an Industrial Civilization***. New York: Macmillan Publishing Company, 1934.

Ost, Edward. "Pursuit of Reality: The Road to Excellence." ***Personnel Administrator*** (January 1986): 51.

Peters, Thomas J., and Robert H. Waterman, Jr. ***In Search of Excellence***. New York: Warner Books, Inc., 1982.

The State of Small Business—A Report of the President. Transmitted to the Congress 1989. Washington, DC: U.S. Government Printing Office, 1989.

Taylor, Frederick W. ***Principles of Management***. New York: Harper and Brothers, 1911.

SUGGESTED READINGS

Farmer, Richard N. ***Business—A Novel Approach***. Berkeley: Ten Speed Press, 1984.

Heilbroner, Robert L. ***The Worldly Philosophers***. New York: Simon and Schuster, 1980.

CHAPTER TWO
PERCEPTION

THE BLIND MEN AND THE ELEPHANT

(A Hindoo Fable)

It was six men of Indostan
  To learning much inclined,
Who went to see the Elephant
  (Though all of them were blind),
That each by observation
  Might satisfy his mind.

The First approached the
    Elephant,
  And happening to fall
Against his broad and sturdy side,
  At once began to bawl:
"God bless me! but the Elephant
  Is very like a wall!"

The Second, feeling of the tusk,
  Cried, "Ho! what have we here
So very round and smooth and
    sharp?
  To me 'tis mighty clear
This wonder of an Elephant
  Is very like a spear!"

The Third approached the animal,
  And happening to take
The squirming trunk within his
    hands,
  Thus boldly up and spake:
"I see," quoth he, "the Elephant
  Is very like a snake!"

The Fourth reached out an eager
    hand,
  and felt about the knee.
"What most this wondrous beast is
    like
  Is mighty plain," quoth he;
"'Tis clear enough the Elephant
  Is very like a tree!"

The Fifth, who chanced to touch
    the ear,
  Said: "E'en the blindest man
Can tell what this resembles most;
  Deny the fact who can,
This marvel of an Elephant
  Is very like a fan!"

The Sixth no sooner had begun
  About the beast to grope,
Than, seizing on the swinging tail
  That fell within his scope,
"I see," quoth he, "the Elephant
  Is very like a rope!"

And so these men of Indostan
  Disputed loud and long,
Each in his own opinion
  Exceeding stiff and strong,
Though each was partly in the
    right
  And all were in the wrong!

Moral

So oft in theologic wars,
  The disputants, I ween,
Rail on in utter ignorance

Of what each other mean,
And prate about an Elephant
Not one of them has seen!

John Godfrey Saxe

OBJECTIVES

After studying this chapter, you should be able to:

1. Explain why people may have different perceptions of the same events, objects, persons, or situations.
2. Use the Johari Window to analyze your relationships with others.
3. Explain the importance of a good self-image.
4. Recognize perceptual defense mechanisms, what can trigger them, and how they hinder our relationships.
5. Explain how perceptions can affect the relationship between employee and supervisor.

WHAT IS PERCEPTION?

Awareness of factors in perception is vital to good human relations.

Perception is an important element in human relations. It is the process by which we acquire mental images of our environment. Through it we organize, interpret, and give meaning to sensations or messages that we receive with our senses of sight, smell, touch, taste, and hearing. Many factors influence perception. Culture, heredity, needs, peer pressures, interests, values, snap judgments, and expectations are only a few examples. All may greatly sway the way that we think and feel about people, situations, events, and objects. Figure 2.1 illustrates how perceptions can differ.

FIGURE 2.1   Is it a bunny or a duck?

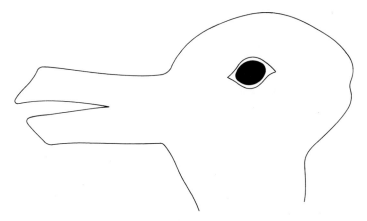

Donald P. Hoffman, "The Interpretation of Visual Illusions." Copyright © 1983 by Scientific American, Inc. All rights reserved.

WHAT INFLUENCES PERCEPTION?

People develop certain attitudes and tend to make decisions based on these attitudes. We should, however, try to view each new problem or situation separately and objectively and base our decisions on the facts. The following is an example of how culture and peer pressure can influence perceptions:

> **When Joe was growing up, his mother had always told him to beware of foreigners. She told him that they were not to be trusted and would lie and cheat. His friends liked to tell jokes about foreigners, calling them stupid.**
>
> **One day at work Joe met Zirka, a young man from abroad. He stared at Zirka and spoke rudely to him when the young man said hello and asked directions to the personnel office. Zirka turned to Joe and said, "What's your problem? What did I do to you to deserve that kind of treatment?"**

Joe's perception of Zirka is based on his upbringing and peer pressure rather than on actual experiences he has had with Zirka. If Joe analyzes his negative feelings, he may be able to understand their origin and to deal with them.

Additional factors can influence perception. The **halo effect** and **reverse** or **tarnished halo effect** are two of them. When the halo effect is operating, we assume that if a person has one trait we view positively, all other traits must be positive. For instance, imagine that you are the owner of an office supplies store. Jane has been a bookkeeper for you for several years, doing an excellent job in the back office, so you promote her to manager. You soon realize to your dismay, however, that she is not an effective manager because she lacks the necessary people skills to meet the public and supervise other employees. You were probably influenced by the halo effect here.

Under the influence of the reverse halo effect, we allow one negative characteristic of a person to influence our whole impression negatively. That is, we consider one behavior or characteristic of a person to be "bad" and, therefore, view all other characteristics or behaviors of that person as bad. For example, you are operating under the reverse halo effect if you believe that people with poor handwriting are not intelligent or will not perform well. Postpone judgment until you see how people function in a variety of situations.

Conditions and characteristics also influence perception. They include the time and place where actions occur, your age or emotional state at the time of an event, and the frequency of the occurrence. Here are examples:

> *Time and place.* Employees sometimes erroneously assume that an order from a supervisor is not as important when it takes place in the hall as when it occurs in the boss's office.
>
> *Emotional state.* We are more receptive to ideas when we are relaxed than when we are feeling nervous or tired.
>
> *Age.* A building or room that you thought was large as a child may seem small when you are an adult.
>
> *Frequency.* If your supervisor starts including you in weekly planning sessions, you may feel uneasy at first but become comfortable after a while.

Stress is another condition that distorts perception. When we are under stress, we are frequently unable to evaluate situations objectively. By learning to recognize situations that are stressful to you, you can make allowances for distortions that may cloud your perceptions.

WHY ARE PERCEPTIONS IMPORTANT?

Perceptual
awareness
allows more
self-control.

Being aware of your own perceptions and what influences them, as well as others' perceptions, is extremely important in today's workplace. With such awareness, you can withhold judgments until you have analyzed situations. Ask yourself why you are feeling the way you are, whether your feelings are justified, and whether you should act on those feelings. Perceiving situations accurately can prevent or resolve human relations problems in your personal life and at work. You may refrain from doing or saying things that could create difficulties.

Understanding perceptions of others will also help you be tolerant. When you accept the fact that their feelings or points of view are legitimate even if you do not agree with them, you can deal with situations better.

Open communication concerning feelings can be helpful in personal and work relationships. If people disclose their feelings to each other, they can develop better mutual understandings. Stronger relationships, built on honesty and openness, can help coworkers develop respect for each other's beliefs and opinions. Respect, in turn, can lead to fewer conflicts, greater job satisfaction, and growth, resulting in higher morale. In addition, productivity may increase because ideas flow more easily.

Self-disclosure
and feedback
increase the
accuracy of
communications.

Others learn about our perceptions when we practice **self-disclosure**, which is the sharing of our thoughts, feelings, opinions, and desires honestly. Self-disclosure can increase the accuracy of our communication and may reduce stress because we no longer have to hide our feelings. Additionally, we can increase our self-awareness by being open to both positive and negative feedback. **Feedback** is information given back to a person that evaluates his or her actions or states what the receiver understood. For instance, someone may tell you, "I missed your point. You are speaking too softly for me." After evaluating their feedback, you may want to make changes within yourself. A theory that may help you understand the importance of open communication and feedback is the **Johari Window**.

WHAT IS THE JOHARI WINDOW?

The Johari
Window helps
us understand
interactions.

The **Johari Window** is a model that helps us understand relationships and interactions among people. It is named for **Jo**seph Luft and **Har**ry **I**ngham who developed it.

Each of us has information within us of which we are aware and habits, attitudes, or talents of which we are not aware. Similarly, information about us or our habits, attitudes, or talents may or may not be known by others. Luft and Ingham combined these concepts to create four windowpanes, depicted in Figure 2.2. These panes are called the arena, hidden area, blind area, and unknown area.

FIGURE 2.2   The Johari Window, a model of awareness.

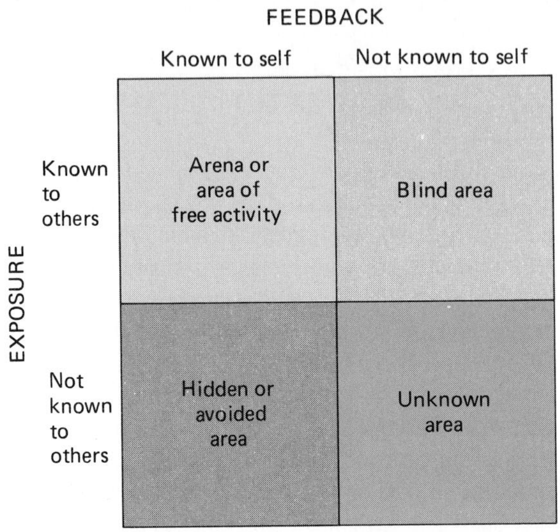

FEEDBACK

Joseph Luft, Group Processes: An Introduction to Group Dynamics *(Mountain View, CA: Mayfield Publishing, 1984). Used with permission.*

Arena

The arena contains information that you know about yourself and that others know about you. This pane will be bigger if you have effectively communicated your thoughts and ideas. It can include information about your job, preferred movies, disliked foods, and many other facts or feelings. An example of the kind of information that can be a part of people's arena is the following:

> **Lisa knows that Helen is a secretary in the real estate department, and Helen is aware that Lisa is an accountant and works on the payroll.**

Hidden Area

The hidden area contains information that you know about yourself but do not divulge to others. The size of your hidden area suggests how trusting you are of those with whom you associate. Experiences, hopes, and dreams can be included in this window if you have not shared them with others. An example of information in the hidden area is this:

> **Mark played the French horn in the band in college and has always dreamed of playing in a symphony orchestra. However, Sam is unaware that Mark has musical abilities and dreams of becoming a professional musician because Mark has never told him.**

Blind Area

The blind area is the section that represents what you do not know about yourself but what others do know about you. Blind areas can get in the way of interactions with others and can make people appear to have poor human relations skills. The size of this pane is an indication of how willing you are to listen to feedback about your behavior. Included in the blind area can be habits, attitudes, prejudices, and strengths. A common example of information in the blind area is the following:

Rene has a habit of tapping her pencil on the desk when she becomes impatient with others. She is not aware that she does this, but Leroy has noticed.

Unknown Area

The unknown area is the undiscovered or subconscious part of you. It contains information about you that neither you nor others know. This information can include unremembered experiences or undiscovered talents:

Stephan has a tremendous dislike of macaroni. Neither he nor Melody knows why he dislikes macaroni so much. One day Stephan discovers a diary that his mother kept when Stephan was little. The diary describes the financial hardship that the family went through for several years and how the family ate macaroni every day to survive.

Using the Window

The ideal Johari Window is one with a large arena and a small unknown area, as shown in Figure 2.3. To achieve this pattern, practice self-disclosure and be willing to accept and learn from feedback (negative or positive). At work, obvious ways in which you can do this include making suggestions and expressing opinions as appropriate and by being receptive to appraisals and suggestions made by your supervisor.

Your relationships away from work can also be improved by enlarging your arena. Ways to do that include accepting feedback from your family and friends about your actions and sharing your feelings and opinions in appropriate ways.

Disclosures, as described in the Johari Window, should be done carefully, particularly in the workplace. Telling too much about intimate matters or revealing personal information too soon can be harmful to careers. We all know people who blurt out their personal problems to almost everyone they meet. Such behavior is considered inappropriate in any setting, but especially so at work. Being critical under the guise of sharing your feelings can also hamper human relations. People who make rude or hurtful or inappropriate comments and excuse their behavior with "I'm just being honest about my feelings" have large blind areas.

Use great caution in sharing intimate information with people at work. Such information may detract from the professional image that you wish to create. Although all of us need people with whom we can share our confidences and problems,

FIGURE 2.3   The ideal Johari Window for effective relationships has a large arena and small unknown area.

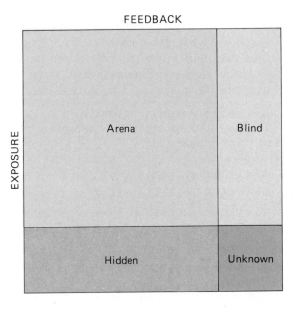

FEEDBACK

EXPOSURE

| Arena | Blind |
| Hidden | Unknown |

Joseph Luft, Group Processes: An Introduction to Group Dynamics *(Mountain View, CA: Mayfield Publishing, 1984). Used with permission.*

people away from work may be more appropriate choices for discussing intimate matters. Subjects shared only with caution include marital problems, financial difficulties, problems with children, many health-related matters, and opinions of coworkers. When deciding to disclose information, consider carefully the individuals with whom you will share information. What will their reaction be? Will they understand and be considerate of your feelings? Will they perceive what you have to tell them as a professional weakness that will inhibit your performance, or will they work with you to enhance your abilities? Is this the right point in your relationship to reveal such information?

Self-disclosure must be done carefully.

If you determine that information can be shared, select an appropriate time and place for disclosures. Look for a time when the other person is most able to pay attention and distractions are least likely to occur. For instance, taking your supervisor's time to discuss a personal problem when the supervisor is working on a deadline project or has others waiting to be seen may create additional stress for the supervisor and hinder your communication.

HOW DO YOU RAISE SELF-ESTEEM?

Self-esteem takes time and practice.

Another aspect of perception important in human relations is how people feel about themselves, their **self-esteem**. Feeling good about ourselves is the key to success. All individuals, even those most confident and secure in their personal and professional lives, must work on their self-perceptions continually. We are never finished with this task. The following are suggestions for developing and maintaining positive self-esteem:

1. Love yourself. We can love and respect others only if we love and respect ourselves.
2. Believe in yourself. Realize that almost everyone is afraid to try new and different experiences. However, we must be willing to take reasonable risks to pursue our goals.
3. Analyze yourself. Know your strengths and weaknesses and set goals to overcome your weaknesses and enhance your strengths.
4. Forgive yourself and accept the fact that you are not perfect. Although we cannot change events of the past, we can learn from them and not make the same mistakes again.
5. Practice positive thinking.

Positive Thinking and Its Importance

Positive thinking is looking on the bright side. Persons who think this way are called **optimists,** whereas persons who always have a negative outlook are called **pessimists.** Research has shown that optimists are more successful than pessimists, and we can certainly understand why. After all, few of us enjoy being around people who are always pessimistic. Then, too, people who are pessimistic probably give up in their endeavors too soon, not believing that positive results can occur. The difference between optimists and pessimists is demonstrated in Figure 2.4.

FIGURE 2.4   Is your glass (and your life) half-full or half-empty? Your perception reflects your degree of optimism or pessimism.

Reach positive thinking by changing thought processes and using positive self-talk and visualization.

Three steps can be taken to develop positive thinking: (1) change your thought processes, (2) engage in positive self-talk, and (3) use visualization. Each step is discussed below.

Change Your Thought Processes   Dr. David D. Burns, in his *Feeling Good*, describes thought processes that prevent us from thinking positively. One is seeing things in black-and-white categories, so that you consider your performance a total failure if it is not perfect. Another is exaggerating or minimizing the importance of your mistakes or someone else's achievements. Some other thought processes that interfere with positive thinking are overgeneralizing so that you see every negative event as part of a failure pattern, disqualifying positive experiences as "not counting," and jumping to conclusions. Being aware of these processes and realizing when we are using them will help us begin to develop positive thinking patterns.

Engage in Positive Self-Talk   Positive **self-talk** involves making favorable statements to ourselves. Statements such as "I can do that job," "I am a winner," or "I performed well" can help us take control of our lives. Taking time daily to say these things to ourselves in front of a mirror will strengthen our positive self-image. Stephen Strasser, in *Working It Out—Sanity & Success in the Workplace*, points out that self-confidence, self-worth, self-direction, self-respect, self-dignity, and self-esteem are necessary before we can solve problems of job and career.

Use Visualization   Taking time to practice **visualization**, or seeing ourselves as good, productive persons, can also help us develop a positive attitude. Take time each day to picture yourself doing well. For example, if you have a test coming up, imagine yourself sitting at the desk, reading the questions, and writing the correct answers. Another example could be a project at work. If you are to make a presentation to your supervisor, visualize yourself successfully making the presentation and seeing your supervisor pleased.

Remember, however, that visualization does not take the place of hard work. If you have studied hard or prepared thoroughly and are rested and healthy, visualization can enhance your performance.

Always Being Positive Is Difficult

All individuals face difficult periods in their lives. The "down" periods can be caused by stress from fatigue, tension, or illness. Other experiences, such as the death of a loved one, loss of a pet, loss of personal belongings through fire or natural disaster, divorce, robbery, moving, loss of a job, and retirement, also trigger stress. When these events occur, we may have difficulty remaining positive. Stress can distort perception and our ability to identify truth or view matters realistically.

The grieving process affects our outlook.

Difficult events can trigger a natural grieving process that was first identified by the Swiss psychiatrist Elisabeth Kübler-Ross. She discovered five stages of grieving—denial, anger, bargaining, grieving, and acceptance. By understanding this process we can work through our grief and return to our positive perspective of life. Follow these stages through the following example:

> **Osami could not believe it! Fired from her job! Not her! The more she thought about it, the angrier she got. She wasn't to blame for being late. "Oh, please, if you'll just give me back my job, I'll never be late again," she thought. After several days Osami became depressed. She lacked her usual energy and enthusiasm and spent time just sitting and staring into space. She sometimes yelled at her family members when they tried to talk to her, and at other times she simply sat and cried.**

Finally, one day Osami woke up and said, "I'm tired of sitting around and feeling sorry for myself. I'm going to start looking for another job."

Individuals enter the stages of grieving at different times. Those persons who do not move through the stages or who stay at one stage too long may need professional help.

HOW DO YOU SEE YOUR ROLES?

Everyone has different **roles** to fill. Employee, parent, church member, student, volunteer, teacher, and friend are examples. Each role has its own acceptable behavior and dress. Realizing which role you are playing and behaving appropriately for that role is important. People feel more comfortable dealing with individuals who fit roles as the roles are perceived. For instance, we expect our auto mechanic to wear work clothes made to withstand oil and grease. A mechanic who is not dressed "appropriately" may be perceived as being unable to perform the tasks necessary to service cars. Parents expect public school teachers not to swear and frequently complain if swear words occur in classroom lectures, even though their children may hear these same words numerous times in a single evening of watching television.

Conformance to expected roles can help us succeed.

Because of this phenomenon, be sensitive to the roles that you play and the perceptions and expectations that others have of you in those roles. Learn what the expected behaviors are and then conform to them when appropriate. Conformance in dress and behavior at work will help you do your job effectively, will enhance your image, and will help you move ahead professionally.

Some people feel more comfortable in one role than in another. For instance, a mother who is returning to school after 20 years will feel more comfortable in her role of mother than in her role of student. The employee promoted to supervisor may feel ill at ease initially. Realize that being uncomfortable in a new role is natural. If you are aware of the behavior that the role requires and keep in mind that changing your behavior to conform to that role is expected and acceptable, you will handle transitions into new roles better.

Sometimes roles are ambiguous. Most people feel awkward the first day on a new job or as a new member of a group because they are not sure what is expected of them. Again, this unease is natural. Learning a new role and developing confidence in it takes time.

Sometimes, too, roles can conflict. A father may need to be at work at the same time that his child's scout meeting is being held. A mother may feel guilty about being at work and not at home with her children. Such conflict can cause anxiety. Recognizing the source of anxiety will help us cope with it.

HOW DO YOU COPE WITH ANXIETY?

All persons face anxiety. Anxiety can be caused by a number of factors, such as role conflict, ambiguity, or low self-esteem. To function satisfactorily, we need to feel

FIGURE 2.5   We all play many roles in life.

Florida Department of Commerce,
Division of Tourism

Copyright © Diane K. Gentry

adequate in our activities and acceptable to others. High feelings of acceptability can compensate for low feelings of adequacy. The weak student who is well liked because of a kind personality is an example. The reverse is also true: high feelings of adequacy can compensate for low feelings of acceptability. An example is the student who makes good grades but has no friends or social life. However, when both adequacy and acceptability are low, a person's overall feelings of worth suffer.

Individuals frequently cope with anxiety through the use of **perceptual defense mechanisms**. These mechanisms serve to protect our feelings of worth. Note that both positive and negative outcomes can result from the use of defense mechanisms. The trouble is that they may prevent us from confronting the real problem.

Perceptual defense mechanisms are used to cope with anxiety.

Denial—denying that anxiety exists.
Work example: "I'm not worried about my upcoming performance appraisal." "I never become nervous before a presentation."
Home example: "Death doesn't frighten me." "I don't become nervous about tests." "I do not have a problem with drugs or alcohol."

Repression—pushing stressful thoughts, worries, or emotions "out of mind" or below the awareness level.
Work example: The cashier at the bank who was robbed at gunpoint cannot remember any of the incident.
Home example: The child cannot remember being abused by a parent.

Rationalization—explaining away unacceptable feelings, thoughts, or motives. This way we protect ourselves from sadness or the full impact of feelings.
Work example: "It's just as well that I did not get that promotion. I would not have been able to spend as much time as I want with my family."
Home example: "I know Joe didn't call me, but I am sure he likes me. He just had important things to do."

Regression—returning to previous, less mature types of behavior.
Work example: Ann's supervisor is reprimanding her for sloppy work. Ann starts to cry.
Home example: Mike wants to be waited on when he is sick, as he was when he was a child.

Scapegoating—blaming another person or group for a problem.
Work example: "It's the Personnel Department's fault. If they would hire better people, we wouldn't be in this mess."
Home example: "It's the Republicans' (or Democrats') fault that we have a budget deficit."

Projection—attributing an unacceptable thought or feeling about yourself to others.
Work example: The supervisor routinely comes in late and accuses employees who are on time of being late.
Home example: The husband accuses the wife of wanting to have an affair when he is actually the one considering an affair.

Displacement—finding safe, less threatening persons or objects and venting frustration on them.

Work example that goes home: The angry manager yells at the supervisor (who cannot yell back), the frustrated supervisor yells at the employee (who cannot yell back), the irritated employee yells at the spouse (who cannot or will not yell back), the furious spouse yells at the child (who cannot yell back), and the upset child kicks the dog.

Sublimation—directing unacceptable impulses into socially acceptable channels.

Work example: A person who is aggressive may make a career in the military, sports, or law enforcement.

Home example: A suicidal person may take up a risky sport, such as sky diving.

Compensation—an attempt to relieve feelings of inadequacy or frustration by excelling in other areas.

Work example: The employee who feels unappreciated by an immediate supervisor may take on tasks in other areas, such as committee or community projects, to experience success or receive positive feedback.

Home example: A physically handicapped person may become a computer expert to show that her mind is not handicapped.

Examine your own thoughts and behaviors. Are you using these defense mechanisms frequently? Are they causing you to avoid dealing with your problems?

While at work, be aware of the behavior of others. *Stop to think before you react.* Perhaps your supervisor has had a fight at home and now seems angry with everyone in the department. If you are aware that displacement is occurring, you will be less likely to take the gruffness personally. Taking a minute to think through interactions before responding can greatly improve your human relations skills.

HOW DO YOU VIEW THE BOSS?

Perception of superiors influences work behavior.

Perceptions play an important role in the relationship we have with supervisors and others above us. How we perceive superiors will determine how we act around them.

Feeling intimidated by authority figures with whom we have not had an opportunity to interact is quite natural. If you become so frightened by authority figures that you cannot communicate comfortably, look for opportunities to interact in casual ways. For instance, you might speak briefly in the hall or, if appropriate, stick your head in their doors for a quick "hello." This type of assertive behavior will help you see authority figures in a new light.

Feeling Unsure of Authority Figures

We may feel unsure of authority figures when a coworker is promoted over us or uncomfortable when we are promoted over coworkers. This type of change creates

FIGURE 2.6   Getting to know your boss may help you feel less intimidated by authority figures.

MOMMA by Mell Lazarus. By permission of Mell Lazarus and Creators Syndicate.

what psychologists call a loss of perceptual anchorages. An adjustment period is normal while everyone involved learns new roles and what is expected of each other in these roles.

Another time that produces anxiety is when we get a new boss. We may miss the old boss and resent having to start from scratch in showing the new supervisor what we are capable of doing. We must remember that some time will be necessary for both of us to become comfortable with each other. Being ready with suggestions if asked and offering to help the new supervisor will encourage a good relationship. Keep an open mind and avoid prejudging the new boss.

Viewing the Boss

The most effective way to view bosses is as humans with their own feelings and own jobs to do. They have their strengths and weaknesses, good days and bad days. Recognize this fact, and learn when to approach them. For instance, if you approach your supervisor about a trivial matter when she is in a hurry or has just arrived late to work because of a flat tire, you can probably expect a less-than-enthusiastic reception.

We should also be sensitive to bosses' moods and viewpoints and not challenge them in front of others or when they are not feeling well. Remember that bosses will appreciate tact and kindness just as much as you do.

Managing the Boss

Managing your supervisor increases job satisfaction.

Just as supervisors manage their staffs to meet goals and deadlines, we can manage our bosses to meet our own objectives. This behavior is called **upward management**. Upward management results in better relationships, increased flexibility in assignments, and a greater understanding of how our work fits in with the overall organizational picture. As a result, we may be more committed to the job, have a higher morale, and increase our productivity.

Walter St. John, in an article in *Personnel Journal*, pointed out that supervisors have the same concerns, fears, and anxieties as others. We can help ourselves by recognizing, understanding, and learning to cope with their fears. Some of the most common fears bosses have are the following:

1. Looking bad or wrong to their own bosses or others and being ridiculed or criticized.
2. Not being respected or appreciated.
3. Appearing inadequate, perhaps because of outdated skills or sharp, aggressive subordinates.
4. Being rejected as a leader.

Government Executive suggests the following steps in managing your supervisor:

1. Present your supervisor with suggestions for solving problems rather than just problems.
2. Keep your supervisor informed of the progress of your work so that those higher than your supervisor can be informed. No one likes surprises. (This step will also help lay the groundwork if you must ask for extra time or help later.)
3. Be honest about problems. Most supervisors will tolerate some mistakes as part of the learning process.
4. Be sensitive to the effect that you have on others and take responsibility for your own behavior.
5. Do not try to change your supervisors. Study their preferences and try to conform to them.
6. Try to make your supervisors look good. Build on their strengths and compensate for their weaknesses.
7. Be sure that your priorities are in agreement with your supervisor's and be aware of changing priorities.
8. Know your supervisor's goals and understand how you can help meet those goals.
9. Recognize that you can learn from criticism. Learn how to ask for specific information and feedback.
10. Try to see things from your supervisor's perspective. Supervisors may not always have the right perceptions, but they do have the power and do determine goals.

SUMMARY

Perceptions differ greatly depending on a number of factors, including your upbringing, values, and culture. Recognizing and appreciating differences in perception is vital to your ability to function in the workplace. Others learn about our perceptions when we practice self-disclosure. We learn theirs by accepting feedback. The Johari Window suggests that ideally we should have a large arena, the result of self-disclosure and openness to feedback. A positive self-esteem, an optimistic outlook on life, and an understanding of the roles people play in life are other important ingredients in a successful career. Positive thinking can be enhanced through changing our thought processes, engaging in positive self-talk, and using visualization.

Learning about the defense mechanisms that individuals use to cope with anxiety can help you deal more successfully with yourself and those around you. Defense mechanisms sometimes have positive outcomes, but they may prevent us from confronting the real problem.

Remember that the most effective way to view bosses is as humans and deal with them accordingly. Learn to manage them by using the concepts of upward management.

KEY TERMS

perception
halo effect
reverse halo effect
self-disclosure
feedback
Johari Window
self-esteem
optimists
pessimists
self-talk
visualization
roles
perceptual defense mechanisms
denial
repression
rationalization
regression
scapegoating
projection
displacement
sublimation
compensation
upward management

REVIEW QUESTIONS

1. Explain why people have different perceptions of the same events, objects, persons, or situations.
2. Name the panes of the Johari Window and explain what they mean.
3. What is self-perception? Why is it important?
4. Name and explain the common perceptual defense mechanisms.
5. How can your perceptions of your supervisor affect the relationship you have?

DISCUSSION QUESTIONS

1. Name three instances when persons view situations differently. Is this difference acceptable? Why or why not?
2. Draw the Johari Window of three persons with whom you interact frequently at work or at school. Explain why you have drawn each pane that particular size, and describe examples of their behavior. How might they enlarge their arenas? What effect would enlarging their arenas have on them? On you?
3. What is your self-image at work? At home? Around friends? What can you do to improve it?
4. Describe an incident from home or work showing each of the defense mechanisms in operation.
5. Why is recognizing that supervisors are human important? How can you allow your supervisor to be "real"?
6. How would you describe an ideal worker? An ideal boss?

CASE STUDY 2.1

THE SCREAMING SUPERVISOR

Isaac stormed into the office and slammed down a pile of papers. "You really messed this up!" he yelled at Bobby and Maria. "I want it done right by noon or both of you are fired!" Isaac turned and stomped out of the office.

"Oh, he makes me so angry!" Maria exclaimed under her breath. "What's been his problem this week? Nothing I have done has made him happy!"

"I heard he's split up with his wife," Bobby said. "They separated last weekend."

"That's true," said Ted, "but you two have really been doing a poor job lately. I don't blame Isaac for being upset."

1. Why do you think Isaac is behaving this way?
2. Is Isaac using a defense mechanism? If you think so, which one? Are Bobby and Maria using a defense mechanism? If so, which one?
3. What would be a more appropriate way for Isaac to deal with Bobby's and Maria's performances?
4. What would be an appropriate action for Bobby and Maria to take if they think that they are being unjustly criticized?

CASE STUDY 2.2

VIEWPOINT

"Don't ever take my hole punch off my desk again without asking!" Ann growled at Dan as she turned to go.

"I don't understand it," Dan said. "I had ten brothers and sisters and I had nothing that was my own. We shared everything."

"Well, I understand," replied Sally. "My mother always taught me to ask permission before I borrowed anything."

1. Which viewpoint is right?
2. Should Dan respect Ann's feelings?
3. Does Dan have to agree with Ann's feelings in order to respect them?

BIBLIOGRAPHY

Baltus, Rita K. *Personal Psychology for Life and Work*. New York: McGraw-Hill, 1983.

"Beyond Positive Thinking." *Success* (December 1988): 31–38.

Burns, David D. *Feeling Good: The New Mood Therapy*. New York: William Morrow and Company, 1980.

Gottesfeld, Harry. *Abnormal Psychology, A Community Mental Health Perspective*. Chicago: Science Research Associates, 1979.

"In the Mind's Eye." *Readings from Scientific American*. New York: Scientific American, Inc., 1986.

"Kübler-Ross, Elisabeth." *Academic American On-Line Encyclopedia*. New York: Grolier, 1988.

Luft, Joseph. *Group Processes: An Introduction to Group Dynamics*. Mountain View, CA: Mayfield Publishing, 1984.

Luft, Joseph. *The Johari Window: A Graphic Model of Awareness in Relations*. Palo Alto, CA: National Press Books, 1970.

"Managing Your Boss." *Government Executive* (April 1989): 34–37.

St. John, Walter D. "Successful Communications between Supervisors and Employees." *Personnel Journal* (January 1983): 71–77.

Sargent, Alice G. *Androgynous Manager*. New York: AMACOM, Division of American Management Association, 1983.

Strasser, Stephen. *Working It Out—Sanity & Success in the Workplace*. Englewood Cliffs, NJ: Prentice-Hall, Inc., 1989.

SUGGESTED READINGS

Applegate, Gary. *Happiness—It's Your Choice*. Sherman Oaks, CA: Beringer Publishing, 1985.

Colgrove, Melba, Harold H. Bloomfield, and Peter McWilliams. *How to Survive the Loss of a Love*. New York: Bantam Books, 1976.

Harris, Thomas A. *I'm OK, You're OK*. New York: Avon Books, 1969.

Kübler-Ross, Elisabeth. *On Death and Dying*. New York: Macmillan Publishing Company, 1970.

Lerner, Harriet Goldhor. *The Dance of Anger*. New York: Harper and Row, 1985.

Peck, M. Scott. *The Road Less Traveled*. New York: Simon and Schuster, 1980.

Rubin, Theodore Isaac. *The Angry Book*. New York: Macmillan Publishing Company, 1969.

Sheehy, Gail. *Passages: Predictable Crises of Adult Life*. New York: Dutton, 1976.

CHAPTER THREE
COMMUNICATION

The psychologist on the morning talk show was driving me bonkers. At first, I didn't understand why.

She spoke forcefully. She made provocative points. But each time she finished speaking, she bared her teeth and smiled like a chimpanzee.

Why was this woman smiling? The smile was out of sync with her serious message. It annoyed me enough to promptly dismiss what she was saying.

Bonnie K. Gangelhoff, *Houston Post*, September 6, 1989

OBJECTIVES

After studying this chapter, you should be able to:
1. Define communication.
2. Explain the difference between verbal and nonverbal communication.
3. Identify barriers to communication and how to overcome them.
4. Define information overload and explain effective ways of handling it.
5. Explain levels of communication and their appropriate and inappropriate uses.
6. List ways to improve your speaking and presentations.
7. Give guidelines for using active listening.
8. Identify the qualities of strong written communication.
9. Discuss forms of nonverbal communication and why it is important.
10. Explain the importance of time, timing, context, and the medium of a message.

WHAT IS COMMUNICATION?

Communication is defined by Webster's as the process by which we exchange information through a common system of symbols, signs, or behavior. This process sends messages from one person to another. Symbols can be written or spoken words; signs can be shapes and colors; and behavior can be any nonverbal communication, such as body movements or facial expressions.

The basic skills in communication are listening, speaking, writing, and reading.

Listening, speaking, writing, and reading are the four basic skills that we use in communicating. Of these skills, the first two are the most frequently used, but unfortunately, they are the two in which we receive the least training.

WHY IS COMMUNICATION IMPORTANT?

Chapter 1 of this book pointed out that the United States has progressed from an agricultural to an industrial society and is now becoming an information society. We can see it happening everywhere we look: computers, satellites, voice processing, and other technological developments are increasing the creation and flow of data. Additionally, employees must interact effectively with a variety of people in a normal workday. Today we spend 70 to 80 percent of our waking hours communicating in one way or another—10 to 11 hours of our day!

The following anecdote demonstrates the great number of people with whom we might communicate in a brief period of time and the different means of communication that we might use:

> **Sharon felt almost crazy. The telephones in the office were ringing off the hook, and no one was answering them. The meeting that she had attended earlier ran longer than expected, and she had not been able to return the five telephone calls that she had received while she was gone. She wondered whether Vicky, who had left her a message to call, had been able to find a speaker for their breakfast club on Friday.**
>
> **Her telephone rang as she was in the process of rewriting a memorandum that was due in one hour for the vice president. It was the school nurse calling to tell her that her daughter was running a fever and needed to be picked up. As Sharon was calling a neighbor to get her daughter, Sharon's secretary stuck her head in the door and began making hand motions and waving a note. Sharon put her hand over the receiver of the telephone and gruffly asked the secretary what she wanted.**
>
> **"You just got a call from Tom," the secretary said. "He's in the fourth floor conference room. They've been waiting for you for ten minutes so they could start the meeting. Did you forget?"**

What happened with Sharon is called a **communication breakdown**. Human beings have a limited capacity to receive and transmit messages. Air traffic controllers in busy airports are well-known examples of people whose capacity to communicate may be stretched to the breaking point. When that point is reached, the ability to communicate deteriorates or fails.

Communication Breakdowns Create Problems

Communication breakdowns create problems that are frequently painful. Sharon is no doubt feeling stress, and her job performance is being affected. Over a period of time, she may develop low morale and become ill, or she may decide to withdraw from the situation through absences or resignation. Frequently, in such situations even minor tasks start seeming major and are, therefore, put aside, causing work to fall even further behind.

When employees in organizations have communication breakdowns, total organizational productivity decreases. Additionally, stress and low morale can cause people to make errors that result in injuries and even deaths. Communication break-downs can be costly for organizations.

Communication skills can be learned, either through experience (which can sometimes be a tough teacher) or through training. Organizations today recognize the importance of communication and are beginning to press schools and universities to turn out people who can communicate. They are also offering their own employees training in communications.

The Connection between Communication Ability and Success

Doris Lee McCoy in the book *Megatraits* identified traits present in all great leaders who have succeeded and risen above the crowd. Good communication skill is one of the traits that helped these individuals obtain positions of power and recognition. Great leaders who did not already have effective communication skills made an effort to develop them.

McCoy points out that creating good ideas is not enough. We must know how to explain our ideas to other people so that they will want to develop and promote them. We must also make a conscious effort to seek and listen to communication from others.

The Role of Communication Skills in Human Relations

Communication is the most important element in human relations. The more sensitive and knowledgeable you are about communication, the stronger human relations skills you will have. Examples of the role communication plays in effective human relations away from work include:

The wife who explains to her husband that she is bothered by the clothes he leaves lying on the floor and offers alternatives rather than yelling at him.

The father who asks his child about a broken lamp and gives his child a chance to explain the circumstances rather than yelling, blaming, and punishing immediately.

The neighbor who calls and asks nicely that the stereo be turned down the first time that it is bothersome rather than immediately calling the police.

Examples of the role communication plays in effective human relations at work include:

The supervisor who gives employees a pat on the back in appreciation for a job well done.

The employee who asks the boss for clarification of a written work order rather than do a job incorrectly and later cause a problem.

The boss who calls employees together to discuss a major company change rather than letting them hear it from coworkers as gossip or sending the information to them in a memo.

The employee who waits for the "right time" to ask the boss for a change in schedule, not when the boss has just arrived late after being snarled in a traffic jam.

The manager with a reputation for having an "open door" and being a good listener.

HOW DOES COMMUNICATION FLOW?

Communication flows upward, downward, or horizontally in an organization.

Notice in the above work examples that communication can flow from the supervisor down to the employee or from the employee up to the supervisor. In any organization communication will flow upward, downward, or horizontally (sideways). Managers will furnish information downward to those under them and upward to their superiors. When they talk to other managers who are at their own level, they are communicating horizontally. Even employees who are not in supervisory positions routinely communicate upward and horizontally.

Sender, receiver, and message are the three elements of the communication process.

In each instance, the communication process includes three elements—the sender, the receiver, and the message. The **sender** is the person who transmits, or sends, the message. The **receiver** is the one to whom the message is sent. The **message**, the content of communication, may be verbal (questions and responses), nonverbal (for example, nodding, smiling, frowning, or eye contact), or written.

Communication can be one-way or two-way. If a sender sends a message to someone and no return message is sent, the communication is considered to be one-way. Common examples are speeches, letters, and memos when no response is expected. In fact, some communication experts classify such one-way communication as information giving only, not true communication. True communication is two-way, with both the sender and the receiver being a part of the process.

To be effective, the message must be understood by the person receiving the information in the same way that the person sending it intended. Whether we are the sender or the receiver, we have a responsibility to determine that the correct message has been received. We check by a process known as **feedback**.

WHAT IS FEEDBACK IN COMMUNICATION?

Feedback should be *t*imely, *o*ften, and *p*recise (*TOP*).

Feedback is information given back to a sender that evaluates the message and states what the receiver understood. Because of the role it plays in clarifying communication, verifying understanding, and overcoming communication barriers (distortions and blockages), it is an extremely important part of the communication process. Figure 3.1 depicts the communication process and the relationship of feedback to the sender and the receiver. To be effective, feedback should be *t*imely, *o*ften, and *p*recise (*TOP*).

Feedback in face-to-face communication can be fast. Both listener and speaker continuously give feedback to each other verbally and nonverbally. Examples of ways in which we do that include frowns, nods, verbal expressions of agreement or disagreement, questions, statements, and silence. The following is an example of communication without feedback:

Michael: Joe, carry this package upstairs to Eleanor in the business office and get a receipt. Then put the receipt in the receipt book in my office immediately, since it's very important.

Joe: Yes, sir.

FIGURE 3.1   Communication process and context.

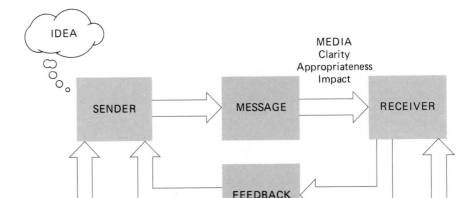

When Joe returns with the receipt, he goes into Michael's office but can find no receipt book. He has to wait until Joe returns, thereby causing delay and possible misplacement of an important piece of paper.

Here is the same situation; however, this time the communication includes feedback:

Michael:	Joe, carry this package upstairs to Eleanor in the business office and get a receipt. Then put the receipt in the receipt book in my office immediately, since it's very important. Understand?
Joe:	I think so. I turn in the package to Eleanor and get a receipt, which goes in the receipt book. Correct so far?
Michael:	Yes.
Joe:	I've never done this before. Where will I find the receipt book?
Michael:	Oh, yes, sorry. It's the blue notebook in my storage closet.

As shown in the second example, feedback can improve communication. It can also save time and reduce the possibility of errors and human relations problems.

As the sender of messages, you will want feedback from the person or persons for whom your messages are intended. Feedback will help you determine whether your message has been received and interpreted correctly. Various ways exist for obtaining feedback. When you are face to face with the receiver, you can ask questions that determine whether the receiver has understood. You can also ask the receiver to restate what you have said, and you can watch for signs of understanding (such as nods) or confusion (such as frowns). When the message is not face to face, feedback is more difficult and, if it occurs, usually takes the same form as the original message. For example, if you send a memo or letter to someone, you can request either a written answer to your message or a written reply specifying when the answer will be available. If a written or oral answer is not received, the most likely ways of obtaining feedback are to follow up and to check for compliance. To follow up means that you repeat your request; to check for compliance means that you see whether the receiver took the action you desired, such as placing an order.

Silence is a powerful form of feedback. Be careful what your silence suggests.

Silence was listed above as a form of feedback. In fact, it is a powerful form, communicating power, uncertainty, agreement, or disapproval. For instance, in couples who are having disagreements, one of the individuals may sometimes use silence as a form of "punishment," thereby attempting to communicate power. When two people meet on the street or in a social setting, one may refrain from speaking to the other, indicating a higher status or more powerful position. We often use silence when we are unsure what the appropriate response is, thereby communicating uncertainty. Silence is also sometimes interpreted as agreement. For this reason, being with a group of people who are gossiping about a coworker is dangerous even if you are not making comments yourself; your presence and silence suggest that you agree. In fact, frequently what happens in such situations is that the silent person is then "quoted" as being one of the gossipers. Finally, silence can also communicate disapproval. Perhaps this interpretation is a carry-over from the adage, "Don't say anything if you can't say something positive."

WHAT ARE BARRIERS IN COMMUNICATION?

Communication experts have identified a number of factors that can cause distortions and blocks in communication. Some of them lie in our senses, in word meanings, and in the emotions and attitudes of the sender and receiver. Others are role expectations, personality, appearance, prejudice, changes, poor organization of ideas, poor listening, and information overload.

Sensory Organs

The first barrier to effective communication is inadequate or distracted sensory organs. Poor eyesight or hearing can cause us to misunderstand or misinterpret messages from others. Also, if other noises or sights distract us, we may be unable to concentrate on sending or receiving messages. For example, have you ever missed seeing your exit sign on the highway because you were involved in a conversation with someone else in the car?

Periodic checkups of your eyes and ears can help you determine whether they are hindering your communication. To improve your communication, try to reduce the number of messages coming at you at one time so that if you must, for example, look for a sign on the highway, you are more attentive.

Semantics

Semantics is the study of the meanings and the changing meanings of words. The fact that words may have multiple meanings can cause difficulty sometimes. Because the meaning of words lies within ourselves and is always subjective, we may interpret a word that someone has said to us in one way when actually the sender meant it in another way. Our understanding of a word depends on our background, experience, and interests.

The more abstract a term, the less likely people are to agree on its meaning. The term *love,* for example, means many things to many different people.

The setting in which the word is used can also alter the meaning. "Loving" chocolate chip cookies is quite different from "loving" your child.

An additional problem with words is that they change. New words are constantly being created, while other words drop from common usage or gain new meanings. For example, *network,* originally a noun, is now commonly used as a verb meaning "to connect with people of similar interests with the intent of helping each other."

The obvious way to reduce misunderstandings is by using feedback. Asking questions such as "Do you mean . . . ?" can prevent future problems.

FIGURE 3.2   We have numerous words for the same object or idea, and the same word can have several meanings.

By permission of Johnny Hart and Creators Syndicate, Inc.

Emotions

Emotions of the sender or the receiver are the most powerful communication barrier over which we have limited control. Our emotional state can cause us to overreact to the speaker's message or prevent us from hearing it at all. Anger, for example, can lead to inappropriate action. If we have just had a fight with our spouse, we may react improperly when our boss tells us that we are assigned a new project requiring overtime. One of the best ways that you can improve your communication and human relations skills is by calming down before you send or receive messages.

Attitudes are our beliefs backed up by emotions. Attitudes cause us to have preconceived ideas about a topic. Negative attitudes about a person or idea can produce resistance to the message, causing communication breakdown. Overly positive attitudes, on the other hand, cause us to hear what we want to hear, and then we fail to evaluate the message effectively. Obvious ways to overcome this barrier are to have an open mind and to withhold judgment until we have adequate information.

Role Expectations

Role expectations, how we expect ourselves and others to act on the basis of the roles played, can distort communication. We may identify others too closely with their roles and discount what they say. For example, a wife may not believe her policeman husband when he tells her that he is afraid.

Sometimes we do not allow others to change their roles and take on new ones. A work group, for example, may expect a coworker who has been promoted to supervisor to continue behaving as before. Family members sometimes overlook the fact that another member has grown in maturity or interests and are uncomfortable with that person's new goals or activities.

Communication is also affected when people use their positions of power to alter the way in which they relate to others. Common examples are people who act superior to others, thereby creating ill will among people below and a bad image of themselves among those above and on the same level. Another common occurrence is the misuse of power. New leaders, for instance, may start telling group members what to do, failing to recognize that leaders are leaders because they have followers who choose to follow. Such demands may backfire, whereas asking for compliance may get greater commitment in the long run.

To overcome this barrier, we should try to separate people from the roles they are playing, recognize that roles change, and be sensitive to the effect that power may have on perception.

Personality and Appearance

Personality and appearance may be barriers to effective communication. Our personalities may cause others to accept or reject our communication. For example, the individual who frequently cracks jokes may not be taken seriously when he presents a budget request for additional people and equipment for his department.

The appearance of the sender or of the message, if written, can make a difference. The man in a ragged shirt and dirty blue jeans who enters the car dealership to buy a Mercedes Benz may not be perceived as a serious buyer. A letter with typographical errors and typed on cheap paper is not considered as authoritative as an attractive, correctly spelled letter on high-quality paper.

To overcome this barrier, we should strive to make our behavior and appearance appropriate to the roles we play. We should also make sure that our correspondence reflects the image we wish to present.

Prejudice

Prejudice based on race, religion, color, sex, national origin, or age can alter perceptions. For example, our society is still unaccustomed to older people in the workplace, and many people tend to view them as "over the hill" and incapable of creative ideas or hard work. However, because of a shrinking population of 18-to-24-year-olds, nearly 40 percent fewer people will enter the work force in the 1990s than in the 1970s. Many companies are beginning to recognize the incredible pool of talent available in retirees and are recruiting them. Other companies, however, still focus development efforts on younger employees. Some of these companies have a "natural tendency" to give critical work—and the training for it—to younger employees.

To overcome the barrier of prejudice in our communication, we should try to evaluate communication on the basis of the message itself, not on preconceived ideas of the sender.

Changes

Failure to recognize the changing nature of people, objects, and situations can cause us difficulties in communication. As pointed out earlier, when people grow in maturity or interests, this change may be unnoticed or ignored by others with whom they interact. This fact can create confusion in roles and misunderstanding of messages.

Sometimes we are so close to objects that we do not notice they have changed. For instance, we may be unaware a coat has become ragged and worn, until someone else points it out to us. Because our appearance does communicate information about us, we should try to be aware of such changes.

A common example of failing to recognize change occurs in organizations that revamp management style to increase employee participation. Often employees who have been with the company for a long time tend to overlook the changes or distrust them, not recognizing that even the leaders may be different.

The obvious way to overcome this barrier is to try to recognize that people, objects, and situations can change and to interpret communication in that light.

Poor Organization of Ideas

Have you ever attended a seminar or class where the speaker presented ideas in such a disorderly fashion that you found following the speaker difficult? What was your reaction? If you are like most people, the speaker probably lost credibility in your eyes. Eventually, you may have lost interest, stopped trying to understand, allowed your mind to wander, or even left the room.

We can experience the same confusion or loss of interest when writing is disorganized. For these reasons, poor organization of ideas is a major barrier to communication. You can overcome this barrier by organizing and revising your correspondence and presentations so that they are clear and logical. If organizing your ideas is a problem for you, help is available in numerous written and oral communications classes and workshops.

Information Overload

Complexities of our busy society, increased communication, and today's hectic pace of life can cause us to experience **information overload**. When we become overloaded with the great number of messages and stimuli coming at us at one time, we lose the ability to continue processing and remembering information, fail to listen carefully, and forget information that has been previously communicated to us. The result is a breakdown in communication.

We cannot normally take in and process information longer than a telephone number. Therefore, we should develop coping strategies for dealing with information overload, such as making notes and grouping activities like telephone calls. Be aware of your own tension, recognize when you are receiving too many messages, then take action to reduce them. Possible ways include reducing noise (turning off radios or closing doors), concentrating on an object in a crowd in the close or middle distance rather than far distance, getting enough rest, and eating well to maintain overall health. Delegating, saying no, getting an answering machine, and doing work before it builds up also help.

Poor Listening

One of the most important elements—perhaps the most important element—in strong human relations skills is the ability to listen; yet few of us have had formal training in listening. The result is the tremendous cost in communication difficulties and damaged relations that poor listening causes. A study at Ohio State University found that 45 percent of our time is spent listening, but that listening is the least taught of the four basic skills. Thirty percent of our time is spent speaking, 16 percent reading, and 9 percent writing. Listening is critical to success at all levels of an organization, and as we move up, listening ability becomes even more important.

Listen for both the message and the speaker's emotions.

We tend to assume that we just know how to listen effectively. Such is not the case. Listening is a skill that can be improved, and it takes effort. To **hear** is to perceive sound with our ears. To **listen** is to make a conscious effort to hear something and to interpret it using reason and understanding. Most of us listen effectively to only about 25 percent of what we hear. Effective listening involves two steps. The first is to determine what the speaker is saying, and the second is to consider the speaker's emotions about the message.

Authorities have identified seven blocks or barriers that create problems in listening:

1. Lack of interest in the subject or the speaker.
2. Outside noises, distractions, or fatigue.
3. Limited vocabulary of the sender or receiver or both.
4. Poor delivery of the message.
5. Thinking ahead to our responses or back to what the speaker said earlier; turning attention away to other matters. (We speak at approximately 125 to 150 words a minute, but we can listen at 400 to 700 words a minute. That means that we usually listen in spurts, paying attention only about 60 seconds at a time.)
6. Lack of knowledge in the speaker or the listener.
7. Prejudices; listening for what we want to hear.

HOW CAN YOU LISTEN BETTER?

To be better listeners, we must want to improve and must engage in **active listening**. Active listening is a conscious effort to listen to both the verbal and the nonverbal components of what someone is saying, without prejudging. Active listening tells the speaker that we are interested and care. If we listen actively, we may also help the other person sort out and solve problems.

Steps to improve your listening skills include the following:

1. Don't anticipate or plan rebuttals. Don't jump to conclusions. Keep your thoughts in the present.
2. Avoid prejudging the speaker. Be aware of your biases and prejudices.
3. Eliminate distractions by providing a quiet, private location for communication. Face the person speaking to you so that you can concentrate.
4. Ask for clarification, and restate important points by paraphrasing the speaker. Ask questions that make the other person go deeper, such as who, what, when, and where. However, you should avoid the use of the word *why*. This word puts some people on the defensive. Remain neutral and restate the person's viewpoint. Put the person's feelings into words.
5. Be ready to give feedback.
6. "Listen" to the nonverbal communication. It is through nonverbal communication that we can pick up the emotional message.
7. Avoid excessive note-taking. (Some may be necessary, as we forget one-third to one-half of what we hear within eight hours.)
8. Listen for major ideas; don't try to remember everything.
9. Don't fake attention; it takes too much work and is distracting.

Here is a conversation without active listening:

Wanda: Gee, there must be something wrong with me. Yesterday I messed up again in doing the monthly report. That's the way it always goes. I never seem to do anything right.

Phil: Oh, well, cheer up; you'll probably forget about it in a few days.

Wanda:	No, I won't. This report has me depressed. I feel like an incompetent. I hurried to get it in on time, and then it was wrong.
Phil:	Well, you're worrying about it too much. It's probably your hurrying that messes things up in the first place.
Wanda:	But I had to hurry. What would you do if your last three reports had been late?
Phil:	Well, what do you think the problem is? Do you start too late? There must be some reason why you mess up.
Wanda:	I don't know. The first thing I do is pull all the necessary information together before writing the report.
Phil:	Well, there's your problem. Pulling the information together is very time-consuming and shouldn't be postponed until the day the report is due. You should gather it throughout the month.

Now compare the conversation using active listening techniques.

Wanda:	Gee, there must be something wrong with me. Yesterday I messed up again in doing the monthly report. That's the way it always goes. I never seem to do anything right.
Phil:	You really sound upset.
Wanda:	Yes, I am. This report has me depressed. I feel like an incompetent. I hurried to get it in on time, and then it was wrong.
Phil:	So you had to hurry. Do you think that is what caused the difficulties?
Wanda:	Probably so. My last three reports were late, too.
Phil:	It sounds as if you have difficulty with late reports. What do you think you could do to keep your reports from being so late?
Wanda:	Well, I guess I could start pulling the information for the report earlier and not wait until the day the report is due.
Phil:	That's a good idea. Pulling the information early will help you not rush. Then your report will be out on time and with fewer mistakes.

Notice that when Phil used active listening, he did not jump to conclusions or prejudge Wanda. He asked for clarification, paraphrased her, and asked questions that made Wanda come to her own conclusions.

HOW CAN YOU IMPROVE YOUR SPOKEN COMMUNICATION?

Verbal communication is any message that we send or receive through the use of words, oral or written. Effective verbal communication requires good listening skills and an ability to use the written and spoken word.

Vital aspects of spoken communication are voice, word choice, using "I" phrases, following up, and speaking up. Also important is finding the right level on which to communicate and being discreet.

Voice

Our voices should be pleasant and appropriate for the situation. For example, an enthusiastic and even loud voice is appropriate in a social setting such as a party or loud restaurant. It would be inappropriate in a formal setting such as church or a quiet dinner in an elegant restaurant.

Word Choice

Correct grammar is important. We should develop an ability to use descriptive, specific verbs, adverbs, and adjectives. Slang should be used sparingly and carefully. Although occasional use of slang can lend color to our communication, it can also confuse listeners. Because the purpose of our speech is to communicate, not to impress, we should exercise care.

"I" Phrases

Beginning your communication with "I think," "I believe," "I feel," or "I don't understand" is much more effective than comments such as "You made me angry" or "You are wrong" or "You are confusing me." These phrases put people on the defensive and make them less open to listening to your whole message. The feelings and opinions belong to you. You formed them. Others do not make you do or feel anything.

Following Up

Verbal directives or complex instructions may need to be followed up in writing. Research has shown that immediately following a ten-minute lecture, college freshmen retain only 50 percent of it and forget half of that within 48 hours. Additionally, we know that about 30 percent of a message is lost or distorted after passing through two people.

Willingness to Speak Up

Sam Donaldson, a television commentator, suggests the following tips on how to talk:

1. Gain some training in speech or drama.
2. Don't worry excessively about what others will think. Everyone has normal fears about inadequacy.
3. Remember that your view is as good as the next person's. Although your opinion may not prevail or you may not have all the facts, you have nothing to be ashamed of in expressing your opinion. (Obviously, you should try to have most of the facts before speaking out, so that your opinions are educated ones.)
4. Don't let the fear of becoming tongue-tied stop you from speaking out. All

people have days when their thoughts will not come out or their subjects and verbs do not agree.

5. Ask precise, sharply phrased questions to gain information.

Other suggestions for improving your communication are shown in Figure 3.3. Review them carefully in relation to your own communication.

FIGURE 3.3   Suggestions for improving communication.

1. Listen to the message in the words and in the feelings.
2. Don't let your own ideas get in the way. Listen to what others are saying.
3. Know when *just* to listen. (Sometimes one person may withdraw, and you will need to be patient and supportive and just wait.)
4. Question assumptions. Appearances can be deceptive. Keep in mind that you are communicating with another distinctly individual human being who feels the need to like and be liked.
5. Tell the truth. (Small white lies such as "I like it" or "I'll be back in five minutes" can create hurt, confusion, and resentment.)
6. Think before speaking. Ask yourself, "What do I want to communicate?" (The key to communication is truly understanding what must be communicated.)
7. Now is the best time to get it correct. "I should have said" will never be enough.

Adapted from Malcolm Boyd, "How to Really Talk to Another Person." Parade Magazine *(February 19, 1989): 14–15.*

Choosing the Right Level

We communicate on many different levels. John Powell, in his book *Why Am I Afraid to Tell You Who I Am?*, describes four levels. The first level is the conventional or cliché conversation or cocktail conversation. This communication with strangers or casual acquaintances is fairly impersonal. An example is "How are you?" "Fine, how are you?"

The second level is exploratory. It is communication about facts or other people. For example, we may report, "John is going skiing." Notice that on this level we are not sharing information about ourselves. Rather, we are "exploring" our relationship with another by sharing neutral information.

Level three is participative. On this level we start talking about ourselves. Example: "I am going skiing." This talk can evolve into self-disclosure, in which we start to express our ideas and feelings.

Intimacy and free sharing make up the last level. At this deepest level we expose our intimate thoughts and feelings. Some risk may be involved. The person to whom we are expressing our ideas, for instance, may not like them.

If we are emotionally healthy and socially adept, we should be able to use all levels and know when each is appropriate. We cannot go through life being impersonal in all of our interactions, nor can we share our thoughts and feelings with everyone we meet. Again, common sense is our best guide in deciding what to say, to whom, and in how much detail.

Having a disagreement with a coworker or family member and telling the service station attendant all the details is inappropriate. However, sharing your opinion about a new procedure after your supervisor has sincerely asked for feedback (and you have no reason to fear reprisal) is. Telling your boss in a loud, angry, aggressive manner that she should fire a coworker immediately when you are unfamiliar with the documentation required before termination is another example of inappropriate sharing of feelings.

Keeping a Secret

Being discreet is extremely important in human relations. The importance of confidentiality in our work and personal relationships cannot be overemphasized. Communications consultant Mark McCormack cites a description millionaire Donald Trump made of Wall Street's Alan Greenberg, the CEO credited with the outstanding success of Bear, Stearns. Trump, one of Bear, Stearns' clients, was asked about Greenberg's most admirable traits. Although Trump might have mentioned Greenberg's stock market skills or other abilities, he named Greenberg's ability to keep a secret.

HOW CAN YOU IMPROVE YOUR WRITTEN COMMUNICATION?

Good writing skills are essential to career success. Writing, the most durable form of communication, is used frequently, particularly at higher levels of an organization.

The purpose of writing, like speech, is to communicate, not impress. Inexperienced writers sometimes think that they must change their personalities completely and write in a showy, unnatural manner in which they would never speak. These changes are neither necessary nor desirable. Every written communication creates a mental image of the sender. Will your writing style cause you to be viewed as disorganized, tedious, and even unreliable, or as an intelligent, clear thinker with a sense of purpose? Here are some suggestions to help you make your writing a positive reflection of you:

Follow the KISS rule in writting: Keep it short and simple.

1. *Sentence length.* Experts suggest that the average sentence length should be 17 words. A variety of means exists for analyzing the reading level of your writing, including computer programs.
2. *Wordiness.* Avoid thinking aloud on paper. Follow the KISS rule: "*K*eep *I*t *S*hort and *S*imple."
3. *Organization.* Think about what you want to communicate. What should be the logical progression of your message? Outlining and creating a rough draft can save your reader time and ensure that you are understood. High-

light your basic information—what your letter is about, what relevance it has to the reader, and what action the reader should take.

4. *Appropriate style or tone for the intended audience.* Know when writing should be formal and when more informal writing would be effective.

5. *Clearly stated purpose.* Ask yourself, "Why am I writing this message?" and then tell the reader. Figure 3.4 humorously depicts getting to the point.

FIGURE 3.4   Get to the Point!

Get to the Point!

"Gee, sometimes
life seems too tough.
I can't go on.
Life seems hopeless
and meaningless."

Shakespeare
HAMLET
Act III, Scene 1
Rough Draft

"To be, or not to be,
that is the question . . ."

Final Draft

Obey 4 C's: be complete, concise, correct, and conversational/clear.

Communications experts suggest that we follow the **4 C's of communication**. Writing should be complete, concise, correct, and conversational or clear.

After you have written a memo or letter, ask yourself the following questions about each of these qualities:

Complete. Have I included all necessary facts and answered all questions?

Concise. Have I deleted unnecessarily long words? Is my message one page or less? Are my paragraphs short and easy? Is important information obvious?

Correct. Is my message accurate? Does it agree with company policy? Are the grammar, spelling, and punctuation correct? Are corrections neat?

Conversational/clear. Is my writing easy to understand and friendly without being flowery? Have I avoided argumentative words or expressions?

Barrett Mandel and Judith Yellen, writing in *Working Woman*, give additional ways to make your writing effective. They suggest that you not say in writing what you would not say in public, not expect writing to remain confidential, not exaggerate, and not criticize coworkers. They also suggest that you wait 24 hours before sending anything written in anger; pay attention to format; be courteous, brief, factual, and specific; and follow the chain of command. Applying these suggestions can help you prevent trouble for yourself later.

HOW CAN YOU USE NONVERBAL COMMUNICATION?

Throughout this chapter, nonverbal communication has been mentioned several times. **Nonverbal communication** is any meaning conveyed through the body (body language), through the way the voice is used, and through the way people position themselves in relation to others. How something is said is frequently just as important as what is said. Tone of voice, facial expression, gestures, or haste may determine how we interpret the words used and may even overshadow them.

Reading the Signals

People with strong human relations skills are usually good at reading others' body language and in using nonverbal communication. Dr. Albert Mehrabian, an expert in nonverbal communication, says that nonverbal communication accounts for at least 93 percent of the impact of our communication and words only 7 percent. That 93 percent is made up of pace, pitch, and tone of voice (38 percent) and facial expressions (55 percent).

Examples of nonverbal communication at work include:

The computer operator who averts her head or turns her body away when the supervisor leans over to explain a graph. This motion may mean that she is uncomfortable with the closeness.

The employee who in a meeting rambles on in long, involved, unfinished sentences. He may feel insecure.

The employee who engages in much unnecessary body, hand, or foot movements. This behavior can signal tension.

The employee who sits at the head of the conference table and participates. He may be signaling confidence and interest. Environment, location, and seating can influence the kind of interaction that occurs.

Examples of nonverbal communication away from work include:

The mother who puts her hands on her hips and looks sternly at her child, indicating that the child had better do as she is told.

The father who smiles as he tells his son that he is disappointed the boy left the house last night without permission. He is sending a mixed message, with his words saying one thing and his body language saying another. When such a split occurs, we tend to believe the nonverbal communication. The message that the son will perceive is that his father approves.

Effective nonverbal communication helps us meet many needs.

Understanding nonverbal communication is important, because people often show their feelings and attitudes by their actions rather than their words. When we appreciate others' thoughts and feelings, we can interact more effectively with them.

Then we can meet our personal needs better on the job. These needs may include belongingness, approval, companionship, recognition, status, self-esteem, achievement, growth, and self-realization. Needs will be discussed in Chapter 6.

Some common means of communicating nonverbally are discussed below. They include posture, facial expressions, eye contact, voice, body movements, personal space, and seating.

Posture   How people sit or stand may reveal something about how they feel. A woman who sits in a chair with her legs wrapped around the chair legs, holding her head rigidly to one side, clasping her hands tightly or holding a clenched fist, is tense. Another tense person may be the man wandering about the room, or continually moving his hands and feet, or twisting his head from side to side.

Attitudes toward others can also be detected from posture. We project a positive attitude when we lean back slightly while standing at a close distance and maintaining eye contact with the other person.

Persons in high-status positions usually display their status through relaxed positions, such as one arm in their laps and the other across the back of a chair. They keep their heads level and straight forward. Those in lower-status positions keep their heads down and hands together or at their sides.

Facial Expressions   When we read facial expressions, we should do so in the total context of what is being said. Examining an isolated expression without being aware of the situation can cause us to make misleading conclusions. Also, some people do not show their emotions on their faces. We cannot always assume that people with no expression have no feeling.

Happiness, anger, surprise, disgust, and fear are the five emotional states that we display most often through facial expressions. The eyes and the lower face reveal these emotions. Individuals may display several of these emotions during the course of a conversation.

Smiling can detract from a serious message, as pointed out by Bonnie Gangelhoff in the opening anecdote to this chapter. Women tend to smile more than men, which can create misunderstandings for them at work and in their personal relations. If we express strong wants or needs but water them down with a smile, they may remain unmet because the receiver will not take our message seriously.

Eye Contact   Eye contact is a direct and powerful form of nonverbal communication. We generally use eye contact to signal a desire for communication, as when we try to make eye contact with a waiter in a restaurant. When we wish to avoid talking to someone, we look away and avoid eye contact.

Think about your eye contact behavior when your instructor asks a question that you cannot answer or when you approach someone in the hall. When you do not want your instructor to call on you, you will avoid making eye contact. When walking down the hall, you may look at the other person as long as you are far away. However, once you are about eight feet apart, you will probably look down or elsewhere until you are almost upon each other. Then you will probably look at each other, and you may or may not speak. Had you continued to look at the approaching person as you drew near, you would have signaled that you wanted or expected interaction.

Voice   The pitch, clarity, breathiness, articulation, resonance, tempo, rhythm, and speech rate all tell us something about the speaker. Insecure people tend to speak in complex, involved, or even unfinished sentences with poor pitch and volume control and with frequent nervous mannerisms. When people feel comfortable or secure, their voices tend to sound smooth and well modulated and their sentences are normal.

A loud voice, a fast rate of speech, and a high pitch may suggest that the speaker is having active feelings such as happiness, interest, surprise, fear, or anger. Passive feelings such as sadness, disgust, boredom, and sometimes fear are usually expressed by a quiet voice, low pitch, and slow rate of speech.

The tone of voice projects authority. A fast but not excessive tempo of speaking is more persuasive and is viewed as more trustworthy and enthusiastic.

Body Movements   Hand, arm, and body movements can reveal openness, suspicion and secretiveness, honesty, confidence, nervousness, or defensiveness. The chart in Figure 3.5 details the meanings of many movements.

FIGURE 3.5   Nonverbal communication clues.

Nonverbal Communication Clues

Shaking Hands
- If the hand is limp, the person is ill at ease or doesn't like to be touched.
- A firm handshake indicates the person has confidence.
- Politicians shake hands with both hands; they grasp the person's hand with their right hand and cup it with their left hand.

Defensiveness
- Arms crossed on chest; can also be a sign of disagreement.
- Closed fists; can also be a sign of nervousness.
- Sitting with a leg over the arm of a chair; can also be a sign of indifference.
- Crossed legs; moving of the crossed leg in a slight kicking motion signifies boredom or impatience.

Openness
- Open hands with palms upward.
- Men who are open or friendly and feel agreement is near will unbutton their coats and take them off.
- Arms and legs not crossed.

Evaluation
- Hand-to-cheek gestures; an interested person's body leans forward, head slightly tilted, supported by one hand.
- A critical evaluation is given with the hand brought to the face, the chin is in

Honesty
- Hand over heart.
- Palms uplifted.
- Looking the person in the eye when speaking.
- Touching gesture.

Frustration
- Short breaths; people who are angry take short breaths and expel air through their nostrils.
- Tsk; the sound usually made to communicate disgust.
- Tightly clenched hands.
- Wringing hands.
- Kicking the ground or an imaginary object.

Confidence
- Steepling (hands or arms brought together to form a church steeple).
- Hands joined together behind the body.
- Feet up on the desk.
- Elevating oneself.
- Leaning back in a seated position with both hands supporting head.

Nervousness
- Clearing throat.
- "Whew" sound.
- Whistling.
- Smoking cigarettes.
- Fidgeting in a chair.

Nonverbal Communication Clues (*continued*)

the palm, the index finger is extended along the cheek, and the remaining fingers are positioned below the mouth.
- A tilted head is a definite sign of interest.
- Stroking a chin indicates a thinking or evaluation process.
- The body leaning forward is a sign of interest.

Suspicion and Secretiveness
- A person who won't look at you is likely concealing something.
- Touching or rubbing the nose, usually with the index finger, is a sign of doubt or nontruth on the part of the speaker.
- Rubbing behind or beside the ear with the index finger when weighing an answer indicates doubt.

- Tugging at pants while sitting.
- Jingling money in pockets.
- Tugging at ear.
- Clenched fist.
- Wringing hands.
- Playing with pencils, notebooks, or eyeglasses in mouth.
- Touching yourself while speaking to others.

Boredom
- Drumming on table.
- Tapping with feet.
- Head in hand.
- Doodling.
- Swinging of crossed foot.

Jan Hargrave, OEA Communique *(March 1988):31. Used by permission of Business Professionals of America.*

Personal Space   We all have a personal space that forms a "bubble" around us. This is the space that we put between ourselves and others. It only becomes apparent when someone bumps or enters it.

We demand a larger personal space when situations are uncomfortable or threatening. The closer we feel to another psychologically, the closer we will stand physically. The size of the bubble varies from culture to culture. People in the United States generally have larger bubbles than people in other countries. A summary of the distances that we tend to maintain during different activities is shown in Figure 3.6.

When our personal space is violated, we may react with bewilderment or embarrassment or move away to create distance. Some of the ways in which we react when our space has been invaded are to turn our heads and place an elbow between ourselves and the intruder, to treat the intruder as a nonperson, or simply to leave the area. Respect for personal space can enhance our communication skills, because it allows others to concentrate on what is being said rather than on their discomfort.

Seating   Seating does make a difference in communication. High-status, dominant individuals tend to sit in the head position and participate more than those who sit along the length of the table. People in positions l, 2, 4, and 7 in Figure 3.7 will tend to contribute more and have greater influence on the decision-making process.

Additionally, the table arrangement can influence conflict development. When a group member stops talking, a person opposite, rather than on the same side, is more likely to begin speaking. For instance, if person 5 says something, person 8 will most likely speak next. Conflict is more likely to develop between persons sitting across from each other than between persons sitting next to each other.

FIGURE 3.6   E. T. Hall identified the distance zones that people maintain in their interactions and the common activities that take place in those zones.

DISTANCE ZONE	SIZE	COMMON ACTIVITIES
Intimate Distance Close Phase	Physical contact or nearly so	Lovemaking, wrestling, comforting, protecting.
Far Phase	6–18″	Crowding in subways, buses, etc.
Personal Distance Close Phase	1½′–2½′	Standing comfortably next to mate.
Far Phase	2½′–4′	Discussing subjects of personal interest and involvement.
Social Distance Close Phase	4–7′	Conducting impersonal business in an involved way; conversing with someone at a social gathering.
Far Phase	7–12′	Conducting formal business matters.
Public Distance Close Phase	12–25′	Speaking with a careful choice of words and phrasing ("formal style").
Far Phase	25′ or more	Setting 30′ distance around important public figures.

Try to sit near the leader during meetings. Also, attempt to speak early. It will help you relax and show that you are a force in the group.

Using the Signals

The National Institute of Business Management suggests that you can make your nonverbal communication work for you by the following means:

1. *Act confident:* Look people in the eye, stand straight with your chest thrust out, move fast and with determination, speak loudly and distinctly, and avoid nervous gestures.
2. *Look efficient:* Dress well and keep a neat but not sterile office.
3. *Get people to open up to you:* Lean forward when listening, look people in the eye, sit with arms and legs uncrossed, and nod occasionally. Smile, move in an open and relaxed manner, have a relaxed posture, and shake hands in a firm but not overpowering way. Mirror the other person's posture or match the voice tempo of the other person to build rapport. The other person will feel more comfortable with you.
4. *Be more effective on the telephone:* At the beginning of the conversation, explain the purpose of your call and indicate how long it will be. End calls gracefully, summarizing key points and thanking the other person, using a rising, upbeat tone of voice. Vary your tone, loudness, and speed. Allowing yourself to use natural gestures may help make your voice sound more natural and expressive.

FIGURE 3.7 Certain patterns of participation and leadership are associated with seating positions in work groups. This figure depicts eight members seated around a conference table.

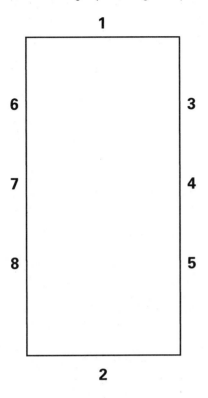

5. *Improve your speeches and presentations:* Be prepared. Practicing aloud in front of a mirror may help. Choose appropriate visuals, examples, anecdotes, and analogies. Keep your message short and simple.

   Look confident and calm, and your voice will relax. During the first half minute of your presentation, smile, walk confidently to the podium or front, establish eye contact by scanning the group, and say thank you to your introducer and audience. Beginning with a humorous or light remark or just a friendly "Hello, how are you today?" encourages the audience to participate and takes the pressure off you.

   Stay relatively centered before the group and change positions to emphasize points. Vary your distances from sections of the audience to stop their talking or to get them to participate. Lean forward when asked a question and look at all people in the group, not at just one part. Try to draw in nonattentive or nonresponsive people by looking at them.

6. *Appear more credible:* Avoid self-deprecating words or expressions such as "This may be a dumb idea" or tag questions such as "Don't you think?" Expressions that hedge, such as "sort of" or "kind of," or excessive superlatives like "really, really great" should not be used. Having notes can build confidence and add security in case you lose your train of thought. Don't

FIGURE 3.8   Effective use of nonverbal communication can make your presentations more successful.

panic if asked a negative question or given a negative argument; be prepared with a short answer.

To make your nonverbal communication further work for you, keep in mind certain cautions. Nonverbal communication must be considered in conjunction with the verbal message and the situation. If we try to interpret meaning from an isolated nonverbal cue, we may be wrong.

Nonverbal communication such as closeness or touching may be misinterpreted at work and may lead to charges of sexual harassment. Even an innocent pat on the back, hand around the waist, or pat on the knee can be mistaken for sexual interest. These types of nonverbal communication should be avoided in the workplace.

We must also recognize that nonverbal communication varies from culture to culture and that persons from other cultures cannot be accurately assessed using the cues presented in this chapter. For instance, the handshake is common in this country between men, women, and men and women. In many other countries customs differ about who shakes hands with whom. In Australia, for example, women do not usually shake hands with other women; in India men and women do not usually

FIGURE 3.9   Nonverbal communication varies from culture to culture. Customs differ, for example, about the handshake.

shake hands with one another; and in South Korea, women usually do not shake hands at all.

WHAT ELSE MAKES COMMUNICATION WORK?

Several other factors make all the difference between failure and success in communication. They include time, timing, context, medium, and humor.

Time, Timing, Context, and Medium

If we are to be effective in our communication, we must remember that at times everyone needs to be left alone or at least have communication demands reduced. At times our supervisors are tired, preoccupied, rushed, angry, or frustrated. If we force them to talk with us at those times, we should not be surprised or hurt if their response seems to be "I don't care" or "I don't want to discuss it." Timing of communication is important.

Most employees feel that they do not have enough communication with their supervisors. Supervisors will not necessarily ask for communication with us, so we must use our own judgment in determining what to tell them and when. You should keep your supervisor informed about matters for which your supervisor is held accountable and about upcoming proposals from you.

The way we use time is also important. People who are frequently tardy say that they are too disorganized to be on time. They also communicate that they lack respect for the person or group with whom they are meeting. Tardiness may also be used by individuals as a manipulative ploy to put themselves in a higher-status position. Whatever their reasons, they will cause frustration and anger and will lose respect. In a job situation, they may be disciplined or even fired. Developing the habit of punctuality can enhance your human relations skills and professional image.

The **context** of messages can markedly change their meanings. Context refers to the conditions in which something occurs, which can throw light on its meaning. Being yelled at to "stop that machine" creates a different response if we are about to be injured than if we are about to be yelled at by a dissatisfied supervisor. Hence, the context of a message must be considered along with its verbal and nonverbal components for accurate understanding.

The **medium** of a message is the form in which it is communicated. A registered letter from an attorney may create feelings that one through regular mail would not, as it seems more important than general delivery.

Humor

A sense of humor can create a favorable long-term impression. People usually like people with whom they can share a healthy laugh. The key is "healthy." Most people dislike sick jokes and lose respect for the person who is constantly clowning around.

A sense of humor can also help us get over some of the rough spots in life. Putting matters in proper perspective and not taking ourselves too seriously becomes easier to accomplish. Some health experts have even suggested that humor can make us physically healthier.

According to Bob Ross in an article in *Management,* a psychologist at the University of Maryland concluded through a study that "workers who have a good time are better at problem solving and are more effective on the job. Having fun at work, therefore, is serious business."

Again, common sense must be our guide. When does humor become silly, sick, or counterproductive? When does it save the day?

SUMMARY

Communication, the process by which we exchange information through a common system of symbols, signs, or behavior, is very important today because we live in an information society and we must interact with a variety of people. When communication breaks down, individuals and organizations suffer. Communication ability is a trait common in leaders and an important element in human relations.

Communication can flow up, down, or horizontally in an organization. It can also be one-way or two-way. Whatever the direction, the communication process includes three elements—the sender, the receiver, and the message. Feedback helps the receiver understand the message as the sender intended it. Feedback should be timely, often, and precise (TOP).

Communication can be distorted or blocked because of barriers. Some barriers are inadequate or distracted sensory organs, semantics, and emotions and attitudes of the sender or receiver. Others are role expectations, personality, appearance, prejudice, unnoticed changes, poor organization of ideas, information overload, and poor listening.

Our verbal communication can be made a strong part of our human relations skills if we develop good listening skills and an ability to use the written and spoken word. An important part of communicating verbally is recognizing that we communicate on many different levels and being able to use all levels appropriately. Careful attention to our voice, word choice, use of "I" phrases, following up, and speaking up will also help our verbal communication. Listening, a key element in strong human relations skills, can be improved through a variety of ways. Use of active listening is one important way. Being discreet is also important. Additionally, because good writing skills are essential to career success, employees should follow the 4 C's of communication.

Nonverbal communication is another form of communication. It is any meaning conveyed through the body, through the way the voice is used, and through the way people position themselves in relation to others. It accounts for at least 93 percent of the impact of our communication. Common means of communicating verbally include posture, facial expression, eye contact, voice, body movements, personal space, and seating. You can make your nonverbal communication work for you.

Time, timing, context, and medium of messages contribute additional dimensions of meaning to messages and communicators. Be careful that the image people receive of you from your use of these elements is the image that you wish to project.

Humor can create a favorable long-term impression, help us get over some of the rough spots in life, and make us more effective on the job. Common sense must be our guide to when it is appropriate.

KEY TERMS

communication
communication breakdown
sender

receiver
message
feedback
semantics
information overload
hear
listen
active listening
verbal communication
4 C's of communication
nonverbal communication
context
medium

REVIEW QUESTIONS

1. Define communication.
2. Explain the difference between verbal and nonverbal communication.
3. Describe common communication barriers and strategies for overcoming them.
4. What is information overload? What are some effective ways of avoiding it?
5. Discuss the levels of communication and their appropriate and inappropriate uses.
6. What are some guidelines to make your verbal messages and presentations more effective?
7. What are some suggestions for using active listening?
8. Name the qualities of strong written communication.
9. Why is an understanding of nonverbal communication important in organizations? What are the different components of nonverbal communication?
10. What do time, timing, context, and medium have to do with the effectiveness of communication?

DISCUSSION QUESTIONS

1. Review the active listening/nonactive listening conversation in this chapter. How are the two communications different? How are they similar?
2. Think of five words that have either gone out of style or are no longer used and five words that have developed new meanings. Share them with your classmates.
3. Think of conversations that you have had with friends or coworkers. Analyze them to determine on which of Powell's levels the conversations were held.
4. Review the opening anecdote in this chapter. Why do you think that Gangelhoff was bothered by the psychologist's smiling?

5. Think of ways in which you have used nonverbal communication today, both as a sender and as a receiver. Share these instances with your class-mates.

CASE STUDY 3.1

WHAT DID I SAY?

Lucy Dorty woke up excited. Today was going to be a big day for her. She finally had a chance to show management that she had some good ideas about how the company could be improved. Because of a new policy requiring open meetings, once a month any employee could speak for five minutes at the management meeting to express ideas or concerns. Having worked in the mailroom for three years, she had seen the great amount of time wasted by sorting and putting mail in individuals' boxes and then retrieving it and handing it to them at the front window. She thought that if each department were given a key to open its own box, much mailroom personnel time could be saved, speeding up distribution of mail and reducing the need for overtime.

Because of Lucy's excitement last night, she forgot to set her alarm and woke up late. Knowing that the meeting was scheduled for 8 A.M., she rushed through her dressing, which was never her strong point anyway. She stopped at the drive-through fast food restaurant on her way to work and ate her sandwich en route. Carrying the still half-full paper cup of coffee with her, she walked into the meeting 10 minutes late, banging the door in her excitement. She then frantically asked those around her whether her name had been called yet.

When her name was called, she jumped up, upsetting her coffee cup, and ran to the microphone. Although she had not made any notes, she knew what she wanted to say and started speaking loudly.

"You know . . ." The sound of her loud voice through the microphone startled her, and she lost her train of thought.

Starting over, she said, "What I mean is, you could, you know, save a lot of money if you let people get their own mail, you know. Don't you think?" Just then, she spotted a part of her breakfast sandwich on the front of her blouse and slapped at it with her hand. Looking back at the managers, she could not think what to say next and ended with "Well, that's all I really wanted to say."

The managers looked at each other blankly and then said, "Thank you, Miss Dorty," and called the next person.

Lucy eagerly waited for some response to her recommendation. Finally, she received a brief memo thanking her for her suggestion and stating that, after consideration, management had decided not to make a change. She later learned that management did not consider her proposal because they did not understand it. They thought she was recommending that everyone, including managers, go to the window to retrieve his own mail rather than having office staff pick it up twice a day.

Amazed, Lucy said, "What? I told them what I thought would work. Why didn't they understand?"

1. What did happen? Why didn't the managers understand what Lucy was recommending?

2. How could she have presented her message better?
3. How could she have made her nonverbal communication work for her?
4. Go back to the beginning of Lucy's day and point out each step that caused her communication to reflect negatively on her and her message.

CASE STUDY 3.2

COMMUNICATION CALAMITY

It was Christmas Eve at the Wonderland Toy Store. The employees were exhausted. Temporary help had been scarce, and everyone had been putting in twelve-hour days. Sleet was beginning to fall outside, which caused Anthony, the manager, to be late arriving. He had hit his car brake to avoid a dog in the road and had run into a ditch. Then he had had to wait 45 minutes for a tow truck to pull him out.

"Great," thought Anthony. "That's all I needed today. My wife has been angry at me for working so much overtime. Wait until she hears how much I had to pay for the tow truck and sees the car."

As Anthony entered the store, he noticed that it was extremely crowded. Shoppers nudged each other in the aisles, fighting over the few remaining toys. The telephones were ringing, and cash register three was malfunctioning.

Suddenly Anthony heard some loud voices. Someone was arguing. As he moved closer, he saw the stock boy, Sydney, and a well-dressed, handsome man. Both had raised their voices and were waving their hands excitedly.

"Buzz off!" Sydney yelled.

"That Sydney," thought Anthony angrily. "He's always causing trouble."

Anthony ran up to Sydney and yelled, "You're fired! Out!"

Sydney looked up at Anthony in surprise and began to protest.

"You're fired!" roared Anthony.

"Yeah!" yelled Sydney, as he stomped off. "And a Merry Christmas to you, too, Scrooge."

A bit later Vicky, the assistant manager, came into the manager's booth where Anthony was filling out Sydney's termination papers.

"You know, Anthony, Sydney didn't start that. The man yelled at him and demanded that he quit helping an elderly lady. When Sydney wouldn't, the man came over and grabbed him by the arm and jerked him away. That's when Sydney told him to buzz off."

1. Identify the communication barriers.
2. How should Anthony have handled the situation?
3. What communication skills should have been used?
4. What do you think the outcome would have been if these skills had been used?

BIBLIOGRAPHY

Body Language for Business Success. New York: National Institute of Business Management, Inc., n.d.

Boyd, Malcolm. "How to Really Talk to Another Person." ***Parade Magazine*** (February 19, 1989): 14–15.

Donaldson, Sam (as told to Laurie Werner). "Talk That Works." ***USA Weekend*** (September 22–24, 1989): 4–5.

Gangelhoff, Bonnie K. "Women Shouldn't Grin and Bear It." ***Houston Post*** (September 6, 1989): D-1.

Hall, E. T. ***The Hidden Dimension***. Garden City, New York: Doubleday, 1965.

Hall, E. T. ***The Silent Language***. Garden City, New York: Doubleday, 1966.

Hargrove, Jan. "Actions Speak." ***OEA Communique*** 12, no. 3 (March 1988): 28–31.

Mandel, Barrett J., and Judith Yellen. "Mastering the Memo." ***Working Woman*** (September 1989): 134–135.

McCormack, Mark. "Create a Good Impression." ***Success Secrets Newsletter***. Cited in ***Spirit*** (September 1989): 22.

McCoy, Doris Lee. ***Megatraits—12 Traits of Successful People***. Plano, TX: Wordware Publishing, Inc., 1988.

Mehrabian, A., and S. R. Ferris. "Inferences of Attitudes from Nonverbal Communication in Two Channels." In ***Nonverbal Communication***, edited by S. Weitz. New York: Oxford University Press, 1974.

Pfeiffer, J. William, and John E. Jones. ***A Handbook of Structured Experiences for Human Relations Training***. Vol. 1. San Diego, CA: University Associates, Inc., 1974, pages 13–18.

Pharriss, Joyce. "Memo Makeover: From Fog to Clarity." ***Working Woman*** (December 1989): 128.

Powell, John. ***Why Am I Afraid to Tell You Who I Am?*** Chicago: Argus Communications, 1969.

Reece, Barry L., and Rhonda Brandt. ***Effective Human Relations in Organizations***. Boston: Houghton Mifflin Company, 1987.

Ross, Bob. "Humor: A Tool for New Age Managers." ***Management*** (October 1988): 24–25.

SUGGESTED READINGS

Eisenberg, Abner M., and Ralph R. Smith, Jr. ***Nonverbal Communication***. New York: The Bobbs-Merrill Company, Inc., 1971.

Knapp, Mark L. ***Nonverbal Communication in Human Interaction***. New York: Holt, Rinehart and Winston, Inc., 1972.

Fast, Julius. ***Body Language***. New York: Evans and Co., 1970.

Martin, Phyllis. ***Word Watcher's Handbook—A Dictionary of the Most Misused and Abused Words***. New York: St. Martin's Press, 1982.

Nierenberg, G., and H. Calero. ***How to Read a Person Like a Book***. New York: Hawthorne, 1971.

Weitz, Shirley, ed. ***Nonverbal Communication***. New York: Oxford University Press, 1974.

CHAPTER FOUR
GROUP DYNAMICS

Anita's alarm goes off at 6:00 A.M. She quickly dresses for work and goes downstairs for breakfast with her two sons, her mother, and the family dog, ChaChi. A horn blast beckons her out the back door into the carpool van already loaded with her fellow workers at the Space Center who live in her neighborhood. Anita is a Branch Chief in the Flight Data and Evaluation Division of NASA's Orbiter Projects Office and has a full day of meetings and activities that will keep her busy well into the evening hours. Today's schedule looks busy with hardly a moment to spare:

MONDAY AUGUST 19

9:00 A.M.	Regular branch staff meeting
10:00 A.M.	Contractor status meeting
11:00 A.M.	" " "
12:00 noon	Lunch—Ralph
1:00 P.M.	Technical manager's staff meeting
2:00 P.M.	Configuration control board meeting
3:00 P.M.	" " " "
4:00 P.M.	Fact finding on escape suit cost proposal
5:00 P.M.	" " " " " " "
6:00 P.M.	Aerobics class—NASA Recreation Center

Another meeting begins at 7:00 P.M. at the Rec Center for the monthly council-level meeting of the National Management Association. Anita is chairperson of the Southwest Regional Conference scheduled for later in the year. The 12 committees she has appointed are to report current status and projected plans for their activities with only one hour to cover the topics.

Anita has made plans to join friends for dinner at the Ambiance Hotel Restaurant and Club afterwards. This dinner spot was chosen as a matter of convenience because at 9:30 P.M. her singles group is scheduled to celebrate a member's birthday and enjoy a festive evening on the terrace with the Harmonics Band and lead singer, Joe. Anita has scheduled a full and busy day, interacting with many groups in a variety of situations.

OBJECTIVES

After studying this chapter, you should be able to:
1. Describe the characteristics of a group.
2. Explain the importance of studying groups.
3. Explain the reasons people join groups.
4. Distinguish among types of formal groups.

5. Explain the importance of recognizing the emergent or informal leader.
6. Describe the cycle groups go through in an effort to mature.
7. Discuss several factors that influence group effectiveness.
8. Recognize the pitfalls of groups.
9. Identify the various roles evident in group interactions.
10. Discuss the importance of using groups in the decision-making process.

WHAT IS A GROUP?

We interact in many groups daily.

A **group** consists of two or more persons who are aware of one another, interact with one another, and perceive themselves to be a group. From the time we wake up each morning, we are involved in group interaction. Anita's busy schedule brought her in touch with many small and large groups, ranging from personal to professional. Her experiences represent the wide range of group activities that many people with today's busy life styles encounter.

Group members usually interact on a regular basis and have a shared desire to attain common goals. Groups take many forms and evolve from many sources. The one common thread in any group is the purpose of satisfying needs—be they organizational needs or individual needs. A group can be as large as an entire textile mill population or a battalion of the U.S. Marine Corps. However, the focus of this chapter will be on the expected behavior and problems associated with small groups whose members interact face-to-face.

WHY ARE GROUPS IMPORTANT TO THE WORKPLACE?

The formation of groups in the workplace is natural. Groups tend to form whenever people are located close together and see and talk to one another on a frequent basis. They are then able to share ideas, opinions, and feelings and to pursue similar activities.

Groups influence behavior and performance at work.

Work groups influence the overall behavior and performance of individuals in the workplace. Figure 4.1 illustrates the relation of behavior and morale to performance and productivity. As can be seen, the behavior of a work group does influence

FIGURE 4.1   Group behavior influences productivity.

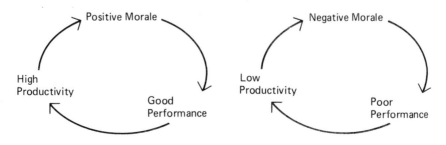

productivity. A positively motivated group can increase productivity. Unfortunately, a negative group can construct roadblocks to an organization's success.

This fact was first substantiated during the late 1920s when the Hawthorne experiments studied several work groups to determine the physical effects of lighting on the productivity of workers in the Hawthorne Plant of Western Electric. Two groups were observed. One experienced various changes in lighting. The other, a control group, experienced no lighting changes. The production in both groups rose because the contact and concern of the individuals doing the observations increased morale, and morale, in turn, increased productivity. The experiment further revealed that the plant workers had definite group norms related to work output, preferred channels of communication, acceptable behavior among group members, and roles for each member.

These and many other studies done from the 1930s to the 1950s left little doubt about the importance of group dynamics in the workplace. Harold Leavitt, an expert on groups, summarized why groups are important and should be taken seriously:

1. Small groups satisfy needs within individuals and are good for them.
2. Groups can promote creativity and innovation and can be used to solve problems.
3. Groups can make better decisions, in many instances, than individuals.
4. Group decisions are more willingly carried out because group members are committed to the decisions.
5. Group members can frequently control and discipline their members more effectively than the formal disciplinary system can.
6. Small groups lessen the impersonality of large organizations, allowing better communication and a sense of belonging.
7. Groups are a natural part of an organization. They cannot be prevented.

For these reasons many organizational and company cultures use team concepts, participative management, and group decision making when appropriate. Additionally, today's work force members are demanding a greater voice in decisions that affect them. Groups will become ever more important in the workplace.

WHY ARE GROUPS IMPORTANT TO INDIVIDUALS?

Groups give us affiliation, power, self-esteem, and accomplishment.

The reasons that we join groups vary depending on our needs and which needs are strongest at any given time. However, studies in the area of need satisfaction have identified the four most common reasons for joining groups. They are social connection, power, self-esteem, and goal accomplishment.

Social Connection (Affiliation)

Groups can provide us with a sense of belonging and reduce our feelings of aloneness. Being a member of a social group gives us an opportunity to share ideas or to exchange information, making us feel needed and increasing our sense of worth.

People tend to feel a stronger sense of affiliation when they join a group on a voluntary basis than when they are formally assigned to a group, as the following example indicates:

> **Rodrigo was reviewing his weekly calendar when he noticed that the meeting of his Hispanic group was scheduled for Wednesday evening.**
>
> **"I enjoy that monthly meeting," he thought. "The people are fun. Carmen was helpful in introducing me to my new employer. I can't wait to share the information from the workshop I attended last week. These meetings are much more enjoyable than our staff meetings at work."**

Power (Security)

Power (security) is another reason for joining groups. The fact that there is power in numbers is no secret. Groups may give us the confidence and courage to speak out and make certain requests. This sense of power and security can also provide us with the confidence to tackle difficult tasks by removing the feeling of facing the task alone:

> **Sarah and John decided to attend the union meeting being held to discuss the removal of the soft drink machines from the snack room.**
>
> **"I'm angry," said John. "The plant superintendent wouldn't listen to me, but I bet he will listen to the union, especially when he hears that the whole membership is up in arms!"**

Self-esteem (Ego)

People frequently join groups for self-esteem or ego satisfaction. Membership in some groups can raise our sense of being "somebody." This is especially true if the group is a prestigious one (known for its power, unique skills, social status, or innovative and profitable ideas). Few people want to be "outsiders." They feel greater satisfaction in being members of the "in" crowd. The following example indicates how participation gives a sense of gratification and satisfies ego needs:

> **"Hey, Mom, I'm running for the position of president of my writing organization," exclaimed Martha. "You know that I have been a member for four years now, and I want the recognition and rewards that come with leading the whole group."**
>
> **Martha's mother smiled. She knew that what Martha also wanted was the prestige of heading this elite group.**

Goal Accomplishment (Strategy)

Joining a group may enable us to accomplish goals more easily because we can learn skills and acquire knowledge from other members of the group. Individual members may either have their own goals and objectives or simply agree with the goals desired by other members of the group and be willing to work toward the same end:

John has always wanted to become involved in community service work but has never done so. Three weeks ago he was offered the opportunity to serve on the United Way fund-raising committee for his organization. He jumped at the opportunity.

"You know," he told Adrian, the committee chairperson, as they were leaving a meeting, "I'm very excited about this committee. I've always wanted to do community service but did not know how to go about it."

Groups, then, are important to both organizations and individuals. Learning how and why groups are formed, what changes them, and when they can be counterproductive is vital to your survival in an organization.

WHAT TYPES OF GROUPS EXIST?

Two basic types of groups exist. The **primary group** consists of family members and close friends, whereas the **secondary group** is made up of work groups and social groups. This chapter focuses on the secondary groups that are essential to workplace operations and evident in our social surroundings.

Within the secondary group category are two types of groups, the formal group and the informal group. Both group types are important in the workplace. Although they may support similar organizational goals, they may also satisfy different needs.

The Formal Group

The formal group is officially set up for a task or objective.

The **formal group** is generally designated by the organization to fulfill specific tasks or accomplish certain organizational objectives. Group members may have similar or complementary skills, responsibilities, or goals clearly related to the organizational purpose. Positions within the formal group are officially identified, usually "assigned" to individuals, and meant to provide order and predictability in the organization.

Two kinds of formal groups exist. The first is the **functional group,** which is made up of managers and subordinates assigned to certain positions in the organizational hierarchy. If you have ever held a job and reported to a supervisor, you have been a member of a functional group. Group positions or assignments in functional groups are usually permanent and serve as the skeleton of the organizational structure:

Alex is a nurse's aide at the Sunny Time Home for the elderly. His functional group consists of individuals assigned to care for the residents who are not able to tend to themselves or walk to the cafeteria for meals. Alex performs this task with five other nurse's aides, one social worker, two janitors, and one registered nurse who is the shift supervisor. The registered nurse, in turn, is supervised by the director of nursing, who supervises the entire nursing staff in the facility.

The second kind of formal group is the **task group**, which is formed for a specific reason with members drawn from various parts of the organization to accomplish a specific purpose. The common example of a task group is the **committee**.

FIGURE 4.2   Formal groups are found in the workplace.

Committees may be formed to develop procedures, solve problems, form recommendations for decision making, or exchange ideas and information. Committees may be considered ongoing or ad hoc.

Ongoing committees are relatively permanent groups that address organizational issues on a standing or continuous basis. Examples include plant safety committees, employee promotion boards, or monthly cost review committees.

Ad hoc committees, on the other hand, have a limited life, serving only a one-time purpose, and disband after accomplishing that purpose. Examples of an ad hoc committee include the Rogers Commission formed to investigate the *Challenger* accident in 1986, a committee formed to plan a going-away party for the department secretary, or a committee gathered to plan a celebration for the birth of the manager's first child.

Informal Groups

Informal groups are formed by individuals to satisfy personal needs.

In addition to formal groups, informal groups may exist in the organizational setting. Unless you are a loner, you, no doubt, are a member of one or more informal groups at work. **Informal groups** are created by the group members themselves because the formal group seldom satisfies all of their individual needs. Although the informal group does not appear on the formal organization chart, it does have a powerful influence on members' behavior. Informal groups exist in all organizations and do not necessarily indicate that the formal group is inadequate or ineffective. Figure 4.3 illustrates the differences between formal and informal groups.

Groups may form to share a common interest.

Informal groups may be peer groups that form because members have common interests, such as politics, recreational preferences, or religion. Peer groups also

FIGURE 4.3   Types of groups.

TYPES OF GROUPS

Formal	Informal
Has recognized authority.	Has little or no authority.
Has a mission or direction.	May have a mission.
Has organized structure.	Has no organizational legitimacy.
Has organizational legitimacy.	Considered a shadow organization.

form to satisfy members' needs for informal job training, to provide them opportunity for status, or to help them gain information concerning the organization. An example of this occurrence follows:

> **Albert, a 26-year-old attorney, is a baseball fan and has joined the company baseball team. He loves playing in the weekly games and enjoys the company of others on the team. Secretaries, engineers, mailroom clerks, accountants, and attorneys for the company can frequently be seen on the playing field or having a hamburger together after the game.**
>
> **Albert also has a task group with which he frequently associates on the job. This group includes Mary, who is an older attorney with years of legal experience. Albert frequently seeks her advice about cases with which he is having difficulty. Marvin, an engineer, is another group member with whom he trades information. Marvin dislikes sports and would much rather spend his days watching movies on his VCR. However, he knows what is going on in engineering and can always answer technical questions. Albert is also able to answer legal questions for Marvin.**

The various peer groups are not mutually exclusive and do overlap at times. While working in an organization you can have relationships on both personal and professional levels that fulfill your needs within the organization. Furthermore, the wider your circle of acquaintances is, the easier time you will have in fulfilling your needs.

WHO LEADS A GROUP?

Within any group may be two leaders—a formal leader and an informal leader. The **formal leader** is the one who is officially given certain rights or authority over other group members and who has a degree of legitimacy. Examples of formal leaders are supervisors, team captains, and organization presidents.

The **informal leader** is the person within the group who is able to influence other group members because of age, knowledge, technical skills, social skills, personality, or physical strength. This leader is also known as the **emergent leader**

FIGURE 4.4 Groups may form to share a common interest.

because he or she will emerge without formal appointment or formal recognition but can, and often does, exert more power or influence than the formal leader. The differences between formal and informal leaders are outlined in Figure 4.5.

The formal leader must be able to recognize the informal leader, determine that person's purposes and goals, and deal with them. If the formal and informal leaders have different objectives, conflict will arise within the group.

FIGURE 4.5 Types of group leaders.

TYPES OF GROUP LEADERS

Formal	Informal
Is the boss.	Recognizable force.
Is appointed to the position.	Unofficial designation.
Has legitimate power.	Emerges because of being
Is officially designated.	• respected
	• likable
Has authority with	• knowledgeable
responsibility.	• technically competent
	• a senior team member
Has a mission.	• large physically
	• older

HOW DO GROUPS DEVELOP?

Groups mature through several stages.

A group is considered mature when its members help each other and address problems that impede its work. Groups go through five different stages to reach maturity. Some never make it to the last stage; others may even move back to previous stages. According to Aldag and Stearns, groups go through the following phases on their way to maturity:

1. *Membership.* During the first stage individuals are deciding how much time, energy, and effort they wish to commit to the group. In addition they are becoming acquainted with other group members and seeing how their goals fit with group goals. Members seldom take strong stands at this stage.

2. *Subgrouping.* Individuals form subgroups with those who have similar interests and backgrounds. Because of subgroup support, individuals are more willing to voice their opinions and take risks. Group goals become more clear, and most individuals have made a commitment to the goals. Group cohesiveness and output increase. However, rivalries may develop among subgroups, which dampens group effectiveness.

3. *Confrontation.* As individuals become more secure in the group, they move from voicing opinions to engaging in disagreements and conflicts. If groups learn how to deal with disagreements constructively, real progress occurs. The group itself becomes stronger and the subgroups less important.

4. *Individual differentiation.* Members now feel free to pursue their own area of responsibility and to be themselves as they work toward group goals. Groups at this stage are effective. Unfortunately, few groups reach this level of maturity.

5. *Collaboration.* Members actively help each other to complete assignments and tasks. If individuals do not successfully carry out their duties, group members will confront them and take action to ensure that no future problems occur.

Group effectiveness depends on behavior of individuals, synergy, cohesiveness, norms, size, status of members, and the task.

Groups are in a constant state of change. Some of the changing factors in group effectiveness are behavior of members, synergy (combined action or operation) of the group, its degree of cohesiveness, group norms that evolve, size of the group, status of group members, and nature of the task to be accomplished by the group.

Behavior of Individuals

The behavior of individuals is in a constant state of fluctuation. As people begin to perceive things differently, they may alter their behavior within the group. Changes in behavior may occur for a number of reasons, such as the influence of family, peers, continued education, or acquisition of new skills. These behavior changes may have a positive or negative effect on the group. For example, you may once have been a member of a group of friends that socialized together every weekend. As individual members became involved in personal relationships, other friendships, or work or school responsibilities, the group grew smaller or broke up.

The group can also cause individuals to behave differently while they are within the group setting. Some people, for instance, behave one way in a one-on-one situation and completely differently in a group atmosphere.

Synergism

Synergism is the interaction of two or more independent parts, the effects of which are different from those they would attain separately. More simply stated, it means the whole is often greater than the sum of its parts. Groups can take advantage of synergism to develop better ideas and make superior decisions through the process of **brainstorming**. Brainstorming involves generating ideas freely without judging the ideas. The group then takes the ideas and forms a plan of action. These decisions are generally more effective because group members have a greater pool of ideas from which to draw. Studies have shown that decisions made by groups generally produce better results. The collective creativity of the group increases the number of alternative solutions generated, and group consensus assures commitment from individual group members. The effort is more likely to become a self-fulfilling prophecy.

FIGURE 4.6   Brainstorming can help groups develop better ideas and make superior decisions.

Reprinted by permission of NEA, INC.

Additionally, our involvement as group members in the decision-making process enhances our feelings of worth (as contributors) and of belonging to the group (as members). These are but a few of the benefits of using groups when making decisions.

Cohesiveness

Another of the factors influencing a group's behavior is cohesiveness. **Cohesiveness** is the degree to which group members are of one mind and act as one body. In general, the more cohesive a group is, the more effective it is, and, as the group becomes more successful, it becomes even more inseparable. This effect occurs because cohesive group members stick together, supporting and encouraging one another. Also, this support helps reduce stress for group members, leading to greater job satisfaction.

Group cohesiveness develops through a number of factors, one of which is group size. Smaller groups tend to be more cohesive because they can more readily communicate and exchange ideas, goals, and purposes.

Similarity of the individuals in a group is also a factor in cohesiveness. The more individuals have similar values, backgrounds, and ages, the more cohesive they tend to be. Cohesiveness is also more likely to be present in groups with high status.

Sometimes groups become more cohesive because of outside pressures. The "It's you and me against the world" attitude draws members together to support and assist each other.

Group Norms

The development of group norms is another of the factors that influences group effectiveness. **Group norms** are shared values about the kinds of behaviors that are acceptable or unacceptable to the group. These norms are standards of behavior that each member is expected to follow—similar to rules that apply to team members. Group norms develop slowly over time and usually relate to those matters of most importance to the group as a whole. Expected conformity to these norms applies only to our behavior and does not affect our private thoughts and feelings.

Deviance from group norms may provoke sanctions, from rejection to violence.

Nonconformity, or **deviance**, from group norms may provoke obvious displays of displeasure, ranging from rejection to physical violence or vicious harassment. The following list represents a few of the more common **sanctions**, actions taken to force compliance with established norms. Each is considered in the context of a work group of four secretaries, of whom only one, Rebecca, smokes. The subtle and not-so-subtle suggestions from the other three secretaries that she not smoke in the office have fallen on deaf ears.

1. *Ostracism* (cold-shoulder treatment). The nonsmokers have quit inviting Rebecca to lunch with them and do not include her in their coffee breaks and informal discussions.
2. *Verbal criticisms.* The nonsmokers frequently make critical comments to Rebecca about her clothes smelling like cigarettes, about ashes on her desk, and about the time she wastes lighting and puffing cigarettes.
3. *Open ridicule.* The nonsmokers have started imitating Rebecca, both in front of her and behind her back, blowing exaggerated smoke rings in the air and brushing imaginary ashes off the front of their blouses.
4. *Malicious gossip.* The nonsmokers begin gossiping about Rebecca's actions both on and off the job.
5. *Harassment.* The nonsmokers begin to save the pleasant tasks for themselves, giving Rebecca the most undesirable jobs to do.
6. *Intimidation.* The nonsmokers threaten to make sure that appropriate persons know about her real or fictitious sloppy work.
7. *Physical violence.* The nonsmokers decide to show Rebecca that they are serious about their complaints and set a mousetrap in the drawer where she keeps her cigarettes. When she reaches in, she suffers a bruised finger.

The type of sanction taken may depend on how important group members perceive the violated norm to be. Some norms are considered more important than others. **Critical norms** are considered essential to the survival and effectiveness of the group as a whole. Others are considered **peripheral norms** because they are not perceived as damaging to the group and its members. The sanctions for violating these norms are less severe than those for critical norms, as the following example indicates:

> **Janet assumed a position of vice-president of a bank in a small town in Kansas. For four months, she routinely appeared at work in bright-colored, flamboyant clothes, heavy makeup, and loud jewelry and sported the latest extreme hairstyle. Eventually she became concerned because none of the local business people asked her to lunch or to parties in their homes as they did some of the other bank employees.**
>
> **When Janet asked the bank president for advice, his response was, "Well, Janet, to be perfectly honest, you just don't fit into the group. This is a conservative town, and people here expect their bankers to dress in a traditional manner."**

FIGURE 4.7   Groups may punish individuals who do not conform to group norms.

The sanctions for violating critical norms can be severe. Often personal safety and career success may depend on an individual's ability to operate within the bounds of established acceptable group norms:

> **Richard returned to his car after a 12-hour shift at the refinery. The windshield was broken, the tires slashed, and the headlights smashed.**

"Scab! Traitor!" yelled the union members who were picketing the refinery for safer working conditions and better benefits. "Don't cross our picket line again!"

We learn about group norms in various ways. In formal groups we learn norms through formal orientation programs, classroom training, and on-the-job training. In informal groups we grasp group norms through conversations with other group members and observation of their behavior.

Often group norms enhance group effectiveness. For instance, the group may ostracize or criticize other members who fail to do their fair share of the work or fail to behave in a way that is constructive on the job. The individuals may react to this unpleasant treatment by increasing their productivity or changing their behavior.

Unfortunately, group norms sometimes prevent members from working toward the goals of the organization. For instance, an assembly line worker may not work as fast as possible because the others at work might reject him. In this case the sanctions and rewards of the informal group are stronger than those of the formal organization. The following example demonstrates how group norms can interfere with the goals of the organization and goals of the individual:

Arthur called Ying into the office. "Congratulations," he said. "You have been chosen to be the new supervisor when I am promoted next month. Your work is superb and my boss and I have confidence that you will be able to handle the group."

Ying was stunned. He was not expecting the promotion, even though he had often thought about it. At first he thought of the power and prestige of the position. Then he began to realize that the relationship with his coworkers, who were his best friends, would never be the same. They bowled on Thursday nights, got together with their families for a cookout once a month, and regularly ate lunch together in the lunchroom.

If Ying became a supervisor, this would end. The gang liked to talk about management during these activities, and he knew everyone would feel uncomfortable talking around him. What if he knew something, such as who was to be terminated, and he did not tell? Would his friends become angry at him?

"Thank you for the offer, Arthur," Ying said, "but I am not interested in the supervisory position."

If you become the target of group sanctions, evaluate your situation carefully. Are the sanctions being applied because you have not followed group norms meant to increase organizational effectiveness? If so, determine why you are behaving the way you are and how you can change your behavior to increase organizational effectiveness.

Nonconformists at work can expect sanctions.

If you determine that the sanctions being applied are counterproductive to the organization and your career, you have several choices. You can conform to the norms (thus jeopardizing your job), attempt through persuasion and the use of effective communication skills to persuade group members to change the norms, tolerate the sanctions, or ask for a transfer to another area that would limit your interaction with the group.

Group Size

The size of a group will also influence its effectiveness. Studies have shown that the preferred group size for maximum effectiveness in problem solving and decision making is five or seven members. Groups of any larger size begin to experience problems with communication and coordination. Groups with even numbers of members may have greater difficulty in obtaining a majority opinion if members are equally divided in their opinions. Having no person to act as tie-breaker can cause increased tension. The uneven-numbered group size offers an easy solution to this problem. Figure 4.8 identifies the characteristics of group interaction in certain group sizes.

FIGURE 4.8   Characteristics of group sizes.

CHARACTERISTICS OF GROUP SIZES

Fewer than five	More than seven
Fewer people to share task responsibilities.	Fewer opportunities to participate.
More personal discussion.	Members feel inhibited.
More participation.	Domination by aggressive members.
Increased tension among group members.	Tendency for "cliques" to form.
Greater sense of satisfaction.	More diverse opinions shared.
Greater cohesion.	Greater likelihood of absenteeism and turnover.
	Coordination of activities more difficult.
	Less cohesion.
	Team effect lost.
	Individual identities tend to be retained.

Status of Group Members

The status of group members can also influence group effectiveness. What gives a person status may vary from group to group. In some groups, higher social class and economic success may create a perception of higher status. In these groups, members who are financially successful, come from "good" families, or have college degrees may be seen to have more status. They may be given more respect, and other group members may pay more attention to them. People in white collar jobs are sometimes seen as being superior to those in blue collar positions. Similarly, salaried workers may be seen as having higher status than those paid by the hour.

Clothing and cars can also make a difference in how much status people are perceived to have. In some groups, individuals who dress fashionably in expensive clothes and drive costly cars are seen as having higher status. In other groups, the reverse may be true; expensive clothing and cars would be considered showy.

Physical appearance is another factor that can influence status. Some studies have suggested that people who are overweight may be viewed negatively. Individuals who are tall are sometimes seen as being more competent and powerful.

Status at work is conveyed in a variety of ways. For instance, those in higher-status positions may have an office with a window, a larger or corner office, reserved parking, and nicer office furniture and decorations. Executives may even have special dining rooms separate from other employees or have memberships in private clubs.

Groups whose members have high status are more effective because they are able to get things done. However, sometimes the status of individual group members can impede the group's brainstorming process. It may cause the group's efforts to be less productive.

Nature of the Task

The last of the factors influencing group effectiveness is the nature of the task itself. When a decision is required on a subject that is simple and uncomplicated, a highly homogeneous group whose members have similar backgrounds and compatible beliefs may be best.

When the task is complex and difficult, group members should be of dissimilar backgrounds and drawn from a variety of sources. This makeup will ensure diversity of ideas, foster creativity among the members, and result in a wider selection of alternatives from which to choose a solution.

WHAT ARE THE PITFALLS OF GROUP DECISION MAKING?

Wasting time, groupthink, and role ambiguity worsen group decisions.

Three factors may negatively influence group decision making. They are wasting time, groupthink, and role ambiguity.

Wasting Time

The group decision-making process is time-consuming. If it is not handled correctly, it can waste time and cause costly delays, indecisiveness, and diluted answers. For this reason, groups must be handled with skill.

Groups should not make emergency or small decisions.

Not all situations lend themselves to group decision making. For example, an emergency situation such as a fire is hardly the time to call the fire fighters together for ideas on how the fire should be extinguished and who should perform which tasks. The fire chief, barking out orders, gets the job done more effectively. Or perhaps the decision is such an easy one that it needs only a quick fix. For situations like this, making the decision yourself is certainly acceptable.

However, if the situation lends itself to group decision making, this process is the preferred method. For example, if office policy is to be revised and enough time

FIGURE 4.9   Small decisions do not need group decision-making skills.

remains to seek office staff opinions, you would do well to apply the participative approach.

Groupthink

Irving Janis identified the phenomenon of **groupthink** and defined it as "the process of deriving negative results from group decision-making efforts as a result of in-group pressures." Through groupthink, a group may be led to a conclusion without fully exploring or even considering creative alternatives.

For example, a supervisor may call a meeting of subordinates to determine how a new office procedure is to be implemented and start the meeting with the statement, "I believe the best way for us to do this is to . . . , don't you agree?" The pressure to accept the leader's approach and to retain group cohesion results in a "rubber stamp" of what may appear as a predetermined conclusion. The supervisor may even interpret the group's silence as a resounding and unanimous acceptance of the "proposed" approach rather than an attempt at retaining group cohesion.

All of us are influenced by our peers, especially those with more status or greater expertise. We should, however, try to avoid falling victim to groupthink.

Role Ambiguity

Roles of individual members are readily apparent when the group is a formal one with certain positions identified. This formal identification helps to define the role an individual is expected to play. However, in informal groups, these roles may not be as clearly designated. Expected behavior may never be stated or in any way formalized.

Role ambiguity occurs when individuals are uncertain about what role they are to fill or what is expected of them. All of us experience some initial feelings of role ambiguity when we join new groups. Figure 4.10 defines several of the roles most frequently expected in group situations. You may recognize some of these roles from groups in which you have been involved. Perhaps you will recognize roles that you have played in group interactions.

FIGURE 4.10   Group members play a variety of roles within the group.

GROUP MEMBER ROLES

Information seeker	Asks for facts, feelings, suggestions, and ideas about the group's concern.
Information giver	Gives the information about the group's concerns, stating facts and feelings; gives ideas and makes suggestions.
Coordinator	Pulls all the group ideas and suggestions together and recommends a decision or conclusion for the group to consider.
Gatekeeper	Keeps communication channels open; facilitates participation.
Harmonizer (police officer)	Reduces tension and reconciles differences.
Observer	Provides feedback on the group's progress; remains neutral and uninvolved in the process.
Follower	Goes along with the group; offers no resistance to suggestions or ideas.
Blocker	Resists any suggestions or ideas of the group; acts negatively toward group purpose and members.
Avoider	Resists interacting with group members; keeps apart from interaction.
Dominator (bulldozer)	Forces opinions, ideas, and desires on the other group members; manipulates group behavior by asserting status or authority, using flattery, interrupting others, and other aggressive and obnoxious measures.

WHAT CAUSES DEVIANCE?

According to Harold W. Berkman and Linda L. Neider in *The Human Relations of Organizations*, deviance can be caused by a number of factors. One is that the sanctions of the group are ineffective. The penalty for noncompliance may not be strong enough to stop the behavior. For instance, if smoking is banned in the office, some employees may continue to smoke at their desks despite the rule. If the supervisor takes no action other than reminding them not to smoke at their desks, they are not likely to change their behavior.

Ignorance is another reason for deviance. A city may have a regulation against walking on the grass. If the sign is not visible and people are not aware of the regulation, they may violate the regulation unknowingly.

Sometimes deviance may be a way for employees to display their frustration and aggression, as the following example indicates:

"That Jane!" muttered Leslie. "She is the worst supervisor I ever had. She embarrassed me in front of the group when she criticized my work. I'll fix her, though. Just wait until she starts to look for the last monthly report. I'll put it where she'll never find it!"

Organizations have formal rules to control deviance. For example, individuals who are tardy may have their pay docked, receive reprimands or warnings, be suspended, or even be terminated. These formal sanctions may help correct the unacceptable behavior. In addition, viewing a coworker suffering the consequences of violating formal rules sometimes has the effect of making individuals try harder to comply with formal regulations.

However, sometimes formal rules backfire and cause more deviance. For instance, if an organization decides that all employees must report promptly at 6 A.M. for work every day when the traditional time to start is 9 A.M., most likely many people will be tardy. Employees may become disgruntled with the new regulations and openly defy them.

If excessive deviance is occurring, management needs to examine its regulations and see whether they can be modified to satisfy the needs of both the company and the employees. A program of flexible time, in which workers begin work at a time that is most desirable for them, may be the answer.

SUMMARY

We all interact with a variety of groups on a day-to-day basis. Organizations encourage groups because they increase productivity and effective decision making. Individuals join groups because they fulfill needs such as power, affiliation, self-esteem, and goal accomplishment.

Secondary groups can be formal groups, which the organization creates for certain purposes, or informal ones, which spontaneously develop because individuals work close to one another. Each group may have two leaders, a formal and an informal (emergent) one. Groups go through various stages on their way to maturity, and many groups never reach the fully mature stage.

Groups are influenced by many factors that can affect their productivity, such as behavior of individual, synergism, group cohesiveness, group norms, group size, status of members, and nature of the task. Although groups do, in general, make better decisions than individuals, pitfalls occur. Groups can be time wasters, give in to groupthink, and produce role ambiguity. Small decisions and emergency decisions are best left to individuals.

KEY TERMS

group
primary groups
secondary groups
formal group
functional group
task group
committee
ongoing committee
ad hoc committee
informal group
formal leader
informal leader
emergent leader
synergism
brainstorming
cohesiveness
group norms
deviance
sanctions
critical norms
peripheral norms
groupthink
role ambiguity

REVIEW QUESTIONS

1. What is a group?
2. What is the importance of studying group dynamics?
3. Why do people join groups?
4. What are the two types of formal groups?

5. Why is it important to recognize the informal or emergent leader in a group?
6. Name the five stages through which groups can evolve as they mature.
7. What are the factors that influence group effectiveness?
8. What are the pitfalls of group decision making? Explain.
9. What roles are open in a group setting?
10. Why is it important today at work to use groups in the decision-making process?

DISCUSSION QUESTIONS

1. Examine the opening scenario and identify the various types of groups Anita encounters.
2. Think of a group to which you belong, such as a social club, church group, civic group, or work group.
   a. What type of group is it?
   b. Who is the formal leader?
   c. Is there an informal or emergent leader? Who is it?
   d. Why is this individual recognized as the emergent leader?
   e. What was the reason that you became a member of this group?
   f. What level of maturity does this group have?
3. Give some examples of group norms and describe the groups to which they belong. How might these norms be violated? What would happen if the norms were violated?
4. Discuss the benefits to the formal group leader of identifying the informal leader. Describe possible negative effects of not identifying this individual.
5. Identify the important roles in group dynamics. Which of these roles do you most often play?

WHO'S THE BOSS?

Robert had just been promoted into his first supervisory position. Initially, a high degree of camaraderie existed among the eight office members. The lead analyst, Sandy, had a long-standing record of good performance, knowledge of the program requirements, and loyalty to the organization. Sandy had become a guiding force to the junior analysts, offering advice on certain topics and showing them the established office procedures of the job.

Robert seemed somewhat uneasy with the guidance being given by Sandy. He frequently challenged her decisions and questioned the approaches that she recommended to the junior analysts. Obviously he did not trust Sandy. Rather than relying on her knowledge and experience, Robert set out to gain absolute control and change the general office operations.

It didn't take long for the junior analysts to get the picture. After all, they did not want to do a job twice—the way Sandy suggested and then again the way Robert would require it.

Eventually, Sandy was left alone and was seldom made to feel a part of the group. The other analysts still went to lunch but seldom invited her. The feeling of being an "outcast" was a painful one to her.

After several months of seeing the situation deteriorate further, more distance coming between her and the other office members, and feeling out of place, Sandy asked to be moved to some other office within the company. After all, her own work reputation and career safety were being threatened.

1. Into what type of group was Robert promoted—formal or informal? What type of leader was he—formal or informal?
2. Was there an informal or emergent leader in the group? What made this person a leader?
3. What factors influenced this group's effectiveness?
4. What could Robert have done differently to minimize the group's disharmony? What could Sandy have done to assure continued group cohesiveness?

CASE STUDY 4.2

THE EXPLOSIVE COMMISSION

The recent explosion at the chemical plant was the worst disaster in the company's twenty-year history, killing five workers. A committee of seven people was immediately formed to study the causes of the accident and prescribe protective measures to eliminate any future occurrence.

The committee members were carefully selected from a wide cross section of appropriate representatives. Ralph Windham was brought in from the company's corporate headquarters to head the committee. He had 47 years of chemical plant experience and had often been used as a troubleshooter in hazardous cases. Bill Schomburg, the plant manager, had been personally involved in a similar accident with a different company. He was considered the expert in chemical plant accident investigation and would bring a great deal of experience to the committee's activities. Bill was to be the local company representative. The plant's local legal representative, Carol Barnett, would be a member, and, of course, the president of the local union, Tom Filbert, would be representing the employees.

Great consideration was given to including other members of the community. The chief surgeon of the local hospital, Dr. Brady Schmidt, was appointed because of the enormous involvement of rescue teams and medical attendants. The mayor, Darren Wilson, and Larry Brown from the Chamber of Commerce would represent the community and its members.

After an extensive investigation, the committee's final report was issued almost nine months after the date of the accident. The report cleared the company of any wrongdoing. From the beginning Ralph Windham's influence on the results was obvious. After all, he was the senior member, the chairman, and a highly respected person throughout the chemical industry for his expertise and knowledge. Other members appeared to have voiced little or no opinion, and the recommendation showed obvious bias toward corporate reasoning.

The industry and community members winced with anger and astonishment that the final outcome was not more representative of all members' interests and fairer in its summation and recommendation.

1. What three factors most heavily influenced the formation and selection of the committee?
2. Which factor undermined the committee, and why did it happen?
3. How might this outcome have been prevented?

BIBLIOGRAPHY

Aldag, Ramon J., and Timothy M. Stearns. *Management*. Cincinnati: South-Western Publishing Company, 1987.

Berkman, Harold W., and Linda L. Neider. *The Human Relations of Organizations*. Boston: Kent Publishing Company, 1987.

Halloran, Jack, and Douglas Benton. *Applied Human Relations*. Englewood Cliffs, NJ: Prentice-Hall, Inc., 1987.

Janis, Irving. *Victims of Groupthink*. Boston: Houghton Mifflin Company, 1972.

Leavitt, H. "Suppose We Took Groups Seriously . . ." In *Man and Work in Society*, edited by E. L. Cass and F. G. Zimmer. New York: Van Nostrand Reinhold, 1975.

Likert, R. "The Nature of Highly Effective Groups." In *New Patterns of Management*. New York: McGraw-Hill, 1961.

Roethlisberger, F. J., and W. J. Dickson. *Management and the Worker*. Cambridge: Harvard University Press, 1939.

Schien, E. H. *Organizational Psychology,* 3rd ed. Englewood Cliffs, NJ: Prentice-Hall, 1980.

Shaw, Marvin E. *Group Dynamics: The Psychology of Small Group Behavior,* 2nd ed. New York: McGraw-Hill, 1976.

PART TWO

PUTTING HUMAN RELATIONS TO WORK

CHAPTER FIVE
ORGANIZATIONAL STRUCTURE

Motorola, Inc. embarked on a daring plan to out-Japan Japan in 1986. Their plan focused on strong research and development, built-in quality, and zealous service. To meet these goals Motorola's management began to restructure its organization. They tore down traditional walls that isolated departments, such as marketing, production, and design, in order to foster team spirit. Individuals from each discipline now become involved early in new projects so that products are more cost-effective and include more features that customers want. The overall strategy has led to a dramatic reversal of Motorola's fortunes.

Businessweek
(November 13, 1989)

OBJECTIVES

After studying this chapter, you should be able to:
1. Explain the purpose and importance of organizational structure.
2. Discuss the hierarchical pyramid, and identify its roots.
3. Describe the ways power is distributed within the chain of command.
4. Define formal communication, and identify the directions in which it can flow.
5. Identify factors that can decrease the effectiveness of formal communication.
6. Discuss informal communication and the dangers of the grapevine.
7. Recognize the types of organizational structures used by businesses today.
8. Describe complex organizational structures and the problems that can arise from their use.
9. Identify corporate life cycles, reasons they exist, and how they affect organizational structure.

WHY DO ORGANIZATIONS HAVE STRUCTURES?

Structure divides and delegates responsibility.

Structure is the relationship among parts. In the case of an organization, structure helps the organization divide its work and delegate tasks. Without structure, employees do not know what their jobs are or who is responsible for what, resulting in frustration, low morale, conflict, and other human relations problems. An effective structure also helps avoid duplication of work and delays that can happen when work must be reviewed by numerous layers of management. For these reasons many organizations study their structure on an ongoing basis and make changes in it to increase efficiency.

Employees need to understand organizational structure to function well within it. Additionally, such knowledge helps employees understand and adjust to organizational changes. The heart of organizational structure is the chain of command, of which all employees should be aware and to which they should be sensitive.

FIGURE 5.1   Organizational structure allows companies to divide work and delegate tasks.

Jeffry W. Myers/STOCK, BOSTON

WHAT IS THE CHAIN OF COMMAND?

The chain of command directs the flow of authority and information.

Organizational structure originally developed around the chain of command. The **chain of command** is the direction in which authority is exercised and policies and other information are communicated to lower levels. Authority begins at the top, and each level gives commands, delegates authority, and passes information to lower levels. Information and requests going up the line follow the chain upward. The idea of the chain of command developed in the military and is prevalent in today's organizations. It forms the classic **pyramidal hierarchy**, illustrated in Figure 5.2.

Using the chain of command for authority is illustrated in the following example:

> **"We're glad to have you here at Maxwell Chemical Company, Joan," said Sheila, the personnel director. "I know you will enjoy working here."**

FIGURE 5.2   The business chain of command can be compared to that of the military.

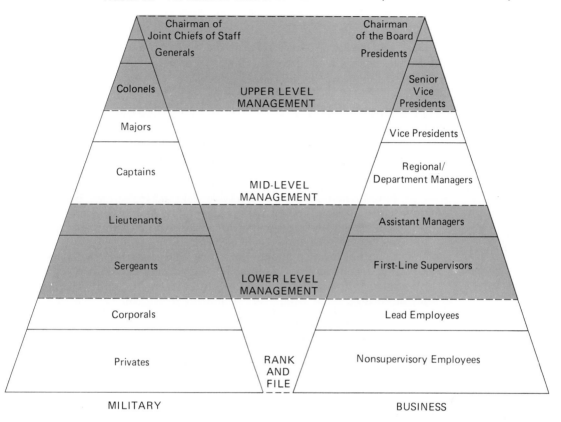

> **"Let me explain a little about your job. You will be assigned
> to work for Alfred. He will be your supervisor, and you will receive
> your job assignments from him as well as your performance ap-
> praisals. Alfred reports to Earnestine, who is the general manager.
> Earnestine reports to Mr. Maxwell, the owner of the company. He's
> the one who calls the shots and makes most of the big decisions
> around here. If you have any questions, please ask Alfred."**

Employees should respect the chain of command and exercise great caution in
skipping levels. Such respect and caution will reduce the potential for human relations problems. One of the few occasions when we can safely ignore the chain is in
emergencies or when time is crucial and our immediate supervisors are not present.

Infrequently employees may be presented with ethical or even legal situations
involving their immediate supervisors. Examples are cases of sexual harassment or
theft by supervisors. Should employees go around their immediate supervisor to the
next level? Such action should be taken only after great thought, as appearances can
be deceiving, and whatever the outcome, the relationship with the supervisor will
probably never be the same again. Ethics will be discussed in Chapter 16.

WHO HAS AUTHORITY?

Authority is
distributed
because orga-
nization heads
usually cannot
make all deci-
sions.

As organizations grow in size and complexity, their heads find that making all decisions becomes increasingly difficult. For instance, the president of a company with ten thousand employees could not possibly make every decision necessary in a day and supervise all employees. Authority to make these decisions must be delegated to lower levels.

Two forms of authority distribution are common. When authority is closely held by those high up in the organization and these people are responsible for making all major decisions, the organization is said to be **centralized**. When important decisions are made at a lower level, authority is **decentralized**. The following example illustrates the two concepts:

> **Barbara is the manager of a local fast food restaurant. Buying power is centralized. When she is running low on hamburger meat or frozen french fries, she calls the local purchasing manager and informs him of her needs.**
>
> **Dick, however, manages in a fast food chain where buying power is decentralized. He places his own orders with suppliers of his choice and negotiates his own contracts. He frequently checks prices to determine where he can get the best deal.**

Centralization and decentralization have their positive and negative sides. A centralized purchasing function, for instance, can ensure that quality of supplies remains constant among locations. Additionally, buyers of large quantities frequently receive discounts.

A drawback to centralization is that decision making can sometimes be slow. Reporting through several layers of managers instead of making the decision immediately and acting on it at the lower level can take time.

Sometimes decentralization faces problems from weak managers. These individuals may not have the maturity or expertise to make effective decisions.

HOW MANY EMPLOYEES TO ONE SUPERVISOR?

You can super-
vise 12 to 21
employees,
depending on
their tasks.

The number of employees that can be supervised effectively by one person generally ranges between 12 and 21. More can be successfully supervised at one time if the employees are capable of working independently and their tasks are very similar. However, the higher up in the organization you go, the more complex jobs become, and the fewer people you can supervise.

The number of people that an individual can supervise is called the **span of control**. The span may be either tall or flat, as shown in Figure 5.3. Not having the appropriate span of control can sometimes result in behavioral or performance problems. Employees may feel unnoticed, and their performance may go uncorrected:

> **Cheryl is a supervisor for a utility company. She supervises 30 employees in charge of checking meters at residences and businesses. All have different routes for which they are responsible.**

FIGURE 5.3   Span of control can be tall or flat.

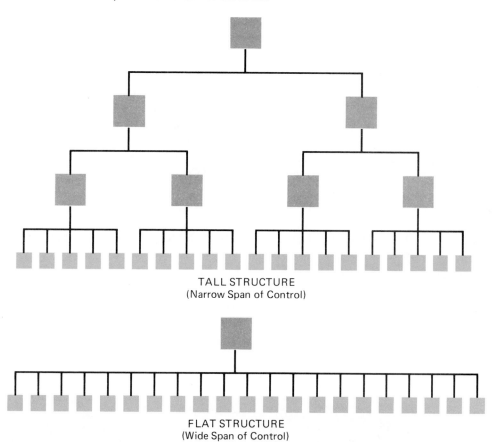

TALL STRUCTURE
(Narrow Span of Control)

FLAT STRUCTURE
(Wide Span of Control)

Cheryl has had a difficult time monitoring everyone's work. She has finally found time to check the paperwork for Angie, one of her new employees. She notices that Angie had incorrectly completed her paperwork for the past two weeks. Cheryl has been so busy dealing with other problems that she has failed to monitor Angie's performance.

Sometimes spans can be broadened by delegating authority to others within the group. Broadening the span can lessen red tape and increase morale. Individuals allowed to perform higher-level tasks feel increased job satisfaction. The following example indicates how authority can be delegated, allowing spans to be broadened:

Lonnie, a supervisor for a local municipality, is in charge of repairs of the wastewater treatment facilities. He has approximately 25 employees under his supervision. Because he is responsible for repair work at as many as ten sites at one time, he has decided to appoint some of the senior employees to the position of

"lead repair person." These individuals are responsible for supervising work at their site, and all other employees at the site are required to take orders from these lead people as if they were actually the supervisor.

If such delegation of authority is to be successful, full communication is essential. The person receiving the authority must understand the new role and be willing to act accordingly. Likewise, the other employees must be informed of what is expected of them and of the person receiving the authority. Without this communication, serious human relations problems can develop. If you are given such authority, ask your supervisor whether coworkers are aware of your new responsibilities. If they are not, suggest that your supervisor inform them. If that does not happen, you should probably communicate this information to your coworkers as early as possible in your new role.

HOW DOES COMMUNICATION FOLLOW STRUCTURE?

Communication flows upward, downward, or horizontally.

Formal communication, communication that flows up or down the formal organizational structure, is controlled by the chain of command. Organizational communication varies in the direction it flows, whether it is one-way or two-way, and in its chance of distortion.

FIGURE 5.4 Various tools can be used to communicate formally within an organization.

Direction and Distortions of Communication Flow

In any organization communication will flow downward, upward, or horizontally (sideways). **Downward communication** is communication that begins at higher levels of the organization and flows downward. Typical forms of downward communication are meetings, memoranda, policy statements, newsletters, manuals, handbooks, telephone conversations, and electronic mail.

Downward communication can become distorted for a variety of reasons discussed in Chapter 3. Long messages not in writing tend to be forgotten or misinterpreted. Furthermore, sometimes so many messages are received that a communication overload results. For example, the employee receiving 20 memos a day may fail to read all of them carefully.

Upward communication consists of messages that begin in the lower levels of the organization and go to higher levels. Upward communication can be in the form of memos, grievances (presented formally or informally), meetings, attitude surveys, or suggestion systems.

Upward communication can also become distorted. Frequently, subordinates who must deliver unpleasant messages misrepresent situations that they are communicating for fear the receiver may "kill the messenger who delivers the bad news," as Figure 5.5 indicates.

FIGURE 5.5   No one likes to be the bearer of bad tidings.

Horizontal communication occurs between individuals at the same level in an organization. These messages can be in the form of telephone conversations, memos, meetings, informal gatherings, or electronic mail. These communications, too, can suffer from distortions discussed in Chapter 3.

One-Way and Two-Way Communication

Communication within organizations is either one-way or two-way. **One-way communication** takes place with no feedback from the receiver. Some examples are memos or videotaped lectures. Although one-way communication can present problems, it is used frequently because it is quick, easy to generate, and orderly. Can you imagine the president of a corporation of thousands of employees attempting to communicate a new benefits program using two-way communication? In addition, one-way communication is less threatening for the sender because no one is present to give negative feedback.

Two-way communication, on the other hand, is communication in which feedback is received. Although two-way communication is slower and less orderly than one-way communication, in general it is more accurate. Greater accuracy is assured because the receiver of the message is able to provide feedback and the sender is able to evaluate whether the message has been correctly interpreted.

HOW ELSE DOES INFORMATION FLOW?

Informal communication is another type of communication that occurs in organizations. This form of communication, the most common type, can either help or hinder an organization's efforts. Discussing a new company policy with someone in another department is an example of informal communication. Informal communication does not follow the formal channels of communication but travels through a

Use the informal grapevine with care.

channel often called the **grapevine**. The grapevine is an informal, person-to-person means of circulating information or gossip. It serves several functions for both employees and management. Many managers have learned to respect and even use the grapevine because of its speed. However, because of its unreliability, it must be used with caution. As employees, we can satisfy social needs through the grapevine, clarify formal orders, and use it as a release for our feelings and concerns. When employees feel that upward communication will be threatening, blocked, or ineffective, they frequently turn to the grapevine.

The problem with grapevines is that often messages are distorted, exaggerated, partial, or even totally wrong. Grapevines are the primary means for transmitting rumors. Additionally, misinterpretation increases with the number of individuals through whom the messages pass, as shown in Figure 5.6. Because downward communication is sometimes ambiguous and upward communication is often nonexistent, rumors too often occur. Such situations are fertile soil for problems in human relations. Because they exist in every organization, you should understand how grapevines work and respect their potential, both good and bad. Be careful that you do not contribute incorrect or inappropriate information to the grapevine. Information can easily be introduced into the grapevine or garbled once it is in, but correcting it is almost impossible. Probably the best rule of thumb for good human relations is to ask yourself the question, "Does this need to be said?" The most valuable asset in human relations is common sense!

FIGURE 5.6   The more individuals involved in repeating a message, the less accurate it is.

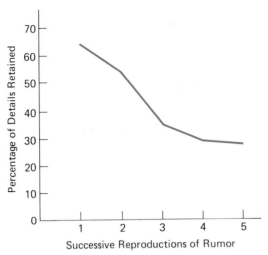

Successive Reproductions of Rumor

Gordon W. Allport and Lee Postman, The Psychology of Rumor. *Copyright ©1947, 1975 by Henry Holt and Co., Inc.*

Barry L. Reece and Rhonda Brandt, two communications authors, have developed the following guidelines and cautions concerning the grapevine. An appreciation of the grapevine can keep you out of trouble.

1. No one can hide from the grapevine, even though it may know only part of the truth. Our reputations are created by the grapevine and are hard to change. Be careful about what information about you makes its way into the grapevine. Watch what you tell others about yourself, choose carefully those with whom you share information, and use discretion in your behavior.
2. The message (gossip) of the grapevine tends to be negative. People who consistently communicate negative information about others ultimately become distrusted or shut out. Exercise discretion about information you contribute to the grapevine. Would you want others to know what you said?
3. Several grapevine networks operate in every organization. Each one is composed of people who have common experiences and concerns. In a particular network, usually only a few people pass on most of the information, and that is usually downward or horizontally. Do you want to be labeled one of these people?
4. The role you play in the grapevine will reflect your ethics, decision-making skills, and maturity. Mature people anticipate the consequences of their actions and words. Think about the image that you create of yourself before you participate in grapevine communication.

WHAT OTHER STRUCTURES EXIST?

Various struc-
tures have
been developed
for large, com-
plex organiza-
tions.

A variety of new organizational structures developed as organizations became larger and more complex. The basic pyramidal hierarchy was no longer meeting organizational needs. However, no one specific type of organizational structure is best. The most efficient structure depends on the size of the organization, whether it provides a service or produces a product, and the number of different products or services involved.

The formal structure can be organized by function (what each department does), by geographic area, by customer, or by product. Large, complex organizations may use a variety of these structures, depending on their needs. Figures 5.7 through 5.11 represent the various ways of organizing. Developing an organizational structure is a complicated process and is a whole study in itself.

Complex organizations have developed other structures to enhance organizational effectiveness. Some use a line and staff structure, others use a matrix structure, and still others mix both.

FIGURE 5.7   Example of a function-oriented organizational structure.

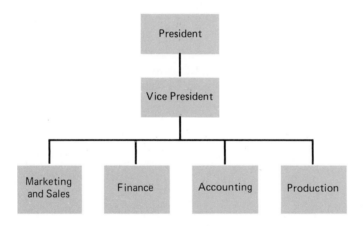

FIGURE 5.8   Example of a geographical organizational structure.

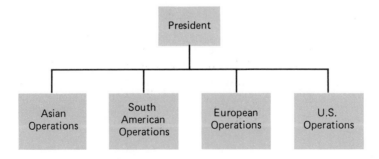

FIGURE 5.9   Example of a customer-oriented organizational structure.

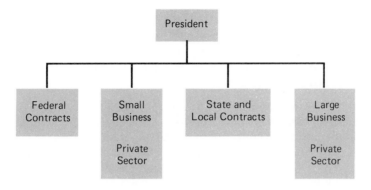

FIGURE 5.10   Example of a product-oriented organizational structure.

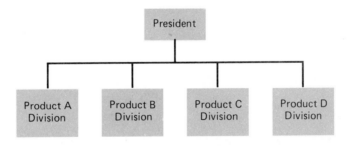

FIGURE 5.11   Example of a company using a variety of organizational structures.

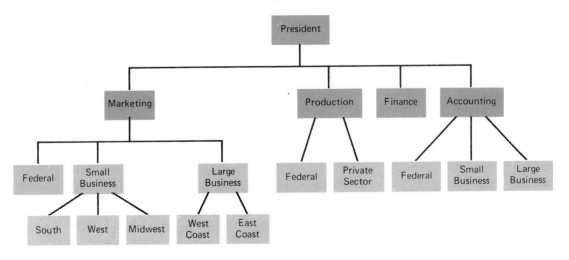

Line and Staff Structure

Line employees are directly involved in production activities. The **staff** support them through advice and counsel on a variety of subjects in their areas of expertise. This support may be in the form of legal, safety, personnel, or computer assistance or may involve maintenance of equipment or facilities. The following example shows the line and staff relationship:

> **Kristin works in the management information system department. She is in charge of seeing that the company managers have all necessary information to operate their computers and generate appropriate computer reports. Chrysaundra, a supervisor in the accounting department, has been asked by top management to submit a special report showing company expenditures on health insurance for the past five years. She calls Kristin for assistance in developing a computerized summary of the requested information.**

Many problems can arise from line and staff relationships, as Figure 5.12 illustrates. One common problem is that staff members usually have no authority to

FIGURE 5.12   Who's the boss?

My supervisor gives my appraisal,
but the computer specialist knows
his job . . .

force line employees to cooperate. Staff people must frequently rely on their skills of persuasion to convince line workers that staff instructions should be followed. For this reason some staff members are given **functional authority**—the authority to make decisions in their area of expertise and to overrule line decisions. Here is what might happen when functional authority is not given:

> **Jim, the superintendent of a construction company, is behind schedule by approximately two months because of unusually**

heavy rains that have plagued the area. He is upset about a memo from Alberto, the company's safety expert. Alberto made a surprise inspection of the construction site yesterday and noticed that many of the workers were not wearing their hard hats and were carelessly operating equipment. After checking employee records, he found that half of the employees were new and had not been given training required by the Occupational Safety and Health Administration. He informed Jim by memo that training would begin for all employees tomorrow on safety policies and procedures.

Jim picked up the phone and, upon reaching Alberto, began to yell. "There's no way I'm going to allow you to give training tomorrow! We're too far behind as it is! Training will just have to wait until we get back on schedule!" Jim slammed the phone down before Alberto could respond.

Alberto thought for a bit. He finally decided he would have to talk to Jim. "I don't believe he's thought this out completely. A serious accident would result in bad publicity and put the project even farther behind. Besides, that would be more costly to the company than being several months behind schedule. I'll go see him when he's had a chance to cool down and discuss all the things that can happen if we don't train workers properly. If that does not work, I may have to discuss this with the president and insist that he give me functional authority on all safety matters."

Problems can, of course, also occur if employees receive contradictory instructions from their line supervisor and their functional staff supervisor. Employees in this situation need to use communication skills to resolve differences. If you ever find yourself in this situation, your most effective approach would be to ask your immediate supervisor for guidance. If a danger is involved and you are not satisfied with the response from your line supervisor, pursue the matter with the functional staff supervisor.

Matrix Structure

Matrix structures are frequently used by organizations that do many projects. Therefore, the matrix structure is sometimes called project structure. A **matrix structure** uses groups of people with expertise in their individual areas who are temporarily assigned full or part time to a project from other parts of the organization. The project has its own supervisor and can last a few weeks or a few years. For instance, an engineering firm may pull together a group of engineers to oversee the design and construction of a new plant and dissolve the group as soon as the plant is finished. The employees then return to their original supervisors, and the plant continues operation under its own management.

Some companies utilize the matrix structure to develop products or operate in markets where decisions need to be made quickly. These groups are given power to make decisions to speed their work, and they may be assigned experts on a number of fronts. The following example illustrates this use of a matrix group:

The Jonston Computer Company president, Allen, returned from a convention where the next generation of computers was exhibited. He called his staff together.

"We've got to do something," he said. "Voice-activated personal computers are the coming trend. We need to create a team to see if they can come up with one that is faster and easier to use than anything that exists today so that we can compete in this new market."

"I'll get a team together," replied Janet. "I'll call in our best research engineer to work on project development. He can recruit a team of engineers to begin designs. I'll include a person from production. We would be wasting resources if we designed something that we could not build. Also, I'll get the marketing team in so that they can find out what customers want. Oh, I almost forgot. I need someone from accounting to develop a budget and monitor costs."

"Tell the group that they can have all the power, money, and support that we can give them," Allen added. "We need to reach market as soon as possible."

Matrix structures can cause difficulty. The individual assigned to head the temporary team may have no formal authority or control over the rest of the group. Power struggles may erupt:

Marie was left in charge of developing a training film for the audit department on how to conduct an audit. She was to head the committee. Three of her peers from another group were assigned to assist her, in addition to the audit manager two levels above her. The audit manager was the expert on using video equipment and was to film the project.

Marie called several meetings concerning the project, but the reception was cool. The manager did not show up for any of the meetings, and two of the peers showed up late.

Marie spoke to her supervisor. "I don't know what to do. No one wants to participate in this project, and I have no idea how to make them help. Do you have any suggestions?"

If you find yourself in a similar situation, the best approach is to discuss it with the person who delegated the project to you and ask for formal authority. Someone higher than the participants in the chain of command should instruct them to cooperate, let them know that cooperation is vital, and emphasize that they will be appraised on their participation and performance.

WHY DOES STRUCTURE CHANGE?

Organizations change for many reasons. New technology brings new products and makes old ones obsolete, new markets open and old markets fade away, and competition or the lack of it increases or decreases demand. All of these changes may call for a change in organizational structure. The economic downturn period of the 1980s saw United States companies adopting new manufacturing practices to remain competitive. Often they changed to a flatter organizational structure that gave employees more responsibility. The new management structures are less military and emphasize a greater team effort.

Another reason organizations change, according to Joseph L. Massie and John Douglas in *Managing—A Contemporary Introduction,* is that they go through **life cycles,** as shown in Figure 5.13. After birth or start-up comes growth. The next stage is stabilization. After that the organization begins to slow down. Then it either closes or it revitalizes.

Structures change as companies go through life cycles.

FIGURE 5.13 An organizational life cycle.

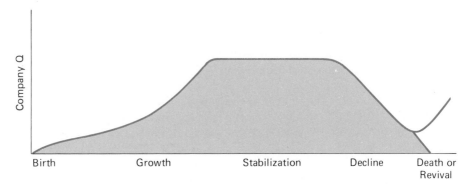

This concept can be illustrated by many companies that once produced only black-and-white televisions for sale in the United States. At first television was a new idea, and the technology was expensive. Sales were low because customers were unfamiliar with television, sets were costly, and few broadcasting stations existed. As the production of televisions increased, the price of production dropped and more stations were established. Then sales rose and television manufacturing companies grew to handle the demand. Soon the majority of households in the United States had a black-and-white television and the demand stabilized. Technology began to change, however, and color television was developed. Sales of companies producing only

FIGURE 5.14 Every employee has a place in the formal organizational structure.

Reprinted with special permission of King Features Syndicate.

black-and-white televisions began to drop. These companies then had two choices. Either they could reduce their production to match demand (taking a risk that they might go out of business) or they could revitalize. Revitalization could mean manufacturing color televisions or locating new markets in countries just beginning to use black-and-white television.

SUMMARY

Organizations require structure to arrange their workload and allow smooth operations. Organizational structure developed because of the chain of command, which controls authority and communication within the organization. The classic business structure, the pyramidal hierarchy, developed from the chain of command.

Authority in an organization can be either centralized or decentralized. Each choice has advantages and disadvantages. Then, too, an organization must consider the most effective span of control for its particular situation. The span of control indicates how many employees a supervisor manages.

Communication in an organization can be either formal or informal. Formal communication can travel upward, downward, or horizontally and can be either one-way or two-way. Each type of communication and flow has its positive and negative aspects. The majority of informal communication is by rumors that travel through the grapevine.

Organizational structure can take many forms besides the classical pyramidal hierarchy. Work can be organized according to function, geography, customer, product, or a mixture of them. Some structures, such as the matrix structure, are complex and can cause difficulties for the employees involved. Organizational structures frequently change as organizations go through life cycles and tailor structures to meet their current needs. Understanding how organizations function and why structural changes are needed can help us in the organization.

KEY TERMS

chain of command
pyramidal hierarchy
centralized management
decentralized management
span of control
formal communication
downward communication
upward communication
horizontal communication
one-way communication

two-way communication
informal communication
grapevine
line and staff structure
functional authority
matrix structure
life cycles

REVIEW QUESTIONS

1. What is the purpose of organizational structure, and why is it important?
2. What is the hierarchical pyramid, and where are its roots?
3. How is power assigned in an organization? How many employees can be supervised effectively at one time?
4. What is formal communication, and in which directions can it flow?
5. What factors decrease the effectiveness of formal communication?
6. What is informal communication, and what are the dangers of the grapevine?
7. Describe the types of structures used by businesses today.
8. What complex organizational structures exist? What problems arise from their use?
9. What is the corporate life cycle, and why does it exist?

DISCUSSION QUESTIONS

1. Describe an organization that restructured of which you are or have been a member. What were the results? Is restructuring always the best step?
2. Have you ever received an inaccurate message through the grapevine? What happened as a result of this misinformation?
3. Should all firms attempt to decentralize authority? Why or why not?
4. Identify a company in your community and describe where you believe it is in the life cycle.
5. Why are we usually more willing to accept authority of those above us than those at our level or below?
6. Think of several organizations with which you are familiar through experience or the news. What organizational structure does each have?

**CASE STUDY
5.1**

NOWHERE TO RUN, NOWHERE TO HIDE

Jacob sat at his desk staring out the window. He did not know what to do. Yesterday his boss, Carlos, had told him to fire Lisa immediately. She had made one too many mistakes. The report that she had just completed contained numerous errors, and the corporate vice president was furious and had threatened to demote Carlos.

However, when Jacob spoke with Janet, the human resources specialist, she voiced concern. Janet did not think that Jacob had followed the company's progressive discipline policy and said that Lisa should be given a final warning before being fired. Janet cautioned Jacob that terminating Lisa without following company policy might result in a grievance from the union and a charge of discrimination filed with the Equal Employment Opportunity Commission.

Jacob reported this concern to Carlos, who exclaimed, "I don't care what those human resources people say! We just can't let lazy, incompetent people continue to work here! I want Lisa fired immediately, and I want anyone else who makes another mistake fired, too!"

1. What type of organizational structure is being used?
2. What problem has the structure caused?
3. Could this problem have been avoided if Janet had been given functional authority? How?
4. Whose orders should Jacob follow? Why?

CASE STUDY 5.2

ORDER FROM CHAOS

Lester's company is growing rapidly, and problems have emerged. He has a T-shirt factory on the outskirts of town and two sales outlets. The T-shirt factory makes 20 varieties of shirts with different logos. A special division does custom orders for sports teams and corporations. The factory employs 60 individuals, and each outlet has 20 employees.

However, matters are getting out of hand. Supplies are late, paychecks are not coming out on time, and employees at the second outlet are sneaking off early after Lester leaves the shop. Yesterday, because Lester forgot to pay the bills, the electricity was turned off at the first outlet and he had to close for the day until power was restored.

Currently, Lester has a plant manager to oversee production in the plant and two lead store clerks, one in each store. Lester takes care of ordering supplies, paying bills, writing paychecks, and hiring personnel. He makes all major decisions at the outlets and most of the decisions at the plant.

1. Does Lester need to restructure his organization? If so, how should he restructure?
2. Should he add more layers of management? Why or why not?
3. Should management decisions be decentralized? Why or why not? In which areas should he add management?
4. What would be an appropriate span of control in the outlets? In the factory?

BIBLIOGRAPHY

Aldag, Ramon J., and Timothy M. Stearns. *Management*. Cincinnati: South-Western Publishing, 1987.

Bittel, Lester R. *What Every Supervisor Should Know*. New York: McGraw-Hill, 1985.

Burke, Ronald S., and Lester R. Bittel. *Introduction to Management Practice*. New York: McGraw-Hill, 1981.

Douglas, John, and Joseph L. Massie. *Managing—A Contemporary Introduction*. Englewood Cliffs, NJ: Prentice-Hall, 1985.

Drucker, Peter F. *Management: Tasks, Responsibilities, Practices*. New York: Harper & Row, 1974.

Halloran, Jack, and Douglas Benton. *Applied Human Relations*. Englewood Cliffs, NJ: Prentice-Hall, 1987.

Harragan, Betty Lehan. *Games Mother Never Taught You—Corporate Gamesmanship for Women*. New York: Warner Books, 1977.

Massie, Joseph L., and John Douglas. *Managing—A Contemporary Introduction*. Englewood Cliffs, NJ: Prentice-Hall, 1985.

Reece, Barry L., and Rhonda Brandt. *Effective Human Relations in Organizations.* Boston: Houghton Mifflin, 1987.

CHAPTER SIX
MOTIVATION

The Allied Plywood Corporation, a small plywood supplier based in Alexandria, Virginia, had been reasonably successful in years past. Allied recently experienced remarkable improvements in company operations and profit margins as a result of a change in corporate philosophies on how to motivate workers. Allied Plywood is now totally owned by its employees!

In 1982, Allied's sales equalled $6 million. By the end of 1988, total sales had risen to $26 million and absenteeism was hardly measurable. Employees watch each other and run the company like a well-oiled machine. Fewer supervisors are required, and the employees hire a new person only if they really need one. Output equals that of competitors using twice the number of employees to do the same job.

As company owners, the employees now receive up to one-third of the company's gross profits as bonus dollars in their personal paychecks each month. In some years, these bonuses have totalled as much as $10,000. Employees do a better job and help each other because it is in their own best interest.

Success
(February 1989)

OBJECTIVES

After studying this chapter, you should be able to:
1. Discuss why understanding motivation is important to organizations and individuals.
2. Describe the basic motivational behavior model from its point of origin through its completion.
3. Identify the major theorists and describe their contributions to the study of human motivation.
4. Describe the two basic categories of individual needs.
5. Discuss the differences between needs and wants.
6. Discuss constructive versus destructive behaviors to fulfill needs.
7. Describe the three motivational source fields in individuals.
8. Discuss motivational techniques that are increasingly important to motivating employees.

WHAT IS MOTIVATION?

Understanding motivation helps individuals and organizations.

Motivation is the emotional stimulus that causes us to act. The stimulus may be a need or a drive that energizes certain behaviors on our part. At work motivation is a combination of all factors in our working environment that lead to positive or negative efforts. If we understand what motivates us, we are more likely to achieve our personal and professional goals. Likewise, if organizations know how to motivate employees, they can increase productivity. This ability to boost production is becoming increasingly important as United States organizations struggle to compete in the global market.

Predicting motivation is difficult. To try to understand what motivates someone, we must guess what physiological and psychological processes underlie behavior. For example, if Allen works much harder than Sid, we assume that Allen is more highly motivated than Sid to achieve some goal—perhaps a bonus, a promotion, or the prestige associated with being the top producer in the organization. Allen seemingly has a stronger need to work hard. However, unless Allen tells us why, we can only presume what his motivation or need may be.

Through studies of motivation and behavior, psychologists have generally concluded that all human behavior is goal-directed toward satisfying a felt need. Figure 6.1 illustrates a basic behavioral model with an unsatisfied need as the starting point in the process of motivation.

FIGURE 6.1   A basic behavior model.

Human behavior is goal-directed toward need satisfaction.

According to this model an unsatisfied need causes inner tension (physical or psychological). The individual engages in some action to reduce or relieve the tension. The individual wants to do something that will satisfy the perceived need. For example, a thirsty man needs water, is driven by his thirst, and is motivated to drink.

HOW DO WANTS DIFFER FROM NEEDS?

People's wants may be very different from their needs, as in the following scenario:

> **Wimberly just graduated from college in June and is about to start her first big job. For five years she lived on her college campus in a dormitory within easy walking distance to and from class and other campus activities. Now, with her new job location almost 20 miles from her modest apartment, she realizes that she needs a reliable car. As Wimberly shops to satisfy this need, she finds several cars that greatly exceed her budget allowance, but are what she calls her "dream machine."**
>
> **Wimberly reasons, "I *want* one of these convertibles with the deluxe option package, but all I *need* is this economical gas-saver. After all, all I need is safe transportation from point A to point B and that doesn't require deluxe extras. Besides, the economy car fits my budget and will be easy on gas, and I can afford the insurance, too."**

Often we are conditioned to think that our "wants" are "needs," when, in fact, the need can be satisfied much more simply. However, everyone does have needs. Although these needs vary greatly in origin and intensity, they fall into two categories—primary (physiological) or secondary (psychological).

Primary needs are the basic needs required to sustain life comfortably, such as food, water, air, sex, sleep, and shelter. Because these needs are so basic to survival, we can easily understand why and how a person's behavior is affected by them.

Secondary needs are psychological and are far more complex. They include the need for security, affiliation or love, respect, and autonomy. Secondary needs are a result of our values and beliefs. These needs are not identical in everyone, nor is the same value or priority placed on satisfying them.

Gary Applegate, in his book *Happiness, It's Your Choice*, states that we have eight secondary needs—security, faith, worth, freedom, belonging, fun, knowledge, and health. Everything else, according to Applegate, is a want. He suggests that wants can be seen as pathways to meeting our needs.

WHAT DO THE THEORISTS SAY?

Maslow, Herzberg, McClelland, and Vroom explain motivation in the workplace.

Many theories have been developed about motivation. Four of these theories apply to individual behaviors in the work setting. Abraham Maslow, Frederick Herzberg, David McClelland, and Victor Vroom have contributed the most to understanding motivation in the workplace.

Maslow's Hierarchy of Needs

Like many other psychologists, Maslow agreed that only a felt need motivates and that once a need is satisfied it ceases to motivate. However, he went on to identify a

hierarchy of needs. Figure 6.2 illustrates Maslow's five need levels and briefly describes the needs associated with each level. The five levels are physiological needs, safety and security, social needs, esteem, and self-actualization.

FIGURE 6.2 Maslow's hierarchy of needs theory.

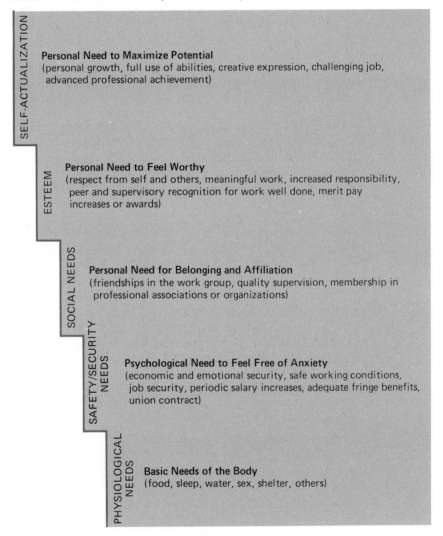

Physiological Needs **Physiological needs** include our desire for food, sleep, water, sex, shelter, and other satisfiers of physiological drives. These are our most basic needs and, until they are satisfied, other needs are of no importance. They are generally satisfied in the workplace by adequate air conditioning and heating, water fountains, cafeteria or snack machines, and other satisfactory working conditions.

Safety and Security Needs   Today **safety and security needs** are more often reflected in our need for economic and emotional security than for physical safety. Examples of how the safety need can be met in the workplace are safe working conditions, job security, periodic salary increases, adequate fringe benefits, or a union contract.

Social Needs   **Social needs** center around our desires for love, affection, acceptance in society, and meaningful affiliation with others. These needs are often satisfied in the workplace by compatible friendships in the work group, quality supervision, and membership in professional associations or organizations. For most people, the need for satisfactory relations with others and a place in society is so important that its lack is often a cause of emotional problems and general maladjustment.

Esteem Needs   Often called the ego needs, **esteem needs** include our need for respect from self and others. Fulfilling these needs gives us a feeling of competence, control, and usefulness. In the workplace, these needs are generally met through meaningful work, increased responsibility, peer and supervisory recognition for work well done, and merit pay increases or awards. People whose esteem needs are not met often feel inferior and hopeless.

Self-Actualization Needs   **Self-actualization needs** refer to our desire to become everything of which we are capable, to maximize our full potential. These needs include the desire to grow personally, to use our abilities to the greatest extent, and to engage in creative expression. In the workplace, these needs are most often met through a challenging job, the opportunity to be creative, and advanced professional achievement.

A common question asked about self-actualization is whether we ever fully actualize. The answer lies in the individual. People actualize at different levels. Some people, for example, are satisfied with a bachelor's degree from a local college, whereas others feel a need for a master's or doctoral degree from a prominent university. Some individuals reach their greatest potential at a simple job; others have a capacity far beyond that level. Satisfying this need level is, therefore, highly individualized.

Maslow believed that we generally satisfy these needs in a hierarchical order, fulfilling the lower-order needs first before moving on to the higher-order needs. However, he added that we can move up and down the hierarchy depending on the situation at hand. For example, during the economic downturn in Detroit and surrounding areas during the early 1980s, many company owners and other corporate leaders operating at the self-esteem and self-actualization levels were suddenly out of jobs. Many companies were forced out of business, and unemployment in that area was at an all-time high. These people were compelled to return to the more basic level of safety and security needs. Most likely, these people resumed their natural progression through the need levels once the security of a paying job satisfied their lower-order needs.

Maslow's hierarchy of needs theory was presented in 1954 in *Motivation and Personality*. This theory became a building block for other theorists.

Herzberg's Two-Factor Theory of Motivation

Herzberg defines two sets of factors in worker behavior.

In 1959, Frederick Herzberg presented his **two-factor theory of motivation.** After questioning over 200 accountants and engineers about what in their work led to extreme satisfaction or extreme dissatisfaction, Herzberg concluded that two sets of factors or conditions influence the behavior of individuals at work. He called the first set hygiene factors and the second set motivational factors.

Hygiene Factors   **Hygiene factors,** also known as maintenance factors, are necessary to maintain a reasonable level of satisfaction among employees. Included in the category of hygiene factors are company policies and procedures, working conditions and job security, salary and employee benefits, the quality of supervision, and relationships with supervisors, peers, and subordinates. Although the absence of these factors may cause considerable dissatisfaction among workers, their presence will not necessarily lead to motivation. Generally, these factors prevent employees from being unhappy in their jobs. However, happy employees are not necessarily motivated workers.

Motivational Factors   According to Herzberg, **motivational factors** build high levels of motivation and job satisfaction. These factors include achievement, advancement, recognition, responsibility, and the work itself. Another important finding in Herzberg's research was that highly motivated employees have a high tolerance for dissatisfaction arising from the absence of adequate maintenance factors. This fact probably has to do with employees' perceptions of motivational factors. A factor that motivates one individual may be perceived as a mere maintenance factor by another. Figure 6.3 compares sets of satisfiers and dissatisfiers and their effects on job attitudes.

Herzberg's theory extended Maslow's ideas and made them more specifically applicable to the workplace. Additionally, it reinforced the concept that while some factors tend to motivate employees, others have little to no effect on worker productivity. We tend to be motivated by what we are seeking rather than by what we already have. Figure 6.4 compares Maslow's hierarchy of needs theory to Herzberg's two-factor theory.

Before we can successfully apply any motivational technique, we must assess the need level of the person concerned. Some people are both satisfied and motivated by hygiene factors, such as an adequate salary and comfortable working conditions. Others are only motivated by opportunities for additional responsibility or advancement to a higher-level position. This variation in need levels has been explored by other theorists with interesting results.

McClelland's Acquired Needs Theory

In 1961 David McClelland developed a theory of motivation that says our needs are the result of our early personality development. Calling it the **acquired needs theory,** he wrote that through cultural exposure, people acquire a framework of three basic needs—achievement, power, and affiliation. These needs are outlined in

FIGURE 6.3 Herzberg's two-factor theory of motivation.

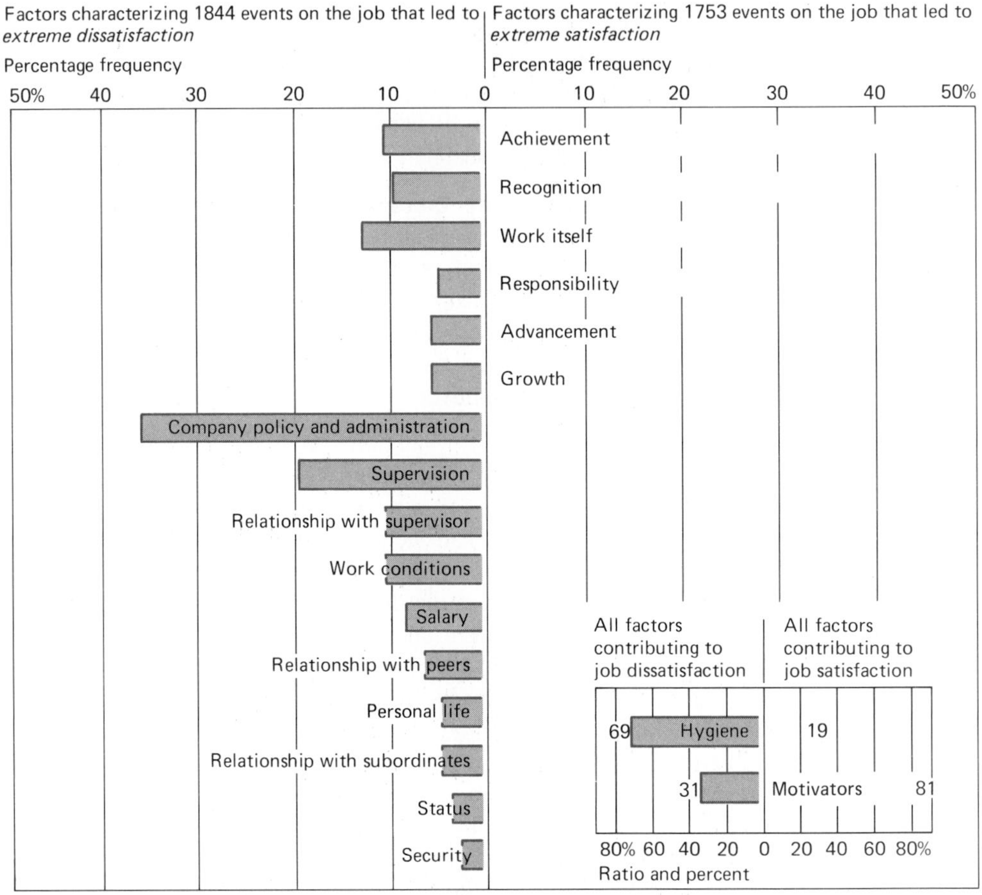

Factors characterizing 1844 events on the job that led to *extreme dissatisfaction* | Factors characterizing 1753 events on the job that led to *extreme satisfaction*

Figure 6.5. McClelland's premise was that these three needs are the primary motives for behavior.

Following McClelland's theory, if we recognize which of the needs is most important to others, we can create the right environment for them. For example, people with a high need for achievement have a natural tendency to become leaders or managers. Planning, setting objectives and goals, and controlling the methods of reaching those goals are a basic part of their work style.

People with a strong need for affiliation are less concerned with getting ahead than they are with developing close relationships and friendships with others at work. They tend to enjoy jobs that require a variety of interpersonal contacts.

People with a strong need for power naturally seek positions with a great deal

McClelland says most people are motivated by achievement, affiliation, or power.

FIGURE 6.4 Similarities in the Maslow and Herzberg theories.

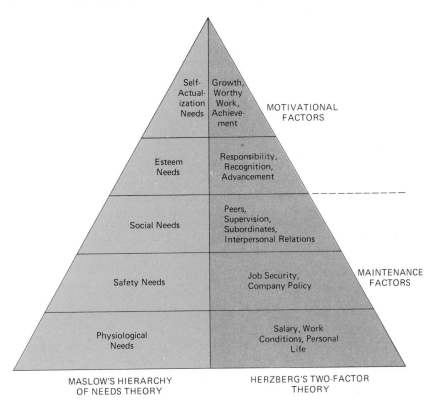

MASLOW'S HIERARCHY
OF NEEDS THEORY

HERZBERG'S TWO-FACTOR
THEORY

of authority and influence. McClelland found that people who are considered highly successful tend to be motivated by the need for power.

McClelland's acquired needs theory provides additional insight into the kinds of needs and motives that drive individual behavior and strengthens our knowledge of how to influence the behavior of others. The theory also helps us determine our own motives and understand our behavior.

Vroom's Expectancy Theory

According to Vroom, we are motivated by expected results of actions.

Victor Vroom, another motivational theorist, took the basic ideas of Maslow, Herzberg, and McClelland one step further. His **expectancy theory** views motivation as a process of choices. According to this theory, you behave in certain ways because you expect certain results from that behavior. For example, you may perceive that if you study long and hard for an upcoming examination, you stand a strong chance of making an A in the course. If you have a need for the prestige or achievement inherent in making an A, you will more than likely study long and hard, expecting to receive the high grade to fulfill your need.

Vroom was careful to emphasize the importance of the individual's perceptions and assessments of organizational behavior. Not all workers in an organization place

FIGURE 6.5   McClelland's acquired needs theory.

Individuals with a High Need for:	Personality Trait Tendencies
Achievement	• Seek and assume responsibility • Take calculated risks • Set challenging but realistic goals • Develop plans to achieve goals • Seek and use feedback in their actions
Affiliation	• Seek and find friendly relationships • Are not overly concerned with "getting ahead" • Seek jobs that are "people intensive" • Require high degrees of interpersonal action
Power	• Seek positions of influence • Enjoy jobs with high degrees of authority and power • Are concerned with reaching top-level, decision-making positions • Need autonomy

the same value on factors associated with job performance. What individual workers perceive as important is far more critical to their choices than what their supervisors view as important. This idea still intrigues researchers, and further work is being done in the area of the expectancy theory of motivation.

The opening story about Allied Plywood's employees is an excellent example of Vroom's expectancy theory. The employees expect good bonuses based on their behavior and are, therefore, highly motivated to be productive in order to gain personally.

Although many other theories on motivation have been developed, these capture the main ideas. The most persistent theme in motivational theories is that all behavior is directed toward some goal to satisfy a need. If the action taken leads to positive outcomes, it will probably be repeated. If the action taken leads to negative results, the behavior will usually not be repeated. Understanding these basic concepts enables us to lead ourselves and others toward desired results.

HOW CAN I APPLY MOTIVATION THEORIES?

Knowledge of motivational theory can help us as individuals in a variety of ways. Understanding the difference between a want and a need, recognizing what motivates us, learning alternative ways to fulfill needs, and learning how to motivate others when we are in leadership situations can help us reach our personal and professional goals.

Mick Jagger of the Rolling Stones aptly sang, "You can't always get what you want, but if you try sometimes, you just might find, you get what you need." Learning to recognize the difference between wants and needs can help us be satisfied with what we have. This lesson can also assist us in being patient and planning alternative ways to fulfill our needs and wants.

Finding Fulfillment

Figure 6.6 expands the behavior model of Figure 6.1 to show possible reactions. Here again an unsatisfied need creates tension and motivates a search for ways to

FIGURE 6.6   Basic motivation model.

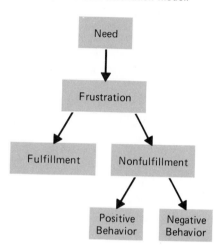

relieve that tension. If the goal is achieved, the individual will usually engage in some form of constructive behavior. If the goal is not achieved, the individual has a choice of behaviors.

The following example illustrates how four employees chose to react when their needs were not met:

Mason was crushed when he did not obtain the supervisory position in his work unit. He had been the lead on the assembly line for the past three years and could hardly believe his coworker, Lani, had received the promotion over him. Mason began to withdraw, keeping to himself during lunch and breaks. When coworkers approached him to ask assistance, he would tell them he could not help. Eventually he resigned to take another position.

Anna, on the other hand, began to behave aggressively when she was not promoted. She criticized the new supervisor, started fights with her coworkers, and complained about many of the company's policies and procedures. She was eventually fired for causing trouble and being insubordinate.

Jackson handled his frustration over not being selected for promotion by deciding to do something about it. First he enrolled in management classes at the local community college. Then he approached his supervisor, explained his goal of becoming a su-

pervisor, and asked for tips and suggestions to meet his goal. His supervisor began to delegate tasks to Jackson. When the next promotion became available, Jackson was selected because he had proven his ability to handle the position.

Linda was extremely upset about not getting the promotion. She sat down and analyzed what she needed that she had thought she would receive with the promotion. She realized that she wanted to feel important to the organization and needed. Linda decided to approach her need fulfillment by volunteering for important projects. She also joined a volunteer organization and assumed a leadership role in order to satisfy her desire to be needed.

Mason and Anna chose to use defense mechanisms to deal with the reality of not satisfying their needs. Their behavior could destroy future hopes of achieving their desired goals. Jackson and Linda, however, found alternatives that would not wreck their careers. Jackson chose to be motivated and try harder, while Linda chose to analyze her real need and find other methods to fulfill it. Understanding why we act and react to any given situation can often help us avoid destructive behaviors than may limit future opportunities.

Motivating Others

Both at work and in our personal lives, we may be placed in positions of leadership and held responsible for accomplishing a goal or become managers of departments at work. For example, you may be elected president of your civic group. Understanding motivation is important in both roles.

Leaders must assess the motivation of followers.

Leaders are frequently judged by the performance of their work group. The output of followers usually depends on their motivation to do what they are asked to do. Performance and motivation are closely linked. Obviously, a large part of any leader's job is to assure maximum output of the group. This task is not easy. Encouraging others to maximize their potential and contribute their enthusiasm and energies at peak levels requires a sound understanding of motivational concepts and techniques. When we are sensitive to what increases motivation and we understand the behavior of coworkers and supervisors, we are able to make the group more productive.

Although motivating followers is one function of the leader, the leader cannot do it alone. Because the decision to move comes from within us, we have a shared responsibility whether we are the leader or the follower. A leader, however, can influence a person's level of motivation.

Through psychological research, three **motivational source fields** have been identified that are believed to influence individual behavior. Figure 6.8 illustrates the fields and their degrees of influence.

Outside motivators include money, praise, and changing the task.

Outside forces offer the greatest opportunity for influencing motivation. A few of these tools are praise, variation of the work task, and financial rewards. Praise involves positive reinforcement for tasks that are completed properly. Task variation can occur through enlargement or enrichment of a job, assignment to special task forces, or rotation through different work assignments.

FIGURE 6.7   A leader works to assure maximum output from the group.

Photo courtesy of Unisys Corporation

Money is not always a motivator.

Financial rewards, which include pay raises, bonuses, and stock options, are the most misunderstood of the outside motivators. Our society is increasingly materialistic, and we are constantly bombarded by advertising telling us what we need. According to Peter Drucker in *Management: Tasks, Responsibilities, Practices,* we are driven to want so much that our income is never large enough to satisfy our needs. For some people, especially knowledge workers (people who earn their livings by what they know rather than from what they produce), money is a form of feedback, equating to their value to the organization. If organizations paid us what we thought we should be paid, they would not be able to function. We begin to see pay raises and bonuses as a "right" rather than a "privilege" and become discontented with our salaries and, ultimately, our jobs. Organizations, then, cannot rely on financial rewards alone to satisfy employees. Other outside motivators must be used.

Inside forces are less easily manipulated. Consider, for example, the company that wants its employees to learn a certain computer software program. Offering training on it may increase a worker's motivation. If the new ability promotes some personal goal, the worker will want to excel in its application.

Influencing people's motivation through the genetic force fields is virtually impossible. These forces were established early in life and are firmly fixed within value and belief systems.

Effective leaders develop an atmosphere conducive to motivation.

Understanding the sources available gives the leader a framework to develop steps that may energize followers. Albert Bernstein and Sydney Rozen conducted research on successful methods that today's corporate leaders use to create environments that will motivate employees. They concluded that the following steps can

FIGURE 6.8   Motivational source fields.

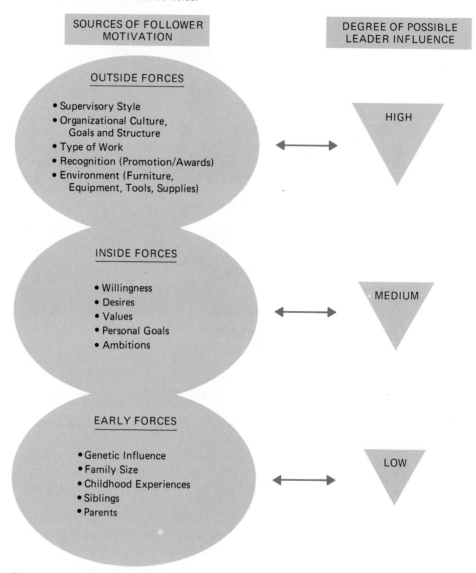

Adapted from Joseph L. Massie and John Douglas, Managing—A Contemporary Introduction
(Englewood Cliffs, NJ: Prentice-Hall, Inc., 1985)

enhance motivation. You may recognize some of these methods as being used in your
organization, or you may choose to apply them in your role as a leader at work and
elsewhere.

   1. *Sell, don't tell.* Selling a course of action by explaining the benefits and the
      reasons for doing it is more likely to persuade employees to act than
      uttering a curt "do it."

2. *Let your followers make their own decisions.* Employees must feel some control and authority over their own jobs. When they must check with a supervisor for every decision, they feel powerless and, consequently, seldom make their own decisions.

3. *Delegate, don't dump.* Delegating only unpleasant tasks is called dumping and is considered an abuse of power. When delegating, give challenges that will develop a subordinate's abilities. Be certain to delegate the authority with the responsibility.

4. *Set goals with your followers.* Regular goal setting improves performance. Define subordinates' work in terms of goals and objectives that become a basic part of each person's job description—not something extra or tacked on.

5. *Listen to your followers and let them know that you are listening.* Schedule regular meetings to let them express what is on their minds. Followers tend to work harder if they feel that you care.

6. *Follow through.* Effective leaders take action to make their promises happen and keep their followers informed on what is happening.

7. *Don't change course midstream.* Followers need continuity. Being consistent in your course of action is important. Communicate any change in course to your employees as soon as possible.

8. *Build in a monitoring system.* Check with your group daily. You should be aware of possible problems to prevent disruption to the work environment. Develop an atmosphere that encourages employees to report potential problems without being asked.

9. *Give criticism gracefully.* Reprimanding or ridiculing followers in public can cause problems. If criticism must be given, it should be done in private and in a constructive manner.

10. *Have a plan for employees' future.* People who cannot envision career growth will probably leave. Even the hope of a promotion can be a powerful motivator. People are more likely to work hard if they see a possibility of growth in their jobs.

11. *Avoid hasty judgments about work style.* Individuals will handle tasks differently than you expect. Allow the freedom of personal choice as long as the task is completed in an acceptable manner.

12. *Use rewards and incentives.* Use praise immediately when a task is well done. Praise is an important method of motivating some individuals.

13. *Encourage camaraderie and friendship.* A team atmosphere can be created by allowing employees time to socialize in the workplace. Given a chance to be sociable, employees can form essential networks and expand their means of being creative and productive.

These suggestions clearly illustrate that our own attitudes play a major role in motivating others. Your personal style of leadership will greatly affect the motivational level of those around you. Understanding our motives is an initial step in realizing how our own behaviors influence the behavior of others. Sometimes called a "self-fulfilling prophecy," your display of positive, energetic behavior about an assignment will have the natural effect of a spark lighting a fire.

HOW ARE MOTIVATORS CHANGING?

Today's em-
ployees are
motivated by
new factors.

Corporate management is recognizing a significant change in what motivates employees in today's workplace. The assumptions that money motivates and that the workplace is of prime importance in workers' lives are no longer valid. Many of the changes are influenced by the "baby boomers" and their different values and expectations.

These individuals, who entered the work force since the 1960s, are demanding much more from a job than their parents did. According to a 1989 Gallup Poll reported by Peter Wittenberg in *The Houston Post,* workers whose jobs give them a sense of identity work longer, harder, and more contentedly than those who see work as just a way to pay bills.

To motivate workers of today and tomorrow, leaders will need to use a variety of methods that help develop a sense of identity. These methods include developing interesting and challenging work, recognizing and appreciating a job well done, allowing more participation in decision making, and providing more leisure time.

In order to develop interesting and challenging work, employers will need to devote more time to employee development in the form of training, job enrichment, and job enlargement. Employees will need continuous training to acquire new skills and knowledge. This training will include classroom as well as on-the-job training. Rotating jobs and increasing the responsibilities of existing jobs will be another way to motivate employees.

Organizations will also need to help employees with career planning and changes. Beginning second, third, or fourth careers will become more common as individuals continue to search for absorbing work.

In one recent survey reported by Bernstein and Rozen, great disparity was found between what people say motivates them and what their companies are actually providing. For example, although 91 percent of the individuals in the survey stated that recognition for good work is important, only 54 percent felt that they were actually receiving appropriate recognition. This finding points out that the old "Attaboy!" still works and that today's managers often fall short by using "management by exception." Under this technique, the boss only says something to you when you do something wrong. One of the key success concepts of the *One Minute Manager* says that the fastest way to motivate individuals is by applying a little praise. In fact, the book's advice is to "catch them doing something right!" It stresses that praise should be specific, appropriate, and immediate.

Smart leaders have discovered that words of encouragement given to a person who has done an outstanding job pay real dividends. By contrast, an old adage states, "Label a man a loser and he'll start acting like one." These practices illustrate the self-fulfilling concept that people tend to act in accordance with their self-image. If they see themselves as successful, respected, and contributing members of the work force, their behavior is likely to reflect this perception.

Participation in decision making will become increasingly important as a motivational tool. Organizations will have to utilize teams more often and allow important decisions to be made at lower levels.

The final motivational factor influencing change in worker behavior today is the desire for more leisure time. Increasingly, employers are finding their workplaces deserted by 2:00 or 3:00 P.M. on Friday. Employees slip away for an early start on the weekend's activities. This practice obviously affects productivity through lost work time, but it can also have an affect on employee morale. Dedicated employees who stay on the job until closing time resent having to handle the work left by those who skip out.

Some methods used by organizations to cope with employees' desires for more leisure time include changing work shifts to four ten-hour work days and instituting more flexible work hours on Fridays to accommodate earlier arrival and departure times. Other employers are allowing individuals the freedom to choose which two days of the week they prefer as their "weekend." For example, employees may choose Sunday and Monday as their days off as opposed to the traditional weekend combination of Saturday and Sunday. For some employees, this choice satisifies a desire for leisure time that is less crowded and ends the "skip out early" syndrome.

One employer's innovative method of using the increased desire for leisure time to solve a different type of motivational problem was reported in *Inc.* magazine. Walter Riley, president and CEO of Guaranteed Overnight Delivery, devised a solution to stop accidents. Tired of the $400,000 a year that accidents were costing his company, he felt that he could reduce costs by instituting a new safety program. First he scrapped the pin, patch, plaque, and $50 driving record award system. He replaced it with a 35-foot-long motor coach for vacation use by drivers who worked one year without an accident. The accident rate dropped by 89 percent the first year that program went into effect. More and more of these innovative approaches to motivating the new age worker may be seen as we adjust to the changing needs of the work force.

SUMMARY

The study of motivation is a complex attempt to understand human behavior. From past studies, we know that a significant relationship exists between needs and motivation. Motivation is defined as the needs or drives within individuals that energize certain behaviors. Only a felt need motivates. Once that need is satisfied, it will no longer be a motivator.

Maslow developed a hierarchy of needs arranged in a specific order. He believed that individuals normally address these needs in a natural order, fulfilling lower-order needs first before moving on to higher-order needs. Herzberg was able to identify two categories of needs. He believed that hygiene factors are necessary to maintain satisfaction among employees, whereas motivational factors build high levels of motivation. McClelland's theory states that individuals acquire needs for achievement, affiliation, or power through cultural exposure during early personality development. Vroom believed that people behave in certain ways based on expected results from that behavior.

The most persistent theme in motivational theories is that all behavior is goal-directed toward satisfying some need. If an action leads to positive outcomes, it will probably be repeated. If it leads to negative results, the behavior will usually not be repeated. Needs vary in importance and intensity with each individual but generally fall into one of two basic categories, primary or secondary. Primary needs are basic to physical survival, and secondary are psychological. By understanding the difference between wants and needs, individuals can learn how to make constructive choices that do not damage careers while fulfilling needs.

Outside, inside, and genetic motivational source fields influence behavior, and leaders can influence motivation by working with the outside source fields. However, we must examine significant changes in factors that motivate workers. Interesting and challenging work, recognition and appreciation for work well done, being included in key decision making, and having more leisure time have replaced some of the traditional motivators such as money and job security.

KEY TERMS

motivation
primary needs
secondary needs
Maslow's hierarchy of needs theory
physiological needs
safety and security needs
social needs
esteem needs
self-actualization needs
Herzberg's two-factor theory of motivation
hygiene factors
motivational factors
McClelland's acquired needs theory
Vroom's expectancy theory
motivational source fields

REVIEW QUESTIONS

1. Why is understanding motivation important to organizations and individuals?
2. What is the basic motivational behavior model from its point of origin through its completion?
3. Who are the major motivational theorists, and what are their contributions to the study of human motivation?
4. What are the two basic categories of individual needs?
5. What are the differences between needs and wants?

6. What are the possible constructive and destructive behaviors that individuals use to fulfill needs?
7. What are the three motivational source fields in individuals?
8. Which motivational techniques are becoming increasingly important to motivate employees today and in the future?

DISCUSSION QUESTIONS

1. Describe a personal situation in which the basic motivational behavior model was evident. What was the need you felt you had to satisfy? What action did you take to relieve the tension?
2. Using the above situation, describe whether the action resulted in constructive or destructive behavior. How might you have handled it differently?
3. Identify several sets of your personal "wants" versus "needs." How do they differ? What other ways can you find to fulfill your needs?
4. Identify a situation in which you were able to apply one or more of the motivational source fields to influence the behavior of a coworker. Which source did you use, and why was it effective?
5. Discuss your personal position on the levels of Maslow's hierarchy of needs. Describe what self-actualization will mean to you.
6. Discuss Herzberg's two-factor theory of motivation. Do you agree with his belief that hygiene factors satisfy only and do not necessarily motivate individuals? Which of the motivational factors most strongly motivates you?
7. Identify which of McClelland's acquired needs most strongly motivates you, and describe why or how you think this need developed in your formative years.
8. Describe a personal situation in which Vroom's expectancy theory may have been the motivational cause. Was the expected result achieved?
9. What changes in your work environment indicate a shift in motivational techniques being used? Describe some of the methods. Describe how you might choose to motivate the new age worker.

CASE STUDY 6.1

THE CASE OF RON THE R.I.P.

Ruby is the supervisor of a small group of resource analysts for a major research and development company. Three of the four analysts have been in her group for less than two years and are highly motivated by opportunities for career growth and promotions to higher salary levels. They have much to learn in their advancement toward a journeyman level position. Ron, the fourth analyst, has been with the company for 26 years. He is 52 years old, financially comfortable, and happily married with no children living at home. He and his wife Marianne travel frequently and enjoy an active social and leisure life.

Ron reached the journeyman level almost 15 years ago. Although his performance is satisfactory, he has become known as an R.I.P. (Retired In Place). He has openly stated to Ruby that he does not want any responsibility added to his current work load. He does not desire a promotion because that would put him into a stress-filled management position, and he has no aspirations to become a star performer. Ron steadily arrives at work on time, works his eight-hour shift with an appropriate lunch break each day, and leaves on time. He strictly avoids overtime hours. When occasional new assignments are added to Ruby's work group, Ron often suggests which of the other analysts is best suited to the task, indicating his obvious disinterest in accepting the assignment.

Ruby has been unsuccessful in her attempts to force Ron to accept any additional work. Assignments made to Ron most often go unattended or result in incomplete products that require more time to redo. The other analysts are beginning to resent Ron's passive attitude and feel that they are having to carry him by shouldering tasks that should be more evenly distributed among all office personnel.

1. According to Maslow's theory, at which need level is Ron operating?
2. At what level of Maslow's theory does Ruby wish Ron was operating?
3. How do you think the others in the group will eventually react if Ron's behavior does not change?
4. What do you think will happen to Ron if his behavior does not change?

CASE STUDY 6.2   THE TIMES, THEY ARE A-CHANGING

David has never been known as a "hay burner" in his six years at Hoffman Manufacturing. He always seems preoccupied with plans for his days off and has been known to call in sick when his shift is due to face heavy periods of production. His supervisor, Carl, expects all employees to carry their load in the shop and to work overtime to meet production output schedules as required.

David's shift was nearly over when a lathe in the shop broke down, requiring a four-hour repair. Carl immediately called in a maintenance crew to make the repair and asked all production shift hands to work whatever hours it took to complete the day's order. David's reply was simply, "I have plans for this Fourth of July weekend, and I'm leaving." Carl was angry and took immediate steps to discipline David. He documented the case against David and found that the company policy requires a three-day suspension without pay as the usual disciplinary action.

When David returned to work and heard the news, his only request was, "Great, can I add the three days to a weekend period so I can plan for the extended time off?" Carl felt defeated but knew David's skilled experience is valuable to the company. He decided instead to try some different method to motivate David. Carl took the challenge of turning this negative situation into a positive one.

1. What motivates David?
2. Why do you think Carl's method of discipline was ineffective in this situation?
3. What will eventually happen to David if he continues to behave in this fashion and Carl continues to motivate him with suspensions?
4. What should Carl try?

BIBLIOGRAPHY

Applegate, Gary. *Happiness, It's Your Choice.* Sherman Oaks, CA: Berringer Publishing, 1985.

Bernstein, Albert J., and Sydney Craft Rozen. "How to Re-Energize Your Staff." *Working Woman* (April 1989): 45–46.

"Bigger Carrot, Better Results." *Inc.* (September 1988): 18.

Bittel, Lester R. *The Nine Master Keys of Management.* New York: McGraw-Hill, 1972.

Bittel, Lester R, and J. E. Ramsey. *Handbook for Professional Managers.* New York: McGraw-Hill, 1985.

Blanchard, Kenneth, and Spencer Johnson. *The One Minute Manager.* New York: William Morrow and Company, 1982.

Burke, Ronald S., and Lester R. Bittel. *Introduction to Management Practices.* New York: McGraw-Hill, 1981.

Drucker, Peter. *The Practice of Management.* New York: Harper & Row, 1954.

Drucker, Peter. *Management: Tasks, Responsibilities, Practices.* New York: Harper & Row, 1974.

Fuller, John. *Behavior Genetics.* New York: John Wiley & Sons, 1964.

Gellerman, Saul W. *Motivation and Productivity.* New York: American Management Association, Inc., 1963.

Herzberg, Frederick. *Work and the Nature of Man.* World Publishing Company, 1966.

Herzberg, Frederick. "One More Time: How Do You Motivate Employees?" *Harvard Business Review Classic.* (September/October 1987): Reprint 87507, 112.

Herzberg, Frederick, Bernard Mausen, and Barbara Block Synderman. *The Motivation to Work.* New York: John Wiley & Sons, 1959.

Jagger, Mick, and Keith Richardson. "You Can't Always Get What You Want." The Rolling Stones Hot Rocks 1964–1971. New York: Abkco Records, 1986.

Maslow, Abraham H. *Motivation and Personality.* Harper & Row, 1954.

McClelland, David C. *The Achieving Society.* New York: Van Nostrand Reinhold, 1961.

McClelland, David C. *Studies in Motivation.* New York: Appleton-Century-Crofts, 1955.

McGregor, Douglas. *The Human Side of Enterprise.* New York: McGraw-Hill, 1960.

Oran, Daniel, and Jay M. Shafritz. *The MBA's Dictionary.* Reston, VA: Reston Publishing Company, Inc., 1983.

Poe, Richard. "Free to Succeed." *Success*, 36, no. 6 (August 1989): 80.

Porter, L. W., and E. E. Lawler III. *Managerial Attitudes and Performance.* Homewood, IL: Richard D. Irwin, Inc., 1968.

Vroom, Victor H. *Work and Motivation.* New York: John Wiley & Sons, 1964.

Wittenberg, Peter. "Baby Boomers See Their Jobs Mainly as a Way to Pay Bills." *The Houston Post* (September 4, 1989): A-1.

CHAPTER SEVEN
GOAL SETTING AND JOB PERFORMANCE

"Lonely-at-top execs want guidance," pointed out the heading in the paper. A study at the University of Toledo and Pennsylvania State University found that executives want to talk about long-term, big-picture issues and desire periodic, thorough, and formal feedback on their performance. The 60 executives in the study said that they receive little feedback and would welcome being told how they are doing on the job, despite the risk of criticism. They wanted ways to improve their own performance and their department's performance and were willing to hear both compliments and complaints from the boss.

The Houston Post (September 25, 1988)

OBJECTIVES

After studying this chapter, you should be able to:
1. Explain the importance of planning to people and to organizations.
2. Name and define the three categories of organizational goals.
3. Describe the characteristics of well-formulated goals.
4. Differentiate long-range, mid-range, and short-range plans.
5. Define four techniques for prioritizing goals.
6. Describe Management by Objectives and name its benefits.
7. Explain what employee performance appraisal is, how it can help satisfy the human need for feedback, why it is done, and how employees can prepare for it.
8. Describe commonly used appraisal instruments.

WHAT IS PLANNING?

The cartoon in Figure 7.1 typifies the way we all too often approach our desires or goals. We might like to accomplish certain things, but we do not think about the steps we must take to do it. Being successful does not have to be a matter of luck or fate. Planning can increase our chances of being successful. Failure to plan is frequently described as taking an automobile trip to a strange place without a road map. You may reach your destination, but getting there will probably take longer and cost more.

FIGURE 7.1   Planning can increase our chances of success.

FRANK AND ERNEST ©by Bob Thaves

Reprinted by permission of NEA, INC.

Planning is important for organizations and individuals.

Planning is important for organizations and individuals (in both our personal and professional lives). Having specific goals gives us a better chance to make events happen and to bring about success than if we just wait, watch things happen, wonder what happened, or criticize what happened. Goals provide direction and assist us in selecting strategies, communicating intentions, and evaluating effectiveness.

Planning is an attempt to prepare for and predict the future. It involves goals, programs, policies, rules, and procedures. Included are decisions about what resources to commit to future action. These resources can include time, money, supplies, material, and labor. Planning should be ongoing and flexible because goals will change as organizations and individuals grow or face new situations.

People fail to plan for a variety of reasons.

Psychologists suggest that lack of planning is a subconscious desire to create crises or even to fail. In our personal lives lack of planning may make us feel more spontaneous and alive because of the temporary heightened emotion:

> **Camille knew from the first day of the semester that she had a written report due at midterm; yet she kept putting it off, saying that she had plenty of time. All of a sudden she realized that she had only two days left in which to do the research and write the report. She stood around in the hall with other classmates, excitedly talking about the upcoming deadline. This talk was "firing her up," and soon she would be ready to tackle the library.**

In an organization, managers may feel more important because they have immediate decisions to make. This kind of busyness is called "putting out brushfires." These are short-term "benefits" and ultimately are harmful. An example of a brushfire follows:

> **Macom knows that budgets are due from all departments on April 1 of each year; yet he never starts working on his budget until his manager announces the deadline in a staff meeting two weeks before.**
>
> **Then Macom rushes back to his employees and tells them that they will "have to hustle because management wants our budgets in two weeks. I'll just have to drop everything so that I can help you prepare your individual budgets to put with the overall departmental budget."**

Some examples of planning in our personal lives include:

Planning our daily schedule.
Planning for vacation this summer.
Planning our classes or job interviews for next semester.
Planning to buy a car by saving for the down payment now.

FIGURE 7.2   Saving to buy a car is an example of planning in personal life.

Planning occurs at all levels of an organization. Examples are:

Daily planning of employee work schedules.
Planning for replacement of inventories.
Planning budgets and finances.
Planning for future human resource requirements.

WHY MUST ORGANIZATIONS PLAN?

Without planning organizations have no sense of direction. No planning or poor planning can result in crisis management (constantly putting out brushfires) and employee frustration. Managers spend their time on emergencies while employees are forced to move from one task to another as emergencies arise.

Proactive management puts you on guard for problems.

Planning is the difference between reactive mananagement and proactive management. **Reactive management** is characterized by supervisors being caught off guard when problems arise and spending their time moving from one crisis to the next. (It is often called crisis management.) **Proactive management** involves looking ahead, anticipating problems, and determining solutions to potential problems before they develop. It may require goal setting by individuals.

HOW DO PEOPLE DIFFER IN PLANNING?

People generally fall into three broad categories when setting goals. Imagine three people playing a game of horseshoes. Here is how each would act if each were in a different category.

The underachiever will stand close to the target. **Underachievers** tend to set goals that are lower than their abilities. This is their way of protecting themselves from risk and anxiety. Because they seldom if ever push themselves, they do not achieve much.

The overachiever will stand so far back from the target that hitting it is almost impossible. **Overachievers** take on goals beyond their abilities. They are uncertain of what they can expect of themselves but cannot admit inadequacy. They lack self-confidence and reduce their anxiety by aiming beyond what they can achieve. Because their goals are unrealistic, they seldom achieve them or feel satisfied.

The realistic achiever will stand just far enough back to be challenged. **Realistic achievers** tend to have a positive self-image. They are usually successful in their endeavors because they set challenging but attainable goals. They, therefore, become high achievers.

David McClelland, a noted psychologist, has identified several traits of high-achieving people:

1. They take moderate risks but not long chances.
2. They like to control situations in which they are involved.
3. They like immediate feedback about how well they have done.
4. They tend to become preoccupied with the job to be done.

Consider the above traits in relation to yourself. Do you set moderate, attainable goals? Do you become involved in situations so that you may influence what is happening rather than just "going with the flow"? Are you receptive to feedback about your behavior and performance? Do you arrange your tasks to be free from interruptions? Do you allow yourself enough time? Do you persevere? If the answers to these questions are yes, you are probably already a realistic/high achiever or well on your way to being one. If the answers are no, analyze what you might do to increase your chances for success.

FIGURE 7.3   Persevering in goals is important to success.

CROCK/by Rechin & Wilder

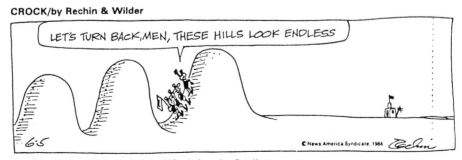

Reprinted with special permission of North America Syndicate.

If you procrasti-
nate, examine
your percep-
tions, coping
skills, tolerance
for disappoint-
ment, assertive-
ness, and task
organization.

If procrastination is a problem for you, think about the pride you feel on accomplishing a task satisfactorily. Giving ourselves credit for our accomplishments can provide "energy" for attempting other goals.

People procrastinate for a number of reasons. Some people procrastinate because they have an unrealistic view of successful people. They do not recognize the great amount of planning, organizing, and hard work required to make success seem "easy."

Other people procrastinate because they have poor coping skills or a low tolerance for disappointment. Instead of analyzing situations to determine alternative actions when complications occur or steps are blocked, they give up and do nothing.

Still others procrastinate as a way of rebelling against expectations, not recognizing the immaturity of such a response. A more effective approach to handling expectations that we consider unfair or inappropriate for us would be to discuss the situation with the person who holds those expectations. Then we can decide for ourselves what is best and proceed accordingly. However, because many procrastinators lack assertiveness skills, they are uncomfortable doing so, hoping perhaps that the problem will go away. Lack of assertiveness can create additional delays or procrastination if people are reluctant to ask others for resources or help necessary to perform a task. The following is an example of problems that can be created when people procrastinate to rebel against expectations and lack assertiveness to confront the real problem:

> **Gail walked out of her boss's office feeling upset. Marsha had made clear that she expected Gail to have the sales report ready by Friday's district meeting. The report would play an important part in planning for the next year. This was already Wednesday, and Gail knew that she had meetings scheduled back-to-back the rest of the day and would be at a seminar downtown all day tomorrow at Marsha's recommendation.**
>
> **"Well," thought Gail, "I can't tell Marsha that I am too busy. She may think that I'm trying to get out of work. I guess I will have to see if I can find time Friday morning. If I don't have the report, Marsha will just have to learn that I can't be in two places at the same time. Besides, she should have given me more advance notice or asked someone else to help me with the report."**

In the above example, Gail could have avoided creating problems for herself, Marsha, and the company if she had tactfully pointed out the short deadline and reminded Marsha of the meetings and the seminar. She could have asked, "Do you think that I should skip the seminar Thursday, or shall we get someone else to work on the report while I'm at the seminar?"

When you find yourself putting off work on a task or goal, a healthy approach will be for you to examine yourself closely to see why. Then decide what you want to do about the situation. Dividing a large task into several smaller ones may be the answer. Do not try to do everything at once. An article in the April 1990 issue of *Working Woman* pointed out that the best way to attack giant projects is to start with small steps and that the key to achievement is to think big but act *now*. A small success can motivate you to move on to the next step. Small, steady steps are the key.

Another factor that may help you overcome procrastination is the support of someone who believes in you, such as a friend, relative, or coworker. Developing supportive relationships takes effective human relations skills. (Procrastination will be discussed more thoroughly in Chapter 19.)

WHAT KINDS OF GOALS EXIST?

A **goal** is the objective, target, or end result expected from the completion of tasks, activities, or programs. In your personal life, your goals may include becoming a college graduate, a successful business person, or a respected community leader.

Organizational goals can be official, operative, or operational.

Much of what is written about goal setting in organizations can be applied to your personal goal setting. Two management authors, Ramon Aldag and Timothy Stearns, have identified three broad categories of goals in organizations: official goals, operative goals, and operational goals.

Official goals are developed by upper management, are formally stated, and may be published in annual reports or newsletters. They are usually the most abstract category of goals. They tend to be open-ended. That is, the goal itself may not include information about quantity, quality, or deadline. Official goals pertain to the overall mission of the organization. A common example in business today is "to provide excellent service."

Operative goals are those goals for which middle management is responsible. They concern the operating policies of the organization. These goals tend to be more specific than the abstract official goals. Operative goals usually include a mix of open-ended and close-ended goals. They are usually redefined on a yearly basis. Common examples of operative goals in business today are "to increase the company's share of the market" and "to hire more minorities."

Peter Drucker, a management expert, has identified eight types of operative goals. They are marketing, innovation, profitability, physical resources, financial resources, human resources, productivity, and social responsibility.

Operational goals are the responsibility of first-line supervisors and employees. They are statements of the expected results of the efforts of the various components of the organization. They include built-in standards of behavior, performance criteria, and completion time. They are concrete and close-ended.

An example of an operational goal is "to increase sales of XYZ chemical by 1995 by 20 percent over the current year by hiring and placing a marketing representative in the Far East." Another example is "to increase the proportion of Hispanic employees in the total work force of the company to one-fourth within three years by active recruiting and training." Notice that these two goals include specific dates for completion and specify how much.

Following the examples of goals in organizations, we can create specific goals in our personal lives. Here are two examples: "to complete an associate degree within two years by registering for and passing 15 credit hours each semester" and "to save $1,000 for a trip next summer by forgoing movies and eating out only once a month."

WHAT CHARACTERISTICS SHOULD GOALS POSSESS?

To be most helpful, goals, whether personal or organizational, should have the following characteristics:

Goals should be written, measurable, time-specific, challenging, and participatory.

1. Goals should be written. Writing increases understanding and commitment.
2. Goals should be measurable. For example, "I want to be more successful in school" is a vague goal because what constitutes success is not specified. Grade point average can be measured; therefore, a better way of expressing this goal would be "I will earn a GPA of 3.0 out of a possible 4.0." If goals are vague and uncertain, they will provide little guidance.
3. Goals should be specific as to time. Otherwise, they are not challenging. At the time specified, they can then be reviewed for correction or revision. Considering the goal above, we can make it time-specific by adding a deadline: "I will earn a GPA of 3.0 out of a possible 4.0 during the next academic year."
4. Goals should be challenging but attainable, to provide satisfaction and reduce frustration. Goals should be realistic, not wish lists, and should be reasonable expectations of what can be achieved over a given period of time.
5. In an organization, goals should involve participation. Participation increases commitment and communication and, hence, understanding and motivation. The most frequent participation is between the employee and supervisor.

Goals are not just a writing exercise to be put aside until the time comes to write goals for another period. They should be used personally and organizationally to monitor progress throughout the period. In organizations this monitoring may be as simple as observation by the employee and the supervisor or as formal as written progress reports. Such progress checks help identify change needed while time still remains. Progress checks must be planned for, and someone must be responsible for them. We should make frequent progress checks of goals in our personal lives as well, recognizing that we are responsible for our own checks and our own progress.

HOW FAR AHEAD ARE PLANS MADE?

Plans can be long-range, mid-range, and short-range. The time involved will vary from level to level in an organization. For top management long-range plans may extend over several years, whereas for supervisors long-range plans may cover only several months. Short-range plans for supervisors may include today or this week, whereas for top management they may cover the current year. In the same way, mid-range plans, which fall between long-range and short-range plans, vary from level to level.

Individuals, too, have long-range, mid-range, and short-range plans. Sometimes we have difficulty completing our long-range plans because we grow tired, forget them, or allow short- or mid-range plans to interfere. Because long-range plans cover a greater period of time, situations and circumstances may change for us, making the long-range plans impractical. In this case, we may need to change them. Psychologists point out that change can be an indication of growth; therefore, a healthy approach for us is to review our plans from time to time to check our progress, modify our strategies if necessary, or perhaps discard the plan as no longer important or possible.

Developing readily attainable short- or mid-range goals can actually help us accomplish long-range goals because they provide us with periodic feelings of accomplishment. For example, if your plans include a bachelor's or master's degree, setting a short-range goal of satisfactorily completing each course in which you enroll or a mid-range goal of getting a two-year associate degree can help. Completion of each course and the two-year degree can provide satisfaction and motivation to continue. Patting ourselves on the back can be psychologically healthy, and completion of short- or mid-range goals provide opportunities to do so.

Goals can become obsolete if we have achieved them. They can also become less important as we grow. Think of how your own goals have changed over the years. We can probably all recall various ways in which we answered the traditional question, "What do you want to be when you grow up?" At four years of age, we may have wanted to be a bunny rabbit, at six a dancer, at ten an astronaut, and in our teens a professional athlete. Somewhere along the line, we lost interest in some of these, decided we lacked the natural ability necessary for others, or found something else of appeal to us. Today we may have a different career goal in mind, one that probably combines dreams and practicality. Then after we have been working a while we may decide to set other career goals. Mid-career switches, for instance, are fairly common.

WHICH GOALS COME FIRST?

Prioritize goals by satisficing, sequential attention, preference ordering, and goal changes.

Both organizations and individuals have multiple goals and priorities. We seldom have the luxury of pursuing one goal at a time. Aldag and Stearns have identified four techniques that managers in an organization can use to decide which goals to emphasize during periods of conflict. We can apply them to our personal goals and plans also. They include satisficing, sequential attention, preference ordering, and goal changes.

Satisficing

When we are faced with numerous goals, we can reduce our stress by identifying a satisfactory rather than optimum level of performance for some of them. In this case, the old adage, "If it's worth doing, it's worth doing well" might better be changed to "If it's worth doing, it's worth doing satisfactorily." Some tasks just need to be done. Excellence here may not be that important and as a matter of fact can be costly or stressful. The desire for perfection can create havoc with goal accomplishment and people's lives if carried too far:

Marvin likes a well-manicured yard. Mowing the grass every week in the growing season is required to keep his yard looking neat. If Marvin waits until he has time to do an outstanding job of mowing, edging, trimming the shrubs, fertilizing, and watering, the yard may become the disgrace of his neighborhood. This condition, in turn, may create anxiety for him and his neighbors, damaging his relations with them. Therefore, some weeks he "settles" for a yard that is less than perfect.

Vanessa is responsible for preparing a report for her supervisor and takes the responsibility seriously. Having accurate information in an attractive, understandable format is the important point. Taking the extra time to set up the report in an elaborate way using desktop publishing when it is a one-time report meant only for her supervisor would probably be an unnecessary expenditure of time. Her desire for perfection could actually work to hurt her should the report be late.

Sequential Attention

When we have multiple priorities, we may need to shift our attention from one goal to the next over periods of time. Successful working parents frequently adopt this tactic. Work priorities sometimes take precedence over family activities, and at other times the reverse is true. The main point is to keep the overall quality of performance in each area acceptable.

Preference Ordering

If we have several goals toward which we wish to work, we may need to rank them according to preference. For example, a company may decide to maximize profit over expansion for a period of time. Individuals may decide to save for a new car rather than take a trip this year.

Goal Changes

As pointed out earlier, we may change goals because they become outdated or inappropriate, such as when we complete a degree or buy the car for which we have been saving. A well-known example is the Foundation for Infantile Paralysis. Its original goal was to develop a vaccine for polio. Once the vaccine was developed, it changed its goal to conquering birth defects and became the March of Dimes.

HOW DO YOU SET PERSONAL GOALS?

The process for deciding where you want to go next with your life requires that you make a frequent, close examination of your preferences. Asking yourself specific questions can help you determine your priorities in life. Consider, for example, how important the following factors are to you:

1. *Affection.* If you are to have your need for affection met, you must obtain and share companionship and affection. Your goals must include other people. Are your other goals practical enough to accommodate others?
2. *Expertness.* If this is important to you, you must become an authority in some area and possess the human relations skills to communicate your expertise to others and have it received. What area? Do your human relations skills need developing?
3. *Independence.* Being independent may require time and at least some money. When will you have that time, and how will you obtain the necessary finances to be independent? Even more basic, what does being independent mean to you? Will it mean the same to others in your life?
4. *Leadership.* To be a leader, you must gain influence. Where? At work? In the community? How?
5. *Parenthood.* Parenthood requires a tremendous investment of time, finances, and physical and emotional energy. Can you afford that investment now? Later? How?
6. *Happiness, contentment.* What is your definition of these concepts? What will it take for you to achieve them? How? Without human relations skills, our lives can be in constant turmoil, which can prevent personal happiness and contentment.
7. *Prestige.* Prestige differs for different people. How will you measure it—by the house in which you live, the organization for which you work, or where you vacation? How will you acquire that house, gain employment at that company, or acquire the money and knowledge for that vacation?
8. *Security.* Security is important for many people but not for others. What kind of security do you need—financial or emotional? If financial security is part of your need, how much will it take and how will you acquire it? If emotional security is important to you, what does that mean—a supportive supervisor? A caring spouse? Concerned friends? What will you have to do to have that kind of relationship with your boss, spouse, or friends?
9. *Personal development.* Personal development can take the form of growth, hobbies, talents, or knowledge. It implies continuing to learn throughout your life. How will you feed this desire in yourself? Where can you find the necessary direction, guidance, and instruction?
10. *Wealth.* If money is important to you, how will you acquire it? How much will it take to satisfy you? How will you take care of it if you gain it? Human relations skills will be necessary to help you earn more and to keep others from begrudging you money for which you have worked hard.
11. *Service to others.* A sense of duty is important to many people and can make the difference in the quality of life in organizations, communities, and countries. If you desire to make such contributions to others, where and how would you like to use your energy and abilities?

Considering the above questions objectively can help you in setting your personal goals. Notice that all of the above measures of success require high levels of human relations skills.

Once you have examined yourself closely, you are ready to set your goals. Below are some guidelines to help you:

1. Remember to be realistic. If your goals are too high, you may lose confidence. In determining how high to set your goals, consider your own past performance and that of others. If your goals are too low, you will have no incentive or challenge to better yourself. Be careful that you do not underrate yourself. Finally, make your goals worthwhile.
2. Once you have determined your goals, openly commit yourself. Letting others know about them can help. Be sure to say specifically what it is you plan to accomplish, when, where, and how.
3. Consider that your goals may have to be coordinated with other people. An examination of your professional and personal relationships is necessary.
4. Visualize success. Get a clear mental image of your objective and think *when*, not if.

Carefully applying the above guidelines can help you establish goals that are both meaningful and achievable. Such application must be an ongoing process to be effective.

WHAT ATTITUDE BRINGS SUCCESS?

Personalities have been characterized as Type A and Type B, based on a person's degree of aggressiveness and passiveness. Type A personalities are usually driven and aggressive, whereas Type B are patient and passive. Both have problems associated with them: Type A people may create stress-related health problems for themselves, and Type B people may not be assertive enough.

Two psychologists, Robert Kriegel and Marilyn Harris Kriegel, suggest that all of us have the potential to perform as a Type C person. Type C behavior is versatile and adaptive. It enables us to perform at our peak and feel vital and full of energy. A Type C attitude combines commitment, confidence, and control.

Commitment

Identifying what you want, knowing your innermost desires, and translating them into action will result in harmony between what you do and what you want to do. The more committed you are to something, the less difficult it seems. Low commitment can make a task overwhelming. When Type C persons look at a task, they see opportunities. Others see obstacles.

Confidence

Confidence in your own worth does not depend on others' moods, your looks, or other external factors. You may hate to fail, but you do not fear it, because you know that with risks come mistakes and failures. Be alert to your own inner signals of fear. When you notice them, stop, take a few deep, slow breaths, hold each to the count of three, and exhale slowly. This practice can help put matters back into perspective.

To do a reality check, measure and rate the difficulty, bring the past into the present, and imagine the worst.

You can do a reality check to determine how serious a problem is in four ways: measure the difficulty, rate the difficulty on a scale of 1 to 10, bring the past into the present, and imagine the worst. Measuring the difficulty may be as simple as writing it down. In bringing the past into the present, think of similar situations and remember your successes. Analyze them: what were your actions, feelings, and thoughts that led you to success? Visualize yourself accomplishing your present goal. In imagining the worst, ask yourself, "What is the worst that can happen if I fail in this endeavor? Will I die, lose my job, or lose my spouse?" Because the consequences are not usually that dire, such a reality check will immediately boost your confidence. In doing your reality check, be careful of false confidence, which can lead to being unprepared. If the reality check shows the problem is indeed major, you can at least now concentrate on dealing with it rather than on your anxieties.

Control

Control is the third component of a Type C attitude. After doing a reality check, concentrate on what you can control to improve your performance and effectiveness. You can include your own thoughts, feelings, attitudes, and actions.

Robert Land, executive vice president of a large national human resources management consulting firm, was quoted in *The Secretary* and pointed out that successful people are generally those who work to maintain control over their work environment and a myriad of unanticipated events. In other words, these people are proactive rather than reactive. He advises that we must be responsible for ourselves and our careers. We cannot expect our bosses to take charge of our careers, because bosses seldom have the time or interest to help us plan where we should be and how to get there.

Two newspaper writers, Thomas Burdick and Charlene Mitchell, in an article dealing with careers in the 1990s, stress that employees must take actions to keep themselves employable, accept change as a partner, and be adaptable. In another article Mitchell and Burdick suggest that successful subordinates make their bosses' jobs easier. Bosses look favorably upon employees who ease their burden and harshly on those who add to it. The more responsibilities we assume and handle competently, the more indispensable we will be. Knowing whether our bosses prefer reports ahead of schedule, uninterrupted mornings, or daily updates can improve our chances of success with our career goals. So can taking unwanted projects, doing more in the boss's absence, and being familiar with the boss's job responsibilities and goals. Ultimately, the most valuable subordinates are those who make their bosses look good. If you are now working, you can check your "progress pulse" to measure your career success by answering the questions in Figure 7.4.

HOW DO ORGANIZATIONS SET GOALS?

MBO emphasizes self-determination for employees.

A variety of approaches and different degrees of formality are used in setting goals in organizations. One popular technique is **Management by Objectives**, originated by George Odiorne. This technique, sometimes abbreviated to MBO, is a method

FIGURE 7.4   Check your "Progress Pulse" to measure career success.

To assess objectively whether your progress pulse is healthy, ask yourself these questions:

1. Have you had a formal or informal performance review within the last three months?
2. Have you asked your boss lately what you can do to help?
3. Do you know what your boss's goals and missions are?
4. Have you taken the initiative to do things your boss hasn't asked you to do?
5. Have you taken on any special projects within the last three months?
6. Have you been sought out recently for information or special advice?
7. Have you created some positive visibility for yourself?
8. Are you keeping notes on your recent accomplishments so you can give them to your boss before your next performance review?
9. Are you a team player and do you help your coworkers meet their goals?
10. Do people, especially your boss, like to work with you?
11. Do people ask you to meetings and copy you on memos?
12. Have you aligned yourself with a confidential peer to get candid feedback on your performance and to determine how others perceive you?
13. Have you set down where you'd like to be in two to five years?
14. Do you know how your progress compares with others in your field at your age?
15. Are you aware of training or experience you'll need to advance to the next position?
16. Are you keeping a list of contacts in your field?
17. Have you been attending professional meetings?
18. Can you name an alternative field where you could transfer your skills if necessary?
19. Have you identified a mentor—someone to help you and to serve as a good role model?

and philosophy of management that emphasizes self-determination. Its chief purpose is to improve employee motivation by having employees at all levels participate in setting their own goals.

Features of MBO

Proponents of MBO say that it helps motivation because of the involvement and commitment of the people participating in the process. It is characterized by three features:

1. Employees participate in establishing the objectives and the criteria by which they will be judged. This step usually involves discussions between the supervisor and the employee. Employees should be aware of overall organizational and departmental goals. Then they can set individual goals that are valued by the organization.
2. Both the supervisor and the employee know what the employee is to accomplish. The employee knows what the supervisor expects and can work toward the correct goal. The supervisor, in turn, can guide the employee correctly if deviation should start occurring.
3. If the goal has been correctly written, it will contain specific descriptions of the end result desired (how much and by when). This feature will make evaluation of the employee's performance easier. Additionally, the employee will be more likely to agree with the appraisal, because the criteria were selected and agreed upon in advance.

Benefits of MBO

The *George Odiorne Letter* summarizes several benefits to be gained from organizations using MBO:

1. Communicating job objectives helps people understand the purpose of their job, which increases the likelihood of success.
2. People today want to participate in decisions affecting them. Because MBO involves superior and subordinate in discussions about responsibilities and expected results, employees develop greater commitment.
3. MBO makes sense psychologically and may help motivation. Various studies have shown that high achievers are those who set goals, that goals have a powerful effect on behavior, that employees with clear goals achieve more than those without them, and that highly motivated people are those who achieve, especially goals to which they are committed. Odiorne points out that goal-centered people are more likely to be mentally healthy than are people driven by fear, intimidation, punishment, or hostility.
4. MBO can save time and money because people know for what tasks they are responsible and accountable.
5. Because individuals are exercising self-control under MBO, they can measure their own progress against the goals they helped create and adapt their behavior appropriately.

6. MBO allows people to present again their past creative ideas not previously accepted when they set their goals for a new period. This opportunity fosters creativity in organizations, considered vital for success today.

7. MBO makes performance appraisal more reasonable and compensation systems more rational. Because people are evaluated against goals and standards that they helped establish, appraisal becomes easier for both the supervisor and the employee.

WHAT IS APPRAISAL?

Both supervisors and subordinates may dread appraisals.

Employee performance appraisal is a measurement of how well an employee is doing on the job. Commonly done at least annually by the immediate supervisor, it is a process that frequently both the employee and the supervisor dread. Being human, supervisors may fear that subordinates will not like them, that employees may do less work if the appraisal is a negative one, that employees may yell at them, or that friendships with subordinates may be jeopardized. At the same time, employees may wonder whether supervisors can be fair, doubt whether supervisors understand the subordinates' jobs, fear an average or below-average rating, or feel that a high rating may interfere with friendships with coworkers.

Organizations appraise employee performance for a number of reasons:

1. To encourage good job performance, to discourage unacceptable performance, and to correct inappropriate behavior that interferes with good performance. If it is conducted correctly, the appraisal session can help communication. It can result in growth and increased motivation or at least a better understanding of what is expected of us.

2. To let us know how we are doing. We want to know where we stand in the organization. Although we may dislike being judged, human beings need feedback, both negative and positive. Negative feedback allows us to make corrections in our behavior and performance, whereas positive feedback lets us know what is appreciated so that we will continue it. (Psychologists say that we quit engaging in a certain behavior both if the behavior is punished and if it is ignored.) Feedback also assists us in making plans for personal improvement.

Feedback reinforces desired behavior, discourages unwanted behavior, and helps us plan improvement.

3. To give the organization information about employees that can be used in later career decisions, such as raises, promotions, demotions, transfers, and terminations. Appraisals also help managers identify the need for training in individuals and in groups of employees.

If performance appraisals are to be effective, both the supervisor and the employee must prepare for them.

Preparing Yourself

You can take several steps ahead of time and during the appraisal session to help make appraisal the positive process that it is supposed to be. Using a proactive, assertive approach is to your advantage.

FIGURE 7.5   Feedback is important. It lets us know what we are doing right and what behavior we need to change.

Steps that you can take *before* the session include the following:

1. Make sure that you understand what is expected of you. Effective supervisors will be preparing for the appraisal session throughout the entire appraisal period. They know what is expected of the employee, make sure the subordinate also knows, observe frequently, and tell you how you are performing. You also can prepare throughout the period. If you participated in the establishment of objectives for your job, you understand what is expected of you. If you did not, do not wait until the appraisal session to ask questions. Keep checking that your understanding of what you are to do is the same as your supervisor's understanding. You can also take the initiative and ask for feedback during the period. This way you will eliminate surprises in the appraisal session. Open communication with your supervisor is extremely important.

2. Become familiar with the evaluation/appraisal instrument to be used. Ideally, you should do so at the beginning of the appraisal period. Then, before your appraisal session, take the time to conduct a self-appraisal by completing the instrument as objectively as you can. This activity will help you remember accomplishments that you want to bring up if your supervisor overlooks them. It also can increase communication and understanding during the session. Identify areas that need improvement also.

Additionally, you can take three steps *during* the appraisal session to make the process effective and to help yourself. They are:

1. Go into the session willing to listen and participate. A defensive, closed mind will sabotage the session before it even starts. The appraisal is a good opportunity to share your career goals with your supervisor.
2. If obstacles have been in the way of your performing satisfactorily, you should have made them known to your supervisor before now. However, if you have not, certainly share them at this time. Are you frequently late in completing a weekly report because the Sales Department is late in submitting figures to you? If so, let your supervisor know what you need to perform better.
3. Make sure that you understand what is expected of you at the conclusion of the appraisal session. For instance, should you continue as you have been, assume other responsibilities, or perform current responsibilities better?

Taking these steps will help you feel more in control of your life and can make the session more effective. Extremely important in each step of this process are strong human relations skills. The greater your skills and those of your supervisor, the better will be the outcome of appraisal. This outcome, in turn, will benefit you, your supervisor, and the organization.

The Supervisor's Role

Understanding the supervisor's role in appraisals can help you prepare.

The effective supervisor will follow a number of steps in conducting the appraisal. Knowledge of these steps can enable you to use them to your advantage. The steps are:

1. The supervisor will schedule the appraisal in advance and ask the employee to think about achievements and areas for improvement to be discussed during the session. This step will allow the supervisor and employee time to prepare. Your objectivity and preparation can make a big difference in how smoothly the session runs and can enhance your supervisor's perception of you.
2. The supervisor will read the employee's personnel file and any other performance information available. If your file is open to you, you should review it periodically. This review will enable you to respond to negative information. If positive comments have been made or written about you that have not been put into the file, bring them to the evaluation session.
3. The supervisor will be prepared and will plan in advance what to say. Realizing that your supervisor is not treating you or the process lightly should make you feel more respected and, hence, more comfortable and receptive.
4. The supervisor will choose a quiet location for the session, free of interruptions, will allow plenty of time, and will give the employee opportunity to speak. If you know that the session will not be rushed, you can take the time to listen fully and communicate openly.

5. The supervisor will not usually discuss salary and performance in the same meeting. Recognizing that money should be discussed in a separate meeting frees you to concentrate on performance matters.
6. During the session, the supervisor will explain the purpose of the meeting, ask the employee's opinion, stay positive, discuss total performance, reach agreement on standards of performance, document the agreement, and get the employee's signature. If you accept these actions as part of the effective appraisal process, each step will seem less threatening to you.

Appraisal Instruments

No one perfect technique or form has yet been designed for recording performance appraisals. You may be evaluated by a variety of means during your career. Numerous kinds of appraisal instruments exist. Some organizations have created their own forms, whereas others use commercially available ones. In general, the most common performance appraisal techniques fall into three broad categories. They are the essay appraisal, the graphic rating scale, and the critical incident method.

Essay Appraisal Using the **essay appraisal** technique, the supervisor writes a paragraph or more about the employee's strengths and weaknesses, quantity and quality of work, current skills and knowledge, and potential value to the organization. The strength of this method lies in the fact that it probably gives a more complete picture of the employee. However, its use has several drawbacks. First, it takes longer to complete, and essay writing is more difficult. Secondly, it is likely to be more subjective than a graph. Finally, it makes comparison of employees almost impossible, because it has no scale. For these reasons it should be used only in appraising middle- and top-management employees.

Graphic Rating Scale As shown in Figure 7.6, the **graphic rating scale** lists the factors to be considered and terms to be used. Its strengths are that it is easy for the supervisor to complete and it helps make comparisons of employees easier. However, the categories and factors in the scale may overlap, making a thorough appraisal difficult. For example, persons appraised with the form shown in Figure 7.6 would almost automatically receive a high score in "effort" if they had been rated high in "quantity of work." Additionally, because descriptions are specified, the scale is rigid and does not give a complete picture of the employee. Because of its weaknesses, the graphic rating scale is often used in combination with the essay method.

Critical Incident Technique Using the **critical incident technique,** supervisors record in writing actual incidents in behavior that they observe in employees. The note or memo is then filed in the employee's personnel folder. Examples of negative incidents include tardiness, careless work, errors in judgment, and insubordination. Positive incidents may be completion of a project ahead of schedule, willingness to assist others, cooperation, or regular attendance at work.

An obvious drawback to the critical incident method is that it is time-consuming. Its advantage is that it provides the organization with the necessary documentation for decisions about transfers, promotions, demotions, and terminations.

FIGURE 7.6   A graphic rating scale lists the factors to be considered and terms to be used in appraising employees.

EMPLOYEE: JOB TITLE: (GRADE)   DEPARTMENT:

DATE OF EMPLOYMENT   DATE OF EMPLOYMENT ON PRESENT JOB: NUMBER OF MONTHS/YEARS ON PRESENT JOB: PRESENT SALARY: $

TO RATERS:

The value of this rating depends upon the impartiality and sound judgment you use when marking this form. Base your judgment of the employee in relation to others doing similar work, keeping in mind the duties and requirements of the job the employee occupies. Consider only one trait at a time. Do not let your rating of the employee on any one trait influence your rating on any other trait. Place a check mark in the block on the scale below the expression that most nearly describes your opinion of the employee. You are requested to note any comments which you believe would furnish additional information concerning the employee's performance on his/her job or to record any significant observations made during the discussion in the space provided at the end of this form.

EFFORT: How well does he/she make use of his/her time? Consider his/her physical and mental application to his/her work, his/her energy and attentiveness.	Wastes considerable time. Does only enough to get by. ☐	Keeps fairly busy. Allows idle conversation to keep him/her from work. ☐	Rarely unoccupied. Is energetic and attentive. ☐	Constantly applying himself/herself. Never seems to have an idle moment ☐
JOB KNOWLEDGE: How well has he/she acquired the knowledge of all elements comprising his/her job? Consider not only his/her own job's fundamentals, but also that of related work: his/her understanding of how and why his/her work is done.	Understands only the simpler or more routine phases of job. ☐	Is steadily acquiring the knowledge necessary to perform the more intricate job phases. ☐	Thoroughly knows most all phases of job. ☐	Has complete mastery of job. Remarkable understanding of all phases. ☐
ACCURACY: How accurate is the employee in performing his/her duty? Consider the number of errors made--the orderliness and thoroughness of work produced.	In need of improvement. ☐	Reasonably accurate. ☐	Very seldom makes a mistake. ☐	Exceptionally precise, orderly and thorough. ☐
INITIATIVE: Is he/she eager and able to attack new problems, advance ideas, better improve his/her work? Consider his/her self-reliance. Aggressiveness--constructive thinking.	Mildly progressive, but lacks certain abilities to go ahead on own. ☐	Possesses a normal amount of initiative. ☐	Usually self sufficient in his/her work enterprise. ☐	A self starter, enjoys solving difficulties and originating better methods. ☐

DEPENDABILITY: What are your feelings toward him/her when you are not at hand to give supervision? Consider his/her reliability in complying with standard procedures on his/her job following instructions and conducting self properly.	Needs occasional follow-up.	Dependable.	Is very dependable, needs little supervision.	Completely trustworthy, can handle job with out supervision.
JUDGMENT: How well does he/she display good common sense in his/her work? Consider how readily he/she grasps a situation and draws a correct conclusion, making best use of his/her experience and the facts at hand.	Apt to make hasty conclusions without due regard for consequences.	Usually displays good common sense.	Is levelheaded, able to draw sound conclusions.	Displays superior discrimination in analyzing facts and coming up with the right answer.
QUANTITY OF WORK: How much work is he/she able to produce? Consider not only his/her regular daily output but also how promptly he/she dispatches those extra or rush assignments.	Pushed to maintain schedule. Sometimes needs help from others.	Turns out satisfactory amount of work.	Keeps well ahead in his/her work-- on top of his/her job.	Extremely rapid--'never seems to get enough to do.'
ATTITUDE TOWARD ASSOCIATES: How well does he/she get along and cooperate with others? Consider his/her relations with fellow workers, his/her supervisors, business contacts.	Frequently uncooperative. Too critical of others.	Average ability to work with others.	A good team worker.	Very well liked and respected. An exceptional force for good morale.
ATTITUDE TOWARD WORK: What interest does he/she take in his/her job or line of work? Consider his/her eagerness to obtain more knowledge about his/her work--his/her enthusiasm in tackling difficulties--his/her pride in a job well done.	Mildly interested in some phases of job.	Shows normal interest.	Eagerness often displayed. Has pride in work.	Extraordinary interest, wants to learn all about job and any related work.

COMMENTS:

RATING REVIEWED WITH EMPLOYEE:

SUPERVISOR:

EMPLOYEE'S SIGNATURE:

DATE:

SUMMARY

Planning can benefit both people and organizations by improving the chances of success. Having goals gives us targets toward which to aim. Without planning organizations tend to become reactive rather than proactive, creating frustration for employees.

Three broad categories of organizational goals are official, operative, and operational. They differ in how specific they are, what activities are included, and which level of management has responsibility for them.

To be most effective, goals should have certain characteristics. They should be written, measurable, specific, and challenging but attainable. In an organization, for the greatest understanding and motivation to occur, they should have been developed with participation of both the supervisor and the affected subordinate.

Goals differ in the time allowed for their completion. They can be long-range, mid-range, and short-range. Long-range goals probably have the least chance of success because of fatigue, forgetfulness, interference, or changes in situations. When goals conflict, four techniques can be used to prioritize them: satisficing, sequential attention, preference ordering, and goal changes.

In setting personal goals, we should consider our priorities in life. They can include affection, expertness, independence, leadership, parenthood, happiness and contentment, prestige, security, personal development, wealth, and service. We should also apply four guidelines: (1) be realistic, (2) openly commit ourselves, (3) coordinate our goals with people important to us professionally and personally, and (4) visualize success. A Type C attitude that combines commitment, confidence, and control can improve our chances of personal success.

We can enhance our success by being responsible for ourselves and our careers, rather than expecting our bosses to take charge of them for us. We should also take actions to keep ourselves employable, accept change as a partner, and be adaptable. Additionally, making our bosses' jobs easier will increase our value as members of our work group. We can do this by assuming responsibilities, carrying them out competently, respecting our bosses' preferences, taking unwanted projects, doing more in our bosses' absences, and being familiar with their job responsibilities and goals.

Management by Objectives is a method and philosophy of management used to formalize goal setting in organizations. It is popular because it helps improve supervisor-subordinate communication, increases employee motivation, and makes employee appraisal easier. Employees like it because they appreciate being able to participate in decisions affecting them, they can monitor their own progress, they have greater opportunity to present their ideas, and they know what is expected of them and how they will be evaluated.

Employee performance appraisal is a measurement of how well the employee is doing on the job. Although both the supervisor and employee may dread them, appraisals are necessary for three major reasons: (1) to encourage good performance, discourage unacceptable performance, and correct inappropriate behavior; (2) to satisfy our need for feedback; and (3) to provide useful information to the organization. Employees can take steps to make appraisal a beneficial experience.

Numerous appraisal forms exist. The most commonly used techniques are the essay appraisal, the graphic rating scale, and the critical incident method. Each has its own strengths and weaknesses.

KEY TERMS

planning
reactive management
proactive management
underachiever
overachiever
realistic achiever
goal
official goals
operative goals
operational goals
Management by Objectives (MBO)
performance appraisal
essay appraisal
graphic rating scale
critical incident technique

REVIEW QUESTIONS

1. Explain how planning can benefit people and organizations.
2. What are the three categories of organizational goals? Whose responsibility is each category? What kinds of activities are included in each category?
3. Describe the characteristics of well-formulated goals.
4. Define long-range, mid-range, and short-range goals.
5. Name and define the four techniques for prioritizing goals.
6. What is Management by Objectives? Name some of the reasons why an organization may use MBO. How would individuals within the organization benefit from its use?
7. What is employee performance appraisal? If it is so dreaded, why do organizations do it? How can employees help turn this process into a positive one?
8. Describe the common performance appraisal instruments.

DISCUSSION QUESTIONS

1. Identify some situations in your personal life and, if you have held jobs, at work that developed because of a lack of planning. What happened? How could the situation have been improved?

2. When setting goals, do you see yourself as an underachiever, over-achiever, or realistic achiever? On what do you base your perception? Do you want to be in a different category? If so, what steps can you take? What steps are you willing to take?

3. Is procrastination a problem for you? Why or why not? If so, what has been the usual result of your procrastination? How might you confront this problem?

4. Write a goal that would be appropriate for a company with which you are familiar. Write a personal goal. Be sure that the goals are complete.

5. Briefly review your goals so far in life. Analyze why the goals have been accomplished or not. How has their status affected where you are today and your current goals?

6. Again considering situations in your personal life and at work, think about periods of conflicting goals. How was the conflict resolved? How might the four techniques described in this chapter have helped you?

7. Review the questions in the section of this chapter dealing with setting personal goals. Choose one long-range goal and develop a plan for accomplishing it. Then write three mid-range or short-range goals related to it.

8. After completing question 7, review the guidelines for setting goals. Examine your goals to see whether you have applied the four guidelines to them.

9. How can you apply the three components of Type C behavior to your accomplishment of the goals you wrote in question 7?

10. Think about a job that you have held. Did you make your boss's job harder or easier? How? Which approach would have been better for you in the long run? What, if anything, would you do differently today?

11. Have you ever worked in an organization that used MBO? If so, what was the process? What was the outcome of that process for the organization and those involved?

12. We have all received evaluations of our performance. We tested for a driver's license, tried out for sports, or completed tests. Think about specific times when you received appraisals, at work or at any other place. How did you react to the feedback? Were some of your reactions negative? Why? How did you use the feedback? Did feedback help you grow in some way? How?

CASE STUDY 7.1

YOU CAN'T HAVE IT ALL AT ONCE

Annette is a part-time student at the local community college. She is afraid that she will once again have to drop her courses even though she wants an associate degree in management very much.

Because Annette is a divorced mother with two children to support, she must work full time as a sales clerk in the nearby mall. Additionally, she feels she should serve as a room mother in her son's and daughter's schools each year. Having no help around the house, she also does all inside and outside painting and yard work. In fact, the appearance of her home is a special area of pride for her. Needless to say, all of this activity leaves little time for friendships.

Annette did not go to college immediately after graduating from high school and feels that she is falling even farther behind by going part time. For the last four semesters, she has tried to play "catch-up" by registering for three or four courses even though her counselor advised against such a heavy load. By the middle of each semester she felt so overwhelmed that she dropped all or most of her courses.

It is now Thanksgiving, and Annette once again recognizes that feeling of hopelessness.

1. What is wrong with Annette's plans?
2. What advice would you give her in setting long-range, mid-range, and short-range goals?
3. How might she prioritize her goals?

CASE STUDY 7.2   MBO GONE AWRY

Mike Aston is an engineer with a large oil and gas company. Four months ago he was asked to participate in the budgeting process for the next year. The corporate office cited use of MBO as the rationale for getting Mike's input. Willingly he spent hours in his office alone, carefully calculating costs for maintaining and operating several oil platforms in the Gulf of Mexico for which his local office in Houston is responsible.

After many hours of hard work, he submitted his budget to his supervisor, Emily Rodriguez, who passed it on to the head of the Houston office, Ronald Wang.

One month after the process began, Mr. Wang gathered the budgets from the different departments in the Houston office and carried them to the corporate office in New York.

Six weeks later the corporate office issued the overall budget guidelines for the corporation. Mike was astonished to see no resemblance between the guidelines and the budget that he had submitted. Emily asked him to redo his budget to fit the parameters issued by the corporate office, which he did.

Exactly four months after beginning the process and after much frustration, Mike received approval of a budget for his next year's operations.

1. Is this application of MBO correct?
2. What happened to create the overly long time involved and the need to prepare a second budget?
3. What could Mike have done to make a more productive process? Emily? Ronald? The corporate office?

BIBLIOGRAPHY

Aldag, Ramon J., and Timothy M. Stearns. *Management*. Cincinnati: South-Western Publishing Company, 1987.

Austin, Nancy K. "Just Do It—The New Job Strategy." *Working Woman* (April 1990): 78–80, 126.

Bittel, Lester. *What Every Supervisor Should Know*. New York: McGraw-Hill, 1985.

Burdick, Thomas E., and Charlene A. Mitchell. "Executives Face Freeze on Fast Track." *The Houston Post* (April 4, 1988): C-1.

"Check Your 'Progress Pulse' to Measure Career Success." *The Secretary* (March 1986): 25.

Drucker, Peter F. *Management: Tasks, Responsibilities, Practices*. New York: Harper & Row, 1974.

The George Odiorne Letter, XIV, no. 20, (October 19, 1984).

Kriegel, Robert, and Marilyn Harris Kriegel. "How to Reach Peak Performance—Naturally." *The Secretary* (March 1986): 22–24.

"Lonely-at-Top Execs Want for Guidance." *The Houston Post* (September 25, 1988): G-14.

McClelland, David C. "Business Drive and National Achievement." *Harvard Business Review,* 40 (1962): 99–112.

Mitchell, Charlene, and Thomas Burdick. "Make Yourself Indispensable." *The Houston Post* (September 26, 1988): C-1.

Perror, C. "The Analysis of Goals in Complex Organizations." *American Sociological Review* 26 (1961): 854–866.

SUGGESTED READINGS

Fiore, Neil. *The Now Habit—A Strategic Programming for Overcoming Procrastination and Enjoying Guilt-Free Play*. Los Angeles: Jeremy P. Tarcher, Inc., 1989.

Shea, Barbara, with Annie Gottlieb. *Wishcraft—How to Get What You Really Want*. New York: Ballantine, 1979.

Waitley, Dennis. *Being the Best*. New York: Pocket Books, 1987.

CHAPTER EIGHT
CHANGE DYNAMICS

When Apple Computer laid off more than 1,000 workers in 1985, they had not counted on the grim aftermath. The company at first assumed that the survivors would be happy just to hold on to their jobs. Instead, most of them felt miserable. Like many companies that cut personnel, Apple followed up with reassignments, demotions, and major changes in the way that the company did business. As a result, employees were depressed and angry, and in many cases, they doubted whether they even wanted their jobs anymore.

Fortunately, Apple managers recognized the crisis and quickly took action. They listened to people's complaints and tried to find solutions. More importantly, they made it clear that Apple was changing and told survivors how they could be a part of that change. That patience and firmness paid off. Apple employees have recovered their famous esprit de corps, and the company is back on track.

Michele Block Morse, *Success*
(September 1987): 58-62

OBJECTIVES

After studying this chapter, you should be able to:
1. Describe significant factors that are changing in today's workplace.
2. Identify who usually recommends and implements organizational changes.
3. Describe three methods of implementing change.
4. Describe several effective methods of planning for change.
5. Identify the common reasons for resistance to change and the methods of reducing or overcoming that resistance.
6. Discuss what individuals who face change can do for themselves.
7. Identify the steps of the change process.
8. Discuss the need for coaching and counseling skills in the change process.
9. Describe the coaching and counseling techniques most commonly used.

WHERE ARE CHANGES OCCURRING?

Mergers, takeovers, buy outs, downsizing, and acquisitions are common today.

Change is a basic condition of today's work world. Never before in business history have so many forces acted as dynamically or changed as rapidly. During the decade of the 1980s, more than 4000 of the largest corporations in the United States were restructured. More than three million jobs were eliminated from payrolls in just a

FIGURE 8.1   This silicone-coated computer wafer is an example of fast-changing technology.

AT&T Bell Laboratories

five-year span, 1985 to 1990. The buzz words "merger," "takeover," "buy out," "downsizing," and "acquisition" became real to a multitude of workers and struck fear in the hearts of many more. This trend is expected to continue into the 1990s as companies prepare to move toward a more competitive global business environment.

Although change is necessary to avoid stagnation, it can be difficult. People are often unwilling to step out of their comfort zones or abandon routines to which they have grown accustomed and which they see no reason to change. However, in today's complex environment, the premium is on adaptability. No person or company will function long or well without deliberate and intelligent planning for change. A planned change is a method of helping people develop appropriate behaviors for adapting to new methods while remaining effective and creative. The key to an organization making a positive transition is getting people involved in and committed to the change at the beginning. Then employees will view change as an opportunity rather than a threat. The application of sound human relations skills by managers and employees will make adapting easier during the transition.

FIGURE 8.2   "Gentlemen, some changes are about to take place."

Change is rapid in the economy, science/technology, transportation, the work force, management styles, and work itself.

Areas experiencing rapid change include the economy, science and technology, transportation, the general work force, management styles, and the work itself. Each area has far-reaching effects on the others. We are bombarded daily with these changing elements in our environment. Figure 8.3 indicates the many forces working to change our work world. Think how each of them affects your world.

FIGURE 8.3   Forces changing the work world.

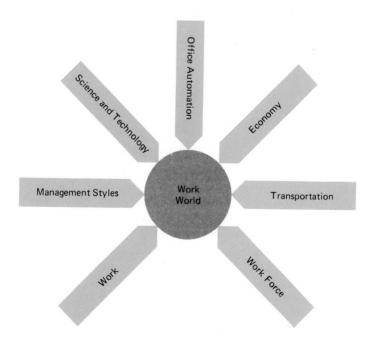

Economy

As we move closer to the globalization of business activities, more opportunities for growth will be realized. The opening of the eastern and western European markets in the early 1990s will cause an explosion in free trade and create a vast array of entrepreneurial opportunities. EC-92 (European Common Market-1992) alone is expected to result in as many as five million new jobs throughout Europe. EC-92 will mean the free movement of goods, services, human resources, and capital across national borders in Europe as easily as they cross state borders in the United States. This change is expected to turn Europe into a unified economic power that will compete as a major economic player with the United States and Japan. Whole nations will not only become linked in economies but will operate as one with global financial ties that bind them.

Science and Technology

Advanced space exploration will result in new scientific discoveries about our universe. New medicines and medical techniques will continue to be developed and will improve our health and well-being. Technological advancements will increase as we share our knowledge and experience through joint ventures with other nations. As we continue to move from the Industrial Era to the Information Age, we will have a greater need for computer competency. John Naisbitt, author of *Megatrends*, labeled this new era "high-tech, high-touch," acknowledging an increase in robotics, automation, and artificial intelligence.

Transportation

Many people alive today have seen transportation evolve from horse-drawn carriages to automobiles and from rapid transit lines to space vehicles shuttling to space stations. The demand for more efficient mass and rapid transit systems has been brought on by a growing population that requires increased mobility in both business and personal areas. New methods of transportation yet to be created will restructure both our personal and professional lives.

Work Force

Numerous changes are occurring in the work force. The "baby boomers" have become the dominant generation and have brought new values into the workplace, requiring new methods of leadership, motivation, and other human relations skills. Workers in the twenty-first century will place stronger emphasis on employment security, career development, training and retraining, and support for job relocation. The general work force will age, but retirements will be fewer. Overall, we will have fewer workers to replace those who do leave the work force, and a critical labor shortage will result. The increase in immigration to the United States will affect the ethnic blend of the work force. Considering the variety of changes foreseen in the workplace, employers are seeking employees who are flexible and adaptable for the work force of 2,000.

Management Styles

Peter Drucker, author of *The New Realities*, predicts that "in so-called knowledge-based companies, hierarchies will give way to something resembling a symphony orchestra with dozens or even hundreds of specialists reporting directly to the conductor/CEO." The age of the standard pyramidal hierarchy is gone. Organizational structures will be more open and fluid, able to adapt quickly. Power will be decentralized, and the use of matrix-style structures will account for an organization's ability to adjust. The horizontal organization in the twenty-first century will be characterized by the absence of a "boss." Leadership will be more team-oriented and participatory.

A 1989 *Fortune* magazine article by Thomas A. Stewart quotes Reuben Mark, CEO of Colgate-Palmolive, as saying, "The more power you have, the less you should use. You can't manage today's work force like yesterday's. The military command and control model went out with red meat." With our rapidly changing work force and workplace, managers are promoting speed, flexibility, and decisiveness. To get these results, they are delegating more tasks to the lowest level possible and empowering others with responsibility.

Work Itself

The Information Age described in Naisbitt's *Megatrends* moves us from manual to mental labor. Work will shift from industrial manufacturing and production to information and knowledge-based goods and services. The increased competitiveness in Europe will force United States employers to achieve productivity with fewer and better-educated workers with different skills. Characteristic of the new skills required is the ability to interpret information using more abstract and creative methods. Within the general labor shortage will be a critical skills shortage. Companies are already realizing a gap between basic skills and the highly technical skills required to operate their rapidly advancing equipment.

The need for improved quality of product or service will continue to be a force shaping the way work is performed. Work performance will take new shape, with decisions being pushed to the lowest level possible in the more horizontal organizational structures of the future.

An equal number of more personal changes will influence the immediate work setting. Predictions for the office of the future include computers that respond to voice commands, paperless office systems, letters and memorandums that are read by an optical scanner and stored or filed on an optical disk, and communications systems that provide instant access to offices, information, and individuals globally.

Further office automation will eliminate approximately 19 million clerical jobs as typewriters and file cabinets are replaced by computers. A 1989 *Wall Street Journal* article cites an example of this trend: an insurance company, Capital Holiday Corporation, reduced its data-entry department staff by 75 percent after introducing a computerized system to record and transmit electronically all claim information. A change like this one can have enormous impact on people on a personal and environmental level.

The coming organizational environment can be summed up in three principal concepts: intense competition, technological advancement and change, and continuing turbulence and uncertainty. An article in the March 1990 *Personnel Journal* points out that in 1985 alone 3,165 mergers worth $139 billion occurred. During the first two months of 1988, takeovers totaled $50 billion, and the trend for the 1990s remains at the same high level as companies continue to streamline. These trends highlight the need for understanding change dynamics.

WHO CHANGES ORGANIZATIONS?

Professional planners, outside consultants, special task forces, and top executives plan most change.

Recommendations for change originate from a variety of sources. These sources include professional planners and outside consultants who may be hired and brought into an organization to define methods and techniques for increasing effectiveness. Additionally, special task forces may be formed of representatives from within the organization to participate in streamlining operations. CEOs and other top-level managers are also the initiators of change within an organization.

The change is usually carried out by mid-level and first-line managers. Methods that they may use in producing change include unilateral, participative, and delegated methods.

Methods for implementing change are unilateral, participative, or delegated.

In the **unilateral method** employees make little or no input to the process. Supervisors dictate the change—what it is, when and how it will be accomplished, and who will be involved. Employees merely follow the directives. In the **participative method**, employee groups are used in the problem-solving and decision-making processes that precede change implementation. Both the supervisors and the employees share in bringing about the change. In the **delegated method**, employees are given the responsibility and authority to effect the change. They diagnose,

FIGURE 8.4   Personal guide for effective change planning.

- Establish consistent goals—consider present and future conditions.
- Have vision—foresee the future and raise expectations of those involved.
- Have "big picture" outlook—take a broad view of change effects.
- Make your intentions known—communicate openly for change acceptance.
- Know your options—develop alternative plans.
- Time your change—introduce processes carefully for least resistance.
- Be flexible—adapt or modify process if necessary.

NASA

analyze, and select the best method for implementation. This method is used most when employees are closest to the situation that needs changing. Figure 8.4 identifies several steps you may find useful in planning and implementing change effectively.

HOW IS CHANGE PLANNED?

The goals in managing change are to anticipate the need for change and to bring the change about effectively. The most common methods for achieving these results include strategic planning, organizational development, job design/redesign, and force field analysis.

Strategic Planning

Strategic planning must be designed to fit the unique characteristics of each organization. The essence of planning is designing a desired future and identifying ways to bring it about. Specifically, **strategic planning** is the systematic setting of organizational goals, defining strategies and policies to achieve them, and developing detailed plans to ensure that the strategies are implemented. The process helps determine what is to be done, when and how it is to be done, who is going to do it, and what is to be done with the results. Because changes in any organization's environment are continuous, strategic planning must be ongoing and flexible.

Strategic planning is not simply forecasting based on trends, nor is it a set of plans that can be carved in stone to be used day after day. This type of planning for change is more a thought process than a prescribed set of procedures and techniques. A formal strategic planning system links three major types of plans. They are strategic plans, medium-range programs, and short-range budgets and operating plans. Figure 8.5 illustrates typical information flow and steps in a strategic planning process.

In the initial steps, consideration is given to the concerns of outside and inside interests and how they may be affected by the planned goal. For example, you may ask how the local community will react to the proposed building site for a factory near the downtown area. Will this company expansion please the stockholders by increasing profits and better serve our customers? Will it generate revenue to pay our creditors and increase orders to our suppliers? Will Rocky Williams agree to leave his current shop foreman job to manage and operate the new facility? What has our past performance capability been in the area of pipe manufacturing, and how will the new factory change that performance? Can we forecast with reasonable accuracy the outcome of making this major investment? What effects overall will this plan for expansion have on the environment and the company? These questions illustrate how the planning begins through a thought process.

Once these questions are favorably answered, the next step is to design a master strategy for implementation. The purpose and objective is clearly defined and policies are established. Then medium- and short-range steps are developed and the plan begins to take shape. With a step-by-step program plan in place, implementation can begin. The land may be purchased and cleared, building specifications drawn to

FIGURE 8.5   The strategic planning process.

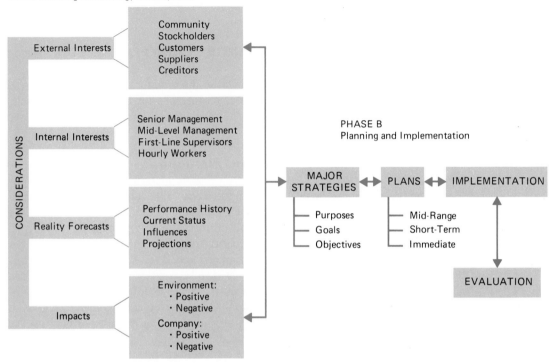

scale, and contractors hired to build the facility. As construction begins, each phase is carefully reviewed and evaluated to assure maximum efficiency upon completion.

The thought process continues throughout the year that building the facility takes. If new facts arise, changes may be made to accommodate them. No plan is absolute. It may best be described as a fluid or dynamic process that allows change to occur as warranted.

Organizational Development (OD)

The approach to organizational change called organizational development (OD) is similar to strategic planning in concept but not in practice. OD takes a holistic approach, involving the entire organization—its people, structures, culture, policies and procedures, and purpose. It also strongly supports the belief that any planned change process must continuously adapt to the ever-changing environment. **Organizational development** is a planned change process for meeting organizational needs through employee participation and management involvement on a continuing basis.

Strongly rooted in human relations management theories, OD relies heavily on methods such as Robert Blake and Jane Mouton's Managerial Grid® (discussed in

Chapter 9) to identify degrees of concern for people and production. This method uses sensitivity training, team development, and goal setting to bring about the desired changes in both the employee and the organization. Other methods used in the OD change process include survey and feedback techniques, confrontation meetings, and teambuilding exercises. Each of these methods involves a high degree of participation by employees and management to improve organizational effectiveness. These activities, known as interventions, are intended to help the adjustment to change.

Instrumental in bringing about any OD change process is the change agent. Also known as an OD practitioner or an OD consultant, the **change agent** attempts to diagnose problems, provide feedback, help develop strategies, or recommend interventions to benefit the organization as a whole.

The role of a change agent in any change process is a powerful one. The challenge is to develop a creative, innovative organization that easily adapts in an ever-changing world, yet remains competitive. To foster such flexibility, employees must be made to feel part of a team rather than just people in charge of a specific set of tasks. Figure 8.6 outlines steps that an agent takes to assure effective change.

FIGURE 8.6   Actions of a change agent.

- Be open, honest about why the change is happening.
- Encourage participation, solicit feelings.
- Allow negative comments but not negative actions.
- Explain benefits of change.
- Involve others in initiation/implementation phases.
- Acknowledge loss of old methods.

Change should be perceived as an opportunity for growth among team members as they accept new challenges and learn new skills.

Job Design/Redesign

Job design changes the makeup of an employee's tasks.

Job design or redesign is a method of bringing about change in the tasks performed by individuals. Job design means changing the makeup of the tasks to make them more interesting and challenging for the employee. Here is an example:

Regina was excited. She had been hired a year ago as a data entry clerk for the data acquisition department. The job had become routine and boring, offering little challenge to her. She was nearly finished with her bachelor's degree in computer science and ready for more advanced systems work. Her boss met with her last Friday to say, "I think you may be ready for additional tasks that will increase your level of responsibility in our organization. Mastering these new tasks will better prepare you for a move into our computer applications group as a computer specialist. This change will be an opportunity to experience our operations in a different

way and broaden your skill base by learning new techniques. We'd like to keep you challenged."

The goal is to relieve boredom, create interest, and obtain a more satisfied and productive worker. The most common methods used in job design or redesign are job enrichment, job enlargement, and job rotation.

Job enrichment builds greater responsibility and interest into task assignments. It means adding tasks that encourage and motivate employees. Job enrichment, also known as vertical loading or adding tasks of increased responsibility, is an excellent means of bringing about positive change within the organization.

Job enlargement, on the other hand, known as horizontal loading, increases the complexity of a job by adding similar tasks to those already being performed. This method may not motivate an employee, but may appeal to higher-order needs within the individual and result in positive change for the employee and the organization.

Job rotation is the shifting of employees from one job to another in hopes of reducing boredom and stimulating renewed interest in job performance. In this situation, the content of a particular job is not affected. This method may also be used to prepare an individual for permanent assignment to a higher-level position.

In a 1990 issue of *Government Executive*, John Bryson describes a program launched at Polaroid, appropriately called "Job Redesign." All employees analyze what they are doing and whether it needs to be done. The plan is voluntary and carries a guarantee that anyone who participates will not be laid off if the job is phased out as a result. The results of this effort have benefited both the organization and the employees. It is a good example of positive change management.

Force Field Analysis

Force field analysis is a technique used to analyze the complexities of the change and identify the forces that must be altered. This useful tool, developed by Kurt Lewin, views any situation in which change is to be made as a dynamic balance of forces working in opposite directions.

One set of forces moves the situation in the direction of the anticipated change. They are called driving forces. The opposite set of forces tends to keep the situation from moving in the direction of the anticipated change. They are called restraining forces. These two sets of forces working against each other create a dynamic equilibrium or a balance that can be disturbed at any moment by altering either the driving or restraining forces.

Using this tool, a change agent can visualize and analyze the forces, can predict the consequences of altering either set of forces, or can go ahead and alter the forces to create the desired change. The forces may include people, tasks, technology, equipment, or the organization's basic structure, as the following example indicates:

Stewart, vice president of production, called the floor supervisors into a meeting. "The head office has told us to increase productivity by 10 percent," Stewart said gravely, "or we will have to close the plant. Does anyone have any suggestions?"

"I don't know how we are going to increase production," Tim

> **commented. "Machine 6 is always breaking. We can keep it run-
> ning only 75 percent of the time. Perhaps if we did not have this
> problem, we could increase production."**
>
> **After the meeting Stewart was thoughtful. "My restraining
> force is that machine. I'm going to get it fixed. This change will
> allow the driving force, increased productivity, to prevail."**

Planning for change is important to ensure a smooth transition with the least resistance possible. Each situation should be analyzed to anticipate the consequences of each step in the change process.

WHY DO PEOPLE RESIST CHANGE?

People are naturally resistant to change. Their feelings create barriers to effective change. Understanding how people feel about change can help us remove the barriers and ensure an easier process. Four reasons for resistance are common:

Fear of the unknown. When situations remain constant, we know what to expect, how to respond, and how things fit together. We have stability, security, and predictability. Change presents us with an unknown and uncertain situation. This disorganization of the familiar often arouses anxiety, fear, and stress.

Fear of power loss. Often our power and status are so tied to the existing situation that any change means a potential personal loss. The change may "cost" us too much.

Fear of economic loss. We may feel threatened by loss of income by reductions in salary or cuts in benefits or the ultimate loss of our jobs.

Conflict of interest. Traditions, standards, values, or norms of a person or a group may be threatened by the change. Social affiliations may also be jeopardized.

The following scenario demonstrates resistance to change:

> **Herbert stared glumly at the shiny new computer on his desk.
> Thinking about it made him break out in a cold sweat. I don't
> know, he thought to himself. This whole thing has me so upset
> that I tossed and turned all night. I don't understand these ma-
> chines. As for that training—all that talk about RAMs and ROMs
> and disks and drives and bits and bytes—it's so confusing! Why
> can't things be the way they were back in the good old days when I
> wrote things by hand and the secretary typed them? I just don't
> know if I can learn all this. What will happen to me if I don't?**

Resistance to change can cause management to examine its process more closely.

Resistance to change can result in some benefits. For example, management may put more thought into clarifying the purpose of the change and identifying the desired results. The fear of the unknown may lead employees to examine possible consequences, both immediate and long-range, with more care. When we find a poor flow of information, we can improve communication systems, a vital link to effective change implementation. Resistance often provides clues for the prevention of failure.

When faced with change, keep the following points in mind:

1. Remember that change is inevitable and that fear of change is normal.
2. Analyze the reasons that you want to resist the change. What fears do you have? What behaviors will you have to adjust in order to effect the change?
3. Search for the positives. How will the changes constructively affect your work?
4. Seek assistance if you are having difficulty adjusting to the changes. A supervisor or a more experienced employee can help.
5. Learn how to learn. According to John Naisbitt in *Re-inventing the Corporation*, "The most important skill to acquire for the future is learning how to learn."

HOW DO LEADERS FACILITATE CHANGE?

Creating a climate conducive to change is an important step in change management. If you are in a position of leadership at work or in other situations and are asked to implement change, the following seven-step process may help you. You can also apply these steps to personal situations in your life. The seven steps, illustrated in Figure 8.7, are as follows:

1. *Present state assessment (PSA).* Diagnose the present situation. "Where am I now, and what are the current conditions?" Examine why you need to change.
2. *Future state assessment (FSA).* Determine the desired results. "Where do I want to be, and how will the conditions change?" Visualize the desired results.
3. *Generation of alternatives.* Identify the possible approaches through use of "What if . . ." questions. Consider the probable outcomes and reactions. Who will be involved and how will they be affected?
4. *Selection of one alternative.* Make a selection from the alternative solutions. Decide which method will best achieve the desired results.
5. *Implemention of change.* Put a plan in motion to assure that the change occurs. Alter whatever conditions are necessary or introduce the change method.
6. *Evaluation of change.* Allow time for implementation and acceptance; then carefully evaluate the results to see whether you have achieved the desired outcome.
7. *Modification of change.* Modify as required. You may make only a minor revision or repeat the entire process with a different alternative.

Modifying or changing an alternative is appropriate if the expected results are not achieved or if they prove undesirable. However, too frequent changes make us appear indecisive. Use of these steps in your change process may reduce the negative effects on people involved.

FIGURE 8.7   Steps in the change process.

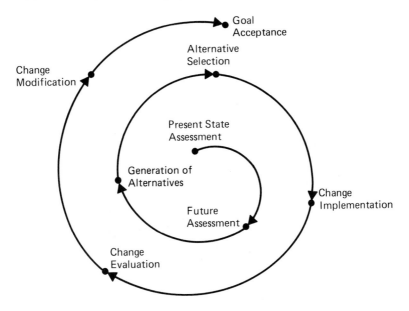

Communication is an important factor in facilitating change. The following suggestions will help those involved adjust:

Discuss the change. Communicate early in the process with those who will be affected. Educate them in how, why, and when the change will occur. Early communication will allow individuals to become accustomed to the idea.

Invite participation. Ask workers to take part in the formulation of the change. Involvement will create "ownership" and commitment to the success of the change. The change becomes partially their own, and they will be much less apt to resist its implementation.

Be open and honest. Share facts and information with those who will be affected. Stick to the facts and avoid what you "hope" or "think."

Accent the positives. Stress the benefits to the worker. Increased pay, fringe benefits, lighter work load, elimination of hectic deadlines, or more flexible work hours may be some of the positive outcomes expected of the change. Although individuals are interested in how the change will affect them, they are even more interested in what benefits it will bring them.

Do not downgrade past methods. A mistake often made when introducing change is to tear down old or existing methods. If you imply that the old or existing method is inadequate, individuals may resent the implication that they have not been doing an adequate job using that method.

Follow up on the process. Frequently resistance to change is shadowed or hidden, only to surface later. Follow up to see whether individuals are having problems accepting it or implementing it, and provide help.

Allow time for adjustments. Changing long-standing work habits can take time. Give individuals a chance to adjust to the change. Be prepared to make adjustments if you hit a snag in the process.

Applying these methods will help those involved accept change. Figure 8.8 illustrates the stages of acceptance they must go through.

FIGURE 8.8 Stages in acceptance of change.

Recognition: Individual must recognize need for change.
Choice: Individual must decide change is beneficial and act to make it happen.
Plan: Individual must think through the change process to develop a specific approach.
Support: Individual must seek understanding and assistance of others to help implement plan.

You may want to try additional human relations approaches when introducing change. For example, you may try the change first on a small scale. Begin the process with some small segment of the whole group to be affected. Other individuals will see the advantages and importance of the change. Their uncertainties will be reduced. A similar approach calls for special timing. Before you begin, find allies who will be supportive of your ideas. This way you may ease the general resistance.

Finally, you can use special human relations skills to facilitate change. Unwelcome change often results in low morale or motivation, apathy, uncertainty, instability, frustration, and symptoms of stress. Even change that is welcomed can cause some of these symptoms. These behavior changes are hardly the ones hoped for in reaching your change objectives. Additionally, changes that tend toward restructuring, compressing, or reducing the work force may result in a mismatch of skills and jobs. In this case, you may notice performance problems and a decrease in productivity while change is being implemented.

Coaching and counseling skills often help you implement change.

The most effective means of dealing with behavioral problems, performance and productivity problems, and employee training and development concerns brought on by change is through coaching and counseling employees. Open communication, which is stressed in these methods, is always a good way to cope with problems.

WHAT IS MEANT BY THE TERM *COACHING?*

Coaching by a senior-level employee is a good employee development method.

Coaching is a method of employee development that closely resembles on-the-job training. Typically, a skilled and experienced employee, usually of high-ranking status within the organization, is assigned to develop or train a junior employee with lesser skills and abilities. A coach may help identify career paths, help define career goals and objectives, explain the organization's culture and established norms, or simply share expertise for skills development. Immediate and continual feedback is provided. Once this relationship is established, it should remain an ongoing part of the employee's development.

A currently popular form of coaching is known as **mentoring.** Whereas a "coach" is often formally assigned, we often find ourselves simply drawn to someone who can help us develop.

Many corporations are recognizing the benefits of establishing formal mentoring programs. Aimee L. Ball describes several success stories about mentoring in *Working Woman.* For example, Ortho Pharmaceutical Corporation began a program in 1981 to help new employees rapidly enter the corporate culture. A mentor and protégé are matched on the basis of backgrounds and interests. In a similar program offered by AT&T, employees can select a senior staff mentor from either the same or a different department. In any case, a **mentor** is usually a senior-level manager with political savvy and an interest in helping employees achieve both career goals and the objectives of the organization.

If you are not assigned a mentor, you should attempt to find one either within your organization or within your profession. A mentor is often selected on the basis of being a kindred soul. You can best achieve the close rapport necessary in this relationship when the ethics, values, and operating styles of both participants mesh. A foundation of mutual respect must exist. A mentor will listen to you empathetically, suspend judgment, probe for your concerns, and offer specific suggestions regarding training and development opportunities. The selection of a mentor can be a wise investment in career planning and development:

> **Joshua, vice president of marketing, and Allison, the new marketing trainee, were having coffee together.**
>
> **"Allison, did you check into a membership in the National Management Association as I mentioned?" Joshua asked.**
>
> **"No, not yet," Allison replied. "I've just been too busy."**
>
> **"You might want to consider joining soon. A promotion may come up in the next several months in Geraldine's section. She is a charter member of that organization and believes that professional organizations are important vehicles for professional development, and so do I. If you are interested in that position, you may want to place some priority on joining the Association."**
>
> **"Thanks for the tip, Joshua," Allison said. "I didn't realize how important the membership might be. I'll check on the membership requirements today. I appreciate your helpful suggestion."**

WHAT IS COUNSELING?

In most organizations, **counseling** is a technique used to assist employees with problems affecting performance on the job. These problems may be personal or work-related. Employee problems may result in unacceptable quality and quantity of work, absenteeism, and low morale, which cost companies millions of dollars.

In an article published in *Manage,* Lin Grensing points out that a six-year study found 18.7 percent of all adults in the United States suffer from at least one mental health disorder during an average six-month period. Not only do problems of this nature affect individuals' performance, but their behavior profoundly affects employees who are in contact with them. A **counselor** may be a supervisor or a trained professional capable of dealing with a wide variety of employee problems.

Once a counselor identifies the problem and documents the specifics to be addressed, a counseling session may be scheduled. During the counseling interview with the employee, any of the three basic types of counseling methods may be used—directive, nondirective, or cooperative.

In **directive counseling** the counselor listens to the employee's problem, allows emotional release, determines an action plan, and advises the employee on what needs to be done.

Nondirective counseling requires the employee to participate more actively. Through a technique known as reflective listening, the counselor will mirror feelings and statements back to the employee and allow the employee to freely define the problem, develop solutions, and choose an appropriate plan of action.

The **cooperative counseling** method is a mutual problem-solving effort. Both parties explore and solve the issues. This process may be more time consuming because of the sharing of ideas and experiences and the evaluation of suggested approaches. The employee is expected to develop the ultimate solution to increase ownership and commitment.

Some supervisors find counseling a difficult part of the human relations skills required in leadership positions. They prefer to have a professional staff counselor take the responsibility. An alternative solution would be to make a referral of the employee to an employee assistance program.

> **Counseling can be directive, nondirective, or cooperative.**

WHAT ARE EMPLOYEE ASSISTANCE PROGRAMS?

Employee assistance programs (EAPs) are formal programs designed to aid employees with personal problems, such as substance abuse or psychological problems, that affect their job performance. These personal problems often result in undesirable behaviors at work, such as absences, errors, tardiness, decreased productivity, accidents, or an inability to operate equipment safely. Problems are generally identified by the immediate supervisor. In some companies the supervisor is expected to take immediate action.

Most companies have specific guidelines for handling these situations. The supervisor is usually required to document incidences of unsatisfactory behavior or performance, counsel the employee on performance expectations, and reach an agreement with the employee on a specific time for improvement of performance. If appreciable improvement is not shown within the time limit, a supervisor is expected to refer the employee to the EAP for assignment to a qualified professional counselor.

The counselor will recommend whatever treatment is required to aid the employee in coping with personal problems. The problem may be marital strife, financial troubles, substance abuse, parenting problems, or care for aging parents:

Juanita entered the EAP office nervously. Her supervisor, Sue Ann, had suggested that she come. Juanita's son had been giving

**her problems lately. Although he was only thirteen, he was skip-
ping school. When he was in school, he seemed to get in trouble
and stay in the detention center most of the time. All this had
caused Juanita to worry. She spent time away from her work making telephone calls to the school and left early to find her son when
the school's office called to report his absence. Her work was slipping and she felt out of control.**

    **"I hope the counselor can help me," she thought. "If I can't
resolve this situation and get back to work, I may lose my job."**

Employees are guaranteed confidentiality when entering an employee assistance program. In most cases, the employee begins to handle the problem and job
performance improves. Grensing, in his *Manage* article, reports these programs
have been so successful that, by 1985, 10,000 EAPs were in place in major corporations throughout the United States.

    Any planned change must give as much attention to the emotional or psycho-
logical dimensions as to the practical and informational aspects of the change process.
The most important condition for effective change management is the certainty that
the climate is conducive to the change being introduced, implemented, and accepted.
The poem in Figure 8.9 puts change in perspective.

FIGURE 8.9   *"The Serenity Prayer."*

God give me the serenity to accept things which cannot be changed;

Give me courage to change things that must be changed;

And the wisdom to distinguish one from the other.

Reinhold Niebuhr, "The Serenity Prayer," in The A.A. Grapevine *(January 1950): 6–7.*

SUMMARY

Never before in business history have so many forces changed as rapidly as
during the past decade. Changes will continue to be a way of life as we move
into the twenty-first century. Areas experiencing rapid change include the
economy, science and technology, transportation, the general work force,
management styles, and work itself. The organizational environment of the
future can be described as intensely competitive, technologically advanced, and
filled with turbulence and uncertainty. Because change can be difficult for
employees, organizations must employ sound human relations skills to facilitate
necessary changes.

    Recommendations for change originate from professional planners, spe-
cial task forces, CEOs, and other top-level executives. However, the change is
usually carried out by mid-level and first-line managers. In effecting change,
unilateral, participative, and delegated methods are used. The most common

methods of planning for change include strategic planning, organizational development, job design/redesign, and force field analysis.

Reasons for resistance to change include a fear of the unknown, a fear of power loss, a fear of economic loss, and a conflict of interest. The steps involved in the change process include a present state assessment, a future state assessment, generation of alternatives, selection of one alternative, implementation, evaluation, and modification if required. Methods of overcoming resistance to change include discussing the change, inviting participation, being open and honest, accenting the positive aspects, and following up on the effectiveness of the change. Coaching and counseling skills are used to help individuals cope with uncertainties of change and attitude and performance problems that it may cause. Coaching and mentoring are methods of developing employees to their maximum potential. Counseling is a method of assisting employees with personal problems affecting their performance. The most common methods of counseling are directive, nondirective, and cooperative. Employee assistance programs are formal programs designed to help employees with personal problems such as substance abuse, marital, financial, and family problems.

KEY TERMS

unilateral method
participative method
delegated method
strategic planning
organizational development
change agent
job design/redesign
job enrichment
job enlargement
job rotation
force field analysis
coaching
mentoring
mentor
counseling
counselor
directive counseling
nondirective counseling
cooperative counseling
employee assistance program (EAP)

REVIEW QUESTIONS

1. Describe the significant factors that are changing in today's workplace.
2. Who usually recommends organizational changes, and who is responsible for their implementation?
3. Describe the three methods of implementing change.
4. Describe several effective methods of planning for change.
5. What are the most common reasons for resisting change, and what are the methods of overcoming that resistance?
6. What steps can you take to deal personally with change?
7. What are the seven steps of the change process?
8. Explain why coaching and counseling are needed in the change process.
9. Describe the most commonly used coaching and counseling techniques.

DISCUSSION QUESTIONS

1. Which of the major factors changing in today's workplace are affecting you personally? How?
2. What changes in your immediate work environment have you resisted over the past year? Discuss why and explain what action you took to adjust.
3. Think of the last major change that was introduced in your organization. Was the method used to effect that change unilateral, participative, or delegated? Describe how you were involved.
4. Do you have a mentor? If so, describe the reasons why you selected that individual as a mentor for your career. If not, think of someone in your organization whom you might select and describe why you would choose that person.
5. Think of a time when you were counseled about a job-related problem. What method of counseling was used to resolve the problem? Was it an effective means?

WOULD SOMEBODY HELP ME, PLEASE?

Marc Tross had been a faithful worker for the Whitaker Transportation Corporation for nearly 20 years. His work record was outstanding with few absences to mar his attendance record and no lateness. He was considered a pillar of dependability and highly respected for the expertise he had developed over the years about the transportation industry.

"I don't understand what's going on with Marc's performance lately," remarked Chauncey, his first-line supervisor. "He has begun to come in late and take excessively long lunch breaks, and he slips out before quitting time. I've spoken with him about the changes in his behavior, but he seems unwilling to admit that he has changed or to commit to correcting the problem."

"Have you documented the circumstances and followed the usual procedures?" asked Gary, the trained counselor from Human Resources.

"Yes, but I don't know what my next step should be," replied Chauncey. "I am not comfortable with this situation."

1. From the behaviors described, what do you think is the problem?
2. Do you think Chauncey has taken the appropriate steps to help his employee in this situation?
3. What do you think Chauncey should do next? Why?

CASE STUDY 8.2

WHERE WILL ALL THE PEOPLE GO?

"This new system will revolutionize your department's operations, increase productivity, and reduce your overhead costs. You can't beat it, and if you plan to stay competitive in this market, you must adopt this system."

Frank knew that he needed to make the decision soon on converting his department to this new system, but it would mean a reduction in his office staff of nearly 60 percent. Then the department would have a period of lost productivity while employees were trained to use the new equipment and establish new procedures. Many factors needed to be considered.

1. What methods should Frank consider using to implement the new system in his department?
2. Is there any evidence that Frank's management had planned for this change in technology and prepared for implementation?
3. What will be some of the typical responses to the implementation of the new system, and how will Frank react to the concerns of his employees?

BIBLIOGRAPHY

Ansbury, Clare. "Labor Letters." *The Wall Street Journal* (March 28, 1989): 1.

Ball, Aimee Lee. "Mentors and Protégés: Portraits of Success." *Working Woman* (October 1989): 134–142.

Bryson, John M. "Extending Strategic Planning beyond Management." *Government Executive* (January 1990): 46.

Coates, Joseph F., Jennifer Jarratt, and John Mahaffie. "Workplace Management 2000." *Personnel Administrator* (December 1989): 51–55.

Drucker, Peter. *The New Realities*. New York: Harper & Row, 1989.

Elliott, Ronald D. "The Challenge of Managing Change." *Personnel Journal* (March 1990): 58–62.

Grensing, Lin. "Employee Personal Problems: Should You Get Involved?" *Manage* (October 1988): 30–33.

Lewin, Kurt. "Frontiers in Group Dynamics: Concept, Method and Reality in Social Science, Social Equilibria and Social Change." *Human Relations* (June 1947): 5–41.

Morse, Michele Block. "Survivor Syndrome." *Success* (September 1987): 58–62.

Naisbitt, John. *Megatrends*. New York: Warner Books, 1982.

Naisbitt, John. *Re-inventing the Corporation.* New York: Warner Books, 1985.

Niebuhr, Reinhold. "The Serenity Prayer." *The A.A. Grapevine* (January 1950): 6–7.

Stewart, Thomas A. "New Ways to Exercise Power." *Fortune* (November 6, 1989): 85–92.

PART THREE

THE LEADER AND THE GROUP

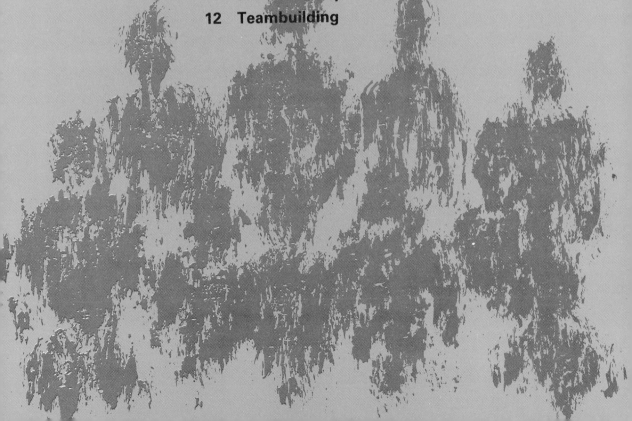

CHAPTER NINE
LEADERSHIP

Since taking the helm of Unocal Corporation from the former chairman who was perceived to be autocratic and outspoken, Richard Stegemeier has gone out of his way to stamp his own less rigid, more communicative personality and leadership style on the Los Angeles-based company. The leadership style change is evident during press interviews when he steps away from his desk to an area of sofas and chairs. He talks about the oil business but also about his wife, two daughters, and home life, mentioning how he wishes that he had time to paint and sculpt again. His predecessor dismissed stock market analysts as "peons," but Stegemeier travels to New York and San Francisco to meet with them regularly. Unocal employees say the corporate culture has changed under his leadership. He is informal and approachable and yet very clearly the boss. They believe that as environmental regulations make the industry more accountable to the public, a more public-conscious executive can be expected to emerge.

Kathleen Murray, *Houston Chronicle*
(February 11, 1990): E1.

OBJECTIVES

After studying this chapter, you should be able to:
1. Define leadership and identify the difference between a leader and a manager.
2. Explain the importance of leadership skills in both our professional and personal lives.
3. Discuss the leadership theories that have developed throughout history.
4. Identify the three traditional leadership styles.
5. Describe the skills required of leaders at different levels of management in an organization.
6. Name the methods of developing leadership skills.
7. Explain how effective followship can help develop leadership ability.
8. Identify and discuss the basic elements of effective leadership.
9. Differentiate between transactional leadership and transformational leadership, and describe the leaders of the next generation.

WHAT IS LEADERSHIP?

Warren Bennis, in *On Becoming a Leader*, says, "One person can live on a desert island without leadership. Two people, if they're totally compatible, could probably get along and even progress. If there are three or more, someone has to take the lead. Otherwise, chaos erupts." He points out three basic reasons why society and organizations need leaders and cannot function without them. First, leaders are responsible for the effectiveness of organizations. The success or failure of all organizations depends on the quality of their leaders. Second, leaders provide a guiding purpose, something greatly needed in today's world. Third, today's concerns about the integrity of our institutions emphasize the need for better leadership in religion, government, Wall Street, and business. The quality of leadership determines the quality of life in society and in organizations.

You do not have to be a manager to be a leader.

Often the terms "leadership" and "management" are used interchangeably. However, a distinct difference can be drawn between the two. A person can be a leader without being in a position of management or supervision. Consider, for example, the following situation:

Norvell is a dedicated engineer with over 23 years of loyal service to the company. He is highly respected by his peers and superiors for the many awards and special recognitions earned in his field of expertise. He is without a doubt a leader in the new and advanced technologies of aeronautical engineering. Norvell is frequently asked to speak to various professional engineering groups to share his knowledge of the newest techniques and methods. Students and colleagues are frequently influenced by his ideas and concepts and use many of his suggestions in their own work.

In the company's hierarchy, illustrated in Figure 9.1, Norvell would be recognized at the worker level rather than the supervisory or managerial level. Although he is neither a supervisor nor a manager, he is a recognized leader, a person with considerable influence over others. From this example several distinctions can be made between leadership and management.

Leadership is the process of influencing the activities of individuals or organized groups so that they follow you and do willingly what you want them to do. To be a leader you must deal directly with people, develop rapport with them, apply appropriate persuasion, inspire them, and thus influence them to cooperate in pursuing your goals. Without followers, leaders do not exist. Sydney Pollack, a well-known film director quoted in an article by Bennis in *Working Woman*, says that people will follow if they honestly believe in the person they are following and if they believe that following is the best action for them at the time.

Anyone can acquire and develop leadership skills, and leaders are seen in many different activities, from politics to play. Not only must leaders be vocationally or professionally competent, but they must also establish and maintain positive relationships with their followers. Such skills will help you understand how people feel, what motivates them, and the best way to influence them. Bennis, in *Working Woman*, says that if you ask successful leaders how they are able to get people on their side

FIGURE 9.1 Levels of management within a typical hierarchy.

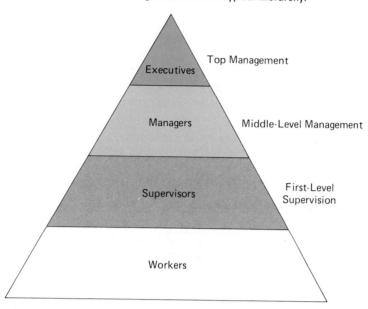

and make their visions of the future happen, they will talk about human values, such as empathy, trust, mutual respect, and courage.

Management, on the other hand, is the use of resources to accomplish a goal. It may be nonbehavioral if it involves using only nonhuman resources. It, too, can occur in many settings, but it is most frequently associated with a formal position within organizations and businesses. A person can be a manager without being an effective leader. Such a person lacks the ability to inspire or influence people.

Influence is a key word in the definition of leadership. Managers can be leaders only if employees allow them to influence their attitudes and behaviors. **Influence** is our ability to change the attitude or behavior of an individual or group. This ability is the result of our power (discussed in Chapter 10), which can come from a number of sources. Leaders vary in their use of the different sources of power. Even formal leaders on the same level vary in their ability to influence others. Although they have the same official title, one may, for example, have greater knowledge or expertise.

Writers such as Bennis contrast leaders and managers, with leaders innovating, challenging the status quo, and "doing things right" and managers administering, accepting the status quo, and "doing right things." John Naisbitt and Patricia Aburdene in *Megatrends 2000* say that any well-trained person can be a manager, but that a leader is ". . . an individual who builds followership by ethical conduct and by creating an environment where the unique potential of one individual can be actualized."

Leadership is a skill that employees at all levels need to develop. To attain goals that we support, whether personal or organizational, we must be effective in directing and coordinating the work of others so that they want to work toward these

An effective leader influences the behavior and attitudes of employees.

same goals. For example, you may support a departmental goal of increasing sales by 15 percent by influencing your department members to sell more, whether or not you are their supervisor. A solid understanding of and a conscientious effort to acquire these abilities can enhance your career even if management is not your career objective. Additionally, leadership skills are needed in situations away from work when we want to influence individuals or groups to work toward certain goals. You may, for example, want a fund drive for the local ballet to succeed and, therefore, try to influence people to contribute by making telephone calls or mailing flyers.

FIGURE 9.2 An effective leader is able to influence groups in setting goals and accomplishing tasks.

Reprinted with special permission of North America Syndicate.

In understanding what leadership is, you should also understand what it is not. It is *not* a form of manipulation. Rather, it involves understanding your followers' motives and providing conditions so that their work-related needs are met while attaining your work goals.

Some of the earliest theories about leadership focused on the origins of this ability to influence others. Is it an innate ability or an acquired skill? Does it have to do with an individual's personality traits or does it rest in certain behaviors? So far, no single theory about leadership has been universally accepted, as you will discover. All, however, have added to our understanding of leadership.

WHAT DOES LEADERSHIP THEORY SAY?

Leadership skill is acquired and developed.

Ideas about leadership have changed significantly over the years. The **great man theory,** the first of these ideas to surface, was based on a belief that certain people are born to become leaders and will emerge in that role when their time comes. According to this theory, because of position, education, or mere exposure to other prominent leaders, these individuals develop a certain style or personality. Today we know that few leaders were born that way. Most people learn to be leaders through study, observation, and hard work. Modern theories of leadership fall into three broad categories—trait theories, behavioral theories, and situational theories. Each of these ideas has evolved with time and research; yet each remains in some way linked to its predecessor.

Trait Theories

Trait theorists sought key physical, personality, and intelligence traits of known leaders.

Wondering whether leaders have certain traits in common, researchers studied the physical, personality, and intelligence traits of prominent leaders in business, military, medical, and other fields. They looked at height, weight, personal appearance, and physique but found no conclusive results. They also looked at intelligence and at personality traits such as confidence, independence, and perception. For example, Edwin Ghiselli, a researcher who spent decades compiling data on the trait theories, concluded that IQ has some bearing on success as a leader. He thought that if leaders were too intelligent or not intelligent enough, followers would not respect them or their decisions.

Lists of desirable traits were formed, giving weights to some believed to be more important than others. These lists were controversial at best and gave little recognition to the effects of the subordinates or the job itself on the success of the leader. The resulting confusion gave way to a belief that perhaps the success of leaders is based on their behavior rather than their traits. Several theories about leadership behavior then developed.

Behavioral Theories

Behavior theorists sought patterns or styles of behavior in leaders.

Theorists in this category believed that successful leaders can be identified by what they *do* rather that what traits they have. In an effort to identify certain behavioral patterns or "styles" of leadership, researchers measured leader behaviors such as amount of control and authority, degree of flexibility, concern for goal or task accomplishment, and concern for subordinates. Several well-known studies developed during this period are still used in identifying the styles of leaders.

In his 1960 book, *The Human Side of Enterprise*, Douglas McGregor suggested that leaders treat followers according to the assumptions they hold about what motivates those followers. The traditional view, known as **Theory X**, contends that people are lazy and unambitious; have an inherent dislike of work, considering it necessary only for survival; will avoid it if they can; and prefer to be directed, wanting to avoid responsibility. Leaders who hold these assumptions believe that workers must be coerced, controlled, directed, and threatened to make them work, resulting in a leadership style that is strict and authoritarian.

The second set of assumptions, **Theory Y**, takes a much more optimistic view of human nature. It contends that the expenditure of physical and mental effort in work is as natural as play or rest and that people will direct themselves toward objectives if their efforts are rewarded. Additionally, most people are eager to work and have the capacity to accept, or even seek, responsibility as well as to use imagination, ingenuity, and creativity in solving problems. McGregor said that under the right circumstances, people derive much satisfaction from work and are capable of doing a good job. The Theory Y leader tends to be less directive and more supportive of subordinates' needs and uses a democratic or participative approach to leading others. McGregor thought that the ideal situation is to integrate the needs of employees with the needs of the organization. He believed that proper leadership helps employees set personal goals that are consistent with organizational goals.

Another of the well-known theories of this period is the two-dimensional **Managerial Grid®** developed by Robert Blake and Jane Mouton. A grid is used to plot the degree to which leaders show concern for people and concern for production (or getting the job done), with 1 being the least concern and 9 the highest concern. Figure 9.3 illustrates the five specific leadership styles identified by Blake and Mouton:

> 1,1 *Impoverished Management.* The leader exerts minimum effort to accomplish the work.

FIGURE 9.3   Blake and Mouton's Managerial Grid® identifies five specific leadership styles with varying degrees of concern for the task and the employee.

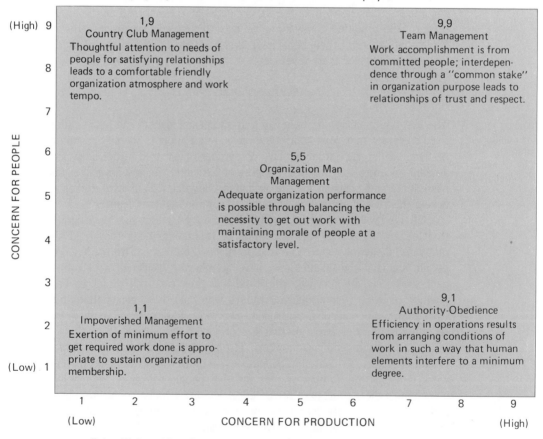

Robert Blake and Jane Srygley Mouton, The Managerial Grid III: The Key to Leadership Excellence *(Houston: Gulf Publishing Company, 1985), 12. Reproduced by permission.*

9,1 *Authority-Obedience.* The leader demonstrates a high degree of concern for accomplishing the task with little or no concern for the development or morale of employees.

1,9 *Country Club Management.* The leader focuses on being supportive and considerate of employees. Task efficiency is not the primary concern.

5,5 *Organization Man Management.* The leader shows concern for both the employees and the task so that adequate performance is possible.

9,9 *Team Management.* The leader shows a high degree of concern for both employees' morale and task accomplishment. The focus is on coordinating and integrating work-related activities and building interdependence, trust, and respect in getting the job done by employees.

> **Blake and Mouton identified the 9,9 leadership style as the best.**

This theory suggests that the the 9,9 Team Management approach is the best leadership style because it results in maximum productivity and positive consequences. It is a goal-directed team approach. However, using a 9,9 leadership style in every situation is difficult. For example, in a conflict with an employee or an emergency job, the supervisor may need to use a 9,1 leadership style. The fluctuations in leader-follower situations, thus, gave rise to the next group of theories, which focus on the situation in which a leader is placed.

Situational or Contingency Theories

> **Fiedler said a leader's success is affected by the leader-follower relationship, the task, and the leader's formal power.**

As theorists continued their research of leadership styles, they realized that in most cases leaders need to adapt their styles to the situation at hand. One of the more important theories from this era was developed by Fred E. Fiedler in his 1967 book, *A Theory of Leadership Effectiveness.* Considerable research evidence supports Fiedler's belief that three important situational factors influence how much power and influence the leader has over the behavior of followers. These factors are the degree of confidence in and loyalty to the leader exhibited by the follower, the degree to which the task is routine or undefined, and the degree of formal or position power held by the leader. Fiedler suggested that some leaders function best in highly directive situations, whereas others are better suited to permissive situations. Therefore, organizations should consider each situation before assigning leaders, because the same person may be effective in one situation but not in another.

An application of contingency theory is **situational leadership,** developed by Paul Hersey. Unlike The Managerial Grid® concept that stresses "one best way" to influence others, situational leadership says that leadership style must be adapted to fit the situation and varies with the "readiness" of subordinates. Readiness, according to this model, does not pertain to age or emotional stability but rather to a worker's desire to achieve, willingness to accept responsibility, ability and experience with the task, and confidence.

> **Situational leadership considers follower readiness, task behavior, and relationship behavior.**

Figure 9.4 illustrates three dimensions of situational leadership. The bar across the bottom of the model describes the first dimension, **follower readiness.** Followers may be unwilling and unable, not able but willing, able but not willing, or willing and able to complete the task. The second dimension, **task behavior,** has to do with the extent to which a leader may or should be directive or "telling." Does the

FIGURE 9.4   Situational leadership suggests varying the leadership style to match the different situations that leaders face.

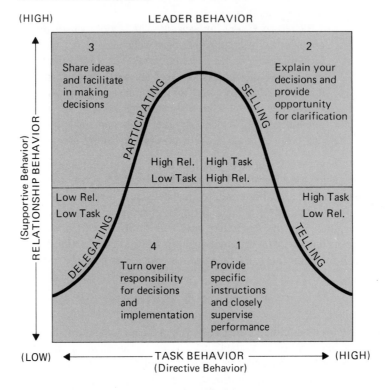

leader closely supervise followers, telling them exactly what to do and when and how to do it, or does the leader allow a great deal of freedom in how followers accomplish the task? The third dimension of this model, **relationship behavior,** describes leader behavior with people, or the extent to which a leader is supportive of followers and engages in two-way communication with them.

Situational leadership suggests that leaders should vary their style as subordinates (either individually or as a group) develop and mature. When a task is new for followers, the leader must engage in many task-related behaviors to instruct them. Once followers begin learning the task, the leader reinforces them with supportive relationship behaviors (such as praise and encouragement) while still offering direction. After followers demonstrate that they are willing and able to perform the task, the leader should stop directing but still offer support and consideration. Finally, when followers are high in readiness in a particular task, the leader reduces both task-related and relationship behaviors *in regard to that task*.

Effective leaders adjust their leadership style to followers' task readiness.

If followers assume additional new tasks, their readiness level may fall because they lack ability or confidence, and the leader must once again move through the cycle. For instance, if your secretary is highly skilled in using an electric typewriter and is suddenly given a new generation computer, that person's maturity level in the performance of typing may decline. You will be required to return to the telling leadership style, providing training on the new equipment with close supervision until the secretary becomes skilled on the computer and regains confidence. This approach allows leaders to handle various situations that occur in the workplace in a flexible manner.

FIGURE 9.5   Your leadership style should allow employees to develop with confidence.

Hersey says that a leader who effectively matches style with followers' readiness motivates the followers and helps them move toward a higher level. The following example shows the four categories of readiness a leader needs to assess:

Kay, a recent high school honor graduate hired in the Human Resources Department, was unfamiliar with the office equipment and departmental procedures. She was insecure about her role in the job at first, but Monica, her supervisor, was careful to super-

vise Kay's activities closely, telling her what was to be done when and showing her how each task was to be accomplished. She often helped her set goals, showed her how to organize the work, established time lines, and directed Kay's daily activities.

After the first few months, Kay began to demonstrate her ability to operate the office equipment efficiently, and she was able to initiate some tasks on her own. Monica realized that Kay was becoming more confident and provided feedback that was supportive and encouraging.

When it was time for Kay's annual review and appraisal, she had fully mastered the functions of the job and received full support from Monica along with a high rating for her performance of the duties. "She will make a fine lead secretary as soon as she becomes confident in her own abilities," remarked Monica to the department chief.

Within two years, Kay had developed into the top secretary in the company, confident of her abilities. She was highly motivated and committed to her job and required little supervision. Many tasks were fully delegated to her with the confidence that she could do the job.

Situational leadership can be applied to individuals or groups.

Referring to the model, you can see the path of leadership chosen by Monica in each of the situations with Kay. Monica assessed Kay's readiness level as low when she was first hired. To use the model, plot a perpendicular line from the readiness assessment scale to intersect with the leadership style bell curve in the model. The point of intersection indicates the appropriate leadership style for that situation, whether dealing with an individual or a group. You can see that Monica accurately applied the "high task and low relationship" leadership style in this situation, providing specific instructions and closely supervising her performance. As Kay moved along the readiness scale, Monica adjusted her style of leadership to be more supportive, facilitating Kay's growth in the job. As Kay reached high readiness, Monica was able to delegate full responsibility to her.

WHAT ARE STYLES OF LEADERSHIP?

A **leadership style** is a particular pattern of behavior exhibited by the leader. Most leaders have a style with which they are most comfortable and that they prefer to use. Studies of leadership behavior patterns have identified three traditional leadership styles. They are the autocratic, democratic, and free rein or laissez-faire styles.

The autocratic leader is highly directive.

The **autocratic leadership** style is also described as authoritarian or directive. Leaders comfortable using this style usually show a high degree of concern for getting the job done. They are task-oriented and tend to provide close supervision, are highly directive, and are not at all comfortable with delegating their authority to others. A close match to this style is the Theory X leader and the 9,1 leader, described above.

An example of this leadership style, described by Kathleen Myler in the *Houston Chronicle*, is the self-professed style of Henry Bloch, chairman of H & R

Block, Inc. After 22 years in the business, he admits that he is a classic example of a leader who cannot let go. "I've got to have my hands in everything. I want to read every report, get in on the advertising, and be involved in every detail. I wish I could delegate, but I can't."

The democratic leader encourages participation by followers.

The **democratic leadership** style is often described as participative and is generally the style preferred by modern management and employees. These leaders tend to share authority with their employees, involving them in decision making and organizational planning. Democratic leaders show concern for their employees, especially in matters that directly affect them in the workplace. A close match to this style is the Theory Y leader and the 9,9 leader.

Typical of the democratic leader is the department manager who says to her work group, "The corporate office has set an overall goal of increasing production company-wide by 10 percent next year. I would like your thoughts about how much we can reasonably try for and how we might do that."

The free rein leader allows followers to lead themselves.

The **free rein** or **laissez-faire leadership** style is sometimes called the integrative style. These leaders allow employees more or less to lead themselves, offering advice or information when asked. Little effort is made by these leaders to either increase productivity or nurture employees. They may integrate the activities by handing out tasks and closing out assignments with a signature at job's end, but for the most part they are uninvolved with directing or controlling tasks or employees. This style can be effective if the task is highly routine or clearly defined and the employees are skilled and responsible in the performance of their duties. This leader is most commonly compared to the 1,1 leader of the Managerial Grid® theory.

Jerry Femina, head of Della Femina, Travisano and Partners, a successful advertising agency, uses a laissez-faire leadership style. According to Myler in a *Houston Chronicle* article, Femina says, "You hire good people, provide them with an arena to be as good as they can be. There is nothing more insane than to hire someone, pay them $200,000 a year, and then tell them what to do." He does little directing and says he makes only three or four major decisions a year.

Although leaders have a preferred style, they should vary their style to fit the various situations that arise in the workplace. Certain factors may influence a leader's preferred style, such as general disposition or personality, skill level or confidence, and perception of others. Failure to adjust to different situations can limit a leader's career.

WHAT ARE THE SKILLS OF A LEADER?

The leader's effectiveness may also depend on demonstrating an adequate level of skills. Fortunately, good leadership skills can be acquired or developed. Substantial research has identified three basic skills most beneficial to competent leaders. If you aspire to be a formal leader in an organization, you will need to pay particular attention to developing your technical, human relations, and conceptual skills, as discussed in Chapter 1. **Technical skills** are those skills required to perform a particular task. For example, a first-line supervisor may need the knowledge and ability to step into the production line and assemble a part or tear down a mechanism to solve a problem or train employees on the process. Obviously, this skill is more important at levels of leadership closest to the actual work being done.

Conceptual skills are often referred to as administrative skills or "big picture" skills. The ability to think abstractly and to analyze problems becomes increasingly important as a person rises in the hierarchy to levels of top management. Planning and coordinating the overall activities of the organization and its personnel requires an ability to view the operations from a total perspective and anticipate as well as solve problems.

Human relations skills cut evenly across all levels of leadership in organizations. This ability to deal effectively with people includes effective communication, listening, empathy, inspiring and motivating, perceptiveness, and fair judgment when dealing with employees. Too often, the lack of this skill is the limiting factor in becoming a good leader.

These skills can be acquired or developed through various means as you progress along your career path. Common ways are exposure and observation, trial-and-error experience, on-the-job training, and some forms of formal education. An important factor in your development as a leader will be your acceptance of the need for lifelong learning or continuing education. John Naisbitt and Patricia Aburdene, authors of *Re-inventing the Corporation*, point out that the constant change created by the new information society requires us to be lifelong learners. We must periodically upgrade our marketable skills and expand our knowledge. We can no longer expect to get an education and be done with it—no education or skill lasts a lifetime now.

FIGURE 9.6   The constant change created by the new information society has made us become lifelong learners. We must periodically upgrade our marketable skills and expand our knowledge, especially if we aspire to leadership.

Rhoda Sidney/STOCK, BOSTON

Coaching and mentoring by a senior person will also help you develop these skills. The way you function as a follower can also help or hurt your development as a leader. A valuable part in becoming a leader is being an effective follower, a role we all play throughout our lives.

HOW SHOULD YOU FOLLOW?

Lester Bittel and John Newstrom, in their book *What Every Supervisor Should Know*, point out that our personalities can determine under what kind of leader we perform best. You can either try to change your personality or seek out leaders who best complement your style:

>If you are an aggressive, cooperative person, you will probably do your best work under a democratic or free-rein leader. Your self-assertiveness will move you constructively in the right direction.

>If you are an aggressive, hostile person, you will probably perform more effectively under an autocratic leader. Such a leader will help channel your feelings toward constructive ends.

>If you are insecure, you will probably depend on your leaders for guidance. Such leaders should ideally be autocratic.

>If you are an individualist who prefers to work alone and if you know your job well, you will probably perform most effectively under free-rein leadership.

Robert N. Waterman, Jr., author of *Adhocracy—The Power to Change*, suggests that followers can have a great influence on how successful a project is. Certainly, such success will reflect well on all members of the project, enhancing your image and potential as a leader. Additionally, working on a successful project is an excellent opportunity to observe effective leadership. Waterman's suggestions include the following:

1. Try to understand the problem from top management's point of view. If you need more information to do so, ask for it.
2. Approach the project as an opportunity to learn and grow. After all, you will have a chance to hear various points of view, see different parts of the organization, interact with different people, and observe new skills.
3. Be committed to the project and show that commitment to your fellow team members.
4. If you believe that the project is doomed to failure, do not sit silently. Discuss this belief with your supervisor.

WHAT ELSE MARKS A LEADER?

Aside from the skills described in the preceding paragraphs, certain other elements have proven critical to effective leadership. These elements include the satisfactory performance of the job functions, common behavioral characteristics, and certain attitudes and behaviors.

Functional Abilities

Early in the research on the basic functions of managing and leading, Luther Gulick, cited in Joseph Massie and John Douglas's management book, coined an acronym that has held through time as a quick reference. The letters in **PODSCORB** each represent a function basic to leadership. They are planning, organizing, directing, staffing, coordinating, reporting, and budgeting. These elements are still needed despite the fact that they were first identified in the 1930s. Leaders and managers must be able to perform these key required tasks before they can motivate others.

Characteristics

A characteristic is a distinguishing feature or attribute that sets you apart from the norm. Successful leaders have consistently been labeled with five characteristics.

Communicator   Leaders are able to express themselves well. Certainly this feature includes good oral and written communication skills but goes far beyond that. It means that they know who they are, what their strengths and weaknesses are, and how to use them to their full advantage. They also know what they want, why they want it, and how to get it. They set goals and achieve those goals by communicating to others what they want to gain support and cooperation. Gloria Steinem, journalist and feminist leader quoted by Warren Bennis in *Working Woman*, says that success as a leader comes from the ability to phrase things in a way that inspires and makes coalition possible.

Decision Maker   Leaders are comfortable making decisions. They are able to gather facts, organize information, and apply good judgment in their choice of action. The willingness to make a choice after considering all possible alternatives is essential. Depending upon the complexity of the decision to be made, decision-making models may be used. These models will be discussed in Chapter 11. Most decisions are made independently, with the decision makers held fully responsible. They take risks that the decision is a good one.

Risk Taker   "Leaders operate on instinct, strike hard and try everything. Leaders are ready to put themselves at great risk," says Warren Bennis in *On Becoming a Leader*. He identifies being a risk taker as tantamount to being a successful leader. Risk takers do not fear failure. They view it as a "temporary setback" or perhaps a "mid-course correction" and feel that failure today does not rule out success tomorrow. Some United States companies are deliberately making risk taking part of their corporate culture. Risk takers tend to be achievement-oriented, goal-directed, and self-confident, as discussed in Chapter 7. They are the great experimenters of life. The willingness to try new ideas often reaps great rewards for the individual and the company.

Motivator   Leaders must be able to influence others to produce good results. In the climate of the 1990s, motivation of employees is leaning away from the autocratic methods of the past toward the new style of inspiring and empowering employees. A good leader recognizes that people are a key resource and should be treated fairly.

John P. Kotter, author of *The Leadership Factor*, says that leadership is "the process of moving people in some direction mostly through noncoercive means."

Motivating employees means getting commitment through the gentle art of persuasion and setting examples of excellence. Former CBS executive Barbara Corday, discussed by Bennis in *Working Woman*, says that empathy helps give leaders power. That power comes from the company's success and the leader's staff working well. In the same article, Bennis points out that followers' trust of the leader is essential to motivation. Leaders can develop trust by being steadfast in their goals, by "walking their talk" (living what they espouse), by being reliable and supportive, and by honoring their commitments and promises.

An example of one-minute motivating, described by Lorraine Calvacca in *Working Woman*, is the work habit of Marilynn Davis, vice president of American Express. Davis inquires about employee's families, acknowledges weddings and graduations, and holds "cake and bull" sessions for employees' birthdays. Such actions inspire followers' loyalty and trust, thus increasing motivation.

Delegator An effective leader delegates tasks to employees to develop their skills and build a stronger team. **Delegation** means assigning tasks to subordinates and following up to ensure that they are completed properly and on time. Leaders often find delegating the single most difficult thing to do. A mistake often made when delegating is giving the responsibility without the authority to get the job done. The steps to successful delegation are to select the person best qualified to perform the task, give good instructions and ask for feedback to assure understanding of the task directions, and then leave the person alone to complete the assignment. If you are the leader, follow up to assure completion but do not interfere with that individual's methods of getting the job done.

An example of effective delegation, described by Laurel Touby in *Working Woman*, is the style used by Sheri Poe, owner of a successful athletic footwear company. Because of the rapid growth of the company, she was forced to start delegating. She lets employees manage their jobs as they think best and keeps tabs on operations through weekly checkup meetings with the department heads. She provides guidance, freedom, and strategic input, and then lets them do the job.

In an amusing analysis of the leadership style of Attila the Hun, author Wess Roberts describes Attila's rules on delegating. Roberts stresses that "delegating demonstrates trust in your subordinates and helps build their skills and improves their loyalty." Specific rules that Attila applied include:

1. Never delegate responsibilities that require your direct attention.
2. Delegate to those people most able to fulfill the assignment, and grant them authority as well as responsibility.
3. Once you delegate a task, never interfere.
4. Do not give your Huns precise direction on how to accomplish their delegated assignments.

Bennis, in *On Becoming a Leader*, adds that leaders seem to share some, if not all, of the following characteristics:

1. *A guiding vision.* Leaders have a clear idea of what they want to do and the strength to persist.

2. *Passion.* Leaders love what they do and love doing it. Leaders who communicate passion give hope and inspiration to others.
3. *Integrity.* The integrity of leaders has three components: self-knowledge, candor, and maturity. Leaders never lie to themselves, know their flaws and assets and deal with them, are honest in thought and action, and experience and grow through following.
4. *Trust.* Trust must be acquired. It is the product of a leader's ability with coworkers and followers.
5. *Curiosity and daring.* Leaders wonder about things, are willing to experiment, and learn from adversity.

Attitudes and Behaviors

Attitudes and behaviors most commonly displayed by successful leaders are listed in Figure 9.7. Sometimes described as states of mind or feelings, attitudes play an important role in the workplace. Followers are affected by the example you set and will react to your enthusiasm and dedication. A showing of empathy for them is important and will gain you their respect. Each of these attitudes has a direct bearing on your success as a leader.

FIGURE 9.7 Typical attitudes and behaviors of effective leaders.

Positive-thinking

Dedicated with a sense of mission

Open-minded

Enthusiastic

Spontaneous

Courageous

Empathetic

Flexible

Responsible

Ethical with high character

Self-denying; willing to forgo self-indulgences, such as showing anger

Competent (both in leadership and technical skills)

Wise

Energetic

Considerate

Fair

WHAT IS THE FUTURE OF LEADERSHIP?

According to Bernard M. Bass, a leadership researcher, leadership can be categorized in two ways—transactional and transformational. **Transactional leadership** encompasses the theories presented in this chapter and requires that leaders determine what followers need to achieve their own and organizational goals, classify those needs, and help followers gain confidence that they can reach their objectives. **Transformational leadership**, on the other hand, motivates followers to do more than they originally expected to do by raising the perceived value of the task, by getting them to transcend self-interest for the sake of the group goal, and by raising their need level to self-actualization.

Richard Boyd, another leadership theorist, suggests that today's business environment requires a variation of transformational leadership. The new leadership skills include the following:

1. *Anticipatory skills*—the ability to foresee a constantly changing environment.
2. *Visioning skills*—the ability to induce people to take action that agrees with the leader's purposes or those of the organization.
3. *Value-congruence skills*—the ability to understand followers' economic, safety, psychological, spiritual, sexual, aesthetic, and physical needs in order to motivate them on the basis of shared motives, values, and goals.
4. *Empowerment skills*—the ability to share power.
5. *Self-understanding*—the ability to understand one's own needs and goals as well as those of followers.

Bennis suggests that we are our own raw leadership material. We must "invent" ourselves by discovering our own native energies and desires and then find our own way to act on them. Numerous experts predict that the days of the "big bad boss" are gone. Bennis says that the next generation of leaders will be more intellectually aware, will be comfortable with and excited by ideas and information, and will anticipate and accept change, seeing it as an opportunity. These new leaders will share the following nine characteristics:

1. They will have a broad education, maintained through lifelong learning.
2. They will have boundless enthusiasm.
3. They will believe in people and teamwork.
4. They will be willing to take risks.
5. They will be devoted to long-term growth rather than short-term profit.
6. They will be committed to excellence.
7. They will be ready for change.
8. They will demonstrate virtue in their integrity, ethics, and respect for self and others.
9. They will be wise, giving followers a chance to look good.

SUMMARY

Leaders, people who influence the behavior of others, may be found at all levels of the organizational hierarchy and in personal life. A person can be a leader and not be a manager and vice versa. Leadership has long been a subject of concern with considerable research to define its origin and identify those traits or behaviors in individuals that single them out to be leaders. From the great man theory, researchers moved into trait and behavioral theories and identified various means of recognizing and even developing leadership abilities. Some of the best-known theories are Theory X and Y, the Managerial Grid®, and situational leadership.

Several distinctive styles of leadership have also been identified. They are autocratic, democratic, and free rein. Most leaders have a preferred style, but change their approach to fit the needs of the situation. An effective leader in an organization must be able to apply technical, conceptual, and human relations skills. These skills can be acquired or developed through exposure and observation, trial-and-error experience, on-the-job training, formal education/continuing education, coaching and mentoring, and effective following. Successful leaders will also display certain functional abilities, characteristics, and attitudes and behaviors known to be critical to effective leadership. Future leaders will be transformational, motivating their followers to transcend self-interest for the sake of the group goal by raising their need levels to self-actualization. Leadership experts predict that the next generation of leaders will possess characteristics that allow this transformation to happen.

KEY TERMS

leadership
management
influence
great man theory
Theory X and Y
Managerial Grid®
situational leadership
follower readiness
task behavior
relationship behavior
leadership style
autocratic leadership
democratic leadership
free-rein leadership

laissez-faire leadership
technical skills
conceptual skills
human relations skills
PODSCORB
delegation
transactional leadership
transformational leadership

REVIEW QUESTIONS

1. Define leadership. What is the difference between a leader and a manager?
2. What is the importance of leadership skills to us at work at any level? In our personal lives?
3. Discuss the various leadership theories that have developed throughout history.
4. Name and define the three traditional leadership styles.
5. What are the three categories of skills required of leaders? How do they vary with the leader's level?
6. What are the methods of developing leadership skills? Why is lifelong learning now necessary?
7. How can being an effective follower help you develop leadership skills? What are some recommendations for being an effective follower?
8. Identify the basic elements of effective leadership. Name the functions, characteristics, and attitudes and behaviors of effective leaders.
9. How do transactional and transformational leadership differ? Which is expected to be more important in the future? What elements are part of it?

DISCUSSION QUESTIONS

1. Think of a situation in which you have been involved and identify the leader's style. Was that style appropriate for the situation?
2. Describe the leadership style from a situational perspective that should be applied to you in your present job situation or in an organization to which you belong. Is that style being used? Why or why not?
3. Identify the leadership characteristics that you believe are most important for you to develop. Why do you place importance on those characteristics? What steps are you taking to develop them?
4. Describe situations that call for each of the three traditional leadership styles. Discuss why that particular leadership style best fits that situation.
5. With what traditional leadership style are you most comfortable? Why is it most effective for you?
6. According to Hersey what situational leadership style would be most appropriate in supervising the following persons and why?
   (a) Martin is a research chemist in a large chemical company. He understands his goals, works hard and diligently, and is very interested in his work.

(b) This is Lew's first month on the job. He is a new patent attorney with the same company. He joins five others who have been with the company from 3 to 15 years.

(c) Nicky is one of the patent attorneys with the same company. She has been there three years, knows patent work backward and forward but still feels a little intimidated by the "old timers."

(d) Francine, another research chemist, has been with the company six months, coming right out of graduate school. She is somewhat unsure of her role and is still learning the ropes.

7. Cite examples from your experience of leaders you perceive to be transactional and transformational. What skills do they demonstrate?

8. Describe follower roles that you now have. How are your behaviors and attitudes in those roles helping you develop leadership skills?

CASE STUDY 9.1

DO WE WANT TO FOLLOW THE LEADER?

Andy ruled his production crew with an iron fist. He had come up through the rank and file and had many years of experience to his credit. His success was based on technical expertise and experience. He had no formal education but knew more about the manufacturing processes involved than any young college graduate in the company. Although the people in the work unit respected his technical knowledge and abilities, they felt that he was a bit heavy-handed in his method of supervising the day-to-day operations.

"He cracks the whip around here and closely supervises every move you make," said Ron, the lead technician. "He wants to be involved with every detail and won't let go of any responsibility. You would think that he doesn't trust us or that maybe he just doubts we would get the job done."

1. What leadership style is Andy using in this situation?

2. What assumptions has he made about his employees, and what typical behaviors of the leadership style is he demonstrating?

3. How do you think his workers feel about his leadership style? How would you feel?

CASE STUDY 9.2

WHAT CAUSED THE BOAT TO SINK?

The Administrative Office had a staff of seven seasoned employees running daily operations. As a service organization, they helped other company employees with questions about policies and procedures and processed all official paperwork on promotions, reassignments, health and life insurance, and many other administrative matters. Wilma, their supervisor for nine years, respected the knowledge and maturity of her employees and normally left them alone to do the job as they saw fit.

When Wilma retired and moved away, Doris was hired from another company to replace her. On her first day as the new supervisor, Doris changed many of the internal office procedures to her way of doing business. She required that all incoming calls from company employees be directed to her. She became the single point of information for the office. She requested a daily prioritized list of activities from each of the staff members for approval by her. She then determined whether the priorities were in order or correct and revised them. Within six months, complaints became common, morale declined, and finally five of the original seven staff members resigned. Doris replaced those employees with members from her previous company's staff, and the operation began to run smoothly again.

1. Using situational leadership, what would you assess the readiness level of the seven office staff members to be?
2. What leadership style had Wilma applied?
3. What leadership style did Doris apply in her new position as head of the Administrative Office?
4. Was Doris's leadership style the correct one to apply in this situation? If not, why not?
5. What might Doris have done to improve human relations in this example?

BIBLIOGRAPHY

Bakker, Jim. "The End of the Big Bad Boss." *Working Woman* (March 1990): 79.

Bass, Bernard M. "Leadership: Good, Better, Best." *Organizational Dynamics* 13, no. 3, (Winter 1985): 25–40.

Bennis, Warren. "How to Be the Leader They'll Follow." *Working Woman* (March 1990): 75–78.

Bennis, Warren. *On Becoming a Leader*. Reading, MA: Addison-Wesley Publishing Company, 1989.

Bittel, Lester R., and John W. Newstrom. *What Every Supervisor Should Know*. New York: McGraw-Hill, Inc., 1990.

Blake, Robert, and Jane Srygley Mouton. *The Managerial Grid III: The Key to Leadership Excellence*. Houston, TX: Gulf Publishing Company, 1985.

Boyd, Richard E. "Corporate Leadership Skills: A New Synthesis." *Organizational Dynamics* 16, no. 1 (1987): 34–43.

Calvacca, Lorraine. "The One-Minute Motivator." *Working Woman* (March 1990): 76.

Fiedler, Fred E. *A Theory of Leadership Effectiveness*. New York: McGraw-Hill, 1967.

Ghiselli, Edwin E. "Managerial Talent." *American Psychologist* 18 (October 1963): 74–77.

Hersey, Paul. *The Situational Leader:* New York: Warner Books, 1985, 63.

Hersey, Paul, and Kenneth H. Blanchard. *Management of Organizational Behavior: Utilizing Human Resources*. Englewood Cliffs, NJ: Prentice-Hall, 1982.

Kotter, John P. *The Leadership Factor*. New York: The Free Press, 1966.

Massie, Joseph L., and John Douglas. *Managing: A Contemporary Introduction*. Englewood Cliffs, NJ: Prentice-Hall, 1985, 38.

McGregor, Douglas. *The Human Side of Enterprise*. New York: McGraw-Hill, 1960.

Murray, Kathleen. "Chairman Stamps Unocal with His Open Style." *Houston Chronicle* (February 11, 1990): E1.

Myler, Kathleen. "Leadership Styles Vary." *Houston Chronicle* (September 25, 1989): H20.

Naisbitt, John, and Patricia Aburdene. *Megatrends 2000—Ten New Directions for the 1990s*. New York: William Morrow and Company, Inc., 1990.

Naisbitt, John, and Patricia Aburdene. *Re-inventing the Corporation*. New York: Warner Books, Inc., 1985.

Roberts, Wess. *Leadership Secrets of Attila the Hun*. New York: Warner Books, 1987.

Stoner, James A. F., and R. Edward Freeman. *Management*. Englewood Cliffs, NJ: Prentice-Hall, 1989.

Touby, Laurel. "The Determined Delegator." *Working Woman* (March 1990): 77.

Waterman, Robert W., Jr. *Adhocracy—The Power to Change*. Knoxville, TN: Whittle Direct Books, 1990.

CHAPTER TEN
POWER

Benjamin Franklin (1706–1790) arrived in Philadelphia at the age of 17, alone and penniless and with less than two years of formal education. By the age of 42, he was able to retire from his successful printing business and live comfortably for the next 20 years. Franklin's sense of humor, gift for compromise, belief in hard work, willingness to take a stand for his personal beliefs, perseverance, optimism, and honesty helped him acquire the power necessary to obtain public printing contracts and establish partnerships with other printers in the colonies. These accomplishments were the cornerstone of his successful business. Building on these characteristics, Franklin became one of the most powerful and influential people in Colonial America. Franklin used his power to the benefit of the citizens of Philadelphia and the United States. Among his contributions are establishing a circulating library, fire department, hospital, police department, and college. His ability to influence others led him to serve his country by helping draft the Declaration of Independence and influencing the outcome of the American Revolution while acting as the first American Minister to France.

*Academic American On-Line
Encyclopedia*, 1988.

Described by *Newsweek* (September 19, 1988) as the man who revolutionized Wall Street, Michael Milken once had extraordinary power in the business world. He allegedly manipulated companies, people, and money markets for enormous personal gain. Milken established a following of investors able to raise billions of dollars for investment purposes. He was viewed as intensely loyal to this network of customers and they were equally loyal to him. Even when the Securities and Exchange Commission alleged that he deliberately defrauded these clients and traded insider information for millions of dollars in personal wealth, many clients openly denied his wrongful intent. This once powerful person was ultimately indicted for securities fraud and forced to leave the firm of Drexel Burnham Lambert.

OBJECTIVES

After studying this chapter, you should be able to:
1. Define power and explain why developing power is necessary.
2. Identify and discuss the basic power sources available to you.
3. Name and discuss the three basic power personalities.

4. Identify and discuss techniques used in the planning and implementation of power positioning.
5. Discuss the importance of applying power politics.
6. Explain the ways that power symbols can be used for power positioning.
7. Discuss the pitfalls of developing power.

WHAT IS POWER?

Power is our ability to influence others to do what we want them to do even if we are not a formal leader. It involves changing the attitudes or behaviors of individuals or groups. Power is exercised by nonmanagement as well as management employees and by people in their personal lives.

Acquiring power and learning to use it are essential to accomplish goals.

Power gives us the clout to accomplish tasks and can help us reach our goals. Many experts point out that people cannot succeed in organizations today without acquiring some power and learning how to use it. Also, an understanding of power can help you recognize when those around you are attempting to influence you through the exercise of power. The appropriate use of power can be a strong factor in how effective your human relations skills are.

A fine distinction exists between influence and power. Influence is the application of power through actions we take or examples we set that cause others to change their attitudes or behaviors. People must possess power from some source before they can influence the behavior of others.

Too often the word "power" brings to mind negative images. Terms such as manipulation, control, domination, exploitation, corruption, and coercion are frequently associated with power. Because of the tarnished image of power, many individuals tend to shy away from learning about and practicing positive power.

Power, sometimes seen as negative, is desirable when used appropriately.

Power can be a healthy, desirable attribute when channeled appropriately. It is most effective when its use is not obvious. Positive uses of power include influence, leadership, control, authority, and direction. These strong behaviors are very necessary in both your personal and professional life. John Phillip Kotter, author of *Power and Influence: Beyond Formal Authority*, states that "professional excellence requires the knack of knowing how to make power dynamics work for us, instead of against us."

Acquiring some power and learning how to use it, then, is essential to your achievement of personal and organizational goals. An understanding of the sources of power available to you and techniques for drawing upon them will assist you in strengthening your power base.

Developing or acquiring power sources is a necessary step in gaining power.

WHAT ARE THE SOURCES OF POWER?

John French and Bertram Raven, two researchers on power, identified five basic power sources: reward, coercive, legitimate, expert, and referent. The first three sources are derived from our position within the organization; the last two are generated from our personal characteristics. Other theorists add derivative and passive power.

Reward Power

Reward power is the ability to give something of material or personal value to others. The rewards may be in the form of promotions, bonuses, supplies and equipment, highly desirable job assignments, or reserved parking places. It may also take the form of valued information, praise for a job well done, or a desired position title. At home reward power may come in the form of an unexpected gift, an allowance, a night to eat out, or a trip to the movies.

Reward power is considered the most important source of power by French and Raven because it places the reward seeker almost totally at the mercy of the reward giver. Only by submitting to the desired behavior can the seeker hope to obtain the reward from the giver. The strength of this power source varies with the amount of rewards controlled by the giver. This power source can be held by a full range of individuals, from the corporate chief executive to the unit secretary who controls the distribution of supplies.

Coercive Power

Coercive power is based on fear and punishment. Demotions, dismissals, reprimands, assignment of unpleasant tasks, and public embarrassment are examples of coercive power. This form of power can be directed toward superiors, coworkers, or subordinates. At home coercive power comes in the form of spanking, scolding, grounding, or loss of privileges.

Coercive power can be used in a positive manner, such as in an emergency, to let others know that you mean business. When an employee's performance is slipping, being firm and pointing out the consequences of continued nonperformance can have a positive effect.

However, open use of coercive power is generally considered unacceptable in the work environment, and the user may risk retaliation, sabotage, or malicious obedience. Low morale may result, because coercive power is a negative motivator. This counterproductive use of power also places the user at great risk of being removed from any position of power. Because of its potential for harm, coercive power should be used with great caution.

Legitimate Power

Legitimate power is derived from formal rank or position within an organizational hierarchy. A company president holds greater legitimate power than a regional vice president, and a general department manager will hold more legitimate power than a first-line supervisor or a technician on the assembly line. This power source is dependent on the formal, established chain of command within the organization and the perceived authority of the individual in that position of power. Examples away from work include a team captain or a committee chairperson. These individuals are perceived to have an "appointed" power.

However, just because you are ranked higher in an organization does not mean that you hold total power over those under you. An example is the security guard who has the legitimate power to request the president of the company to present identification to enter a secured facility.

Expert Power

Expert power develops when an individual possesses specialized skills, knowledge, or expertise. This power source is limited in that it is only useful when the knowledge is of value to the seeker. This power source is not dependent on appointed rank or position. It can be held by individuals ranging from the chief executive officer to the computer technician to the janitor. For instance, when the building heat is malfunctioning, employees will turn to the janitor rather than the company president, who may have no knowledge of machinery or equipment.

Expert power can also be found off the job. You may, for example, defer to a neighbor with extensive mechanical experience when dealing with an automobile that will not start or a dishwasher that does not work.

Referent Power

Referent power is power based on respect or admiration for the individual. This respect or admiration may result from personal charisma and "likable" personal traits. Sports heroes, political leaders, and dynamic religious or business leaders can influence the behavior of others who have a desire to emulate their heroes' perceived success.

Derivative and Passive Power

Derivative power comes from close association with a powerful person. We are all familiar with signs and symbols of people using this power technique. Name dropping and use of the "good old boy" system are examples of using derivative power to gain advantages.

Passive power, the last of the power sources, stems from a display of helplessness. A child often uses this power source effectively on a parent to gain attention or solicit help with some undesirable task. Unfortunately, we sometimes see this same technique carried into adulthood and used in the workplace. For example, an employee will act incapable in order to gain help in accomplishing a task or to escape it altogether. A simple statement that says, "I cannot possibly manage this all by myself and, besides, you are so much better at this sort of thing than I am," will often subtly but powerfully gain the desired results.

Derivative and passive power sources are not dependable in the long haul. They tend to damage the image and credibility of the user. Recognizing that these power sources exist and avoiding their use will aid you in developing more desirable power sources. Being knowledgeable will additionally help you avoid being the pawn that gets duped in the game of passive power.

CAN YOU COMBINE SOURCES OF POWER?

The power sources are highly linked. They tend to occur in combinations, as the following example indicates:

> **Thomas, the head of the accounting department, glared down at the junior accountant sitting in the chair beside him. He was angry at his antics and felt that he had to show him he could not get away with foolishness that reflected badly on the company. Thomas's brow was furrowed, reflecting a scowl. When he spoke, it was in low-toned, slow phrases that revealed his anger. He was the department chief with full authority to administer the punishment due for the embarrassment caused the company and to delay any promotion until the junior accountant's behavior matured.**

FIGURE 10.1   What are the power sources for these individuals?

Albert Einstein   *Indira Gandhi*   *Martin Luther King, Jr.*

Jerry Lewis   *Your mother*

The Bettman Archive

Thomas has legitimate power given to him through his position in the organization. Additionally, he is exercising coercive power through his intimidating body language and threats of consequences for the behavior of the junior accountant.

The type of behavior response in different situations will depend on what the receiver perceives the power source of the sender to be. For example, individuals with a high degree of expert power are usually admired and respected and, therefore, have a high degree of referent power. Similarly, individuals with a high degree of legitimate power may wield strong reward and coercive power over others.

Many combinations can be developed. A particularly powerful combination to acquire is expert, legitimate, and reward power sources. Obviously, the more power sources you acquire, the stronger your influence will be in the work environment and on a personal level.

Our ability to use these power sources individually or in combination relies heavily on the perception of those involved. They must believe that our power source is genuine. Kotter, as summarized by James Stoner and R. Edward Freeman in *Management*, suggests that, in order to develop the perception in others that you are truly powerful, you must use your power sources wisely and appropriately. Recognize what sources you do not have and avoid their use. Using undeveloped sources or abusing your power sources weakens your credibility and strips you of what power you do have. Understand the risks and benefits of using each of your power sources and develop your skills accordingly.

WHAT IS YOUR POWER PERSONALITY?

Some theorists believe that power is based on personal characteristics.

Some behavioral theorists believe that a person's use of power is based more on personal characteristics, charisma, and acquired personality traits than on other factors. These traits vary in intensity in different people, resulting in three basic power personalities: the power-shy, the power-positive, and the power-compulsive.

Power-shy individuals tend to avoid being placed in positions that require overt use of power. They quickly sidestep or totally shun responsibility and leadership, feeling extremely uncomfortable with decision making and influencing or controlling the behavior of others. Power-shy persons make excellent followers and will usually excel in positions that require them to operate independently and rely on individual skills and abilities.

On the other hand, **power-positive** persons genuinely enjoy accepting responsibility and thrive on the use of power. Highly power-motivated, these individuals enjoy controlling situations and directing and influencing the behavior of others. They express strong views and opinions and are usually risk takers and adventurers. Power-positive individuals can be valuable resources when placed in leadership roles requiring the described qualities. Only when the need or desire for power becomes compulsive and is a driving force directing all actions toward selfish goals does it take on negative overtones.

Power-compulsive persons have a lust for power and are seldom satisfied with the amount of power they have. These individuals constantly seek increased levels of control and influence over others and have a strong need to display power plays for personal gain in all situations. This use of power is destructive and intimidating, seldom benefiting the organization or the individual.

Fortunately, the need and desire for power does vary greatly in individuals. The power-shy and power-positive personalities are both needed in the work environment to create balance. We acquire power in varying amounts, from different sources, and at different times in life. How we choose to use it reflects our positive or negative motives.

The short self-inventory in Figure 10.2 will rate your power personality. Does the need for power control you, or do you use the power that you have constructively for growth and advancement? As in any self-test, you must be honest in your responses to get a true reflection of yourself. You may also want to have your spouse, close friend, or coworker answer the questions about you. Seeing yourself as others see you is an excellent method of *gaining insight.*

FIGURE 10.2 Power personality test.

INSTRUCTIONS: Answer each question with **2** (often true), **1** (sometimes true), or **0** (seldom or never true). The scoring interpretation appears below.

1. "Get the last word in" is my motto.
2. It is important to me to "wear the pants" in my family.
3. It disturbs me when things are disorganized.
4. It angers me when somebody tries to take advantage of me.
5. When I entertain, it is important that plans go smoothly.
6. For my leisure time, I usually plan things/activities well in advance
7. People who don't behave the way I expect really irritate me.
8. Nothing angers me more than people trying to dominate me.
9. In my position, I feel it is demeaning to do subordinate tasks.
10. I always conceal my true feelings.
11. I do not tolerate my child publicly displaying poor manners or bad behavior.
12. In a public or business meeting, I make certain my viewpoint is known.
13. I cannot tolerate others humiliating me.

14. I would turn down a tempting job offer with another firm if the position had less prestige and power than my current one.
15. I agree with Michael Korda's quote about the workplace, "Without power we're merely cogs in a meaningless machine."
16. I feel good when I can make others perform menial tasks for me.
17. To show others "who's the boss," I will sometimes humiliate them undeservingly.
18. When people get "out of line" at work, it really irritates me.
19. I never allow other people to push me around.
20. Inconveniencing others, forcing them to adhere to my schedule, or keeping others waiting provides me with a certain degree of enjoyment.
21. It angers or depresses me when a rival at work upstages me.
22. I will feel like a failure if I do not achieve my targeted key executive position in my company.

SCORING INTERPRETATION:

Control Scale   Total the scores for your answers to questions 3, 5, 6, 7, 10, 11, and 18. Your total score reflects the degree to which you seek or need control and order in situations.

	Total Score of:	
	0–3	Little to no need
	4–6	Moderate need
	7 or more	High, compulsive need

FIGURE 10.2   (*Continued*)

A high score in the control scale means you seek consistency and prefer predictability. You need or desire the security of certainty. You seldom "go with the flow" or allow yourself the freedom of spontaneity. You prefer rigid control. Learn to be more flexible. Decrease your need for control by enjoying your emotions. Allow your feelings to surface.

Power Scale   Total the scores for your answers to questions 1, 2, 4, 8, 9, 12, 13, 14, 15, 16, 17, 19, 20, 21 and 22. You total score indicates the degree to which you have a need for or seek power.

	Total Score of:	
	0–6	Little to no need
	7–14	Moderate need
	15 or more	High, compulsive need

A high score on the power scale means your need for power may be excessive and may require some self-evaluation of your motives. In your interpersonal actions with others, examine your behavior to better understand the origins of your power compulsion. What did you do, and what were the effects of your actions? Why did you feel the need for power in that situation? Did your dominance decrease your overall effectiveness? Compulsive power needs can be destructive to the development or use of good human relations skills. Plan and implement change in your behavior to lessen a strong compulsive drive for power if necessary.

Adapted from Robert Meier, "Power—Do You Lust for It?" Success *(May 1984): 35–36, 40.*

HOW DO YOU DEVELOP POWER?

Building power is a complex process that requires planning and careful execution.

Building power is a complex process and seldom comes without planning and careful execution. Some individuals may operate from a totally subconscious level in their quest for power, whereas others consciously and methodically plan their steps to the top. Building and maintaining a strong power base usually requires a thorough understanding of power positioning, power politics, and power symbols.

Power Positioning

Power positioning is the conscientious use of techniques designed to position yourself for maximum personal growth or gain. Achieving success is sometimes attributed to luck or being at the right place at the right time. (How often have you heard the cliche, "It's not *what* you know, but *whom* you know"?) However, you can apply specific techniques of power positioning that do not rely on luck or influential others.

Some 20 years of research by behavioral scientists have resulted in the identification of major techniques that strongly influence the degree of personal power that we attain. These techniques should be cultivated in your quest for power, as they will greatly enhance your chances for success. They are:

1. Be goal-oriented. Know what power sources you have and how you plan to strengthen them and add others.
2. Learn to take risks. Show that you are willing to take action and make decisions. (Risk taking was discussed in Chapters 2 and 9.)
3. Look for ways to become visible. Volunteer for special projects and other activities that expose your strengths and capabilities.
4. Acquire positions of authority and knowledge. Controlling resources and information strengthens power.
5. Develop communication skills, including the ability to negotiate. They are crucial in learning to persuade and influence others.
6. Learn to make decisions. Think through issues on which you wish to take a stand. Taking a stand just for the sake of winning and being right can backfire in the long run.
7. Develop commitment. Show through your determination and will power that you are committed to your cause. Display that inner drive that shows you are dedicated to excellence.
8. Network. Learn to call on individuals inside and outside your organization who can help you accomplish your goals. They can be superiors, subordinates, or colleagues. Discover how to ask for and return favors that will help you build your coalition.
9. Learn how to be a team player. Help others reach their goals and objectives. Do not be afraid to delegate authority to others. Display a cooperative attitude.
10. Create a following. Be sensitive to the feelings of others and be careful not to abuse your power. Establishing a reputation for being credible, reliable, and ethical will draw others to your side.
11. Select a mentor. Choose a successful person with whom you can develop rapport to give you advice and guidance. Having a mentor with political savvy is advisable, particularly for those women who lack experience in organizational politics.
12. Develop confidence. Sharpen public speaking and other communication skills that will enhance your positive self-image. Portray a professional impression through appropriate dress. (Self-confidence was discussed in Chapter 2.)
13. Develop advanced skills. Become an authority by developing and maintaining advanced skills in some area that is perceived as important to others.
14. Understand your organization. Be knowledgeable in the philosophy, politics, communication channels, and structures of your organization. Discover where the power lies and how it is used.
15. Anticipate resistance. Realize that others may resent your use of power or view you as a threat to their own goals. Develop an information feedback system that lets you know how others perceive you. Then deal positively with the situation.

Seldom are individuals fully proficient in all these techniques. Self-assessment is an important first step in identifying which technique needs attention and which already is fully developed in you. Effective power positioning requires skillful planning and careful implementation.

Power Politics

In his book *Unlimited Power,* Anthony Robbins says, "The meeting of preparation with opportunity generates the offspring we call luck." Success is not an accident, and **power politics** allows us to develop opportunities for success.

FIGURE 10.3   Some individuals would prefer to avoid politics altogether.

"It was a power struggle but I won!"
Reprinted with permission of Joseph Farris.

Not all decisions for promotion and rewards are made on the bases of merit, fair play, rationality, or even ethics. The only defense you may have against unfair practices is becoming politically astute. This means developing an awareness of power politics, understanding how it works, and applying those techniques with which you are most comfortable.

A first step in this process is to determine how politically inclined you are. Figure 10.4 is a quick self-test that will give you some insight into your political inclination. It is an abbreviated version of the Organizational Politics Scale developed by Andrew J. DuBrin in *Winning with Office Politics.*

DuBrin's complete test consists of 100 comprehensive questions that provide an in-depth index of an individual's political tendencies. He places the scores in five categories that illustrate a person's identity as a politician. The shortened test in

FIGURE 10.4   How political are you?

Directions: Answer each question "mostly agree" or "mostly disagree," even if it is difficult for you to decide which alternative best describes your opinion.

	Mostly Agree	*Mostly Disagree*
1. Only a fool would correct a boss's mistakes.	____	____
2. If you have certain confidential information, release it to your advantage.	____	____
3. I would be careful not to hire a subordinate with more formal education than myself.	____	____
4. If you do somebody a favor, remember to cash in on it.	____	____
5. Given the opportunity, I would cultivate friendships with power people.	____	____
6. I like the idea of saying nice things about a rival in order to get that person transferred from my department.	____	____
7. Why not take credit for someone else's work? They would do the same to you.	____	____
8. Given the chance, I would offer to help my boss build some shelves for his or her den.	____	____
9. I laugh heartily at my boss's jokes, even when they are not funny.	____	____
10. I would be sure to attend a company picnic even if I had the chance to do something I enjoyed more that day.	____	____
11. If I knew an executive in my company was stealing money, I would use that against him or her in asking for favors.	____	____
12. I would first find out my boss's political preferences before discussing politics with him or her.	____	____
13. I think using memos to zap somebody for his or her mistakes is a good idea (especially when you want to show that person up).	____	____
14. If I wanted something done by a coworker, I would be willing to say "If you don't get this done, our boss might be very unhappy."	____	____
15. I would invite my boss to a party at my house, even if I didn't like him or her.	____	____
16. When I'm in a position to, I would have lunch with the "right people" at least twice a week.	____	____
17. Richard M. Nixon's bugging the Democratic Headquarters would have been a clever idea if he hadn't been caught.	____	____
18. Power for its own sake is one of life's most precious commodities.	____	____
19. Having a high school named after you would be an incredible thrill.	____	____
20. Reading about job politics is as much fun as reading an adventure story.	____	____

Interpretation of Scores. Each statement you check "mostly agree" is worth one point toward your political orientation score. If you score 16 or over, it suggests that you have a strong inclination toward playing politics. A high score of this nature would also suggest that you have strong needs for power. Scores of 5 or less would suggest that you are not inclined toward political maneuvering and that you are not strongly power-driven.

Andrew J. DuBrin, Human Relations: A Job-Oriented Approach, 4th ed. (Englewood Cliffs, NJ: Prentice-Hall, 1988), 273–274.

Figure 10.4 may help you determine where you would fall in the category scale. Dubrin's five categories are:

1. *Machiavellian.* A power-hungry, power-grabbing individual. Often ruthless, devious, and power-crazed. Will try to succeed at any cost to others.
2. *Company Politician.* A shrewd maneuverer and politico. Most successful individuals fall into this category. Company politicians desire power, but it is not an all-consuming preoccupation. Will do whatever is necessary to address their cause except deliberately defame or injure others.
3. *Survivalist.* Practices enough power politics to take advantage of good opportunities. Not concerned about making obvious political blunders and will stay out of trouble with others of higher rank than self.
4. *Straight Arrow.* Not particularly perceived as a politician, nor seen as a person intent on committing political suicide. Fundamentally believes that most people are honest, hardworking, and trustworthy. Favorite career advancement strategy is to display job competence and may neglect other important career-advancement strategies.
5. *Innocent Lamb.* Believes fully that good people are rewarded for their efforts and will rise to the top. Remains focused on the tasks at hand, hoping that hard work will be rewarded.

Obviously, some individuals are well suited to applying whatever methods and techniques will advance them toward their goals. The Machiavellian and Innocent Lamb types are extremes to avoid, but falling somewhere in the middle of these categories may prove valuable in power politics.

Office politics are unavoidable and must be played like any game.

Organizational politics are unavoidable. The political implications of your actions, and the actions of others, must be taken into consideration whenever operating within an organization, be it large or small. Playing power politics can be negative or positive. Negative methods are manipulative, coercive, exploitive, and destructive. Positive methods are used to achieve common goals, empower others, build cooperation, develop effective personal contacts, and gain credibility and leadership.

Figure 10.5, The Political Power Checklist, provides a quick reference to methods that you may use to become politically powerful. It can be used to check your progress or map your strategies.

Power Symbols

Power symbols come in the form of physical traits and personality characteristics as well as external physical factors, such as clothes or cars. Power symbols are everywhere. We turn on the soap operas and watch as the rich, handsome tycoon and his ex-model wife, who is draped in minks, are driven in their Rolls to a romantic weekend on their 80-foot yacht. We then pick up the paper only to see that another corporation has built an even larger building designed by a popular architect.

Power symbols influence perceptions.

Do individuals acquire these power symbols after they obtain power? Do some persons with little power use them to portray the illusion of power? If you do not have power, will use of power symbols speed your ability to obtain it? The answers

FIGURE 10.5 Political power checklist.

Use this checklist to assess your progress in building a power base.

_____ Do you have a mentor?
_____ Are you sought out for advice or information?
_____ Are your achievements visible?
_____ Do you present your major accomplishments at performance appraisal time?
_____ Have you set your mid- and long-range goals?
_____ Are you tracking (and remaining ahead of) your competition?
_____ Are you paying attention to power dynamics?
_____ Do you attempt to influence others?
_____ Do you get credit and recognition for your ideas?
_____ Are you developing and increasing your power sources?
_____ Do people like to work with you?

are unclear. One thing is certain, however—our perceptions are influenced by these symbols. Understanding power symbols will help us decide how we wish to use them and recognize their use by others.

Traits and Characteristics Do some characteristics identify the potential of an individual to hold power over others? High achievers are generally perceived as powerful, and their traits have been associated with power. These individuals are seen as self-confident, ambitious, dominant, attractive, selfish, ruthless, decisive, strong-willed, determined, accomplished, and goal-directed.

Whether individuals start with these traits or acquire them is undetermined. However, most theorists believe that they are learned abilities nurtured from infancy. Individuals gain these strengths through exposure and experience and cultivate them because of benefits that they derive from their use. The desire for some of these traits is no doubt strengthened through the constant reinforcement by the media that these are the dynamic traits of success and power.

Some studies have supported the idea that being tall makes a more powerful impression. Individuals do make a mental connection between height and power, as reported by a *Houston Post* article in 1988. Wayne Hensley, a scientist who has done research on whether height provides any real advantage, found in a 1988 survey of 243 executives that 90 percent of them were taller than the average 5-foot-9-inch male. He also found through a sampling of male university professors that the taller the teacher, the higher the academic ranking. Full professors averaged a two-or-more-inch advantage. The same pattern held true in his research on the last 21 presidential elections. The taller candidate was chosen to be our nation's chief executive in 17 of the 21 elections.

Additionally, some studies have shown that specific nonverbal behavior patterns differ between high- and low-power persons. These behaviors deal with direct eye contact, facial expression, body gestures, and body positioning. For example, a less powerful person is more likely to *be* touched, whereas the more powerful person is far more likely to do the touching.

External Physical Factors   Clothing is an external physical factor that may send power signals. The famous adage "Clothes do not the man make" does not hold completely true. Certainly, the idea of "dressing for success" has merit. Personal appearance does seem to carry some importance. The way we dress, from hair style down to shoes, is believed to make a statement about the degree of power we either hold or seek. This aspect of power should be kept in mind while shopping for clothes and in our daily grooming.

Powerful people generally have large zones of personal space. For example, the corporate CEO may be seated behind a large, executive-style desk issuing orders to a subordinate standing in front of the desk nervously receiving those orders. A less powerful person will usually make an appointment and wait to be ushered in by invitation to see the power holder, whereas the more powerful person is far more likely to walk right into the smaller office area of a subordinate and be given immediate recognition and respect. Although these cues are subtle, they do leave the impression that an individual is powerful.

Other benefits may be acquired by the power person. As an individual rises to a position of power, certain symbols clearly set that person apart from others. The

FIGURE 10.6   External physical factors send power signals.

kind of car we choose to drive and the size and location of our home are also believed to give the desired appearance of status and power. These silent symbols say, "I have arrived!"

Power symbols provided by organizations may include a company car, a personal secretary, and a large office with plush carpet. These extras, or perks, are seldom enjoyed by the mail room clerk who holds a considerably less powerful position.

WHAT PITFALLS SHOULD YOU AVOID?

Wise use of power allows you to become even more powerful.

The more power you are able to exert, the more easily you will accomplish your goals. With each goal accomplishment, some degree of additional power is gained that enhances further accomplishments. Each cycle increases the ability to go beyond the previous level, as the power spiral in Figure 10.7 indicates.

FIGURE 10.7 The power spiral.

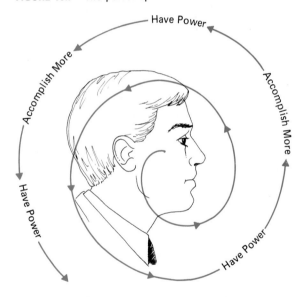

PERSONAL POWER PROFILE

A number of behaviors, however, can block the development of power. Individuals who are so eager to be liked that they bend over backwards to please others will find the development of power difficult. Being eager to please includes being unwilling to face a conflict for fear of offending others or refusing to take some action that will displease others.

On the other side of the coin, being aggressive and coming on too strong at inappropriate times can reduce your power. Refusing to share power by being unwilling to delegate is also viewed negatively.

A truly powerful person has the ability to recruit allies and harness resources to accomplish a mission or goal. Power use is most effective when it is an exercise of strength that enables you to achieve your goals and objectives without harm or damage to others and least effective when it is abused for selfish, personal gain.

SUMMARY

Power is the ability to influence others to do what we want them to do. Despite its sometimes negative image, experts agree that the acquisition and appropriate use of power is necessary for individuals at all levels of an organization if they are to accomplish goals and objectives.

Many sources of power are available and need to be cultivated for maximum effectiveness. These sources include reward, coercive, legitimate, expert, and referent power. Derivative and passive power are sources best left uncultivated. In addition to these power sources, research has defined three basic power personalities, the power-shy, the power-positive, and the power-compulsive.

Developing power is not a matter of luck. It must be planned. Part of this planning and development involves a thorough understanding and respect for power positioning, power politics, and power symbols. Crucial to power development is avoiding the power pitfalls and ensuring that you have used power in a positive manner.

KEY TERMS

power
reward power
coercive power
legitimate power
expert power
referent power
derivative power
passive power
power-shy
power-positive
power-compulsive
power positioning
power politics
power symbols

REVIEW QUESTIONS

1. What is power, and why is developing power necessary?
2. Which basic power sources are available to you?
3. What are the three basic power personalities?
4. What techniques can you use in the planning and implementation of power positioning?
5. Why is applying power politics important?
6. How are power symbols used for power positioning?
7. What are the pitfalls in developing power?

DISCUSSION QUESTIONS

1. Think of individuals who are powerful or have power over you. Which power sources do they possess? Which ones are most effective?
2. Review the power sources available to you. What is your strongest source, and which is your weakest? Do you have linkages?
3. Do you effectively plan the use of your power to gain personal advantages? How and why?
4. Which of the power personalities best fits you? Are you comfortable with your assessment? Why or why not?
5. What power symbols do you possess? How do you use these symbols in your power building?
6. How many of the power techniques have you cultivated? How have they benefited your power positioning?
7. Do you agree that playing power politics is an unavoidable means of assuring personal and professional success? Why or why not?

CASE STUDY 10.1

LINDA LOOPHOLE, THE LEGAL EAGLE

Linda is the best lawyer the firm has. All the junior associates admire her abilities and pattern their courtroom style after hers. She has been at the business longer than most of them have been living. She is known to be able to "persuade Eskimos to buy ice." Just her physical presence in a courtroom demands attention. Her nearly 6-feet-tall, slender frame displays her immaculate and expensive clothing to its maximum flair. She really has it together. Linda knows exactly when to exert her strengths and when to let others have their opinions heard.

Everyone is aware of how she has used every legitimate method available to her to reach the pinnacle of success that seems rightfully hers. She was mentored by the firm's founder, gained high visibility by landing two highly controversial cases early in her career, and outpaced most of her peers with little effort.

1. What power sources has Linda developed during her years with the law firm? How are they linked?
2. What power symbols does Linda use to add to her power positioning?
3. What power techniques has she used to aid her in becoming a success?

4. Do you think that Linda used power politics to acquire her status as the best lawyer in the firm? If so, why do you think that?

CASE STUDY 10.2

DANIEL DOORIGHT, THE DEVIOUS DUPER

Daniel had started with the agency only a few years ago and had already risen to the management ranks. He was intelligent, no doubt about that, but his career had taken off like a rocket, and now everyone wondered how they could have not recognized his limitations before it was too late. Sally said, "You know that he was Willy's fair-haired star from the beginning. He stuck to Willy like a tick on a hound dog and used his name anytime it would gain him any advantage."

Bill agreed and added, "I have even seen him get out of budget planning assignments by claiming that he was not all that familiar with the procedures on company acquisitions. He has certainly been here long enough to know them. I just don't think that he likes having to work the long hours the rest of us do and that's an easy out for him."

"Well, I don't like it, and I don't think he'll last long before he's put out to pasture. That is no way to get ahead around here," Sally remarked.

Some evidence existed that Sally was right. Daniel had already begun to have morale problems in his work unit, and talk was circulating of his reassignment to another area where he would not have a negative effect on others who had already demonstrated their expertise and value to the agency. He had certainly gotten all the mileage he was likely to get in this job.

1. What power sources had Daniel used to assure his rise to a position in management?
2. Why did the other agency employees resent his rise to power?
3. What might Daniel have done differently?

BIBLIOGRAPHY

Allen, Robert W. "Organizational Politics: Tactics and Characteristics of Its Actors." *California Management Review* (Fall 1979): 77–83.

"Benjamin Franklin." *Academic American On-Line Encyclopedia.* New York: Grolier, 1988.

Bogorya, Yvonne. "Office Politics: Game or War?" *The Secretary* (March 1987): 10–13.

Collins, Robert F. "Why I Was Fired: To Survivors, Learn the Art of Politics." *Success* (September 1988): 14.

Davis, Lisa. "In Business, There's Link between Stature and Status." *The Houston Post* (April 24, 1988): G1, 14.

DuBrin, Andrew J. *Winning at Office Politics*. New York: Van Nostrand Reinhold, 1978.

Edwards, Owen. "Office Politics." *GQ* (October 1988): 267–272.

Feinberg, Mortimer R. "Point of View: A Few Kind Words about Fear." *Working Woman* (August, 1990): 20.

French, J. R. P., and B. Raven. "The Bases of Social Power." In D. Cartwright and A. F. Zander, eds., *Group Dynamics*, 3rd ed. New York: Harper & Row, 1968.

Hagberg, Janet O. *Real Power*. Minnesota: Winston Press Inc., 1977.

Klienfield, N. R. "Tall Executives Say Height Gives Them Sizeable Help in Business." *The Houston Post* (March 15, 1987): Section 5, 18.

Kotter, John Phillip. *Power and Influence: Beyond Formal Authority*. New York: Free Press, 1985.

Korda, Michael. *Power! How To Get It, How To Use It.* New York: Random House, 1975.

Martin, Norman H., and John Howard Sims. "Power Tactics." *Harvard Business Review* (November–December 1956): 25–29.

McClelland, David C. *Power: The Inner Experience.* New York: Irvington Publishers, 1975.

Meier, Robert. "Power—Do You Lust for It?" *Success* (May 1984): 35–36, 40.

Powell, Bill, and Carolyn Friday. "The Feds Finger the King of Junk." *Newsweek* (September 19, 1988): 42–44.

Robbins, Anthony. *Unlimited Power*. New York: Simon and Schuster, 1986.

Satran, Pamela Redmond. "Short Power." *Working Woman* (June 1987): 98–100.

Schwartz, Judith D. "Radical Management: How to Overpower Politics in the Office." *Success* (November 1985): 18.

Stechert, Kathryn B. "Power Skills: Raising Your Power Consciousness." *Working Woman* (April 1986): 117–123.

Stoner, James A. F., and R. Edward Freeman. *Management*. Englewood Cliffs, NJ: Prentice-Hall, 1989.

Wiseman, Dan. "How to Survive Office Politics." *Houston Magazine* (October 1988): 26–28.

CHAPTER ELEVEN

PROBLEM SOLVING, DECISION MAKING, AND CREATIVITY

The 3M Corporation encourages creativity by allowing staffers to spend up to 15 percent of their time each week doing anything they want as long as it is product-related. This practice produced Post-its. The original idea was to invent a bookmark that would not slip out of a book, and the adhesive was developed during the free, creative time. Revenues for Post-its alone are now estimated at around $300 million a year.

Business Week
(April 10, 1989): 58–63

OBJECTIVES

After studying this chapter, you should be able to:
1. Define a problem and explain how one occurs.
2. List the steps in problem solving.
3. Explain the relationship between problem solving and decision making.
4. Discuss various approaches to decision making, including decision trees, cost-benefit analyses, ABC analyses, PERT charts, and quality circles.
5. Discuss the role of creativity in problem solving.
6. List the basic steps in the creative process.
7. Name the sources of creativity in organizations and describe ways to get new ideas through organizations.
8. Explain how to encourage creativity in organizations and in ourselves.
9. Discuss the blocks to creativity and how to overcome them.

WHAT IS A PROBLEM?

A popular definition of a problem is a puzzle looking for an answer. Whether the **problem** is an organizational one or a personal one, it can be defined as a disturbance or unsettled matter that requires a solution if the organization or person is to function effectively. Problems become evident when expected results are compared to actual results. The gap is the problem that needs solving. Determining that solution involves decision making.

Problems may be of three types. They may be occurring now and have to be addressed now. They may be expected in the future, and plans must be made for dealing with them when they do occur. They may be foreseen for the future but be so serious that action must be taken immediately to prevent their developing. The following are organizational and personal examples of each type:

Problems occurring now

The economy is forcing the XYZ Company to lay off several employees.
You have returned to school, requiring that you allocate part of your budget to school expenses.

Problems expected in the future

The ABC Company has a deadline of May 1 to complete a project and is now behind schedule.
You have a major paper due in two weeks and have not started writing it.

Problems that are so serious that action must be taken to prevent their developing

Earnings projected for a company reveal that it will be unable to meet its payroll by the middle of the last quarter.
The term paper that you have not yet started and that is due next week is a minimum requirement to pass the course.

Once a problem has been identified, specific steps should be taken to solve it. Decision making is an important part of the problem-solving process. Deciding which solution to choose is always necessary.

HOW ARE PROBLEMS SOLVED?

Regardless of your position in an organization, you are or will be faced with problems and the need to make decisions. Your personal life also requires problem solving and decision making. Human relations, if they are effective, can prevent or help solve problems. If they are not effective, they can create problems of their own. For this reason, problem-solving skills are considered an important part of human relations.

Problem solving and decision making are related. Effective decisions must be made if problems are to be solved satisfactorily. Identifying a problem and its possible solutions is important, but the process is incomplete until we decide which option(s) to implement.

Numerous ways exist for making decisions, some more effective than others. You should understand and be able to use a systematic approach to problem solving so that you do not have to rely on generalizations, snap judgments, or intuition. The following process can help you attain personal and career success.

Step 1—Identify the Problem

Following these steps can increase your problem-solving skills.

The first step in the problem-solving process is to define the problem clearly and specifically. A helpful maxim says that "A problem well defined is a problem half solved." Defining a problem clearly and specifically requires that you first be objective—see the situation as it actually is, not as you think it is. To do so, use the information presented in Chapter 2 and do not let emotions or other factors color your perception. Then quantify the problem if possible. Instead of saying, "We are behind schedule," say, "We have only two weeks in which to complete this project."

Examine all facets of the issue and identify the exact source of the problem. Collect and analyze all information pertinent to it. Although you do not want to overwhelm yourself with information, try to uncover all relevant objective data. You want factual information about the real problem, whether it deals with people, processes, materials, equipment, or other matters. In looking at information related to a project that is behind schedule, for example, you may find that absenteeism has been high, materials have been late in arriving, and the new computer system used on the project has had start-up difficulties.

Then list as many possible causes for the problem as you can. Try to think of what change caused the gap between the expected and actual results. Considering the example above, try to imagine the impact of each change—the absenteeism, late materials, and new computer system.

Select the cause or causes that seem most likely. Using a process of elimination, imagine what difference returning a changed factor to its original condition would make. If that does not solve the problem, keep checking. Continuing the example above, would the project be on time if absenteeism had been at its usual rate, or if materials had arrived on time, or if the computer system had not been changed? After considering these options, you may decide that the most likely cause was the late materials.

Step 2—Generate Alternative Solutions

Once you have identified the cause or causes, develop alternative solutions for removing the causes. Because seldom only one solution exists, think of as many as possible. Frequently the second or third solution will actually be more realistic. In the example above, what can you do to assure the timely arrival of materials in the future? You may, for instance, consider ordering earlier, or ordering from a different source, or even changing the design so that other materials can be substituted for the late ones.

Brainstorming generates as many ideas as possible in a nonjudgmental setting.

Generate ideas through brainstorming. **Brainstorming** is a group problem-solving technique that involves the spontaneous contribution of ideas from all members of the group. The aim of brainstorming is to generate as many ideas as possible. The more ideas presented, the better the results. No ideas should be initially considered too unreasonable or silly. One idea that may seem ridiculous may trigger a feasible idea in someone else. By throwing ideas back and forth and adding to them, members can form a plan. Brainstorming is a freewheeling, fun activity that encourages creativity.

The following discussion demonstrates how brainstorming can work:

Susan, Jeff, and Allison work in the children's wing of the public hospital. During their break Susan commented that the children had no toys with which to play.

"Yes," said Jeff. "Little Johnny was bored today. He is tired of the TV. I know that he will be glad to go home."

FIGURE 11.1 Brainstorming is a group problem-solving technique that involves spontaneous contribution of ideas in a nonjudgmental environment. It is freewheeling and fun.

Allison looked thoughtful and remarked, "Well, I don't understand why we couldn't get them some toys."

"Where would you get them, Allison?" asked Susan. "I don't get paid enough to buy a room full of toys!"

"Oh, I don't know . . . ."

"Wait!" interrupted Jeff. "I saw a news show the other night and the announcer told about the plight of a family who had lost everything in a fire. After the report, they received tons of donations."

"That's a thought," said Susan. "You know . . . we could get the union to organize a committee to see about getting toys."

"Yes, and we could have each employee donate one toy and make a big deal out of it. We could invite the television stations to the party. Then we could ask for public donations over the TV," said Allison excitedly.

"What a great idea, Allison. I'm going to call the union steward right now and see if we can get the committee organized," replied Jeff.

At this point, the ideas should be evaluated for *practicality*. Some of the ideas may sound good but simply cannot be executed.

Step 3—Evaluate Alternatives

Analyze the implications of each alternative by evaluating the pros and cons. Rather than just saying that one solution is better than another, define "better." Develop criteria such as cost and speed. Consider the information gathered in Step 2 and possibly discuss the criteria with experts. Then anticipate the likely results of each alternative. You may discover that some alternatives create more problems than they solve. For example, if you choose to substitute materials in the example above, you may create design problems. Although ordering from another source seems reasonable, you may find that the second source is more expensive.

Step 4—Select a Solution

Select your "best" solution. This step is the decision phase in the problem-solving process. Weigh all the chances of success against the risks of failure. The strengths of your solution should exceed its weaknesses. You may, therefore, in the above example, decide that ordering earlier seems the best alternative. However, because you may not always have advance notice of the need, having an alternative source in mind will be helpful.

Then develop a plan of action for carrying out your solution. What will be done, how, by whom, where, when, and at what cost? You may, for example, develop a plan that says when you have at least two months lead time, you will order from Source A, but with less time you will order from Source B, pay the higher price, and build the extra expense into the cost of the project.

Step 5—Implement the Solution

Implement the idea by carrying out your "best" solution. Consider that you may have to alter your plans and be ready. Again considering the above example, you may choose to order from Source A two months before the start of a new project but cancel your order when that source has not verified delivery two weeks before you need the materials. You then place a new order to Source B and pay the difference.

Step 6—Evaluate Results

The final step in the problem-solving process is to follow up and modify when necessary. Make sure that your actions accomplish your objectives by examining the situation carefully. If your goals are not being met, you may have to study the problem further and apply other alternatives. In the example above, the basic question is whether your projects are being completed on time using the specific plan for ordering supplies. If you are still running behind, you need to study the situation further and try other solutions.

Problem solving has several pitfalls.

When trying to solve a problem, be alert to pitfalls or problem areas. Common ones are the following:

Overanalyzing, which can lead to inaction.

Not taking necessary action or acting too quickly.

Erring in judgment or execution.
Not having a backup plan.
Not involving others.
Perceiving the problem incorrectly.

Following the above steps in the problem-solving process can help you avoid these pitfalls.

HOW CAN WE MAKE BETTER DECISIONS?

All organizations and people are faced with the need to make decisions. In fact, we make dozens of them daily. What time should we get up today, what should we wear, should we eat breakfast, what route do we drive to work, do we have coffee first or start work immediately upon arriving at work, what task do we attack first, when is the best time to try to reach someone by telephone, and on and on. Whenever we have more than one way of doing something, we must make a decision. Sometimes the decisions we must make include problem solving, as discussed above. In such cases, we are trying to overcome the gap between expected and actual results. At other times, we must choose among a number of opportunities facing us. For example, at some point you considered whether to go to college, to go to work, or to combine the two. Each is an opportunity with its own rewards. Once you decided to go to college, either full time or part time, you then had to consider your major field of study. You may have considered several occupations or professions, each of which offers different kinds of rewards (for example, travel, money, control over your time, or interaction with other people).

Decisions are made when we must choose actions, opportunities, or solutions.

Many people overlook opportunities for decisions, both personal and professional ones. Managers and individuals alike become comfortable with the status quo. We should, however, keep in mind the important point that *no decision is a decision.* By not making another choice, we have, in effect, chosen to remain with the status quo. People sometimes fail to make conscious decisions because they fear change, as discussed in Chapter 8. If that is a problem for you, reread that chapter and check the bibliography for recommended reading.

To make decisions, use decision trees, cost-benefit analyses, ABC analyses, PERT charts, or quality circles.

Several well-known techniques exist for helping us make personal and work-related decisions. They include decision trees, cost-benefit analyses, ABC analyses, PERT charts, and quality circles.

Decision Trees

A **decision tree** is a graphic depiction of how alternative solutions lead to various possibilities. It helps people and organizations see the implications that certain choices have for the future. The decision tree illustrated in Figure 11.2 shows various decision points and chance events that may occur in the growth of a company. Should additional employees be hired, should employees be asked to work overtime, or should the owner decide not to increase business?

Decision trees can be used formally by actually drawing them or informally in our heads. Many people find that putting something down on paper is more helpful,

FIGURE 11.2   A decision tree shows various decision points and chance events that may occur.

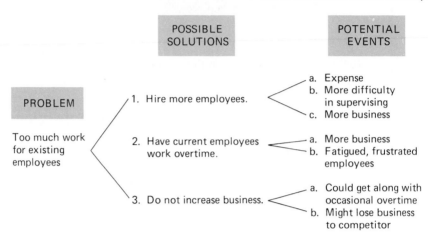

as it prevents them from overlooking some points and helps them keep factors in perspective.

Cost-Benefit Analyses

A **cost-benefit analysis** is an examination of the pros and cons of each proposed solution. A popular technique in the public sector, it is frequently used for evaluating proposals to provide a nonprofit service to the community, such as hospitals, playgrounds, or child care facilities. The analysis involves comparison of all costs against value of the service to the community.

ABC Analyses

An **ABC analysis** is the concentration of decisions where the potential for payoff is greatest. Because you are faced with a multitude of decisions every day, you simply cannot devote much time, thought, or effort to all of them, nor should you want to do so. Economists point out that only a few problems or opportunities (considered vital) account for the greatest loss or gain. They call this fact the 20/80 syndrome, meaning that 20 percent of your problems will account for 80 percent of your losses or gains. It is the 20 percent to which you should attend. In ABC analysis, the vital few are called "A" items; the inconsequential many, "C" items; and those that fall somewhere in between, "B" items. Astute decision makers concentrate on the vital few items, not the trivial many. For instance, in choosing a builder for your home or office, you would do well to concentrate on the quality of the construction first rather than the choice of paint colors. Quality would be considered an "A" item, paint color a "C" item, and brand of appliances probably a "B" item. Anyone who has ever been faced with the pressing need to study for a test coming up the next morning, in effect, has used ABC analysis. If you are like most people, when the time comes to study, you may remember that you need to run to the grocery store for milk, pick up

FIGURE 11.3   The use of decision trees in solving problems can help prevent further problems.

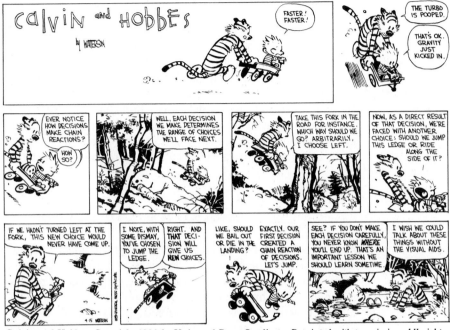

Calvin and Hobbes. Copyright 1990 by Universal Press Syndicate. Reprinted with permission. All rights reserved.

around your house or apartment, run a load of wash, call a friend with whom you have not visited in a while, arrange your photos in the album, or do any number of other tasks. The use of ABC analysis would probably result in considering studying as an "A" item, arranging the photos as a "C" item, and everything else as "B" items.

PERT Charts

As discussed in Chapter 1, Program Evaluation and Review Technique or **PERT charts** are graphic techniques for planning projects in which a great number of tasks must be coordinated. They can aid in problem solving and decision making because they show the relationships between tasks and help identify critical bottlenecks that may delay progress toward a project's completion. Look back at the example of a PERT chart in Chapter 1. The critical path is the sequence of activities that must be done one after another and that requires the longest time for completion.

Quality Circles

Quality circles are committees of 6 to 15 employees who meet regularly to examine and suggest solutions to common problems of quality. Widely used in Japan since the 1950s and in the United States since the mid-1970s, they are a form of participative management because employees provide input to key decisions.

Because quality circles are used frequently in organizations today, you may have an opportunity to serve as a member of one. Typically, the committee consists of volunteers from the same work area. They usually receive some training in group processes, problem solving including brainstorming, and statistical quality control. Statistical quality control is the use of statistics as tools. They are used in frequency distribution charts, quality control charts, and sampling tables. Computers, tools themselves, may be used to help with the statistical analyses.

Quality circles use problem-solving and decision-making techniques, including brain-storming.

Because quality circles focus on improvement of quality, problem-solving and decision-making techniques discussed throughout this chapter are used in them. Proponents of quality circles point out that as a member of a quality circle you are involved in challenging and fulfilling work; therefore, quality circles not only improve product quality and productivity, but they can also improve the quality of your work life.

SHOULD A GROUP DECIDE?

Whatever decision-making technique is being used, most work-related problems and many personal ones require that decisions be made by groups of people rather than by individuals alone. Such situations require strong human relations skills, skills that can be enhanced by a knowledge of group decision making.

In general, groups make better decisions than individuals because of the increased input and suggestions. However, pitfalls can occur, such as wasting time and engaging in groupthink. The first step, then, is deciding whether a group should be used in making a decision. Factors to be considered are shown in Figure 11.4.

Review the factors in the figure carefully. Notice that group decision making assumes that members are knowledgeable, will participate, can be creative in their solutions, and are likely to support what they help create. Human relations skills can help groups arrive at consensus decisions.

HOW DO GROUPS AGREE?

Group decision making seeks consensus, a solution all members can support.

The goal of group problem solving is to reach **consensus**—to develop a solution with which all members can agree. Webster's defines consensus as "group solidarity in sentiment and belief" and "the judgment arrived at by most of those concerned." It does not mean that the final solution is the one each member thinks is the best one, but the solution is one that all members can at least support.

For a group to have the greatest likelihood of reaching consensus, certain guidelines should be followed. Consider these recommendations when you are working with a problem-solving group:

1. State the idea or proposal in the clearest terms possible. Writing it on a chalkboard or flip chart will help.
2. Poll *each* member for opinions by asking, "What do you think of the idea (or proposal)?" Use an open-ended question such as this one rather than "do you agree?"

FIGURE 11.4   Individual versus group decision making.

Situational Factors Supportive of Individual Decision Making	Situational Factors Supportive of Group Decision Making
1. When time is short.	1. When creativity is needed.
2. When the decision is relatively unimportant.	2. When data for the solution rest within the group.
3. When the leader has all the data needed to make the decision.	3. When acceptance of a solution by group members is important.
4. When one or two group members are likely to dominate the discussion.	4. When understanding of a solution by group members is important.
5. When destructive conflict is likely to erupt among group members.	5. When the problem is complex or requires a broad range of knowledge for solution.
6. When people feel they attend too many meetings, don't feel they should be involved, or are pessimistic about the value of group meetings.	6. When the manager wants subordinates to feel part of a democratic process or wants to build their confidence.
7. When the relevant decision-making data are confidential and cannot be shared with all group members.	7. When more risk taking in considering solutions is needed.
8. When group members aren't capable or qualified to decide.	8. When better group member understanding of each other is desirable.
9. When the leader is dominant or intimidates group members.	9. When the group as a whole is ultimately responsible for the decision.
10. When the decision doesn't affect the group directly.	10. When the leader wants to get feedback on the validity of his ideas and opinions.

Lyle Sussman and Samuel D. Deep, COMEX: The Communication Experience in Human Relations *(Cincinnati: South-Western Publishing Co., 1984), 120. Used with permission.*

3. If everyone expresses positive opinions for the idea or proposal, you have total consensus.
4. If someone disagrees, ask why and ask for an alternative idea or proposal.
5. Restate any opposing ideas or proposals to ensure understanding.
6. Use problem-solving techniques to resolve the differences. For example:
   a. Find common ground and work toward another suitable alternative.
   b. Use a best-estimate approach to weigh alternatives, such as a decision tree or ABC analysis.
   c. Strive for a substantial agreement among group members and encourage willingness to try the idea or proposal for a limited time.
   d. Use negotiation that results in a "win-win" situation. **Negotiation** is discussion that leads to a decision acceptable to all.
7. Avoid forcing unanimity, voting, "averaging," "majority rule," or horse trading ("I'll do this if you do that"). Voting divides the group into a win-lose situation.
8. If one group member changes his or her mind, poll opinions from *each* member again.

FIGURE 11.5   Successful negotiation leaves all parties feeling that they have won.

Reprinted with special permission of King Features Syndicate.

9. If someone still disagrees, return to step 4.
10. If only one person, or a small subgroup, continues to disagree, get that person or group to give permission to try the idea or proposal for a limited time period, with the stipulation to test the counter idea or proposal if the first one fails to accomplish its objective.
11. If all parties now agree, consensus has been achieved.

A healthy **"win-win" situation** occurs when both sides on an issue feel they have won. If one side runs roughshod over the other, the situation is considered to be a "win-lose" one. Aggressive, bullying people, in the long run, are not effective negotiators because other people are not likely to feel satisfied at the end of the negotiations. Because negotiation is a part of our daily lives, learning to negotiate properly will increase your effectiveness on the job and the satisfaction of everyone involved. Establishing a reputation of trust will also help you in negotiating. If you are seen as someone who can come through in a tight spot, keep your word, and never betray confidences, you are ahead in the process. Phrases such as "How do you think this idea would work?," "What are your feelings . . .?," and "Have you ever considered . . .?" are helpful during negotiations. Other aspects of commmunication useful in negotiations are listening carefully, finding out what the other person wants, and watching that person's body language.

WHAT IS CREATIVITY?

As pointed out above, an important factor in problem solving is the need to be creative. In fact, creativity is so important in today's economy that many experts are suggesting that it is the only way for businesses to survive.

Creativity is a thinking process that solves a problem or achieves a goal in an original and useful way. Simply stated, it is the ability to come up with new and unique solutions to problems. A creative person has the ability to see practical

FIGURE 11.6 Creativity comes in many forms. Devising a better filing system and a more effective office procedure are worthwhile examples.

relationships among things that are not similar and to combine elements into new patterns of association. Imagination, rather than genius, is a necessary ingredient. Research at Berkeley in the 1960s and 1970s showed that creative professionals were no different than others in intelligence. However, they had learned how to respond spontaneously to their intuitions and to investigate ideas that aroused their curiosity without immediately judging the ideas too harshly.

We all have the potential for creativity. Some people simply develop their potential more than others. Cultivating the vivid imagination that we have as children allows creativity to occur later in life. If we listen to Maslow's advice that creating a first-rate cake is better than creating a second-rate poem, we may be less judgmental of ourselves and others.

Creative persons have been found to have several characteristics and traits in common. Figure 11.7 summarizes them. Of course, not all creative people will possess all of these traits, and some of the traits or characteristics may be found in other people.

Innovation, the end product of creative activity, is vital to the success of organizations and individuals today. Businesses must be able to respond quickly to today's changing world in order to stay competitive. Failing to change and develop new products or techniques will eventually lead to the deterioration of a company.

FIGURE 11.7   Characteristics and traits of creative persons.

Creative people:
1. Can make "leaps of reasoning" from one fact to a seemingly unrelated fact and build a bridge of logic across the two.
2. Ask seemingly naive questions that frequently begin with "Why . . ."
3. Were nurtured to be creative by their social and educational environment rather than being born creative or intelligent.
4. May be of any age. Many of the most creative people in the computer industry today are in their 20s and 30s.
5. May be of either sex but probably have less rigid male and female role identification.
6. View nature as fundamentally orderly.
7. Engage in divergent rather than convergent thinking first. They use divergent thinking to search for answers in many directions and convergent thinking to make choices based on analysis, reason, and experience.
8. May appear highly sensitive, self-centered, and unconventional with chaotic lives and an unconventional morality. Because they are inner-directed, they do not worry about the approval of society.
9. May be "loners" with few close friends.
10. Tend to be introspective, open to new experiences, less emotionally stable, spontaneous, compulsive problem seekers, anxious, with an inner maturity.
11. On the job, may prefer ideas and things to people, have a high regard for intellectual interests, a high level of resourcefulness, high tolerance for ambiguity, be less concerned about job security, not enjoy detail or routine, and be persistent.

Innovation cannot take place without creativity. Many business experts point out that the ability to come up with new ideas and make them work is, for most companies, the only way to stay alive today. Companies are, therefore, interested in learning more about creativity, how to identify it, and how to foster it. For this reason, employees who develop their own creativity skills and produce more and better ideas for their organizations will become more valuable members.

WHAT ARE THE STAGES IN CREATIVITY?

The stages of creativity are perception, incubation, inspiration, and verification.

Although the creative process is still somewhat mysterious, researchers have identified four stages. They are perception, incubation, inspiration, and verification. The **perception** stage requires that we view matters differently than others do. Sometimes it simply involves looking for relationships; at other times it means questioning accepted answers.

Incubation is the most mysterious part of the creative process. Numerous people have compared this stage to a bird sitting quietly on a nest of eggs waiting for them to hatch. Although not much action can be observed, much is happening below the surface. So it is with the innovator. This person may be mentally reviewing many ideas and much information, even in dreams. This stage can range in length from a few hours to many years.

Several major concerns are now in the incubation stage at many companies and in the minds of many people. They include how to deal with the European Common Market, how to solve food and water shortages, how to find new sources of fuel, how to develop effective mass transit systems, and how to market United States goods in changing economies like eastern Europe, the Soviet Union, and Africa.

The **inspiration** stage is the flashing light bulb that cartoonists like to use. We usually experience inspiration as an "aha" feeling. This breakthrough to conscious thought lasts for only a few moments, but it is the result of lengthy thought. Its occurrence is unpredictable and can come at totally unexpected times.

The last stage of the creative process is **verification**. Thomas Edison once said, "Creation is 1 percent inspiration and 99 percent perspiration." Once an idea comes to us, we must begin the hard work of verifying it—that is, testing it, evaluating it, revising it, retesting it, and reevaluating it if necessary. Productivity is the ability to make new and unique solutions effective. This stage often requires working closely with others and, hence, having finely tuned human relations skills.

HOW DO NEW IDEAS GET ACCEPTED?

Organizations should listen to their customers, clients, and employees, who can identify the drawbacks to products and point out needs for new products or services. Ideas can then be developed based on these findings. For example, according to *Business Week*, 3M inventor Richard Drew noticed that painters on automobile assembly lines had a hard time keeping the borders straight on two-tone cars, so he invented masking tape. Thomas Edison invented wax paper because he became tired of chocolates sticking to the tissue paper in which they were wrapped.

As a worker in an organization, you may be more familiar with the processes involved in the performance of your job than anyone else. Therefore, you are in a good position to be able to identify creative approaches. What should you do if you think of what appears to be a better procedure or better product? Knowing how to successfully present ideas and get others to act on them is a crucial skill for creative individuals.

New ideas are not usually immediately embraced in a company. They must be cultivated and supported from conception to implementation. The idea must have a champion, someone who is willing to speak up for it and to commit to it. Being a champion of an idea takes enthusiasm and the willingness to take risks. After all, the idea may prove to be fruitless. The champion, who may be you or someone else such as your supervisor, must put together a team to develop the idea. Few ideas and projects are implemented by one person alone. Working as part of a creative team will not only require creativity, but it will also require well-developed skills in human relations, including problem solving, decision making, and communication.

If you are trying to get an idea through an organization, be prepared to persist. Even the most successful projects have their down sides when the going is tough and participants become discouraged. As the champion of an idea or as a member of a team developing an idea, you should be emotionally prepared for these periods. Having supportive family, friends, or coworkers can help tremendously.

Ideas must be sold to others. Effective communication and networking skills will help the champion develop a coalition and gather others who are willing to support the idea. You or the person serving as the champion must then work to maintain their support.

The above discussion points out the importance of effective human relations skills and explodes the myth that creative people work alone and, therefore, do not need people skills. Creative people have a much better chance of bringing their ideas to fruition if they are able to work effectively with others.

Getting an idea accepted takes human relations skills.

A strong trait in people with effective human relations skills is the willingness to share credit. When a creative group project or idea is successful, the person in charge must be sure to share the credit. While patents and copyrights exist to protect individuals' creations, taking individual credit for a group project is an excellent way to ensure that no further successful group projects will be completed.

HOW CAN SUPERVISORS STIMULATE CREATIVITY?

If you are a supervisor in an organization, you have a responsibility to stimulate creativity among your employees. Several methods for accomplishing this are suspending judgment, tolerating a reasonable amount of failure, supervising carefully, offering constructive criticism, and tolerating some different behavior.

The National Institute of Business Management has pointed out that managers skilled in stimulating creativity among workers make it to the top faster than anybody else. They have overcome several common myths about creativity. Being aware of the myths shown in Figure 11.8 can help you move up in your organization.

Supervisors interested in stimulating creativity must be sure that they suspend critical judgment during brainstorming sessions. They should also make sure that employees understand they are not responsible for any "crazy" comments they might make during the session.

Supervisors must also stress that failure will be tolerated. Failure is a natural part of innovation and risk taking. As individuals and as employees, if we never fail, we are probably setting goals that are too "safe," as discussed in Chapter 7. Unfortunately, many companies stifle creativity because they do not tolerate a certain amount of failure or reward those persons who develop creative ideas. Employees then become afraid to present a project or product that might not be successful.

Supervising creative people takes some practice. Creative persons find breaking, stretching, or overlooking rules to be natural. For this reason they must be supervised carefully. Goals and timetables need to be set for them while they work at their own pace. If your supervisor does this to you, view it as an attempt to help you succeed professionally, not hinder you.

Creative persons also need quiet time to allow their unconscious mind to work. Supervisors should help ensure that such times are available.

FIGURE 11.8   Myths about corporate creativity.

1. **MYTH:** Creativity is only important in the arts.
   FACT: Creativity is essential to any organization's success, and managers skilled in tapping their employees' creativity rise faster in the organization.
2. **MYTH:** Only a small number of people are creative, and they are weirdos.
   FACT: Actually, most people can be creative. Companies should learn to spot creative ideas and use public recognition and money as incentives.
3. **MYTH:** Creativity is intangible and uncontrollable.
   FACT: Although people cannot be made to produce brilliant ideas on demand, an innovative spirit can be nurtured.
4. **MYTH:** Creative thinking is needed only in the creative fields of an organization, such as research and product development.
   FACT: Innovation can occur in policies, processes, and techniques as well as people's activities and behaviors. Additionally, innovation in one area can set off a creative chain reaction throughout the organization.
5. **MYTH:** Creative thinking is play, not work.
   FACT: Intensive thought about innovative problem-solving strategies can be draining. Companies should convey the message that creative work will be rewarded.
6. **MYTH:** Creative thinking is risky and leads to unnecessary change.
   FACT: Creativity is necessary for companies to survive today.

Adapted from "How to Harness Creativity," in Personal Report for the Executive *(New York: National Institute of Business Management, July 1, 1989), 2.*

Feedback in the form of constructive criticism, praise, and evaluation must be given even if the project is indefinite or long postponed. As pointed out in the discussion about Maslow's hierarchy of needs in Chapter 6, self-actualizing people (who tend to be creative) thrive on feedback.

Finally, creative people can be eccentrics, and others in the company may become impatient with their progress or be bothered by their behavior. Creativity is not always a visible process. The person who is staring out the window with feet on the desk may indeed be working very hard. At times a supervisor may need to defend creative persons, protect them from harm, and nurture them in the corporate political environment:

Lawrence, the vice president of marketing, cornered Barbara, the advertising manager, near the water fountain. He began to complain about Harry, one of Barbara's employees.

"Harry is strange. He wears those wrinkled shirts to work,

and he is always walking around with his nose in a book or magazine. Every time I see him and try to say hello he looks at me as if I were crazy. Yesterday I saw him staring out the window. I stood there for five minutes before he noticed me. I don't think that he is fitting into the department. Perhaps we should see if personnel can help him find a job elsewhere."

Barbara responded, "I realize that Harry is a bit different from our other employee, Virginia. However, he is very talented. He has produced some of the best ideas that our department has had. Why don't I bring some of his work for you to see? I think that he is valuable to my team, and I would hate to lose him."

Barbara also later suggested to Harry that he might close his door when he felt the need to reach a solution to a problem. She also suggested that if he wishes to move up into management, he will probably need to control aspects of his behavior that appear eccentric to others.

WHAT BLOCKS CREATIVITY?

Creativity can be developed and nurtured. It can also be hampered in a variety of ways. Blocks to creativity include thought processes, emotional blocks, cultural blocks, and environmental blocks.

Thought Processes

To stimulate creativity, we must learn to modify our problem-solving habits and develop new ways of thinking that enhance creativity. The first block to overcome is the inability to isolate the real source of a problem. People often stereotype a dilemma and see only what they expect to see. To overcome this limit, develop the habit of taking a "big picture" perspective. Look at every angle and take a wide view of the dilemma, as demonstrated in the following example:

Marcus stormed into Denise's office. He began to yell at her because he did not have the report that he needed to make his presentation tomorrow. Denise reminded him that she could not finish the report until the accounting office sent her the statistics. She had checked on them three times already today. Marcus left in a huff, telling Denise that she should stay until the report was completed, even if it meant she had to stay all night.

Denise began to think about the problem. She had tickets to a concert and did not want to stay late. Mentally stepping back from the immediate problem of not receiving the statistics from accounting, she took a "big picture" view and asked the following questions: Can I obtain the information elsewhere? How vital are the statistics to the report? Can I prepare the majority of the report without the statistics?

Sometimes we become overloaded with information, as discussed in Chapter 3, and cannot recall familiar information because our minds are cluttered with trivia that we are unable to clear away. Needless to say, this clutter can interfere with our creativity. Changing our activities can frequently help us overcome this block. For example, if you have been working in your office, you might go to the library for a short period; or you might temporarily put the problem out of your mind only to have the solution come to you when you are out walking that evening.

Thought processes that block creativity can be overcome.

Failing to use all of our senses is an additional way that thought processes block creativity. Using sight, sound, and feel as inputs into the creative process can help. Many people, for example, find that watching playful kittens or happy children stimulates their creativity. Others are inspired by the sights, sounds, and smells of nature.

Think about your own thought processes in light of information in this section. Do you look at the big picture? What settings inspire your creativity? Are you more creative when you are alone or when you are around other people? Do you tend to be more creative in the mornings or evenings? Have you developed habits for remembering your ideas, such as writing them down? Concentrate on these aspects of your own creativity to see it increase.

Emotional Blocks

Fear of taking a risk or making a mistake is one of the biggest emotional blocks to creativity. Not all ideas are successful, and the creative individual must be willing to risk negative outcomes. We should, therefore, refrain from letting others (or ourselves) engender such fear in us. If fear is a problem for you, go back and reread the section dealing with risk taking in Chapter 7.

Being overly critical will also kill creativity. Most people would rather judge an idea than generate one. Many ideas die because they are judged too early, before they have been fully developed. Review the steps in the creative process and recall that generation of ideas and evaluation of them are two different parts of the process.

The ability to tolerate ambiguity is also essential in the creative process. When something is ambiguous, it can be understood in two or more possible ways. That is precisely what you want in creativity. If you are able to look at a problem in a different way, you are closer to coming up with a novel solution. As you will recall from Chapter 3, black/white, either/or thinking is a communication barrier. If such thinking impedes communication, it will certainly inhibit creativity. Most people have an overriding desire for order and predictability, but the creative process is a "messy" one. New ideas or projects are not orderly or predictable, and people working on them can become frustrated if they cannot tolerate ambiguity. Being aware of this emotional block may help you overcome it.

If we are to be creative, we must unlock our unconscious minds. When we are tense or preoccupied, we are unable to be creative. Relaxation and the ability to "sleep on it" are helpful. Many ideas have been conceived on the golf course, in the shower, on the way to work, or during routine chores.

Another emotional block is fear of change. Some people find tradition more comfortable. Because creativity by its nature is newness and change, we should develop a positive attitude toward change if we wish to be more creative. Engaging in new activities, sports, or hobbies can help our creativity.

Egos, too, can be the source of emotional blocks to creativity. People who feel that they can never be wrong and will not back down or who will not support an idea presented by another person even when it is a good one stifle creativity. Be careful of such behaviors in yourself.

> We must become aware of emotional blocks to creativity.

Finally, some persons are unable to distinguish fantasy from reality. The creative person needs to be able to distinguish what is feasible from what is not. Remember that an important step in the problem-solving process is the evaluation of ideas for practicality.

Cultural Blocks

> Cultural blocks to creativity include taboos against daydreaming, intuition, and humor.

Cultural taboos can stand in the way of creativity. The old adage that "an idle mind is the devil's workshop" reflects the idea that fantasy is wasteful and lazy. Playing is seen as an activity for children only, not for adults, and pleasure is considered sinful ("Waste not, want not"). To be creative we must rid ourselves of such notions and allow our minds to float in a random fashion sometimes, to see figures in clouds.

Other cultural biases lock out the use of intuition and qualitative judgment in favor of logic, reason, numbers, and practicality. Reality, however, dictates that a balance be maintained between these two sets of forces. Another cultural block is the idea that problem solving is serious business. Humor, however, can unlock creativity.

Environmental Blocks

A lack of trust and cooperation among colleagues can short-circuit creativity. Group interactions are particularly vulnerable when members of rival groups are thrown together to resolve a problem:

> **The engineering department and the accounting department have been at odds. The engineers continue to order supplies and fail to complete correctly the forms necessary to allow the accounting department to keep track of the materials. Also, they are ordering materials before checking to see whether excess material is at another location. The engineers say that the forms are too long and cumbersome and that it takes days to check other locations.**
>
> **Martha decides to call a task force together that consists of engineers and accountants to solve the problem. She includes Jeffrey from accounting and Ronald from engineering. They recently had a loud argument over the issue that they are to resolve. When Jeffrey and Ronald enter the room, they stare at each other and sullenly sink into their chairs. Neither wants a compromise because each thinks his side is right. They sit silently, failing to contribute to the discussion.**

Autocratic bosses and those who provide little or no feedback can also hinder creativity. They may value their own ideas and not support those of subordinates, blocking contribution to the brainstorming process. Their inability or unwillingness to provide feedback "starves" employees.

In some situations, groups become merely a rubber stamp and approve ideas without exploring them. This block may happen for two reasons. Sometimes people

Supervisors and subordinates can set up environmental blocks to creativity.

are afraid to speak up and present opposing views. At other times they fear jeopardizing harmony, so they make a decision that satisfies both sides but that is not the most practical or realistic.

HOW CAN YOU BECOME CREATIVE?

Ways to improve your creative ability, suggested by Jimmy Calano and Jeff Salzman in *Working Woman* and Eugene Rauidsepp in *Nation's Business*, include the following:

1. Believe that you have the ability to be creative.
2. Listen to your hunches, particularly while relaxed.
3. Keep track of your ideas by writing down your insights and thoughts. Keep a pad near your bed, in your car, and in your pocket or purse on which to record your ideas as they occur.
4. Learn about things outside of your specialty to keep your thinking fresh.
5. Avoid rigid set patterns of doing things. Change your rhythms. Draw your problems instead of writing them down. Change your scene or environment by taking a trip or walking. Try a different route to work occasionally.
6. Observe similarities, differences, and unique features in things, whether they are situations, processes, or ideas.
7. Engage in an activity at which you are not an expert and that puts you outside of your comfort zone, such as tennis or playing a musical instrument.
8. Engage in hobbies, especially those involving your hands. Keep your brain trim by playing games and doing puzzles and exercises.
9. Take the other side occasionally in order to challenge and scrutinize your own beliefs.
10. Have a sense of humor and learn to laugh easily. Humor helps put you and your problems into perspective and relieves tension, allowing you to be more creative.
11. Adopt a risk-taking attitude. Nothing is more fatal to creativity than fear of failure or resistance to change.
12. Think positive! Believe that a solution is possible and that you will find it.
13. Turn your ideas into action; follow through. Use positive reinforcement with yourself and reward yourself as a payoff for completing a project.

SUMMARY

Problems are disturbances or unsettled matters that require solutions if the organization or person is to function effectively. They occur because change is inevitable. Problems become evident when expected results are compared to actual results.

Problems can best be solved by following these steps: Define the problem clearly and specifically. Explore the problem, list possible causes, and evaluate the ideas for practicality. Develop alternative solutions for removing the causes. Analyze the implications of each alternative. Select the "best" solution and develop a plan of action. Implement the idea. Follow up and modify when necessary.

Decisions are needed when we must make choices among actions, opportunities, and solutions. Well-known techniques for making personal and work decisions are decision trees, ABC analyses, cost-benefit analyses, PERT charts, and quality circles. A decision tree is a graphic depiction of how alternative solutions lead to various possibilities. A cost-benefit analysis is an examination of the pros and cons of each proposed solution. ABC analysis is the concentration of decisions where the potential for payoff is great. PERT charts are used with projects in which a great number of tasks must be coordinated. Quality circles are committees of 6 to 15 employees who meet regularly to examine and suggest solutions to common problems of quality.

Decision making may be done by individuals or by groups. The goal of group problem solving is to reach consensus—to develop a solution with which all members can agree. Negotiation, discussion that leads to a decision acceptable to all, is important. To be an effective negotiator, you should try for win-win solutions.

An important factor in problem solving is creativity, the ability to come up with new and unique solutions. We all have the potential for creativity, but it must be nurtured and developed. Innovation, the end product of creative activity, is vital to the success of organizations and individuals today.

Creativity involves four steps: perception, incubation, inspiration, and verification. Creative ideas can come from many sources. For organizations these sources can include customers, clients, and employees. An employee trying to get a new idea through an organization must be prepared to persist, develop a coalition, sell the idea, work as part of a team, and share credit.

Supervisors wishing to stimulate creativity among their workers must be aware of the myths about corporate creativity. They must also suspend critical judgment during brainstorming sessions; stress that failure will be tolerated; supervise creative employees carefully; arrange quiet time for such employees; provide constructive criticism, praise, and evaluation; and be willing to defend them.

Blocks to creativity include thought processes, emotional blocks, cultural blocks, and environmental blocks. Thought processes that can block creativity are the inability to isolate the real source of a problem, information overload, and failure to use all of our senses. Emotional blocks include fear of risk, being overly critical, inability to tolerate ambiguity, not unlocking the unconscious mind, fear of change, ego, and inability to distinguish fantasy from reality. Cultural blocks are taboos against daydreaming, intuition, and humor. Lack of trust and cooperation among colleagues, autocratic bosses, and "rubber stamp" groups are environmental blocks to creativity.

You can take several steps to develop your own creativity, starting with believing that you can be creative. Thinking positively helps, and following through is essential.

KEY TERMS

problem
brainstorming
decision tree
cost-benefit analysis
ABC analysis
PERT chart
quality circle
consensus
negotiation
"win-win" situation
creativity
innovation
perception
incubation
inspiration
verification

REVIEW QUESTIONS

1. What is a problem, and how do problems occur?
2. What are the steps in the problem-solving process?
3. What is the relationship between problems and decision making?
4. Define decision trees, ABC analyses, cost-benefit analyses, PERT charts, and quality circles.
5. What is the role of creativity in problem solving?
6. List and explain the basic steps in the creative process.
7. What sources of creativity do organizations have? How can new ideas get through an organization?
8. Explain how organizations can encourage creativity among workers. How can you develop your own creativity?
9. Name the different categories of blocks to creativity, give examples of each, and explain how to overcome them.

DISCUSSION QUESTIONS

1. Think of a problem with which you were recently confronted. Apply the problem-solving process to it. Would you take the same action now that you did at the time? (Remember that no decision is a decision!) Share the answer with the class.
2. Think of two problems that you are currently facing. Apply a decision tree to one and ABC analysis to the other.
3. Think of a time when you came up with what you considered to be a novel solution to a problem. Think back carefully to the process you used. Try to identify the four basic steps in your creative process. Share this experience with the class.
4. If you are currently working or have worked, think about your organization. What is the level of creativity in it? What steps is the organization or your supervisor taking to stimulate creativity? What are you doing to develop your own creative ability?
5. Review the different blocks to creativity. Name examples of each kind and consider them in relation to yourself. Are they blocks to your own creativity? (Try to be objective!) If not, good for you. If so, identify what you can do to overcome each block.

CASE STUDY 11.1

20/80 SYNDROME

Brad, the head of the continuing education program at the local community college, finds that summer is the best time for him to develop new programs and courses. In looking at his "to do" list for this summer, he sees so many projects that he cannot possibly do all of them. In reviewing the list he finds the following:

1. *Courses for professional groups.* Some professional groups are required to complete state-mandated continuing education hours each year in order to remain licensed or certified. The state expects community colleges to provide such training, and Brad is interested in offering courses if they will have satisfactory enrollments. These groups include real estate sales people, Certified Public Accountants, and insurance agents.

Brad has tried to run some courses for CPAs in the past, but enrollments were low, yet he knows that other community colleges are experiencing high enrollments. One of these colleges said that it set up an advisory committee made up of members of the local CPA society. The advisory committee recommends courses, helps find instructors, and assists in publicizing the courses. Brad thinks that perhaps he should set up an advisory committee before offering additional courses for CPAs.

Brad has not yet offered courses for insurance agents, but he knows of a college nearby that does. That school reports low enrollments. Brad is uncertain whether he should try courses in this area, set up an advisory committee, or even devote effort to it.

2. *Other new courses and programs.* Brad also has several other program and course possibilities on his list. They include classes for senior citizens and a "fear-of-flying" course for white-knuckle flyers. Other colleges report great success in

targeting classes to local citizens over 55 years of age. Brad does not know of any colleges that offer the flying course or even who would teach it for him (his college does have a pilot training program). He is also considering a dental assistant program and a gerontology program. His community has several medical complexes in it, and students would probably be able to do internships in them.

3. *Business/industry contracts.* Brad would also like to devote some time to developing additional training contracts with businesses and industries in the community. He has been successful in building up a good working relationship with a number of companies around his college and would like to do more. Such contracts develop good will in the community, bring in additional money to the college, and provide jobs for teachers. Besides, Brad enjoys setting them up.

Although Brad can ask some of the other people at the college for input, he has to do most of the work himself in designing and marketing courses and programs. As Brad looks at his list of potential projects, he grows both excited and frustrated. He enjoys creating new programs and courses, but he also knows that he will not be able to do all of this work in two and one-half months.

1. Apply ABC analysis to Brad's dilemma. Categorize each task, label it A, B, or C, and explain your reasoning.
2. Based on your ABC analysis, what recommendation would you make to Brad about his priorities for the summer?

CASE STUDY 11.2

HELP! HELP!

Two years ago Kathleen started a word-processing service. Most of her clients are individuals, other small business owners, or large companies with overflow or rush jobs. Her business has been so successful that six months ago she hired an employee to help her. She was lucky enough then to find someone who is experienced and fast.

Last month Kathleen hired a second person when she found that work was stacking up and deadlines were not being met. The second employee is not experienced but is eager to learn and, in fact, seems to learn fast. However, because of all the rush projects, Kathleen has not had much time to train him and, hence, has to give him the less complex jobs.

Kathleen is beginning to feel overwhelmed. One of her computers has been acting up for the last two weeks, resulting in some downtime. The office also frequently runs out of needed supplies. Another common problem is realizing that a job is to be printed on a particular company's letterhead, and the company representative did not bring in the letterhead when she brought in the job. Kathleen is dismayed to find that even though she has an additional person on the payroll, deadlines are still not being met and jobs are backing up. In fact, some projects have even been put aside and not remembered until the client came by for them, causing much embarrassment. Kathleen feels that she cannot blame anybody in particular, as whoever is free is the one who takes requests from clients, orders supplies, and moves on to the next project.

1. Imagine that you are a consultant hired by Kathleen to try to bring order to her business. Using the problem-solving process described in this text, summarize your conversation with Kathleen. Be specific.
   a. What do you think is the real problem? What information are you using to determine it?
   b. What do you think are the possible causes for the problem? Again, what information are you using?
2. Based on the conversation with Kathleen and the application of the problem-solving process, what advice would you give her? Be specific.
   a. How practical are the ideas you have generated?
   b. What alternatives for removing the causes of the problem would you suggest? What are the implications of each alternative?
   c. What would you recommend as the most likely solution to her problem? Next most likely?
   d. What plan of action do you advise?
   e. How should the plan be implemented and followed up?

BIBLIOGRAPHY

Cleese, John. "No More Mistakes and You're Through." *Forbes* (May 16, 1988): 126, 128.

Calano, Jimmy, and Jeff Salzman. "Ten Ways to Fire Up Your Creativity." *Working Woman* (July 1989): 94–95.

Feinberg, Mortimer R. "Manager's Tipsheet—The Special Art of Managing Creative People." *Working Woman* (April 1989): 40. (Reprinted from "Management Letter," 1988, by the Bureau of Business Practice, Inc., Waterford, CT.)

Halloran, Jack, and Douglas Benton. *Applied Human Relations*. Englewood Cliffs, NJ: Prentice-Hall, 1987.

"How to Harness Creativity." *Personal Report for the Executive*. New York: National Institute of Business Management, July 1, 1989.

Kanter, Rosabeth Moss. "How to be an Entrepreneur without Leaving Your Company." *Working Woman* (November 1988): 44, 46, 48.

Kossen, Stan. *The Human Side of Organizations*. New York: Harper & Row, 1983.

Maslow, Abraham H. "The Scientific Study of Inventive Talent." *A Source Book for Creative Thinking*. Edited by S. J. Parnes and H. F. Harding. New York: Scribner, 1962.

Mitchell, Russell. "Masters of Innovation—How 3M Keeps Its New Products Coming." *Business Week* (April 10, 1989): 58-63.

Raudsepp, Eugene. "How Creative Are You?" *Nation's Business* (June 1985): 25–26.

Sussman, Lyle, and Samuel D. Deep. *COMEX: The Communication Experience in Human Relations*. Cincinnati: South-Western Publishing Company, Inc., 1984.

Webster's New Collegiate Dictionary. Springfield, MA: G. & C. Merriam Company, 1976.

SUGGESTED READING

Adams, James L. ***Conceptual Blockbusting***. Reading, MA: Addison-Wesley Publishing Company, 1986.

Bennis, Warren. ***On Becoming a Leader***. Reading, MA: Addison-Wesley Publishing Company, 1989.

Bennis, Warren. ***Why Leaders Can't Lead***. San Francisco: Jossey-Bass Publishers, 1990. (Part Three: "Parts of the Problem"; Part Four: "Parts of the Solution.")

Gamache, R. Donald, and Robert L. Kuhn. ***The Creativity Infusion***. New York: Harper & Row, 1989.

Greene, Richard M., Jr. ***The Management Game***. Homewood, IL: Dow Jones-Irwin, Inc., 1969. (Chapter 3, "Creativity and Productivity.")

Jandt, Fred E. ***Win-Win Negotiating***. New York: John Wiley & Sons, 1985.

Moskowitz, Robert A. ***Creative Problem Solving***. New York: AMACOM, 1978.

Nanus, Burt. ***The Leader's Edge—The Seven Keys to Leadership in a Turbulent World***. New York: Contemporary Books, 1989. (Chapter 7, "Creative Leadership.")

CHAPTER TWELVE

TEAMBUILDING

General Foods found inspiration by applying a teamwork approach to product development. In 1984, they set up a team of nine people to launch a new line of ready-to-eat desserts. These team members were treated like entrepreneurs with the freedom to start and operate their own business within General Foods. Developing the basic idea from concept through product distribution included the responsibility of overseeing the construction of a new-technology factory capable of manufacturing the new food product.

The process of fully developing a new product from design to shipping normally takes a food company five to seven years. This high-performance team took only three years to put Jell-O Pudding Snacks on grocery store shelves across the nation and capture the leading market position. The ready-to-eat dessert sales at General Foods now exceed $100 million.

Using this successful role model, General Foods has implemented the team concept throughout the company. The employee productivity teams are even used with employees on the factory floor to improve conditions and lower costs. General Foods' management believes that "the teams create higher motivation and commitment, more innovation, and better performance."

Pamela King, *Psychology Today* (December 1989): 16

OBJECTIVES

After studying this chapter, you should be able to:
1. Discuss the need for effective team concepts in today's work environment.
2. Explain how effective teams increase productivity.
3. Identify the steps in building an effective team.
4. Explain the reasons communication and networking are important ingredients in effective teambuilding.
5. Discuss some of the benefits and drawbacks of team use for individual team members.
6. Describe what you can do to be an effective team member.
7. Explain the difference between conflict and competition and discuss why they both can be healthy for an organization.
8. Describe the most common techniques used in conflict resolution.

WHAT IS A TEAM?

Webster defines a **team** as "a number of persons associated together in work or activity." We commonly think of a team as a group of individuals doing the same thing, such as playing basketball or hockey. In today's work environment, however, teams may be made of representatives from a variety of disciplines, departments, or even different lines of business coming together to achieve common goals and objectives that will enhance all their specific areas. An example is the cooperation and combined efforts in the Amish community when a family needs a new home. Carpenters, painters, bricklayers, roofers, and finishers come together to achieve a common goal, and the house is raised in just one day.

Teamwork is a key to improved quality, productivity, and efficiency.

Teamwork, the combined effort of several disciplines for maximum effectiveness in achieving common goals, is important to organizations because it can increase productivity. An excellent example of effective teamwork that increased productivity occurred within United States car manufacturing over the past few years. Companies strove to recover in a market that was threatened by quality Japanese products. The goal was to speed up the cycle time in product development and get a better product out to the customers faster. The solution was to form a team of marketing, design engineering, quality, and manufacturing people to attack the problem from the beginning.

The old process involved having one group do the design, hand it off to the manufacturing team, and then forward the work to the quality crew. The final step was to have marketing people decide how to sell or market the final product. This process was slow and cost the industry dearly in such a highly competitive marketplace. With the use of the new team concept, product designs and quality were greatly improved, and total product cycle time was reduced, resulting in a comeback for a failing industry.

WHAT IS TEAMBUILDING?

Organizations have found that effective teamwork does not just happen. It evolves through the deliberate efforts of team members working to strengthen the group's purpose. For this reason many organizations have begun a conscientious effort to develop competent teams through teambuilding. **Teambuilding** is a series of activities designed to help work groups solve problems, accomplish work goals, and more effectively function through teamwork. Constructive teambuilding requires that each team participant accept the team goals and objectives and take ownership of the results. A high degree of cohesion develops within the group, and the open environment improves the quality of problem solving and decision making. **Synergism** involves cooperative action to achieve an effect that is greater than the sum of the individual effects.

The team concept, which involves the application of teambuilding and teams bonding together for effective teamwork, is a generic term used to describe the workings of teams in achieving common goals and objectives, with all their human relations complexities. The concept is not new to the work environment.

FIGURE 12.1 Teams are a vital part of work.

Virginia Blaisdell/STOCK, BOSTON

HOW HAS THE TEAM CONCEPT GROWN?

Teams have been used since people began to perform complex tasks. The early Egyptians, for instance, used large teams to construct the pyramids. Major corporations in the United States began experimenting with team concepts on a small scale as early as the 1920s and 1930s with the introduction of problem-solving teams. **Problem-solving teams** generally consisted of 5 to 12 volunteers from different areas of a department who met once or twice a week to discuss ways of improving quality, efficiency, or work conditions. Initially they had no power to implement ideas, which limited their effectiveness. However, more widespread use of this team concept blossomed in the late 1970s based on Japanese quality circles, as discussed in Chapter 11.

Problem-solving and special-purpose teams evolved into the self-managing teams of today.

   Special-purpose teams evolved in the early to mid-1980s. Worker and union representatives collaborated to improve quality and productivity. These teams introduced work reforms and new technology and actually met with suppliers and customers, linking various disciplines and separate functions. Special-purpose teams are frequently used today in unionized organizations.

The most common team in the modern work environment is the **self-managing team**. These teams usually consist of 5 to 15 employees who produce an entire product in a truly entrepreneurial sense. This approach fundamentally changes how work is organized and gives employees control over their own destinies. Organizational hierarchies are flattened by eliminating tiers of middle management and supervision. The use of self-managing teams usually increases productivity and substantially improves quality in the end product or service.

Abigail Reifsnyder points out in her 1986 *Success* article that by early 1980 more than one-third of the Fortune 500 companies had some form of team concept within their corporate structure. The use of teams has steadily grown and has become an integral part of the operation of any company that hopes to remain competitive in today's marketplace. The former authoritarian, single-focus individual driving a company has given way to clerical, engineering, financial, and sales employees working as a team to accomplish the job.

The team concept is ever more important in an increasingly competitive global market.

The use of teams involving diverse employee resources is necessary for the United States to remain competitive in a global marketplace. Companies are having to revamp ways of doing business to include more team efforts in order to cope with the rapidly changing economic environment. Studies indicate that work-team systems that allow workers real participation in decision making produce better quality products, improve efficiency, increase productivity, and yield more satisfied employees. Workers who are a part of a team find their jobs more rewarding and stimulating than the usual fragmented or production-line job. Additionally, today's workers are demanding a say in decisions that affect their work environment and want greater responsibility. Building productive teams is, therefore, becoming increasingly important in today's organizations.

HOW DO YOU BUILD AN EFFECTIVE TEAM?

When people cooperate in a true team effort, powerful results are achieved. Several key ingredients are necessary to assure the kind of synergism that a competent team can produce. The specific ingredients are described in the following paragraphs.

1. Vision. To build an effective team, whether at work or elsewhere, you must have a clear idea of the team's purpose, where you want to go, and what you must do. Allowing the team to contribute to the planning and setting of specific goals promotes teamwork. Goals should be specific and result in a mission statement through which team members can clearly understand their purpose. For example, President John F. Kennedy provided NASA's team with a clear and compelling vision that demonstrated the power of purpose. By committing to "place a man on the moon by the end of the 1960s," President Kennedy inspired team members of the Apollo Program to achieve their mission. The clarity and conviction generated strategies and an execution that in fact achieved the goal in the prescribed time frame.

2. Interdependence. Clearly identifying each person's role is essential in reducing conflict and negative competitiveness. Once individuals are comfortable with their role and mission, true team identity can arise. Members will feel like teammates. Teammates will feel comfortable sharing and will come to rely on one another rather than operate as independent entities. The use of "we/us/our" terms becomes noticeable, replacing the typical "I/me/mine" individualistic view. This togetherness reflects a sense of ownership in what the team is doing and builds team spirit.

3. Leadership. The leadership role in a team is a critical and often difficult one. Certainly, a leader is needed, but it need not always be the formal, legitimate leader. Sharing the leadership role with other team members when appropriate serves to strengthen the team feeling. Today's formal leader must learn when to let go and allow others to lead.

However, the formal leader does have several obligations to the team. Assigning the right people to the right task is one of them. For example, people-oriented individuals do their best work when they have interaction with others. Project-oriented people tend to function best dealing with analysis, design, and technical parameters rather than people. Individuals should not be "pigeonholed" into exclusive assignments, but their natural strengths should be used.

Involving "rookie" employees in the team is another strong play that can greatly benefit the team. Too often the newcomers' abilities are underestimated because of their lack of experience or exposure. This inexperience can prove to be a plus in bringing a fresh outlook or approach to a problem. Often new team members can more objectively view the situation than current team members who may have become enmeshed in the task details.

Effective leadership is particularly important in the initial phases to encourage full participation and get the ball rolling. Leadership is also needed to administer rewards for performance by teammates. People tend to respond positively to positive reinforcement. If team members are made to see themselves as important contributors, they will keep up that image. Effective leaders will make clear what is expected, and team members will most often live up to and frequently exceed those expectations. Self-confidence has a proven influence on performance. People do as well as they believe they can. Good leaders are important in fulfilling this necessary role of "cheerleader" to encourage people to be significant contributors.

4. Coordination. Given the dynamic conditions of the team approach, coordination of information is a critical point. All members need to keep up with changes in direction and new facts. Establishing effective communication lines is essential. Something as simple as notification of meeting times and places can play a key part in the process.

Sharing information is also important. All team members should be informed of important events, from policy changes to new technologies and priority modifications. Team members should be encouraged to cross traditional departmental boundaries and establish networks with other team members and other external sources. Maximum cooperation occurs when people know they will have to deal with each other again.

5. Adaptability. Keeping pace in the rapidly changing workplace requires adaptability and flexibility. In a 1988 article by Nancy K. Austin, Buck Rodgers, former vice president of marketing at IBM, is quoted as saying that "one of the things needed most urgently today is a company's ability to respond quickly. People working shoulder-to-shoulder in teams can get things done much faster than individuals out to protect their own turf or those who may be required to obtain dozens of approvals of higher-ups before they can proceed." Meeting the challenge of change can serve to inspire team responsiveness and heighten synergism.

Studies have shown that employees like participating in group or team activities and appreciate opportunities to contribute their ideas and knowledge toward improving operations. Increasing an employee's sense of responsibility translates directly into greater job satisfaction and loyalty.

Formal team leaders must be willing to share control.

John Naisbitt, in his book *Megatrends*, states that being a formal leader in the Information Age is different from leading in the traditional Industrial Era, when assembly-line workers each performed a specific independent task daily. Working as a team requires new management methods. It does not mean that the formal leader never leads. Today's formal leader must learn to allow others to assume a guiding role when appropriate. The choice of leaders in a truly effective team is made by consensus, and the team will usually select the leader based on strengths. Decisions are based on logic and agreed to by team members rather than dictated by authority or position power. The ability to acknowledge others' leadership ability and let go is a sign of an effective formal leader.

Identifying Effective Team Members

Donna Lopiano, director of women's athletics at the University of Texas, in a speech on effective teambuilding presented at a National Management Association conference, recommended acquiring "Blue Chippers" or the best team members possible. She suggested tolerance for "fatal flaws," allowing team members to make occasional mistakes. The freedom to make mistakes allows growth through trial-and-error learning.

Encourage team members to contribute their strengths and expertise.

If you are selecting team members, a cross-section of talents with each member representing expertise in a separate discipline is desirable. However, when drawing a team from an existing group, you may need to rely on the strengths of certain individuals and develop abilities in others. You may choose to cross-train or rotate employees to enhance their knowledge of operations. You should recognize valuable traits in individuals and encourage them to flourish. Figure 12.2 identifies characteristics of good team players whom you should enlist or develop.

FIGURE 12.2   Characteristics of a good team player.

A good team member generally:
- Thinks in "we/us/our" terms versus "I/me/mine."
- Is flexible.
- Is willing to share information, ideas, and recognition.
- Gets along well with others.
- Exhibits interest and enthusiasm.
- Remains loyal to team purpose and team members.

Importance of Communication, Networking, and Human Relations Skills

Once team members understand their roles and mission, communication, networking, and other human relation skills become important. One of the key ingredients for any team effort is open communication. It enhances creativity and camaraderie among team members and adds to the bottom line of improved productivity.

Open communication and networking enhance the team's creativity.

In a study done by Arthur D. Little, Inc., a research and consulting firm, researchers found a common positive attribute in ten of the United States' most innovative companies. The key was an organizational style stressing easy communication and networking. Innovation increased when collaboration disrupted the hierarchical power flows. Successful corporations such as 3M, IBM, AT&T, and General Foods place emphasis on internal communications and networking with the belief that the enormous information base thus created fosters new ideas and stimulates innovation and creativity.

Because an effective team is able to communicate openly and is highly cohesive, good human relations skills are in constant use. To examine some of these aspects, you need only ask the following questions about your team and its members. Are we supportive of one another? Do we share how we feel about important things? Are we effective listeners? Do we confront individuals who take unfair advantage of situations? Developing these basic human relations skills can go a long way toward improving your team's overall output.

HOW DOES A TEAM AFFECT ITS MEMBERS?

Teamwork strengthens ownership, involvement, and responsibility.

Being on a team has advantages. It creates a cycle of positive dynamics with each part reinforcing the other. This enables individual team members to reach high levels of performance. Teams are the most effective means to stimulate participation and involvement by employees. Most individuals have difficulty feeling a strong sense of identity with or loyalty to an organization when they think that their impact is minimal. However, as team members, they have a sense of making real contributions and feel that their impact is direct and appreciated. This increased feeling of worth improves their commitment to the goals and objectives of the team and the organization:

> **Josh grinned as he hung the certificate on the wall of his office. His group had again been honored for being the most productive unit at the agency. He enjoyed the attention and respect he received for being a member of the best team in the office.**
>
> **"Well," he thought, as he sat back down at the desk, "let's see what I can do on the Bryers' file. Doing a good job on this file will help meet the group goals for next quarter. I know that Janice and the other team members will appreciate my efforts on this one."**

Figure 12.3 identifies the many benefits derived from teamwork. The benefits listed were developed by Mark Bassin in an article on teamwork at General Foods.

FIGURE 12.3 Benefits of teamwork.

- Increased commitment and ownership of goals
- Higher sustained effort toward goal accomplishment
- Improved self-confidence and sense of well being for team members
- Increased levels of team member motivation, enthusiasm, and job satisfaction
- Improved decision-making and problem-solving results
- Greater emotional support within team structure
- Greater endurance and energy levels from team members
- Greater reservoir of ideas and information
- Increased sharing of individual skills
- Increased productivity
- Improved quality and quantity output
- Improved loyalty to goals and objectives

General Foods, one of several large companies using self-managing work teams, has discovered that its best chance for reaching levels of peak performance is to establish business work teams throughout its operation.

Disadvantages

However, drawbacks do exist in the teamwork process. For example, some team members feel anonymous. Employees frequently believe that teamwork is fine for others but not for them and say that "I have to stand out or I'm going to be overlooked."

This reaction seems to be directly tied to promotion and reward systems currently in place in most organizations. Few are structured to allow adequate recognition of exemplary performance of a "team." The current hierarchical structure prevents everyone from being promoted en masse. In fact, one study found that most people at the top of the pyramid got there by being rugged individualists who merely paid homage to the idea of teamwork and rose to positions of power and influence through personal accomplishment and recognition.

Team membership gives individuals less recognition.

Another drawback to teamwork is having to promote the team's purpose and goal before or in place of personal career goals. Often individuals have to be concerned with areas outside their specific interest, compromising their individual desires. Strong commitment to a team is often viewed as a restriction on career movement and mobility:

Laura tapped her pencil on the desk impatiently. "I'm not going to share my idea with the group," she thought. "I'm tired of sitting here in this position, not getting promoted."

No one ever seemed to notice her, even though she worked hard and came up with some good ideas to save the company

money. In fact, Laura was the informal team leader, and without her contributions and expertise the team would not have gotten the award for the most innovative group last year.

"This time I'm going to present my idea directly to the vice president. I'm not even going to tell Alex because he will just give me a hard time about not sharing it with everyone else."

Figure 12.4 captures the major drawbacks of team involvement. These factors show that a team approach is not always welcome.

FIGURE 12.4   Drawbacks of team membership.

- Fear of individual anonymity
- Restricted opportunity for personal career advancement
- Loss of power and authority
- Need to be generalists versus specialists in career field
- Team commitments overshadow personal desires
- Current leadership not geared to team concepts
- Duplication of effort
- Time wasted in team interaction
- Conflict and infighting

DO TEAMS FIT ALL OCCASIONS?

The team approach is not always the best strategy.

For a teamwork approach to work, participants must buy into the premise that, in order to succeed, they must commit to helping those around them succeed and that all the team members will be held personally responsible for the outcome. This adjustment is difficult for most individuals. Douglas McGregor identified the most common characteristics of effective and ineffective teams in *The Human Side of Enterprise*. Figure 12.5 identifies his key team effectiveness factors.

Part of the problem occurs because organizations are in transition. Current structures and operating styles do not lend themselves readily to the universal use of teamwork. However, in situations where team concepts can be used, the benefits are well worth the effort of implementation and adaptation. Teams inspire peak performance and confer a critical, competitive edge.

HOW CAN YOU BE AN EFFECTIVE TEAM MEMBER?

When you are a member of a team, at work or elsewhere, you can help make the team effective and the experience pleasant if you remember certain suggestions:

1. Know your role. Be aware of your strengths and weaknesses and what you can contribute to the group effort. If you are unsure about team goals and objectives, ask.

FIGURE 12.5   McGregor's key factors in team effectiveness.

Characteristics of an Effective Team

1. The "atmosphere" is a working atmosphere that tends to be informal, comfortable, and relaxed. People are involved and interested.
2. There is a lot of discussion in which virtually everyone participates, but it remains pertinent to the task.
3. The task or objective of the group is well understood and accepted by the members.
4. The members listen to each other!
5. There is disagreement. Disagreements are not suppressed or overridden by premature group action.
6. Where there are basic disagreements that cannot be resolved and action is necessary, it will be taken but with open caution and recognition that the action may be subject to later reconsideration.
7. Most decisions are reached by a kind of consensus in which it is clear that everybody is in general agreement and willing to go along.
8. Criticism is frequent, frank, constructive, and relatively comfortable.
9. People are free in expressing their feelings as well as their ideas both on the problem and the group's operation.
10. When action is taken, clear assignments are made and accepted.
11. The leader of the group does not dominate it, nor on the contrary does the group defer unduly to him or her.
12. The group is self-conscious about its own operation.

Characteristics of an Ineffective Team

1. Domination by the leader.
2. Warring cliques or subgroups.
3. Unequal participation and uneven use of group resources.
4. Rigid or dysfunctional group norms and procedures.
5. A climate of defensiveness or fear.
6. Uncreative alternatives to problems.
7. Restricted communications.
8. Avoidance of differences or potential conflicts.

Douglas McGregor, The Human Side of Enterprise *(New York: McGraw-Hill, 1962). Copyright 1962. Reproduced with permission of McGraw-Hill, Inc.*

An effective team member needs extensive human relations skills.

2. Be a willing team player. At times you may be asked to perform tasks that you dislike or with which you disagree. Realize how performing these assignments will contribute to the group productivity and perform them willingly.
3. Cooperate with other team members. Harmony is enhanced by using open communication and solid human relations skills.
4. Support other team members by giving them encouragement and assisting them when necessary with their tasks.
5. Share the praise. Do not claim all of the credit for yourself if a team effort was involved.
6. When conflict occurs, attempt to turn it into a positive experience.

FIGURE 12.6   Participation can help individuals achieve productivity and recognition that they could not attain individually.

IS CONFLICT BAD?

Introducing change sets the stage for conflict. Although conflict is often regarded as a barrier to teamwork, it is actually an essential part of the process. **Conflict** is defined as disagreement between individuals or groups about goals. It is inevitable. If no conflict occurs in a group, the group may actually be ineffective because members do not care about outcomes or make suggestions. Conflict does become a problem, however, when it is excessive, becomes disruptive, or causes a team to become dysfunctional.

Competition is a healthy struggle toward goal accomplishment without interference, even when the goals are incompatible. Competition can stimulate beneficial and creative ideas and methods by team members, whereas excessive conflict typically limits creativity. The difference between the two is highlighted in the following example:

Archibald did not know what he was going to do. His team was literally falling apart. A promotion had opened up in another section and both Wilma and Charles wanted the position badly. A decision would not be made until next month. In the meantime the two of them were fighting constantly. Wilma began by refusing to answer Charles's telephone while he was away from his desk. This caused Archibald to receive several calls from irate customers. Then, to strike back at Wilma, Charles accidentally "lost" the big report Wilma was to submit on Wednesday. Wilma had to stay late three nights to reconstruct the data. "This conflict has to stop," Archibald thought.

He wished that the team were the way it used to be. Wilma and Charles had always competed with each other. The competition had not been harmful, however. Wilma would always want to know how many customer complaints Charles was going to resolve for the week and would try to better his mark. Charles kept a watchful eye on Wilma's ability to write reports and would ask Archibald for some assistance so that he could learn to write better reports than Wilma.

Archibald shook his head. He dreaded hearing who got the promotion. He hoped that it wasn't either one of them. Then maybe the situation would return to normal.

Conflict can be healthy and positive if handled properly. Team members may be inspired or stimulated to resolve issues and reach new heights of creativity. Although too much conflict may be disruptive or destructive, too little conflict generally results in apathy or stagnation. A moderate amount of conflict controlled through resolution techniques can be of benefit to both the organization and the team members and can assure peak performance.

WHAT CAUSES CONFLICT?

You must identify the cause of conflict before you can resolve it.

Conflict can be experienced by any team member or by the team as a whole. Five causes are common:

Incompatibility. Personality conflicts may arise within the team or even between two teams. Within the team, a conflict may occur between a supervisor and a subordinate or between any two or more team members.

Between teams, ill feelings may exist for a variety of reasons. For example, plant operators may resent corporate engineers who design and implement changes that do not work well. The engineers may look down on the plant operators. Such conflict may create considerable trouble.

Organizational Reliance. In most organizations, teams rely upon one another. For example, machine operators depend upon the maintenance crews to perform periodic maintenance on equipment. A production team may rely on the sales team to provide orders from customers to keep the production line in full operation. Conflict may arise between the teams if maintenance is slipshod or if sales orders force production into overtime to meet unrealistic schedules.

Goal Ambiguity. Team goals may differ from the goals of the organization. For example, the organization may want to hurry processes and jeopardize quality of product in order to get the job out and turn a profit. The work teams may want to take time to assure quality. The goals of the two groups clearly conflict.

Labor-Management Disputes. Labor and management have long had disagreements over work conditions, hours, and wages. However, the trouble often goes deeper. Conflicts may be based on roles that each feels necessary to portray. Management representatives may believe that "squaring off" with union representatives just prior to contract negotiations is necessary to set the stage. These situations are normal when the union and management have opposing views.

Unclear Roles. The uncertainty brought on by constant changes in roles and missions breeds conflict. These environmental changes cause instability among team members, and conflict will occur. Good communication among team members helps control this type of conflict.

HOW IS CONFLICT RESOLVED?

Various methods resolve conflicts in the workplace.

Conflict resolution is the active management of conflict through defining and solving issues between individuals, groups, or organizations. Given the fact that conflict is part of any team environment, understanding how to manage it is important.

In a study conducted by Ronald J. Burke on methods of resolving conflict, five techniques proved to be the most common and effective ways of handling conflict:

Avoidance. This technique involves totally refraining from confronting the conflict. Avoiding the situation can buy some time to learn additional facts surrounding the conflict or provide a "cooling off" period. It does not resolve the conflict but is often of immediate help.

Smoothing. Accommodating the differences between the two parties, smoothing plays down strong issues and concentrates on mutual interests. Negative issues are seldom even discussed.

Compromising. This technique does address the issue but seldom resolves it to the complete satisfaction of both parties. There is no clear winner or loser.

Forcing. Forcing results when two groups reach an impasse and allow an authoritative figure to choose one preference rather than work toward a mutually agreeable solution. This is considered a win-lose situation.

Confrontation. Although it sounds like a negative approach, confrontation is actually the most positive. It can create a win-win situation. Openly exchanging information and actively working through the differences assures that some agreeable resolution is reached.

These techniques give you some choices for dealing with conflict. The critical message when confronted with confusion or disagreements among team members is to be alert and aware that the conflict exists, look for the causes, understand the reasons as much as possible, and then meet the conflict head on to bring it to resolution.

SUMMARY

Organizations use teamwork because it increases productivity. This concept was used in corporations as early as the 1920s, but it has become increasingly important in recent years as employees demand more direct involvement and companies strive to gain a competitive edge in the ever-changing marketplace.

Five basic ingredients must be present for a team to be effective. The team must have a vision, feel interdependence, have good leadership, use effective means of coordination, and have a high degree of adaptability.

Although a formal leader will be present in most teams, leadership is commonly shared without fear of loss of power. Good team members can be selected or developed and can be coached to share responsibility in achieving the team's goals and mission.

Effective networking systems and open communication are both required for maximum team effectiveness. The benefits derived from the use of teams outweigh the drawbacks and point to the usefulness of teamwork when increased productivity and improved quality are desirable. Occasionally, the team approach is not the best method to use, but these occasions are dwindling as companies seek new ways to meet the challenge of the future.

Competition among teams and team members can stimulate creative ideas and methods for accomplishing goals. Conflict, an active ingredient in the team process, can be healthy and positive. Conflict may also be disruptive or destructive. Excessive conflict typically limits creativity and should be properly managed. Major sources of conflict include incompatibility, organizational reliance, goal ambiguity, labor-management disputes, and unclear roles. However, the five common techniques of conflict resolution (avoidance, smoothing, compromising, forcing, and confrontation) can bring positive results.

KEY TERMS

team
teamwork
teambuilding
synergism
problem-solving teams
special-purpose teams
self-managing teams
conflict
competition
conflict resolution

avoidance
smoothing
compromising
forcing
confrontation

REVIEW QUESTIONS

1. Why are team concepts necessary in today's work environment and why are they successful?
2. How do effective teams increase productivity?
3. What are the steps in building an effective team?
4. Why are communication and networking important ingredients in team-building?
5. What are some of the benefits and drawbacks of team membership?
6. What can you do to become an effective team member?
7. What is the difference between conflict and competition? Why can they both be healthy for an organization?
8. What are the most common techniques in conflict resolution?

DISCUSSION QUESTIONS

1. You are responsible for building a team to improve quality and productivity in your work unit. Outline your approach and describe your reasoning.
2. Describe a conflict that you have experienced within a team setting. Identify the causes and discuss what conflict resolution techniques might have been used.
3. Identify a problem within your community. If you were the formal leader assigned to correct the problem, what types of individuals would you choose for your team? How would you approach the task of team formation?
4. Think of a team with which you have been involved recently. Identify the disciplines or areas of expertise that were represented in the team. How did they serve the team's purpose?
5. Identify tasks in your work or volunteer organization setting that are more efficiently performed by teams than by individuals.

CASE STUDY 12.1

THE MAGIC AT MAGILL MANUFACTURING

Anita Magill took over as chief executive officer at Magill Manufacturing after her father retired from running the business for 32 years. Magill Manufacturing was a keystone company in Lisbon, Ohio, and provided jobs to a large number of the citizens in the community. She took great pride in continuing the family business but knew that she would run the operation differently than her father had.

After only a short period of time in her new position, Anita realized the company was suffering from symptoms of high absenteeism, chronic tardiness, and low morale. Frequent complaints had been filed, employee attitudes were poor, and a general discontent existed among workers. Management was viewed as coercive, with "little dictators" running isolated kingdoms throughout the company. Employees felt that managers gave little support to their ideas or suggestions. Working at Magill Manufacturing had become a way to draw a paycheck and little more. These conditions were reflected in slumping productivity and declining quality of the products.

Anita knew that she needed to act quickly if she were going to turn this situation around. She felt a strong commitment to improving the quality of product, increasing productivity, and creating company loyalty. Her course was clearly charted.

1. How can Anita use team concepts to improve conditions at Magill Manufacturing?
2. What positive changes might be expected from the use of teams in the problem-solving process?
3. Do you think that the employees will respond to the new methods? Why or why not?

CASE STUDY 12.2

THE LEFT-HANDED PRESSURE VALVE

The engineering office issued design drawings for the installation of a pressure valve in the plant. The design had been developed by the corporate engineers without consulting the users of the valve. Reviewing the design drawings, the operations people noticed problems with the design. They said nothing, however, because the engineers had not asked for their input.

The operators waited until the valve had been fabricated and installed before they told the engineers why the valve would not work. Indignantly they demonstrated that the valve could only be accessed from the left side and could not even be seen if approached from the right side. The entire operation had to be returned to the drawing board and redesigned, refabricated, and reinstalled incorporating the suggestions made by the operators.

1. What was the relationship between the two team groups? How effective was the approach taken by the engineers?
2. What did this conflict cost the company?
3. What techniques might have been employed to prevent the conflict in the first place? How might future conflict be prevented?

BIBLIOGRAPHY

Austin, Nancy K. "How to Position Yourself as a Leader." ***Working Woman*** (November 1988): 140–144.

Bassin, Marc. "Teamwork at General Foods: New and Improved." ***Personnel Journal*** (May 1988): 62–70.

Belzer, Ellen J. "Twelve Ways to Better Team Building." ***Working Woman*** (August 1989): 62–70.

Burke, Ronald J. "Methods of Resolving Interpersonal Conflicts." In ***A Contingency Approach to Management Readings***, edited by John W. Newstrom. New York: McGraw-Hill, 1975.

Calano, Jimmy, and Jeff Salzman. "Lead Your Team to Victory." ***Working Woman*** (August 1989): 86–90.

Hoerr, John P. "Is Teamwork a Management Plot? Mostly Not!" ***Business Week*** (February 1989): 70.

Kanter, Rosabeth Moss. "How the Kinder, More Cooperative Corporation Wins." ***Working Woman*** (May 1989): 120.

King, Pamela. "What Makes Teamwork Work?" ***Psychology Today*** (December 1989): 16–17.

Lopiano, Donna. Speech on "Effective Teambuilding" presented at The National Management Association's regional conference in Austin, TX, May 1988.

McGregor, Douglas. ***The Human Side of Enterprise***. New York: McGraw Hill, 1962.

Naisbitt, John. ***Megatrends***. New York: Warner Books, 1982.

Reifsnyder, Abigail W. "Who's in Charge?" ***Success***. (November 1986):49–52.

Webster's Ninth New Collegiate Dictionary. Springfield, MA: Merriam-Webster Inc., 1985.

PART FOUR

LAWS AND ETHICS

CHAPTER THIRTEEN
EMPLOYEE RIGHTS

A federal jury awarded $3.8 million in damages to former Quasar employees in an age discrimination suit. In *Fortino* v. *Quasar Co.* (No. 87-C4386, N.D. Ill. 11/14/88)), three plaintiffs were awarded back pay, front pay, and liquidated damages for a number of actions ruled to be Quasar's willful violations of the Age Discrimination in Employment Act. Quasar had discharged three senior middle managers during a reorganization of the company. The company had also hired new people under 40 while eliminating the jobs of more senior people. A sales meeting videotape had been shown in which an executive boasted, "Because of a change in our TV group organization at headquarters, our average age of employees has become a lot younger, and that means we will be ready to spend many hours day and night to help you out in your work." The personnel manager had also made a list of employees over 55 years old when he heard about the reduction in force.

Resource (March 1989): 15
prepared by David Israel

The Occupational Safety and Health Administration announced on November 25, 1988, that IBP Inc., the nation's largest meat packer, agreed to pay $975,000 as part of a settlement. IBP Inc. had been charged with illegal safety practices that caused hand, wrist, and arm injuries to employees.

Resource (December 1988): 16
prepared by David Israel

The United States District Court, Eastern District of New York (*Robert Capaldo* v. *Pan American Federal Credit Union*, F.2d., 43 EPD (CCH) (¶ 37,016) ruled in 1987 that the credit union did not commit sex discrimination when it discharged a male employee for refusing to remove an earring. The plaintiff, Robert Capaldo, was a loan counselor whose job duties included taking loan applications and conducting loan interviews. The president of the credit union said that he did not think Mr. Capaldo was presenting an appropriate professional image. Mr. Capaldo was then discharged for refusing to remove the earring.

The court further stated that deciding the issue of whether wearing an earring constituted symbolic speech was not necessary because Mr. Capaldo only asserted this claim as an afterthought. However, the court seriously questioned this defense and doubted that the credit union's action would be constrained by the First Amendment.

Employment Practices Decisions
43 ¶ 37,016

OBJECTIVES

After studying this chapter, you should be able to:
1. Identify and discuss federal employment discrimination laws.
2. Explain how OSHA protects employees from safety and health hazards.
3. Demonstrate a working knowledge of fair labor standards.
4. Name benefits available to employees and distinguish between those that are required and those that are optional.
5. Identify and discuss other employee rights at work.

WHAT LAWS PROTECT WORKERS?

Local, state, and federal laws regulate five aspects of employment. These regulations cover employment discrimination, employee safety, fair labor standards, employee benefits, and miscellaneous employee rights. Both individuals and organizations need to understand these regulations.

Individuals should understand what their rights are and how to take appropriate action when those rights are violated. Sometimes employees assume they have rights on the job that they, in fact, do not. Problems may arise when employees act on these assumptions. The consequences can range from lost promotions or raises to disciplinary action or termination.

Organizations also need to be aware of, and respect, employee rights. Violating employee rights can lead to costly investigations by federal and/or state agencies. These investigations require the submission of paperwork and can disrupt the workplace by removing employees from the job to provide witness statements. In addition, employees may spend time discussing or worrying about the impending investigations rather than working. Violations may require payment of fines or back pay and reinstatement of employees. Payment for damages may be required as a result of a lawsuit. More important, employees whose rights are abused will be unhappy and less productive.

Because laws in the area of employee rights change rapidly, both employees and organizations must keep track of changes. *Consult a lawyer for recent changes* in legislation discussed in this chapter and for an explanation of state and local laws.

WHAT IS EMPLOYMENT DISCRIMINATION?

Abraham Lincoln abolished slavery on January 1, 1863, by signing the Emancipation Proclamation. However, the freed slaves continued to be deprived of their liberty and blocked in their pursuit of happiness through **discrimination**, or a difference in treatment based on a factor other than individual merit. A grassroots movement began in the 1950s, demanding that these inequities be corrected. As a result several acts were passed in the 1960s and 1970s to protect blacks and others against discrimination in the workplace.

FIGURE 13.1   Various laws regulate the workplace.

Which Federal Laws Regulate Discrimination in the Workplace?

Title VII of the Civil Rights Act of 1964, the Pregnancy Discrimination Act, the Equal Pay Act, and the Age Discrimination in Employment Act were enacted to stop discrimination in the workplace. The **Equal Employment Opportunity Commission** (EEOC) is the federal agency responsible for enforcing these laws. These acts are briefly summarized below.

Federal law requires equal treatment of workers, regardless of color, religion, sex, race, age, or national origin.

Title VII of the Civil Rights Act (1964)   Title VII of the Civil Rights Act of 1964 prohibits discrimination by companies that have 15 or more employees. Discrimination based on race, color, religion, sex, or national origin is forbidden. All terms, conditions, and privileges are covered—hiring, placement, training, promotions, transfers, layoffs, compensation, and terminations. This act also prohibits sexual harassment. The following examples demonstrate Title VII at work:

> **Susan (White), Juanita (Hispanic), and Joan (Black) have applied for a position as an accountant at a local firm. The position requires a college degree and two to five years of accounting experience. Joan has five years of experience and a degree in accounting. Susan has not yet completed her degree but plans to do so next year. Juanita has a degree but no experience. All three women have excellent human relations skills and interview well. The employer is required to hire the best qualified candidate, which is Joan. Failure to do so could be ruled to be discrimination**

based on race. (Some companies that are federal contractors or are under a court order are sometimes required to promote individuals who may not be the best qualified candidates in order to correct inequities in the work force. This process is known as *affirmative action*.)

Jason (White) is a member of a road construction crew. His boss is Miguel (Hispanic). All other members of the crew are Black or Hispanic. Miguel allows other crew members several breaks a day. However, when Jason tried to take a break along with his coworkers, he was told to get back to work. Jason has been discriminated against because of his race.

James belongs to a religious sect that worships on Thursdays. His employer works shifts 24 hours a day, 7 days a week. His employer must attempt to accommodate James's religious schedule, provided that it does not cause undue hardship on the company. James has found another employee who has agreed to switch shifts with him. This accommodation must be allowed provided that the switch does not require more than ordinary administrative costs. Not to do so would constitute religious discrimination.

Karen is the only female engineer in her section. Five male engineers also work under her male boss, Calvin. One secretary (female) has been assigned to assist the group. When the secretary is ill or out to lunch, Calvin requires Karen to perform the secretary's duties, such as answering the telephone. None of the male engineers, some of whom have been with the company less time than Karen, is required to perform secretarial duties. Calvin is discriminating against Karen in terms and conditions of employment based on sex. (If Calvin makes all engineers take turns answering the telephone and performing clerical duties, no discrimination exists. Even though clerical work is not in their job description, he has treated them equally by assigning these tasks to all.)

Hong-Ling speaks English with an accent. She has been denied a promotion to the position of senior data entry clerk. Although she is the best qualified, she is not promoted because of her accent. Her position requires little oral communication. She has been discriminated against because of her national origin.

These actions are discriminatory because they are based on factors other than individual merit. Actions based on presumptions, such as that an individual is not capable because of color or accent, are outlawed in the workplace.

Some employers attempted to get around Title VII by setting specific qualifications for a position. For instance, some police departments set height and weight requirements that effectively eliminated females from the position of officer. These practices were curbed by requiring a **bona fide occupational qualification (BFOQ).** The employer must show a legitimate business necessity for eliminating certain groups of individuals from a job. Requiring proof that restrictions are bona fide has limited the use of discriminatory occupational qualifications by employers. However, some restrictions have been found to be valid. For instance, a producer may hire only females for a female role in a movie. Legitimate age limitations may be placed on some occupations, such as airline pilot. The courts have ruled, however, that preferences, such as females for airline attendants, are not BFOQs.

Pregnancy Discrimination Act (1978)   The **Pregnancy Discrimination Act** is an amendment to the Civil Rights Act of 1964. An employer cannot refuse to hire a woman because of pregnancy as long as the woman is able to perform the job.

A pregnant woman may work as long as she is able to perform the job and may not be required to stay out a certain length of time after the baby is born. Pregnant employees are to be treated the same as nonpregnant employees who are temporarily disabled, as the following example indicates:

> **Sylvia held a job at a local lumber mill, pulling logs off a conveyor belt. During her fourth month of pregnancy, Sylvia presented her employer with a doctor's statement that she could not perform the heavy work required. She was immediately terminated. Her co-worker, Don, was in a car wreck and, due to his injuries, was unable to perform his work. Upon presentation of his doctor's notice, he was reassigned to the weigh station to log trucks in and out. Discrimination exists because the pregnant employee has been treated differently from the nonpregnant employee.**

Federal law does not require that special considerations, such as light duty, be made for pregnant women. It does, however, require that pregnant women be treated the same as others who are temporarily disabled. If nonpregnant individuals are given light duty, pregnant individuals must be allowed the same privilege.

A company is required to hold a job open for a woman on maternity leave the same length of time that jobs are held open for other employees who are on sick leave or disability leave but are not pregnant. This law does not guarantee a position upon return from maternity leave. If the company routinely fills positions of persons who are sick for other reasons, it may legally fill positions of persons who are on maternity leave. Some states, such as California, require that a position be held open for a certain length of time after the start of maternity leave.

Equal Pay Act (1963)   The **Equal Pay Act** requires that men and women be paid the same for equivalent work. For instance, a male and female teacher with similar backgrounds and experience are to be paid equal salaries.

The inequities that the Equal Pay Act are designed to correct are not found as frequently in the workplace as they once were. However, a new issue, which revolves around the differences in salaries paid in traditionally female occupations versus salaries in traditionally male occupations, has emerged. This issue is known as **comparable worth.** For instance, a female-dominated position such as secretary that requires skills and responsibility may command lower wages than a male-dominated position such as janitor that requires fewer skills. This issue is expected to command more attention in the future.

Age Discrimination in Employment Act (1967)   The **Age Discrimination in Employment Act** prohibits employers with 20 or more employees from discriminating based on age. The law covers persons 40 years of age and older. As long as employees are able to perform their jobs, they cannot be forced to retire. However, an exception for highly paid corporate executives does exist.

Sexual Harassment   Sexual harassment in the workplace is prohibited by the Civil Rights Act of 1964. **Sexual harassment** includes any *unwelcome* sexual advances, requests for sexual favors, or verbal or physical conduct of a sexual nature. Examples are telling sexually oriented jokes, standing too close, touching and making physical contact, displaying sexually oriented material, or making sexual comments about a person's body if these actions are unwelcome.

Either sex can commit sexual harassment. Men can harass women, and women can harass men. Additionally, men can harass men, and women can harass women. Harassment can be from a coworker, supervisor, an agent of the employer, or a nonemployee such as a repair person who comes on the company premises to perform work. Organizations are responsible for stopping the harassment from a coworker, nonemployee, or agent of an employer as soon as a management official becomes aware of the harassment. Furthermore, they are responsible for the harassment from a supervisor whether other management officials are aware of the harassment or not.

Employees must make clear that sexual harassment is unwelcome and report it immediately.

The law requires that employers provide an atmosphere free of sexual harassment. However, employees must make it clear that the harassment is unwanted. The individual being harassed, for example, should tell the harasser in no uncertain terms that the comments or actions are not appreciated and to stop. If the harassment continues, the victim should report the harassment to a management official or the human resources department.

How Should I Respond to Discrimination?

If you think you have been the victim of discrimination, you should attempt to settle difficulties within your organization before resorting to outside sources. If your company has a grievance or complaint procedure, use this process. If such a procedure is unavailable, approach your supervisor or a responsible individual in the human resources department. Explain your concerns and difficulties in a calm, clear manner, using the communication skills from Chapter 3. Listen carefully to the explanations of the company officials. External circumstances of which you are not aware may exist. Work with your organization in good faith, giving the company a chance to correct the problem. Such action on your part demonstrates a belief that a person, not the company, is the problem.

If companies do not take action, employees have the right to file charges.

If the company will not take action, you should file a charge of discrimination with the Equal Employment Opportunity Commission or your state commission on equal employment. Employers, by law, cannot retaliate against persons who have filed a charge of discrimination with the EEOC. However, companies can continue disciplinary action that is reasonable and expected and is administered to other employees not filing charges.

What Are Trends in Discrimination Laws?

Employment discrimination legislation is rapidly changing. As our work force becomes more diverse with more minorities and women, a renewed interest in minority rights can be expected. Currently bills are pending in Congress to substantially strengthen present civil rights legislation. A number of Supreme Court cases issued in 1989 made proving discrimination more difficult. Legislation is being developed that would reverse these court decisions. Additionally, a new civil rights bill is being considered that would, for the first time, allow for punitive damages in Title VII cases and extend the time limits for filing complaints.

Other efforts are being made to legally protect individuals who are not traditionally considered to be in the mainstream of the work force. The Americans with Disabilities Act (ADA), effective by 1992, extends the protection afforded under Title VII to those individuals who are disabled. The act defines a disability as a physical or mental impairment that substantially limits one or more of the major life activities of the individual. Individuals with a record of such impairments or those regarded as having such impairments are covered. Additionally, the ADA requires employers to make a reasonable accommodation for a person with a disability unless it poses an undue hardship on the company.

HOW ARE SAFETY AND HEALTH REGULATED?

More than 14,000 workers were killed and over two million were injured in industrial accidents in 1970. Estimates suggested that 300,000 new cases of occupational disease were being discovered annually. These work-related injuries had steadily increased since the 1960s, and no end to this trend was seen. Although many companies were concerned with safety and taking action to provide their employees with a safe environment, these individual actions were not considered sufficient. The public demanded action, which came in the form of the Occupational Safety and Health Act.

The Occupational Safety and Health Act

Federal law requires employers to provide a safe work environment.

The **Occupational Safety and Health Act** was passed in 1970 to "assure so far as possible every working man and woman in the nation safe and healthful working conditions and to preserve our human resources." The act sets health and safety standards for United States businesses. **Safety** standards address hazards that can result in a direct injury, such as broken bones and cuts. **Health** standards address the role of the work environment in the development of diseases and illnesses, such as asbestosis and black lung. (Black lung, or pneumoconiosis, is a disease coal miners acquire from breathing air filled with coal dust.) These types of diseases are known as occupational diseases.

The **Occupational Safety and Health Administration** (OSHA) was established as a federal agency to ensure that each employer provides a place of employment free of recognized hazards causing or likely to cause death or serious harm to

FIGURE 13.2   Companies are responsible for providing a safe work environment.

THE WIZARD OF ID   by Brant parker and Johnny hart

By permission of Johnny Hart and NAS, Inc.

employees. Almost all businesses that affect commerce (except government) are covered. However, only businesses with ten or more employers are required to keep records concerning occupational illnesses or injury.

OSHA establishes standards for safety and health in the workplace. These standards cover many facets of the work environment, such as training and safety procedures for operating hazardous machinery and equipment, instructions for handling dangerous chemicals, permitted noise levels, designation of protective equipment and clothing, and sanitation regulations.

In order to enforce the act, OSHA makes inspections of company sites. These visits may be unscheduled. Unscheduled visits may be in response to complaints of imminent danger or to deaths or catastrophes. Other visits are scheduled in advance. These visits can be prompted by a high injury rate or a specific type of injury reported. Sometimes OSHA chooses a certain industry to monitor.

If violations are found during the visit, citations are issued. These citations must be posted in a public location in the workplace. In the case of gross violations, OSHA can secure a court order to close the facility. Failure to correct the infractions immediately can result in fines or jail sentences.

OSHA further requires that companies give training to employees handling hazardous chemicals. Currently, approximately 32 million workers are exposed to one or more of the estimated 575,000 existing chemicals in the workplace. Material Safety Data Sheets (MSDS), which describe the chemical and the proper first aid treatment, are to be kept where all employees have immediate access in an emergency.

How Do I Assure My Safety?

Every employee has a responsibility to follow OSHA and company rules concerning safety. If you work in an environment that requires goggles or a hard hat, your compliance with these regulations is extremely important. These measures may prevent you from losing an eye or suffering a concussion. Even though workers' compensation helps support an employee who has been injured, payment in any amount can never make up for a lost hand or a damaged back. Specific tips for on-the-job safety are listed in Figure 13.3.

FIGURE 13.3   Tips for working safely.

1. Observe all safety rules.
2. Wear personal protective equipment correctly.
3. Know how to operate all equipment properly. If you do not know, ask.
4. Check equipment before using to be sure it is in proper working condition.
5. Be alert for unsafe conditions.
6. Report any hazardous conditions or malfunctioning equipment immediately to your supervisor.
7. Do not participate in or condone horseplay while working in hazardous areas or while using equipment.

Accidents can be caused by incorrect lifting of equipment or supplies; careless operation of saws, lathes, or machinery with gears, pulleys, and belts; inattention while using hand tools; negligence while working with electricity; or falls on stairs, ladders, and scaffolds.

Office workers also need to be alert to safety. Time has been lost from injuries that occurred when file cabinets tipped over because too many drawers were opened at once. Falls on floors made slick by spilled coffee are another source of injury.

OSHA also gives employees rights under the law. An employee may request an inspection and have a representative, such as a union member, accompany the inspector. Employees may talk to the inspector privately. In addition, regulations can be posted regarding employee rights under the act, and employees can have locations monitored for exposure to toxic or radioactive materials, have access to those records, and have a record of their own exposure.

Employees may have company medical examinations or other tests to determine whether their health is being affected by an exposure and have the results furnished to their personal doctors. Furthermore, employers may not retaliate against employees for exercising their rights under the Occupational Safety and Health Act.

If you ever feel unsafe on the job, you should discuss the problem immediately with your supervisor or the safety committee if your facility has an active one. Should you feel that the danger is life-threatening, you have the right, by law, to refuse to work. If the problem cannot be resolved by working through the company, you should, of course, contact OSHA.

What Are Future Health and Safety Issues?

Health and safety of workers will continue to be a focal point of concern for both employers and employees. Employers, faced with spiraling insurance and worker compensation premiums, will be searching for ways to reduce employment-related injuries and diseases. Furthermore, fit employees are more productive employees, adding incentives for organizations to provide a healthy work environment.

Advanced technology brings with it new dangers and concerns. For instance, employees are raising disturbing questions about exposure to low-level radiation such as that received from video display terminals. Potential health hazards that have been alleged but not proven are reproductive hazards and cataracts. Additionally, new chemicals, whose effects from long-term exposure are unknown, are another source of worry for workers. As medical science advances, the relationship between exposure to certain chemicals and radiation and diseases will most likely be better defined, generating a flurry of new, protective legislation.

The prevalence of computer-related equipment in the workplace brings new health problems, such as eye strain, backaches, headaches, and computer stress. Future technology will most likely bring more problems of this nature that must be resolved. As a result of these changes, the focus will most likely move away from safety and towards health.

WHAT ARE FAIR LABOR STANDARDS?

At the turn of the century children and women were exploited in the nation's factories, farms, and mines. Very young children worked long hours, sometimes 12 to 14 hours a day or all night. They were paid less than adults, which tended to lower the adult wage. Women also were exploited by being subjected to low wages and long hours of work. Public concern mounted, and states began to pass laws restricting child labor and providing a minimum livable wage.

The mass unemployment of the Great Depression of the 1930s brought a public outcry to regulate hours of work in order to allow more individuals to be employed. The result was the first national legislation to regulate working hours, wages, and child labor, which is known as the Fair Labor Standards Act.

The Fair Labor Standards Act (1938)

The **Fair Labor Standards Act** of 1938, as amended in 1966, 1974, 1977, and 1985, sets the minimum wage, equal-pay, overtime, and child-labor standards for several types of employers and employees. They include employers engaged in interstate commerce or the production of goods for commerce and employees who are employed in enterprises engaged in commerce or the production of goods for commerce. Employers in retail and services whose sales volumes exceed a certain amount and agricultural workers are also covered. Certain employees, however, are exempt from minimum wage and/or overtime requirements. They are listed in Figure 13.4.

The minimum wage has slowly increased over the years. In 1981 it was set at $3.35 an hour. The first increase since that time occurred on April 1, 1990, when the minimum wage was raised to $3.80 an hour and then to $4.25 an hour on April 1, 1991. A subminimum training wage allows employers to pay individuals aged 16 to 19 85 percent of the minimum wage (but no less than $3.35) for three months provided that the employer has a certified training program.

FIGURE 13.4 Fair Labor Standards Act exemptions from minimum wage and overtime.

Exempt from Minimum Wage and Overtime

Section 6(f) and 7(l)	Domestic service employees not covered by the Social Security Act nor employed for more than 8 hours per week in the aggregate, from minimum wage, and live-in domestics, from overtime.
Section 13(a)(1)	Outside salesmen, professional, executive, and administrative personnel ("including any employee employed in the capacity of academic administrative personnel or teacher in elementary or secondary schools").
Section 13(a)(2)	Employees of certain retail or service establishments which do not qualify as or are not in an enterprise engaged in commerce or in the production of goods for commerce.
Section 13(a)(3)	Employees of certain seasonal amusements or recreational establishments.
Section 13(a)(4)	Employees of retail establishments which customarily manufacture goods they sell if such establishment would otherwise qualify as an exempt retail establishment.
Section 13(a)(5)	Fishing and first processing at sea employees.
Section 13(a)(6)	Agricultural employees employed by farms utilizing fewer than 500 man-days of agricultural labor, employed by a member of their immediate family, certain local seasonal harvest laborers and seasonal hand harvest laborers 16 years of age or under, and employees principally engaged in the range production of livestock.
Section 13(a)(7)	Employees exempt under Section 14 of the Act (certain learners, apprentices, students and handicapped workers).
Section 13(a)(8)	Employees of certain small newspapers.
Section 13(a)(10)	Switchboard operators of certain independently owned small telephone companies.
Section 13(a)(12)	Seamen on foreign vessels.
Section 13(a)(15)	Babysitters employed on a casual basis and persons employed to provide companion services.

Exempt from Overtime

Section 7(b)	Certain employees under collectively bargained guaranteed annual wage plans and wholesale or bulk petroleum distribution employees.
Section 7(i)	Certain commission salesmen in retail or service establishments.
Section 7(n)	Local transit employees when performing certain charter activities.
Section 13(b)(1)	Motor carrier employees.
Section 13(b)(2)	Railroad employees.
Section 13(b)(3)	Airline employees.
Section 13(b)(5)	Outside buyers of poultry, eggs, cream, milk.
Section 13(b)(6)	Seamen.
Section 13(b)(9)	Announcers and news editors of certain small radio or television stations.
Section 13(b)(10)	Certain salesmen, partsmen, and mechanics.
Section 13(b)(11)	Drivers and drivers helpers paid on a trip basis.
Section 13(b)(12)	Agricultural employees.

FIGURE 13.4 *(continued)*

Section 13(b)(13)	Farm workers engaged in livestock auction operations.
Section 13(b)(14)	Employees of certain country elevators.
Section 13(b)(15)	Maple sap employees.
Section 13(b)(16)	Employees engaged in transportation of farm products.
Section 13(b)(17)	Taxicab drivers.
Section 13(b)(21)	Domestic service employees residing on employers' premises.
Section 13(b)(24)	Substitute parents for institutionalized children.
Section 13(b)(27)	Motion picture theatre employees.
Section 13(b)(28)	Employees of small loggers (crews with fewer than nine employees).
Section 13(b)(29)	Employees of amusements or recreational establishments located in a national park or national forest or on land in the National Wildlife Refuge system.

Reprinted with permission from Labor Relations Reporter—Wages and Hours, *90:4. Copyright by The Bureau of National Affairs, Inc.*

Overtime provisions require payment of time and one-half of the employee's regular rate for all hours worked in excess of 40 hours per week. This base rate must include incentive pay or bonuses received in that week. A workweek is considered to be seven consecutive days and may begin on any day of the week. State and local governments are allowed to pay compensatory time in lieu of overtime.

The law exempts four basic groups of employees from the overtime requirements—executive, administrative, professional, and outside salespersons. The regulations concerning who is exempt are complex, and the Department of Labor should be contacted concerning these exemptions.

Individuals under 18 years of age are not allowed to work in hazardous occupations. Individuals 14 to 16 years old are allowed to work in industries other than manufacturing, but their duties cannot conflict with school. Exceptions to the age limitations are for newspaper carriers, farm workers, and wreath makers.

If you feel your rights to fair wages and hours have been violated, attempt to work it out with your employer first. If this attempt fails, contact the Wage and Hour Division of the Department of Labor.

What Are Future Issues Concerning Fair Labor Standards?

One area of growing concern is parental leave. Legislation is currently pending that would require employers to grant leave for birth, adoption, disability, or serious illness of a child or parent. This type of legislation would ease the burden of single parents and with two working parents.

Issues concerning payment of overtime are developing as companies are forced to become more competitive in the workplace. They are finding that working a skilled work force a bit more is less expensive than hiring and training new workers. Additionally, some professionals who are exempt from overtime are routinely putting in 70 to 80 hours a week. Many feel individuals working excessive hours are being

FIGURE 13.5   Younger employees are being hired to work in fast food establishments.

exploited. Suggestions have been made to limit hours of work for everyone or to raise overtime pay to double pay.

The abuse of child labor, an issue once considered under control, is again appearing. The General Accounting Office reported that in 1989 the number of violations of child labor laws was up 250 percent from 1983. Most of the violations occurred in the retail trade industry, which includes fast food establishments. These employers, who are faced with labor shortages and a declining number of teenagers who are able to work, are hiring younger employees and working them longer. The result is that schools are reporting students who are too tired to learn.

Lastly, the idea of a livable minimum wage will always resurface. Stories abound of the working poor, individuals who work 40 hours a week but who earn so little that they are unable to afford decent housing and other basic necessities of life. Periods of inflation will fuel this debate again as we search for a balance between the need for employers to remain competitive in the global economy and the need of the worker to survive.

WHAT ARE EMPLOYEE BENEFITS?

Most employers must provide social security, unemployment compensation, and workers' compensation.

Traditionally, care of those too infirm or too old to work was left to charitable organizations or to families. This method of caring for those unable to help themselves worked fairly well in an agrarian society where an extra mouth could be supported by planting another row of crops or raising extra livestock. However, urbanization and industrialization began to put a strain on the ability of individuals to care for extended families. Some organizations initiated benefit programs for their employees, but the majority of employees were left without assistance.

The Great Depression intensified the crisis, leaving a great many individuals without work and unable to provide the basics for themselves, much less for their dependents. As a result, legislation was enacted that required organizations to provide retirement benefits, benefits to those who became unemployed, and compensation to those injured on the job.

What Retirement Benefits Are Mandated by Federal Law?

The **Social Security Act** was passed in 1935 and has been amended many times since. Social Security benefits include retirement insurance, survivor's insurance, disability insurance, and Medicare. These benefits are mandatory for approximately 95 percent of all United States workers. The benefits are summarized in Figure 13.6. Social Security was founded to replace a portion of earnings lost as a result of old age, disability, or death—not all lost wages.

FIGURE 13.6   Social Security benefits.

Who May Draw Retirement Benefits
1. Individuals who are fully insured and at least 62 years old.
2. Wife or husband of retiree.
3. Children of retiree if under 18 or disabled.
4. Divorced spouse if 62 or over and married ten years or more.

Who May Draw Disability
1. Individuals who have a physical or mental impairment which lasts or is expected to last one year or more or expected to end in death and who meet the requirements for being insured.
2. Dependents of the disabled individual.

Who May Draw Survivor's Benefits
1. Widow or widower at 60 (50 if disabled) or any age if caring for entitled children under 16 or disabled of a fully insured wage earner.
2. Divorced widow or widower if married over ten years or if caring for entitled child.

Who May Be Covered by Medicare
1. Insured individuals age 65 and over.
2. Disabled individuals who have been entitled to Social Security benefits 24 or more months.
3. Insured workers and their eligible family members who need dialysis or kidney transplant because of permanent kidney failure.

Consult your local Social Security office for details concerning wage credits needed to be fully insured and specific requirements for drawing benefits.

Social Security is funded through payroll taxes. Effective January 1990, employees contribute 7.65 percent of their salary up to a $51,300 maximum. The company matches this contribution. Regardless of the number of companies for whom an employee works, benefits will accumulate in the employee's account.

The Social Security program is administered by the Social Security Administration. You may contact the Administration to review your earnings statement to be sure that your earnings have been correctly recorded and to inquire about details of benefit programs.

What Assistance Is Available after Losing a Job?

Unemployment compensation was created by the Social Security Act of 1935. The federal government set up minimum standards for unemployment compensation, and the states developed their own standards around the minimums. For this reason the state agency governing unemployment compensation should be contacted concerning specific benefits and qualifications.

In most instances employees who quit voluntarily are unable to receive unemployment compensation. Employees also are denied benefits in most states if they have been discharged for misconduct. Misconduct is discussed in Figure 13.7.

Individuals receiving unemployment compensation must be actively seeking employment and must accept suitable employment when offered. States may interpret these terms differently; therefore, you should consult your local unemployment agency when you have specific questions.

FIGURE 13.7   What is misconduct?

Is Misconduct	Is Not Misconduct
Failure to perform work after having demonstrated ability to do the work.	Incompetence; genuine inability to do the work.
Deliberate damage to equipment; willful failure to follow safety rules.	Accidents; negligence; errors that are not the result of reckless conduct.
Unreasonable or excessive use of obscene language in violation of employer's rules.	Isolated incident using obscene language.
Excessive and unjustified absences and tardiness; failure to inform supervisor.	Justified absences and tardiness.
Lying; stealing; using equipment without permission of supervisor.	Age; physical condition; illness; pregnancy.
Failure to obey reasonable rules and follow reasonable orders.	Failure to obey unreasonable rules and follow unreasonable orders.
Unjustified assault on coworker or supervisor.	Justified assault on coworker; self-defense.
Spending too much time socializing at work after being told not to.	Associating with coworkers or marrying coworker in violation of employer's rules.
Refusal to work on the weekend.	Refusal to work on the employee's Sabbath day.

Darien McWhirter, Your Rights at Work *(New York: John Wiley and Sons, 1989)*

The unemployment compensation system is funded through employer taxes. The amount of tax depends on the total wages and the number of former employees drawing unemployment compensation. For this reason employers have an incentive to keep undeserving former employees from drawing unemployment benefits.

What Benefits Are Available after an Injury?

Workers' compensation is a system that compensates individuals who have been physically or mentally injured on their jobs or who have developed an occupational disease. The compensation can include cash payments, reimbursement for medical costs; and, in some cases, the costs of rehabilitation or compensation for survivors of those who have been killed on the job.

Employers are required either to purchase insurance to cover workers' compensation or to become self-insured, and state regulations vary on how they can acquire coverage. Employers do, however, have an incentive to reduce injuries, because injuries mean not only lost time from the job but higher premiums.

Each state has its own compensation laws. Federal employees are covered by the Federal Employees' Compensation Act, and federal coverage is extended to maritime workers on navigable waters of the United States. As with unemployment insurance, the state agency should be contacted for specific details.

Do Employers Offer Voluntary Benefits?

Employers typically offer a number of benefits voluntarily. They have found that attractive benefit packages help draw and keep qualified employees, allowing them to remain competitive in the workplace. The variety of benefits that may be offered by employers is listed in Figure 13.8.

Voluntary plus mandatory benefits can amount to 35 percent of an employee's salary.

These benefits may be paid for in part or in full by the employer. An employer may give employees a choice of benefits so that they can design their own benefit packages. All benefits together, mandatory and optional, average 35 percent of salaries.

In 1974 the federal government enacted the Employee Retirement Income Security Act (ERISA). This act regulates benefit plans for health insurance, group life insurance, sick pay, long-term disability income, pension plans, profit sharing plans, thrift plans, and stock bonus plans. It sets legal standards around which employee benefit plans must be established and administered. In addition, ERISA requires that employees be given a summary plan description and have access to plan financial information. Plan termination insurance, which guarantees benefits if certain types of retirement plans terminate, is another provision of ERISA.

If you have questions concerning your benefits or options, consult your supervisor or the Human Resources Department. The company will have literature or other information that will explain the benefits available in detail.

What Is the Future of Benefits?

Employee benefits will be a controversial topic in the twenty-first century. An aging work force will bring with it the need to revise Social Security regulations that specify

FIGURE 13.8 Voluntary company benefits.

Financial Plans

Pension plans
Profit sharing
Thrift plans
Employee stock ownership plans
Individual retirement accounts

Insurance

Health—hospital, medical, dental, vision, prescription drug
Life insurance
Disability insurance

Payment for Time Not Worked

Vacation
Holidays
Sick leave

Other Benefits or Services

Housing or moving assistance
In-house health services
Flexible work hours
Parental leave
Child care programs
Social or recreational services
Employee assistance plans
Legal services
Financial planning
Assistance or discounts on purchasing food or other goods
Credit unions
Transportation services

how much work an employee is allowed to perform and still draw benefits. Funding can be expected to be an issue because of the large number of individuals who will be drawing benefits.

Already a crisis is brewing concerning medical benefits offered by employers. Many are hiring only part-time workers in an effort to avoid paying medical insurance premiums. Others are shifting the burden of rising premiums to employees, making the cost of health care soar. In a further effort to reduce medical costs, some insurance carriers are dropping the amount of coverage allowed on some claims, which leaves the employee paying an increasing share of medical bills. Legislation is currently being considered that would require employers to provide a minimum package of health benefits to their employees.

WHAT ARE OTHER EMPLOYEE RIGHTS?

In general, our rights as employees differ from those we have away from the workplace. Understanding our rights as employees is crucial to function in the work world. Using sound communication and human relations skills is important as we attempt to work out problems on the job.

The rights of employees of governmental bodies and union members are usually better defined than those of other employees. The rights discussed in the following sections are controversial at this time. Many areas are gray and subject to change. Changes in rights evolve from court and arbitration decisions. At times, court cases can be inconsistent, with one court deciding for an issue while another court is ruling against it.

As an employee, you should be aware that standing on principle over some of the issues discussed below may result in termination. A court case may be needed to decide who is right, and years may pass before the case comes to trial.

State and local law varies in the areas discussed below, and a familiarity with your local law is advisable. *Consult a legal expert for details in these areas of the law.*

What Are Current Employee Rights?

The principle of employment at will is eroding in the United States.

Employment at Will   **Employment at will** means that an employee serves at the discretion of an employer and can be terminated at any time for any reason even if the employee is performing well. The employee also has the right to quit at any point. Presently the legality of this practice is in question, and the law is rapidly changing in this area. In general, most states support the concept of employment at will. However, employees who have contracts or implied contracts should consult an attorney.

The exceptions to employment at will are persons who assert their rights under certain federal legislation, such as the equal employment laws, Occupational Health and Safety Act, Fair Labor Standards Act, Vietnam Era Veterans Reemployment Act, Clean Air Act, and Federal Juror's Protection Law. These people cannot be terminated for exercising those rights.

Courts have also ruled that employees cannot be terminated for filing for workers' compensation benefits, obeying a subpoena, leaving for jury duty, refusing to participate in an employer's lobbying efforts, or reporting an employer's illegal acts.

New employees must prove their identity and their authorization to work.

Proof of Eligibility to Work   The Immigration Reform and Control Act (IRCA) of 1986 bans employment of unauthorized aliens and requires employers to document the identity and authorization to work for all new employees. Employers are required, within three days of hire, to complete an employment eligibility verification form called an I-9 on all new employees. The documents that may be used for identification are listed in Figure 13.9.

FIGURE 13.9 Establishing authorization to work in the United States.

List A Documents that Establish Identity and Employment Eligibility	List B Documents that Establish Identity	**and**	List C Documents that Establish Employment Eligibility
☐ 1. United States Passport ☐ 2. Certificate of United States citizenship ☐ 3. Certificate of Naturalization ☐ 4. Unexpired foreign passport with attached Employment authorization ☐ 5. Alien Registration Card with photograph	☐ 1. A State-issued driver's license or a State-issued I.D. card with a photograph, or information, including name, sex, date of birth, height, weight, and color of eyes. (Specify State)_____) ☐ 2. U.S. Military Card ☐ 3. Other (Specify document and issuing authority)		☐ 1. Original Social Security Number Card (other than a card stating it is not valid for employment) ☐ 2. A birth certificate issued by State, county, or municipal authority bearing a seal or other certification ☐ 3. Unexpired INS Employment Authorization

Employees must provide either one document from List A OR one document from List B and C. This list is an abbreviated list. Consult the Immigration and Naturalization Service for a list of alternative documents.

Form I-9, U.S. Immigration and Naturalization Service, 1987

All individuals seeking employment should be sure that they have the correct documentation to provide proof of authorization to work in the United States. If you have any questions concerning your documentation, consult the Immigration and Naturalization Service.

Freedom of Speech Public employees in general cannot be terminated for speaking on matters of public concern. This right, however, can be limited if the speech interferes with the efficient operation of the government. They can be terminated for speaking on matters of personal interest.

Public employees are not allowed to campaign for people who will become their bosses. The Hatch Act was passed in 1940, limiting the political activity of federal civil servants. Many states and large cities have passed their own Hatch acts.

The rights of free speech for private employees vary from state to state. Some states offer broad protection, whereas others offer little or none. In general, individuals in high positions in a company have fewer rights than individuals at lower levels. The potential impact of statements coming from persons in higher positions of authority or prestige is greater.

AIDS AIDS (acquired immunodeficiency syndrome) is one of the most serious health problems facing this country today. The disease destroys the body's ability to fight other diseases that eventually kill the AIDS victim. To date no known cure for AIDS has been found.

According to the Surgeon General, AIDS cannot be transmitted through normal everyday contact at work. An employee cannot acquire it from saliva, sweat, tears, urine or bowel movements, a kiss, clothes, a telephone, or a toilet seat. AIDS is transmitted through sexual contact with someone infected by the AIDS virus, by sharing drug needles and syringes with an infected person, by a mother with AIDS to her baby before or during birth, or through transfusion of infected blood. Individuals cannot acquire AIDS by giving blood, and the chance of receiving the virus through a blood transfusion has been greatly reduced.

The rights of AIDS victims to work are generally given priority over the rights of co-workers.

In general, the courts have ruled in favor of the rights of the employee infected with AIDS rather than in favor of the rights of noninfected employees. They have also ruled that AIDS is considered a handicap under the Rehabilitation Act of 1973, which extends rights to the disabled who work in the federal sector or whose organizations are federal contractors. AIDS is also considered a disability under the Americans with Disabilities Act.

A private employer cannot require that an employee with AIDS leave the workplace while still able to work. Additionally, a company faces substantial legal risk in revealing that an employee has AIDS and in testing new or current employees for AIDS.

Defamation of Character   **Defamation** is the open publication of a false statement tending to harm the reputation of a person. If the statement is oral, it is called slander. If it is in writing, it is called libel. If you feel that your character has been defamed, consult an attorney to determine your rights.

Truth is considered a defense in defamation charges. Most courts consider a statement protected if it is made in good faith in the discharge of a public or private duty to someone else who has a corresponding interest, right, or duty. For instance, if a security guard reported to the manager and assistant manager that an employee had attempted to steal the employer's property, the courts would most likely not consider this action defamation of character.

Smokers' Rights   Courts are tending to side with the rights of nonsmokers. At present an employer may totally forbid smoking on the job and discriminate against smokers by not hiring them. Some companies that do not totally ban smoking may identify smoking and nonsmoking areas. Often this is prompted by local ordinances that require the designation of nonsmoking and smoking areas in the workplace.

Employee files store documentation on performance and behavior on the job.

Personnel Files   Employers are compelled to protect themselves from charges of discrimination and unjust punishment or termination. Many resort to documentation in the personnel file to protect themselves in this area.

Employees can expect to find reprimands, warnings, or writeups concerning performance or behavior in their files. Most states allow access to personnel records by employees at reasonable times. Some states allow employees to correct documents or remove erroneous materials or insert explanations of disputed materials. Employees should consult their employee handbook and state laws to determine whether access to their personnel files is allowed.

Drugs on Personal Time   Currently the courts do not give employees in private enterprise many rights in this area. Terminations of employees who test positive for drugs whether used on or off the job are upheld. Governmental employees have more rights concerning drug testing than those in private industry. Even though

FIGURE 13.10   Employers have the right to search employee belongings.

some drugs can stay in the system up to 72 hours after use, the courts have made no allowances for use of drugs on personal time.

Search of Work Areas   In general, employers have the right to search employee packages, files, desks, and cars in order to prevent theft and control operations. Court restrictions on search and seizure are limited, particularly if the employer has warned employees that they are subject to search.

Employers can generally search work areas at will.

Polygraphs   The Employee Polygraph Protection Act of 1988 prohibits most private employers from using lie detector tests to screen applicants. The tests cannot be the sole reason for discharge and can only be used if a reasonable suspicion of guilt exists. Because polygraph use is limited, some employers have turned to the use of pencil and paper tests concerning honesty and substance abuse in order to screen job applicants.

Companies are concerned with employee honesty for several reasons. First, employers lose billions of dollars yearly through employee theft. Then, substance abusers cost companies billions of dollars more in higher benefit costs, lower productivity, and absenteeism. Additionally, because of the "negligent hiring theory," employers can be held liable for crimes that an employee commits on the job if they fail to screen the employee for past misdeeds or personality quirks.

Currently these tests are legal, and employers can use them to make decisions concerning hiring and firing. However, many see the tests as intrusive, subjective, and unreliable. Employers who administer the test may offend potential applicants and send a message to future employees that they are not trusted.

Plant Closings   The Worker Adjustment and Retraining Notification Act of 1988 requires that plants with 100 or more workers give 60 days advance notice of a shutdown affecting at least 50 workers. Layoffs of more than one-third of the work site employees for more than six months must also be announced in advance.

Dress Codes   Dress codes that are reasonably related to the business needs of the company and that are clear, consistently enforced, and communicated have generally been upheld by courts and arbitrators. Some reasonable accommodation, however, must be made if the employee asks to deviate from the dress code for religious reasons.

Blowing the Whistle on Illegal Activities   This protection is generally afforded by law only to federal and state employees. These employees cannot be terminated for reporting illegal activities within their organization.

Electronic Surveillance of Employees   Currently employers may legally survey employees electronically, particularly if they have advised the employees that surveillance may occur without the employees' knowledge and that refusal to permit it may be grounds for discipline. Some companies have employees sign waivers; others post copies of search policies. Some companies perform electronic surveillance to prevent theft and reduce unproductive time of employees not closely supervised. Employers may eavesdrop with hidden microphones and transmitters attached to lockers or telephones that pick up office conversations or spy with pinhole lenses in walls and ceilings. Some companies record the length of telephone calls, when the calls were made, and where the calls were placed. They may also monitor the content of the telephone calls.

What Are Future Rights?

The future will most likely bring extensive changes in the area of miscellaneous employee rights. As technology becomes more sophisticated and inexpensive, enabling companies to perform even more thorough surveillance on employees, a push to curb this "big brother" type of activity will most likely occur. Additionally, the courts are expected to continue to move away from the employment at will doctrine, granting employees even more rights.

SUMMARY

Various federal, state, and local laws regulate the workplace. Federal laws protect employees from discrimination based on race, religion, sex, color, age, and national origin. Health and safety of workers is regulated through the

Occupational Safety and Health Act. Federal laws also mandate fair labor standards, retirement, disability, survivor's benefits, and unemployment compensation through the Social Security Act. State laws control compensation for employees injured or killed on the job.

Many employers offer additional benefits, such as health insurance, retirement, savings plans, or child care. These benefits, along with required benefits, can average 35 percent of an employee's salary.

In general, miscellaneous employee rights at work differ from those enjoyed away from the job. Public employees tend to have better-defined rights than private employees. Employees should learn what they can and cannot do in their locale.

KEY TERMS

discrimination
Equal Employment Opportunity Commission
Title VII of the Civil Rights Act of 1964
affirmative action
bona fide occupational qualification (BFOQ)
Pregnancy Discrimination Act
Equal Pay Act
comparable worth
Age Discrimination in Employment Act
sexual harassment
Occupational Safety and Health Act
safety
health
Occupational Safety and Health Administration (OSHA)
Fair Labor Standards Act
Social Security Act
unemployment compensation
workers' compensation
employment at will
AIDS
defamation

REVIEW QUESTIONS

1. Which federal laws regulate discrimination in the workplace? What types of discrimination do they prohibit?
2. What is OSHA? How does it protect employees' safety and health?

3. Which major laws regulate fair labor standards? What do these laws specify?
4. Identify three benefits that are required by law and five that may be offered voluntarily to employees.
5. What miscellaneous rights do employees have at work?

DISCUSSION QUESTIONS

1. Review the employee rights discussed in the last section of the chapter. Do you think employees should have more rights or fewer rights?
2. Have you ever been confronted by an unsafe working condition on the job? What did you do about it?
3. Should an employer have the right to search your work area? Why or why not?
4. Social Security was not intended to support fully individuals who have lost income through death, disability, or retirement. Explain what other benefits companies provide to help fill the gap. Have you begun to plan for your retirement? Why or why not? If so, how?
5. Do you agree with the teenage training wage? Why or why not?
6. Does your school or place of work have designated smoking areas? Should smoking be banned altogether? Why or why not?
7. Should employers be able to tell you what to wear to work? Why might an employer care about what you wear?
8. What are your feelings about electronic surveillance in the workplace? Should employers have the right to monitor employees to see that they are working during business hours and to assess the quality of their work?

CASE STUDY 13.1

IT'S YOUR THING. CAN YOU DO WHAT YOU WANT TO DO?

Dora had been employed at Seymour's Shop for five years. She and her supervisor, Herbert, had been at odds for months. Dora thought that he was obnoxious and disliked his ordering her around and making demands.

Dora began to complain about Herbert to others in her group. She criticized his decisions to Manuel and made fun of his clothes when talking to Janice. Other workers began to pick up on this behavior and made fun of Herbert behind his back.

One evening Dora noticed Herbert in the cafe across the street from the office. A young woman was with him. The next day she reported this scene to the group, and they began to speculate concerning the woman's identity and why she and Herbert were together. Dora and the group were standing in front of the water fountain, laughing and talking, when Herbert walked up.

"Dora, I want to see you in my office right now," he said abruptly. Dora followed him in and Herbert shut the door.

"Dora, I'm going to have to let you go because you are a troublemaker. Every time I turn around, you are in someone else's office gossiping and interrupting work. You are causing too much trouble."

1. What employer right did Herbert exercise?
2. Should Dora have been allowed freedom of speech? How would you have felt if you were Dora?
3. How would you have felt if you were Herbert? Should the right to free speech be more important than the right of the company to run an efficient and effective business?
4. How do you think the other members of the group will react?

CASE STUDY 13.2

EQUAL AND FAIR ARE TWO DIFFERENT THINGS

"I've had it," Carmelita said as she sat down next to Jose. "That Elvin is a real monster. He yells at me, returns my work, and makes me do it over. He's always telling me that I'm stupid when I make mistakes. He makes me so nervous that I can't think straight. I'm tempted to go to the EEOC and file charges on him. I don't think he likes Hispanics."

"I know what you mean," Jose said. "He chewed me out in front of the whole office. I was so embarrassed that I felt like hiding."

Just then Jan walked up. Carmelita and Jose began discussing the situation with her.

"You can try EEOC if you want," Jan said. "But he treats everyone that way. I was in Alice's office yesterday when Elvin came in and told her what a simpleton she was because she had incorrectly added a column of numbers. He threw the report on her desk and yelled 'Do it right or else!' and stormed out. Alice is White and she gets that treatment, too. I guess he's just treating everybody equally!"

1. What discriminatory treatment do federal laws prohibit? Would they be applicable to Carmelita and Jose?
2. Does being equal mean that treatment is fair or as you would like it to be?
3. How do you think Carmelita and Jose might handle their difficulties with Elvin?
4. Do any governmental regulations dictate the type of treatment to be received by employees?

BIBLIOGRAPHY

Ahern, Eileen, et al. *Federal Policies and Worker Status since the Thirties*. Madison, WI: Industrial Relations Research Association, 1976.

Bittel, Lester. *What Every Supervisor Should Know*. New York: McGraw-Hill, 1985.

Bureau of National Affairs publications:
  OSHA Reporter
  Policy and Practice Series, Wages and Hours
  Reporter

Chemical Hazard Communication. Washington, DC: U.S. Department of Labor/OSHA, 1987.

Commerce Clearing House publications:
  EEO Manual
  Human Resource Management, Employee Relations
Conrad, Pamela J., and Robert B. Maddux. *Guide to Affirmative Action: A Primer for Supervisors and Managers*. Los Altos, CA: Crisp Publications, 1988.
Dantico, John A. "Wage-Hour Law Clarifies Exempt/Nonexempt." *HRNews* (January 1990):3.
"Employment-at-Will Erodes, Union Membership Shrinks." *Resource* (December 1989): 10.
Employment Practices Decisions. Chicago: Commerce Clearing House, Inc., 1987, volume 43, ¶ 37,016.
Equal Employment Opportunity Commission publications:
  Facts about National Origin Discrimination
  Facts about Pregnancy Discrimination
  Facts about Religious Discrimination
  Facts about Sexual Harassment
Fundamentals of Employee Benefit Programs. Washington, DC: Employee Benefit Research Institute, 1987.
Immigration Reform and Control Act of 1986 (IRCA): Your Job and Your Rights. Washington, DC: U.S. Department of Justice, 1988.
Klinberg, Christine. "Violations of Child Labor Laws Up 250 Percent." *HRNews* (March 1990): 9.
Lorber, Lawrence A., and J. Robert Kirk. *Fear Itself: A Legal and Personal Analysis of Drug Testing, AIDS, Secondary Smoke, and VDTs*. Alexandria, VA: The ASPA Foundation, 1987.
May, Bruce D. "Law Puts Immigration Control in Employers' Hands." *Personnel Journal* (March 1987): 106–111.
McWhirter, Darien. *Your Rights at Work*. New York: John Wiley and Sons, 1989.
Meisinger, Susan. "House Passes Americans with Disabilities Act." *HRNews* (June 1990): 3.
Nackley, Jeffrey V. *Primer on Workers' Compensation*. Washington, DC: Bureau of National Affairs, 1987.
Novit, Mitchell S. *Essentials of Personnel Management*, 2nd ed. Engelwood Cliffs, NJ: Prentice-Hall, 1986.
Overman, Stephenie. "New Civil Rights Bill Expands Title VII." *HRNews* (March 1990): 1.
Overman, Stephanie. "Mandated Health Insurance Reality in Some States." *HRNews* (August 1990): 9.
Scheuch, Richard. *Labor in the American Economy.* New York: Harper & Row, 1981.
Social Security Administration publications:
  Retirement
  Survivors
  Disability
Sherman, Arthur W., Jr., George W. Bohlander, and Herbert J. Chruden. *Managing Human Resources*. Cincinnati: South-Western Publishing Company, 1988.
Thornburg, Linda. "Bush Signs Disabilities Act." *HRNews* (August 1990): 1.

Twomey, David P. ***A Concise Guide to Employment Law: EEOC and OSHA***.
    Cincinnati: South-Western Publishing Company, 1986.
Twomey, David P. ***Labor and Employment Law: Text and Cases***. Cincinnati:
    South-Western Publishing Company, 1989.
Understanding AIDS. Rockville, MD: U.S. Department of Health and Human
    Services Publication no. (CDC) HHS-58-8404, 1988.

CHAPTER FOURTEEN
UNIONS

In 1989 at a Pittston Company plant in southwestern Virginia, company guards were forced to retreat to shelter in a nearby office building while 98 camouflage-clad, unarmed men and a minister seized the coal-producing plant. This takeover was aimed to highlight the plight of the five-month-old strike by the United Mine Workers (UMW) against Pittston. The intruders were able to occupy the plant for 21 days, successfuly preventing the company from producing coal.

For the first three days, nearly 2,000 sympathizers and supporters kept state troopers from entering the plant to rescue the guards and arresting the strikers. The strikers left peacefully after a court order was issued to end the seizure.

This type of physical takeover coupled with strong community support has seldom happened since the sit-down strikes of the early 1930s. These tactics are, however, common in the intense labor-management dispute between the UMW and Pittston Coal.

John Hoerr, *Business Week*
(October 9, 1989)

OBJECTIVES

After studying this chapter, you should be able to:
1. Describe the differences between unions and employee associations.
2. Describe some of the methods used by companies to prevent union formation prior to passage of the Wagner Act.
3. Discuss the key federal legislation to establish and govern labor-management activities.
4. Discuss the steps involved in a typical grievance procedure.
5. Describe the key differences between mediation and arbitration.
6. Discuss whether unions are strengthening or weakening in their representation of today's work force.

WHAT IS A UNION?

Many unions today are literally fighting to stay alive. A recent example is the case between the United Mine Workers (UMW) and a leading coal mining company, Pittston Coal. While Pittston was mounting a massive public relations campaign accusing the union of using "terrorist" tactics, the union was countering with head-lines that Pittston was attempting "a classic case of union-busting." Although it was a relatively small strike involving only 1,700 miners in Virginia, West Virginia, and Kentucky, this contract dispute has far greater importance in that it raises basic questions about our current national labor laws and the direction of future union activities.

A **union** is a group or association of workers who collectively bargain with employers to improve working conditions and to protect employees from unfair or arbitrary treatment by management. The working conditions in question are usually hours, wages, and benefits. When representatives of a union and management are unable to reach agreement on improvements to these working conditions, union members may use a technique known as a strike to improve their bargaining position with a company's management. A **strike** is the refusal to work under the current conditions until some agreement can be reached toward the desired improvements:

A union bargains on behalf of members for improved conditions of employment.

> **Wallace and Sylvia waited expectantly for the local's vote. The mood was upbeat, and Wallace thoroughly expected a strike to be approved by the membership.**
> **"What will it be like if we strike?" Sylvia asked.**
> **"We'll shut down the whole plant," Wallace declared. "I don't think any of the other union members will cross our picket line. We need to be out with our signs before the shift starts in order to encourage them not to work." Wallace paused a minute, and then said thoughtfully, "I'm afraid this will be a long strike."**

Management, on the other hand, may respond to the strike by hiring new employees to take the place of the strikers. Replacing strikers is exactly what President Ronald Reagan did to crush the 1981 strike of the Professional Air Traffic Controllers Organization (PATCO). The President fired the 12,000 striking federal employees, who by law are not allowed to participate in work stoppages, and filled in the gap by using nonstrikers, supervisors, and military air traffic controllers.

Strikes can be costly for both the union members and management. Union members usually suffer income losses during the strike period. Although the union provides compensation benefits from union dues paid by members during nonstrike periods, the income is less than normal wages. Union members will most often take some other full- or part-time job to supplement their income until the strike is settled.

Companies may also suffer income or profit losses during the strike. Often the company is forced to operate with a skeleton crew of managers and nonstrikers who may not be fully trained and able to keep productivity levels constant with prestrike levels.

Today little distinction exists between unions and employee associations. His-torically, **employee associations** were made up of group members from the white-collar and professional sectors of the work force, such as teachers, nurses, public sector employees, doctors, lawyers, and clerical workers. These individuals seldom engaged in collective bargaining activities, and a key distinction for some associations was the denial of the right to strike. Many federal and state employees, for instance, took an oath of employment that stated they would not strike against the government. However, because most employee associations have evolved to function much

Unions and employee associations perform virtually the same functions.

FIGURE 14.1   Many retail occupations, such as cashier, are sometimes covered by union contracts.

the same as unions, the U. S. Department of Labor no longer makes a distinction between the two.

HOW DID THE LABOR MOVEMENT BEGIN?

Prior to the 1930s, working conditions for most of America's workers were unfavorable. Early in the Industrial Era, factories were little more than sweatshops, exploiting the worker with long hours, child labor, unsafe work conditions, and low wages. As discussed in Chapter 1, management emphasis was placed on the scientific approach popularized by Frederick W. Taylor that maximized productivity output, and workers' needs were ignored. Employers showed little concern for human relations, and workers had no voice in influencing their work environment. Attempts by workers to unionize were resisted by management and routinely brought before the courts, which customarily ruled against labor union activities. Companies habitually used injunctions to halt strikes and boycotts to inhibit union activity.

Early attempts to unionize were marred by conflict and controversy.

FIGURE 14.2   Children were exploited in the early Industrial Era.

The Bettmann Archive

Other anti-union techniques used by management included firing labor agitators, blacklisting, yellow-dog contracts, and lockouts. These methods are briefly summarized below.

1. *Labor Agitators.* Union hopefuls would occasionally send influential persons capable of rallying workers toward unionizing into a workplace to help a union effort to organize. These people were considered **labor agitators** by management and were immediately fired when identified.

2. *Blacklists.* The names of labor agitators and any other persons known to be sympathetic to unionizing efforts were placed on a list referred to as a **blacklist.** The blacklists identifying those whom management perceived as potential troublemakers were exchanged among company managers to assure that union organizers were denied employment. The threat of unemployment had the desired result of discouraging active support for the labor movement.

3. *Yellow-dog Contracts.* **Yellow-dog contracts** were a condition of employment that required would-be employees to sign a statement that they would not start or join a union. Use of these contracts was one of several anti-union methods outlawed by the **Norris-LaGuardia Act of 1932** as a softening of anti-union attitudes began in the early 1930s.

4. *Lockouts.* When workers made demands for improved conditions or threatened early forms of strikes, company management would simply lock the

doors of the factory and shut down operations. This technique was known as a **lockout**. Because companies could usually economically outlast the now unemployed worker, it was another effective means of discouraging union activities.

Other equally effective methods were used by management to deter the pro-union activities of employees. Some of these methods were brutal and blatantly illegal. Mounting public and congressional disfavor of these activities gave rise to the trend toward legalizing unions. Further federal legislation would drastically change the labor movement and form the basis for union activities as we know them today.

HOW DID FEDERAL LAW AFFECT THE LABOR MOVEMENT?

Several key pieces of congressional legislation laid the framework for the labor movement and the unionization rights of workers. The Wagner Act of 1935, the Taft-Hartley Act of 1947, and the Landrum-Griffin Act of 1959 are of primary interest.

The right of employees to form unions and collectively bargain with management on employment issues was established in 1935 through passage of the National Labor Relations Act. More popularly known as the **Wagner Act**, this legislation ordered management to stop interfering with union organizing efforts and defined what constituted an unfair labor practice by management. Figure 14.3 identifies some of the practices that developed from the Wagner Act.

The Wagner Act legitimized labor unions.

FIGURE 14.3   Practices that have developed from the Wagner Act.

1. Management cannot fire or refuse to hire because individuals are union members.
2. Management cannot discriminate against a union member who files an unfair labor practice complaint or testifies before the National Labor Relations Board.
3. Management must bargain in good faith with a union and, once a union is elected, cannot recognize any other union.
4. Management can talk about the disadvantages of a union but cannot threaten, interrogate, or spy on individuals concerning union activities or joining a union.
5. Management must allow union members to meet on their own personal time such as lunch or breaks to discuss union business but can deny union activities on company time.
6. If employees strike for wages or working conditions, employers may hire replacements and, when the strike is over, are not required to hire back the strikers unless provided for in the contract.
7. If employees strike over unfair labor practices (activities that violate the act), the employer must fire the replacements and take the strikers back after the strike ends.

The **National Labor Relations Board (NLRB)** was also established by the Wagner Act. The NLRB is a government agency responsible for enforcing the provisions of the Wagner Act. Regional offices throughout the United States are often called upon to help resolve disputes.

The UMW/Pittston strike described in the opening case became known as the most confrontational strike of the 1980s. This reputation is primarily based on the issuance by the NLRB of more than 400 charges of unfair labor practices against Pittston and the union. This constitutes the largest number of charges levied by the NLRB ever before in a single dispute. Nearly 3,000 miners and supporters were arrested for picket-line misconduct and isolated episodes of violence. The NLRB policed the strike activities for violations of federal legislation.

Because the Wagner Act was so sweepingly pro-union, unions gained enormous power and frequently called strikes to force desired improvements in work conditions. In 1946, 113 million workdays were lost in union strikes, causing a major shift in public opinion about unions. Many industries were paralyzed, which affected the general public and set the stage for more restrictive labor legislation.

The **Taft-Hartley Act**, also known as the Labor Management Relations Act of 1947, was a series of amendments to the Wagner Act. It imposed certain controls on union organizing activities, internal union activities, and methods used by unions in collective bargaining attempts. Figure 14.4 outlines the key provisions of the Taft-Hartley Act. Several of these provisions are worth exploring in more detail because of their significant impact on union activities.

For example, the closed shop was outlawed. A **closed shop** required a person to belong to a bargaining unit before being hired, and job loss was automatic if the person was expelled from the union for any reason (such as nonpayment of dues).

> The NLRB remains active in policing labor-management activities.

FIGURE 14.4 Key provisions of the Taft-Hartley Act.

1. Enables states to pass right-to-work laws that prohibit union shop contracts. (Known as Section 14b.)
2. Forbids discriminatory or excessive dues or fee charging of prospective employees.
3. Forbids makework and featherbedding practices that force employers to pay for services not rendered.
4. Invokes the "cooling-off period," which allows the Attorney General at the request of the President to put an 80-day freeze on any strike that might threaten national health or safety.
5. Requires labor to bargain in good faith with management.
6. Requires unions or management to give 60-day notices of any impending contract termination.
7. Forbids unions to use coercive means for recruiting members.
8. Empowers individual employees to settle grievances informally with management.

This setup gave the union a strong control over the worker and the employer. Abuse of this control led to negative public opinion that unions were too powerful and corrupt in their dealings and forced demise of closed shops in the Taft-Hartley legislation.

Another means of assuring union membership was use of the union shop agreement. In a **union shop**, the worker need not be a union member at the time of hiring but is required to join the union within a specified time, usually within 60 to 90 days after employment. The union shop is permitted by the Taft-Hartley Act.

Closed, union, and agency shops protected the union's rights to membership dues.

The **agency shop** requires workers to pay union membership dues whether or not they choose actually to join the union. This rule serves to protect the union from would-be free riders. **Free riders** enjoy the same benefits afforded dues-paying members because they are a part of the greater bargaining unit represented by the union.

Use of these shop agreements helped to protect the rights of the union, the worker, and the company. As part of most contract agreements, a company will deduct union dues directly from a worker's paycheck and forward them to the union. This process is called a **checkoff** and must be authorized by the employee's signature on a routinely used form. The union automatically gets the dues, the member remains in good standing with the union, and the company does not have to fire a worker for nonpayment of union dues. The benefits to all parties are obvious.

The right-to-work law grants states the option of imposing union membership.

In addition to prohibiting the closed shop, the Taft-Hartley Act contains a provision that individual states may pass right-to-work laws. The **right-to-work law** allows states to prohibit both the closed and the union shop contract agreements, giving the worker the choice of union membership without compromise. Because most companies discourage union representation and most workers do not like being forced to join any organization, this law is viewed favorably by the two. However, the law is not well received by union representatives, who feel that it is financially burdensome to them to represent all members of a **bargaining unit** — the group of employees the union may be bargaining for—if they are not required to be union members and pay union dues.

A peculiar fact about the right-to-work law, Section 14b of the Taft-Hartley Act, is that it allows a state law to supersede a federal law by giving the state the right of choice in the matter, rather than the federal law imposing the decision. Of the 21 states that are currently right-to-work states, most are located in the southern, midwestern, and western United States. Figure 14.5 identifies the states with right-to-work laws as of 1986. Interestingly, eastern states, who have long been the staunch supporters of union activities, are not on the list.

Corruption and misuse of funds by some union officials led to the Landrum-Griffin Act.

One other federal law that had significant impact on labor activities was passed by Congress in 1959. Driven by reports of alleged corruption by union officials, extensive congressional investigations were held and resulted in the passage of the Labor Management Reporting and Disclosure Act, also known as the **Landrum-Griffin Act**. This act requires unions and employers of union members to report certain matters to the Department of Labor. Unions must disclose the sources and disbursements of their funds, hold regularly scheduled elections of union officials by secret ballot, and restrict union officials from using union funds for personal means. This legislation remains an effective control over possible corruption in union activities and misuse of union funds.

FIGURE 14.5   States with right-to-work laws as of 1986.

Alabama	Nevada
Arizona	North Carolina
Arkansas	North Dakota
Florida	South Carolina
Georgia	South Dakota
Idaho	Tennessee
Iowa	Texas
Kansas	Utah
Louisiana	Virginia
Mississippi	Wyoming
Nebraska	

WHOM DO UNIONS REPRESENT?

In the early years, unions represented two major segments of the working population. The **craft unions** represented skilled workers, such as shoemakers, carpenters, and stonemasons, and were primarily concerned with training apprentices to be masters of their craft. The **American Federation of Labor (AFL)** was formed in 1886 of a small number of these craft unions and led by Samuel L. Gompers.

The other segment of workers represented by unions in the early years was industrial workers who were unskilled or semiskilled, such as mine workers, steel makers, and laborers. This group of **industrial unions** formed the **Congress of Industrial Organizations (CIO)** in 1936 and was led by John L. Lewis.

The two groups merged in 1955 to form the **AFL-CIO** as a show of strength to improve bargaining power. A few of the larger unions later withdrew to become independents. Examples include the Teamsters, Auto Workers, and Warehousemen.

These situations remained fairly constant until 1965, when unions made significant gains in membership among government workers, white-collar professionals, and farm workers.

Unions have expanded into almost all segments of the labor force.

Today, union members may be teachers, politicians, police, fire fighters, professional athletes, grocery store workers, nurses, or clerical workers. The number of these types of workers represented by unions is increasing while the membership of the craft and industrial unions is declining.

HOW DO UNIONS WORK?

Unions come into existence in a precise way and their functioning involves specific processes.

Formation

Unions develop through an election. At least 50 percent of the employees in what is called a bargaining unit must vote to have the union represent them. The voting is monitored by the National Labor Relations Board. If the union is successful in the election, it then has the right to bargain for all employees in that bargaining unit. The units are usually drawn up according to job categories, with those doing similar work in the same unit. Supervisors are considered part of management and are not allowed to vote or join the union.

Union members may also vote to decertify a union. If successful in their attempt, the union would no longer represent the employees in the bargaining unit. The employees would then be free to certify another union or to have no union representation.

A **union steward** represents union members' interests and protects their rights on the job. Many times this person acts as a go-between, representing the union member to the company supervisor in settling disagreements. The steward is usually a senior employee elected by the union to act in this capacity. The steward may assist in grievance procedures and act as a watchdog to ensure company compliance with the union contract.

Local unions generally have a **business agent** who helps run the affairs of the union. A business agent's responsibilities may include negotiating and administering the agreement, collecting dues, recruiting new members, and performing other day-to-day activities.

Many unions are large, national organizations with full-time staffs to conduct general business. Wage issues may be negotiated by the national organizations on a national or regional level, leaving the individual local union to bargain over local issues. However, local unions sometimes do all their own bargaining and negotiate critical issues for their members.

Workers choose union representation by voting.

Bargaining

Once a union has been elected to represent the workers, union representatives meet with company management representatives to establish a mutual agreement on hours, wages, and working conditions. This process of negotiation to reach a written agreement is called **collective bargaining**. Both union and management are expected to bargain in good faith to reach a mutually acceptable agreement. This written agreement is known as a **contract**. Once signed, the contract is legally binding to both parties. A contract usually covers a one- to three-year period. It then will be renegotiated for renewal as is or with changes. Figure 14.6 outlines the various topics most commonly addressed in collective bargaining.

By no means is the bargaining process a stagnant one. The contract is a written document. Written documents are often interpreted differently depending upon a reader's perception of the meaning. Interpretations of the contract's terms and conditions may take place daily as some portion is questioned as to its proper meaning. Disputes between a supervisor and a union worker over contract wording often result in what is called a **grievance**. Careful attention to the wording of the

FIGURE 14.6 Typical collective bargaining topics.

WAGES	HOURS	WORKING CONDITIONS	GENERAL
Wage rates	Shift hours	Employment requirements	Contract length
shift-work rates	Lunch lengths	Work load/division	Grievance procedures
Overtime rates	Lunch times	Work rules/policies	Strike clause
	Break times	Safety rules/policies	Arbitration policy
Promotions	Vacation days	Seniority policies	
Cost-of-living increases	Sick days	Disciplinary policies	
Retirement plans	Holidays	Firing policies	
Health insurance			
Life insurance			
Checkoff (dues)			
Unemployment benefits			

written contract can help reduce the frequency of these disputes; however, they are inevitable.

Resolving Grievances

Ideally, disputes between workers and supervisors should be resolved informally, using effective human relations skills. However, if these first attempts fail, the dispute becomes part of a grievance system designed to handle these problems.

Most contracts have a specific **grievance procedure** written into the contract that carefully outlines the formal steps for resolving contract disputes. These procedures are not standardized in all contracts but follow a three- to seven-step process. Figure 14.7 identifies the typical steps of a grievance procedure.

The number and order of steps in a grievance procedure is determined during negotiations of the contract. Specific time limits are established for each of the steps to ensure timely processing of the dispute.

A formal grievance is usually filed in writing on a grievance form. Figure 14.8 is an example of such a grievance form. At this point, the bargaining process officially begins, with each party responsible for presenting its position. As we discussed in Chapter 12, such conflict can be healthy if good human relations skills are used to reach a solution that represents growth for both parties.

Mediation and Arbitration

Contracts can include both mediation and arbitration as final steps in resolving conflicts. The two steps are quite different in their approaches and results.

Mediation brings both groups together under the influence of an unbiased third party who may skillfully guide the opposing parties toward new ideas or meth-

FIGURE 14.7   Typical steps of a grievance procedure.

1. Supervisor, employee, and union steward attempt to resolve the dispute informally.
2. Formal written grievance is filed by employee with management representatives.
3. Management representatives meet with employee and union representatives to hear case facts.
4. Management presents written position to employee and union representatives.
5. If not resolved, employee and union representative may appeal to next higher-level management.
6. Top levels of management and union officials meet with employee to reach agreement, with occasional use of a mediator.
7. If not resolved, grievance is submitted to an arbitrator for final, legally binding decision.

A mediator leads informal sessions to resolve a dead-locked griev-ance.

'An arbitrator's formal decision is legally bind-ing to both parties.

ods of resolution. This unbiased third party, known as a **mediator**, can only be summoned if both parties agree to try mediation. Upon agreement, a list of media-tors is requested from the **Federal Mediation and Conciliation Service (FMCS)** or from state labor departments.

Mediators are usually highly skilled in the art of negotiation and conflict resolu-tion techniques. They may carefully select the date, time, and place of the next meeting and wisely restrict attendance at the meeting for maximum effectiveness. Ground rules are quickly established on how the sessions will be conducted, the basic problem issues are reviewed for proper identification and understanding, and both parties must commit to resolving the conflict. The mediator then helps develop alternative solutions in hopes that one will be mutually agreeable.

If a solution is reached, it is written down and signed by both parties and the grievance is considered resolved. No further action is necessary.

Arbitration is a formal process similar to a legal court hearing. The sessions are led by an **arbitrator**, whose professional services are usually requested from the American Arbitration Association (AAA). During the hearing, both sides present their cases, call witnesses, and submit other supporting facts. When all the facts have been presented, the arbitrator is given a limited time to develop a written decision on the matter. In the determination process, the arbitrator must consider any similar arbitration cases that have set precedents.

Once the decision is made, it becomes legally binding on both parties. This fact is the key difference between mediation and arbitration. The final decision made by the arbitrator can only be challenged by taking the issue to court, which is seldom done.

Arbitration can be a costly process. Arbitrators are paid a daily fee for their services plus expenses for travel, lodging, food and other incidentals during the

FIGURE 14.8 Sample grievance form.

GRIEVANCE

(FOR GRIEVANCES OVER INTERPRETATION OR APPLICATION OF THE NEGOTIATED AGREEMENT BETWEEN JSC AND LOCAL 2284, AFGE)

NAME OF EMPLOYEE		POSITION TITLE	
GRADE	ORGANIZATION CODE	EXTENSION	DATE INCIDENT OCCURRED
NAME OF SUPERVISOR WHO RECEIVED INFORMAL COMPLAINT OR GRIEVANCE		ORGANIZATION CODE	DATE INFORMAL GRIEVANCE PRESENTED TO SUPERVISOR

1. SPECIFIC PROVISION OF THE AGREEMENT WHICH IS AN ISSUE IN THE GRIEVANCE:

2. SPECIFIC REASONS SERVING AS THE BASIS FOR THE GRIEVANCE: *(Including how, when, and by whom it is alleged that the provision of the Agreement was misinterpreted or misapplied)*

3. RELIEF OR ADJUSTMENT REQUESTED:

4. NAME ADDRESS AND TELEPHONE NUMBER OF REPRESENTATIVE, IF ANY:

SIGNATURE OF EMPLOYEE	DATE
SIGNATURE OF REPRESENTATIVE, IF ANY	DATE
SIGNATURE OF UNION OFFICIAL (APPROVING REPRESENTATIVE)	DATE
SIGNATURE OF SUPERVISOR ACKNOWLEDGING RECEIPT OF FORMAL GRIEVANCE	DATE

(Use reverse side if more space is needed.)

JSC FORM 1347 (Rev Mar 78)   NASA-JSC

FIGURE 14.9 A mediator attempts to resolve difficult conflicts between the union and management.

arbitration process. Most contracts require that this cost be split evenly between the union and management. Because of the cost, only grievances on issues of considerable importance are brought to arbitration. Today, costs can be a key factor in any decision unions make, with the diminishing numbers of members paying union dues. Union funds historically used for enhancing union purposes and promoting union growth have been drastically reduced, and new strategies may need to be developed to counter the situation.

WHAT IS THE STATUS OF UNIONS TODAY?

United States Labor Department statistics indicate that in 1980 approximately 23 million employees were represented by unions from diverse labor fields. By 1990 the Labor Department reported a decline in union membership to only 17 million. Another indicator of union changes is the decline in numbers of strikes. John Hoerr in a *Business Week* article states that in 1969 more than 400 strikes were recorded. In 1979 only 235 strikes occurred, and by 1989 the reported count was down to only 40 work stoppages. Although a general increase in total employment has occurred, union representation has declined.

Additionally, unions have experienced notable shifts in representation. The number of Hispanics and Blacks belonging to unions remains roughly the same. However, female union membership has increased. Labor analysts attribute these gains to the general increase in the numbers of women in the work force and to the shift in our economy from manufacturing to service industries. Service industries traditionally employ larger numbers of women. The declining numbers of manufacturing jobs have been largely male-dominated, which accounts for the overall decline in male union membership.

Labor activists are quick to identify two major factors that they feel have contributed to the overall union membership declines in the decade of the 1980s. Social change brought the government and laws into the picture. James Flanigan, writing in the *Houston Chronicle*, said that the Equal Employment Opportunity Commission (EEOC), the Occupational Safety and Health Administration (OSHA), and the Employee Retirement Income Security Act (ERISA) have been critical legislation that "took decisions on hiring, work conditions, and pension fund investing out of the hands of both union and management." Businesses are now forced to face lawyers and government specialists rather than unions on these issues.

Social and legal changes have reduced union popularity.

Additionally, employer attitudes toward workers have improved, as evidenced by the more participative approaches to the overall management of company activities. Workers have not felt a strong need to join unions. Quality circles and increased employee involvement programs have lessened the need for employee representation by union staff members to improve conditions. Clearly, the purpose of unions as envisioned in the 1930s has not met the requirements of the changing work environment.

What people perceive or believe to be true is frequently what will be. Individuals have a generally negative attitude about the worth of a union in today's participative and teamwork-oriented work environment. Perhaps inflation or major changes in union philosophies will change this attitude, but for now no noticeable upward trend in union membership is expected. However, unionism in the United States is not dead.

ARE UNIONS WEAKENING?

Whether unions are weakening is a highly controversial question. Some labor analysts readily point out examples that support a downward trend in labor unions. They claim that labor organizations are experiencing tough times with no relief in sight. There are two major problems. One is inability to draw members, and another is the trend toward labor-management cooperation.

Unions have historically chosen to hang their hat on their ability to obtain higher wages, and in today's labor market that is just not a broad enough agenda to satisfy the needs of modern workers. Their reputation for being able to provide higher wages was seriously damaged when the economy took a downturn in the 1980s, forcing employers to cut costs. Wage increases promoted by the unions were the first to go. These cuts weakened their ability to draw membership.

Unions may need new priorities to attract members.

An area that is having devastating effects on weakening unions is employee involvement (EI) programs. In the past few years, General Motors has been successful in acquiring labor-management cooperation headed by the union's leadership. Labor leaders have been willing to risk involvement in EI programs such as quality circles in hopes of making their employers more competitive in the do-or-die fight against Japanese competitors. This cooperative spirit may make the union members' jobs more secure and lessen the need for the traditional worker protectionism offered by unions.

At a United Auto Workers (UAW) convention in 1989, delegates favoring labor-management cooperation overwhelmingly voted down the old-line traditionalists who staunchly opposed the movement. The disagreement has been touted as the UAW's fiercest internal debate in over 40 years. When the convention was over, the UAW's leaders were more strongly committed to supporting the Big Three auto makers' EI programs. The UAW is not the only union making similar concessions. Other unions are joining in efforts to improve the country's competitive edge.

The use of work teams is creating significant changes in work practices, and unions are struggling to find a new role in teamwork plants. Teamwork reduces the influence of the union on traditional matters such as seniority and grievance procedures. Some labor experts see these trends as the major forces weakening unions.

Labor-management cooperation could further weaken traditional unions.

ARE UNIONS STRENGTHENING?

The 1990s may hold surprises as unions struggle to recover from decline.

Other expert labor analysts see several bright spots on the horizon for the strengthening of unions. The two major areas of hope are a perceived resurgence of support by union members and the successful attempts at unionizing new segments of the work force.

As management gets "leaner and meaner" through mergers, cutbacks, and downsizing, workers are unionizing in self-defense. A typical young man in today's work force actually earns less than his father realized at the same age in his career history, and the young man's job and future are far less secure. The changing work force is seeking representation for new demands, such as adequate retirement plans, health benefits, federal support for child care, and more flexible work hours to address the needs of families with two working parents. If the unions can aggressively address these issues with employers and make gains, opinions about the worth of union representation could make a major swing.

Additionally, strong union member support for strikes has shown a renewed commitment to union activities. When three Eastern Airline unions recently combined strike efforts in a show of labor strength, they shut down most of Eastern's activities. This show of unity resulted in forcing Eastern to reorganize under Chapter 11 of the federal bankruptcy laws. This intense type of labor unification has not been seen in decades. Similar types of strikes at Boeing Aircraft, Pittston Coal, and AT&T have added to the show of strength that unions are perceiving as a positive sign of an upswing of the labor movement.

New markets for union membership are being successfully tapped by union organizers. For example, at the Russell Stover candy plant in Cookeville, Tennessee, the union was voted in by a two-to-one margin. This instance is one of many new union representations in the southern states, which have for many years been opposed to unions. Unions have also been successful in organizing Hispanic workers in California recently.

New organizing approaches are being used by unions. Unions are becoming increasingly sophisticated in their approach to gaining new members through the use of college-educated, professional recruiters. These organizers are using what Kenneth Gilberg and Nancy Abrams refer to as the "Norma Rae" or "Tupperware" approach. The organizers are beginning with small groups in grassroot movements in order to generate enthusiastic support.

Additionally, the AFL-CIO is extending support to local organizing efforts by providing prepared television and radio spots, written scripts for advertising, videotapes, decals, and logos. These efforts provide local groups with polished and professional advertising that is a draw to membership.

While unions continue to dominate the craft and industrial sectors, they are also winning representation of more public sector, clerical, and white-collar professional employees. More than two million school teachers have become politically active union members. With continued efforts by organizers to tap these new markets and a shift in bargaining strategies, unions could realize a strengthening in membership numbers. The battle is far from over, but one thing is certain—unions are not dead.

SHOULD YOU JOIN A UNION?

If faced with becoming part of a union, you will be required to weigh the union and management positions. The union will tell you that you will have strength in numbers, your work and personal life will improve, and you will gain dignity and respect through membership. Additionally, office politics and favoritism will be eliminated, and your rights will be protected because your concerns will be heard.

Management will argue that you will pay dues for rights you already have. They may point out that unions tend to establish strong work rules, making the workplace rigid and causing the relationship between supervisors and workers to deteriorate. Management may also mention that the international union's highly paid officers control dues and how the money is spent, and that you will not be paid if you strike. Finally, it will be noted that the union often makes promises it may not be able to deliver.

The decision will be yours alone.

SUMMARY

A union is a group of workers who collectively bargain with employers for improved hours, wages, and working conditions.

When unions first developed, they typically represented blue-collar craft and industrial workers. Employee associations represented the white-collar and public sectors. Public sector workers were denied the right to strike against the government. Little difference exists today.

Prior to the 1930s, working conditions were unfavorable for workers. Unions formed to call with a collective voice for improving the situation. However, management used such tactics as obtaining injunctions, firing union agitators and blacklisting them from being hired elsewhere, forcing employees to sign yellow-dog contracts not to join a union when employed, and locking the doors to the factory to prevent workers from coming to work to make demands on management.

The Wagner Act of 1935 was the first federal legislation that prohibited management from interfering with union activities. Because this act was so sweepingly pro-union and provided unions with unchallenged power, the Taft-Hartley Act was passed restoring some rights to management and putting some restrictions on union activities. The National Labor Relations Board was formed to police labor-management activities and enforce the provisions of federal legislation. States were given the choice of adopting the right-to-work law, which prevented unions from forcing workers to join a union as a condition of employment. The Landrum-Griffin Act, which was passed after fraud and corruption by some union officials was uncovered, required unions to report their financial activities and hold elections for new officers to reduce the corruption alleged in union ranks.

The first unions represented skilled craftspeople who formed the AFL and unskilled workers who formed the CIO. These two groups later merged to form the AFL-CIO and reported a total membership of 14 million workers. Some large unions withdrew from the AFL-CIO to become independents.

Collective bargaining between labor and management representatives results in a written agreement, known as a contract, which is binding on both parties. Disputes over interpretations of the contract are called grievances and are resolved through a grievance procedure outlined in the contract. When a grievance is difficult to resolve, the matter is often taken to mediation, and a mediator assists in developing alternative solutions to the disputes. If this attempt is unsuccessful, the grievance is taken to arbitration, and an arbitrator makes a ruling that is legally binding on both parties. The key difference between mediation and arbitration is the legal standing of the arbitrator's decision. A mediator can only help in developing solutions acceptable to the parties involved.

Unions have seen significant shifts in membership in recent years and a decline in representation. In the decade of the eighties, union membership fell from 23 million employees to approximately 17 million. Male membership declined as female membership increased with the increased numbers of women in the general work force.

Labor analysts differ in opinion as to whether unions will revive and once again become an effective force in the workplace.

KEY TERMS

union
strike
employee association

labor agitator
blacklist
yellow-dog contract
Norris-LaGuardia Act
lockout
Wagner Act
National Labor Relations Board (NLRB)
Taft-Hartley Act
closed shop
union shop
agency shop
free rider
checkoff
right-to-work law
bargaining unit
Landrum-Griffin Act
craft union
American Federation of Labor (AFL)
industrial union
Congress of Industrial Organizations (CIO)
AFL-CIO
union steward
business agent
collective bargaining
contract
grievance
grievance procedure
mediation
mediator
Federal Mediation and Conciliation Service
arbitration
arbitrator

REVIEW QUESTIONS

1. Discuss the differences between unions and employee associations.
2. What were some of the methods used by management to prevent unions from forming prior to the passage of the Wagner Act?
3. What are the three key federal acts passed that still govern labor-management activities?
4. Describe the sequence of steps in a grievance procedure.
5. What is the key difference between mediation and arbitration?
6. Discuss whether unions are growing stronger or weakening today.

DISCUSSION QUESTIONS

1. If your current work unit were voting for union representation, would you vote for or against it? Why?
2. If your current work unit is not union, have you noticed any effort on the part of your management to avoid unionization? What methods are being used and by whom?
3. Think of the hours, wages, and working conditions in your current place of employment. Which of them do you think would be worth negotiating for improvement?
4. Would you be willing to be a union steward? Why or why not?
5. Do you think unions have a positive image in your community? Why or why not?
6. Do you think that unions in your region are strengthening or weakening? Why?

CASE STUDY 14.1

MAURICE, THE MASTER MECHANIC

Maurice was a member in good standing of the locally strong mechanics' union and had always been a good worker for the company. His union contract defined specific disciplinary actions for repeated or excessive absences from the job. The shop was a small one, and one person's absence caused work stoppages that crippled the work flow and created delays in finished products.

Maurice's supervisor noticed a drastic change in attendance by Maurice in the matter of a two-week period. Almost every other day he was either late or absent. The supervisor began immediate disciplinary procedures according to the contract terms and conditions.

When he confronted Maurice with his plans, Maurice reacted in a hostile manner. "That's certainly not the way I read that part of the contract. How in the world could you be so unfair to me? You let Carole take off whenever she needs to. What's the difference here? I'm not going to take this lying down! You'll be hearing from my union steward!" Maurice put down his tools and went to find his union steward immediately.

1. From the behaviors described, do you think that Maurice will be willing to resolve this dispute informally? Why or why not?
2. Did Maurice's supervisor respond appropriately to the situation? Should he have handled the situation any differently?
3. What will the union steward do as his first steps of involvement in the process?

CASE STUDY 14.2

THE BANANA'S REALLY RIPE

Horace Lynch had seen his banana import/export company triple in size in just the five short years since he started the company. He had moved into the new warehouse location only a couple of years ago. Sure, he had been forced to cut some corners to afford the new place, and unfortunately he had not been able to give his employees a raise these past two years, but they did not really seem to mind. Frankly, they seldom mentioned it at all. He had also had to raise the air conditioning temperature by several degrees to reduce the electrical bills that were a real drain on his operating budget. Hardly any of the employees had mentioned much about it, and he had joked it off by suggesting they wear cooler clothes.

The only other action he had taken to be able to afford the move to the larger warehouse had to do with some of the unfair safety rules that that government agent had tried to force on him. Why did he have to provide safety glasses for all his machinists when they had hardly ever had a serious accident? And the very idea that he should hang fire extinguishers near all possible flammatory locations! Why couldn't the workers just call the fire department if something like that should happen? After all, that is what fire departments are for. Horace had felt so strongly about these silly rules that he had made very clear to all his employees what would happen if they squawked about the possible safety hazards.

"If you don't like the conditions here, you can always go somewhere else. And if you complain to that government guy, I'll fire you on the spot and see to it that you are never hired in this line of work again."

1. Is Horace in danger of his workers desiring union representation?
2. If the workers did gain union representation, what conditions ripe for improvement would be taken to the bargaining table?
3. If you were one of Horace's employees, how would you handle this situation?

BIBLIOGRAPHY

Alpert, Mark. "Bonus Battles at Boeing." *Fortune* (November 6, 1989): 9.

Beal, Edwin F., and James P. Begin. *The Practice of Collective Bargaining*. Homewood, IL: Richard D. Irwin, Inc., 1982.

Beasley, J. Ernest. "U.S. Steel, Union Are at Odds on Eve of Talks." *The Wall Street Journal* (June 11, 1986): 20.

Blowen, Mildred S. (Executive Vice President of PTI Human Resource Management, Inc.). Personal interview, July 2, 1990.

Carley, William M. "Flight Attendants, Unions are Losing Strength." *The Wall Street Journal* (April 8, 1986): 9.

Connerton, Peggy. "The Union's Future Is Bright." *Personnel Administrator* (December 1989): 99–100.

Flanigan, James. "Workers Losing Job Security." *Houston Chronicle* (March 4, 1989): 1.

Freedman, Audrey. "The Union's Future is Bleak." *Personnel Administrator* (December 1989): 98–100.

Gilberg, Kenneth, and Nancy Abrams. "Union Organizing: New Tactics for New Times." *Personnel Administrator* (July 1987): 52–56.

Hoerr, John. "The Payoff from Teamwork." *Business Week* (July 10, 1989): 56–92.

Hoerr, John, Michael Schroeder, Todd Schroder, and Todd Vogel. "The Mine

Workers Must Win This Fight to Survive." **Business Week** (October 9, 1989): 144–148.

Holly, William H., and Kenneth M. Jennings. **The Labor Relations Process**. New York: CBS College Publishing, 1984.

McDonough, Paul A. "Maintain a Union-Free Status." **Personnel Journal** (April 1990): 108–114.

McWhirter, Darien A. **Your Rights at Work**. New York: John Wiley and Sons, 1989.

Mills, D. Quinn. "Reforming the U.S. System of Collective Bargaining." **Monthly Labor Review** 106, no. 1 (March 1983): 18–22.

Mintz, Bill. "Battle Unites Unions: Eastern Provides Common Enemy." **Houston Chronicle** (March 12, 1989): G1.

Statistical Abstract of the United States 1989, 109th Edition. Washington, DC: Bureau of the Census, 1989.

"Unions Today: New Tactics to Tackle Tough Times." Washington, DC: Bureau of National Affairs videotape, 1985.

Zellner, Wendy. "The UAW Rebels Teaming Up against Teamwork." **Business Week** (March 27, 1989): 32.

CHAPTER FIFTEEN
SUBSTANCE ABUSE

A federal jury convicted three former Northwest Airline pilots of flying a jetliner while intoxicated, even though the Boeing 727 jet with 91 passengers aboard arrived safely. The pilots had been drinking heavily the night before the 6:30 A.M. flight, with one pilot downing 19 rum and cokes and the other two sharing at least 7 pitchers of beer. The pilots were terminated by Northwest for drinking within 12 hours of a scheduled flight. Their licenses were revoked by the Federal Aviation Administration for violating regulations that prohibit flying within eight hours of drinking or with a blood-alcohol content above 0.04 percent.

Facts on File 1990 (August 20, 1990)

From 1975 to 1985, according to the Department of Transportation, U.S. railroads had 48 accidents that were directly linked to drug-impaired employees.

Dorothy Langley, *Drug Testing: The Right to Privacy vs. The Right to Test,* 1988.

These accidents resulted in 37 deaths and $34 million in property damages.

Robert B. Maddux and Lynda Voorhees, *Job Performance and Chemical Dependency,* 1987.

OBJECTIVES

After studying this chapter, you should be able to:
1. Identify the costs of substance abuse to organizations.
2. Describe what organizations are doing to combat substance abuse.
3. Name the types of drug testing schedules organizations use.
4. Discuss the downside of employee drug testing.
5. Identify substances that may be abused and their effects.
6. Describe the behavior of a substance abuser in the early, middle, and late phases of abuse.
7. Describe the actions a supervisor may take to handle an employee who is under the influence of drugs.
8. Explain the actions an employee can take when a coworker or supervisor is abusing substances.

WHAT IS SUBSTANCE ABUSE?

Substance
abusers cost
companies
money.

Substance abuse is the misuse of alcohol, illegal drugs, and prescription drugs. It has become a great concern for organizations because of the millions of dollars lost each year through decreased productivity, absenteeism, industrial accidents, and benefits used. Estimates are that employee drug use costs United States businesses between $33 billion and $81 billion a year.

FIGURE 15.1 Two train workers tested positive for drugs immediately following this 1987 railway collision that left 16 people dead and 175 injured.

Marty Katz/GAMMA LIAISON

According to Robert Maddux and Lynda Voorhees in *Job Performance and Chemical Dependency*, substance abusers are less effective workers. The authors estimate that:

A chemically dependent employee works at only 75 percent capacity.

Chemically dependent employees use three times as many sickness and accident benefits as other employees.

Substance abusers have two to four times more accidents on the job.

Substance abusers are absent twice as often as other employees.

Substance abusers file more grievances than nonabusing employees.

Nonalcoholic family members of alcoholics take more sick leave than the norm.

Approximately one out of six workers in the United States misuses sub-

stances. Companies average one or more drug dealers in their work
population for every 100 employees.

Most important, substance abuse is found in every level of a company.
Approximately 45 percent of all alcoholics are 15- to 30-year veterans in
management and professional positions.

In short, substance abuse costs companies money. The federal government
has become so concerned that in 1988 it issued **Executive Order 12564**, which
establishes a drug-free federal workplace and a drug testing program for federal
employees. The federal government also passed the **Federal Drug-Free Workplace Act** in 1988. This act requires federal contractors and grantees who receive
more than $25,000 in government business to certify that they will maintain a drug-
free workplace. These companies must establish and communicate to employees an
antidrug policy, notify employees that compliance with this policy is a condition of
employment, establish a drug-awareness program that educates employees on the
dangers of drugs and identifies assistance available to those with substance abuse
problems, and make a good-faith effort to maintain a drug-free workplace. Many
organizations not covered by these regulations are taking similar actions to reduce
costs associated with substance abuse.

HOW DO ORGANIZATIONS FIGHT ABUSE?

Organizations
fight substance
abuse by drug
testing, em-
ployee assis-
tance pro-
grams, and
education.

Organizations are using a variety of techniques, such as drug testing, employee
assistance programs, and employee education, in an effort to curtail substance abuse
at work. Testing can be performed on potential employees as well as current employees.

Pre-employment drug testing requires job applicants to pass a urinalysis examination for drugs in their system prior to employment. Applicants who do not pass the
examination or refuse to take the examination are not hired. The following is an
example of how pre-employment screening might be conducted:

> **Joan has just passed her typing test, and her interviews are
> favorable. However, before she can be hired at the TIV Corpora-
> tion, she must pass a drug test. The personnel department sends
> her to a clinic for the test, where a nurse asks her to list all the
> medications she has recently taken so that they will not be mis-
> taken for illicit drugs. Then Joan provides a urine specimen. She
> may possibly be monitored while she produces the specimen so
> that she cannot dilute it with water or switch samples with some-
> one else.**
>
> **The nurse and Joan watch while the sample is sealed and
> Joan's name is taped on the specimen, ensuring that her sample
> will not be mixed up with someone else's. The nurse will then send
> the specimen to the lab for processing. Later, Joan will be notified
> whether she will be hired by TIV.**

A growing number of organizations are also testing current employees for
substance abuse. A variety of testing schedules is used, depending on the preference

Organizations are testing employees for substance abuse.

of the organization. One type of schedule is known as **expected interval testing**. Under this method, employees are informed ahead of time when testing will occur. It is then performed at the same time on a continuous basis. For example, the test may be scheduled for the first workday after each payday.

Random interval testing involves giving tests at random to a particular group of employees. For instance, all employees in the accounting department may be informed that they are to report immediately for a drug test.

A third type of testing schedule is called **"for cause"** testing. Under this method, individual employees may be tested when they appear to exhibit signs of substance abuse, such as slurred speech or dilated pupils. Testing is sometimes done after industrial accidents or for reasonable cause:

> **Lee works on the assembly line at the TIV Corporation. She is 45 minutes late in returning from lunch. Her supervisor, Jim, notices that when Lee returns, her eyes are red, she appears disoriented, and she stumbles as she tries to sit down at her work station. She does not appear coherent when he attempts to talk to her. Jim speaks with her often enough to be able to determine that she is not ill, and he suspects that she is under the influence of some substance. He asks Lee to report to the company clinic for a drug test. Once there, Lee may be asked to submit to a blood test or breath test if the company suspects that she is under the influence of alcohol because alcohol intoxication cannot be measured through urinalysis.**

Other organizations test only employees who are transferred or promoted or employees who are in critical positions. Examples of employees in critical positions are factory employees who work with dangerous equipment and airline pilots.

Companies take action against employees who abuse substances.

Company policies and procedures vary on what happens to an employee who fails or refuses to submit to a substance abuse test. Many companies require termination on the spot. Others may require mandatory enrollment in a substance abuse program. Employees should be familiar with their company policy on this matter. Figure 15.2 summarizes drug testing results by industry, showing abuse by current employees and job applicants.

Many companies reserve the right to search all areas and property over which the company maintains control without consent of the employee. On occasion organizations have been known to call local law enforcement agencies or use dogs trained to locate illegal substances in an effort to curtail substance abuse.

Employers are also taking actions other than policing employees in order to reduce substance abuse. Many firms are establishing employee assistance programs. These programs, which are discussed in detail in Chapter 8, provide short-term counseling to employees and assist them in obtaining appropriate treatment for substance abuse.

Companies are also establishing employee education programs concerning drug and alcohol addiction as part of their employee wellness programs. These programs are discussed in Chapter 19. Employee education includes alerting employees to the dangers of substance abuse and encouraging those who are abusing to seek treatment.

FIGURE 15.2   Drug testing results—Breakdown of drug test results by industry.

Industry	% of Current Employees Tested Positive	% Job Applicants Tested Positive
Mining	6.1%	12.7%
Construction	12.0	11.9
Durable goods mfg.	12.1	11.2
Nondurable goods mfg.	8.9	12.7
Transportation	5.6	9.9
Communications and public utilities	7.8	5.5
Wholesale trade	20.2	17.4
Retail trade	18.8	24.4
Finance, insurance, real estate	—	6.7
Services	3.1	9.9
TOTAL	8.8	11.9

Bureau of Labor Statistics, Summer 1988

IS DRUG TESTING APPROPRIATE?

Although proponents of testing say drug testing saves companies money, opponents say that testing is intrusive, humiliating, and an invasion of privacy. Some civil libertarians see drug testing as an invasion of Fourth Amendment rights, which protect us from unreasonable search and seizure. Employees who feel violated may suffer from low morale, which may lead to decreased productivity.

Random testing subjects many innocent employees to degrading urinalysis tests. The acquisition of the specimen, to ensure that it is not altered and that it belongs to the individual who is doing the test, must be observed. Blood tests can also be intrusive. Because random testing targets many individuals who are not abusers, the cost of testing is extremely high in proportion to the positive results uncovered. According to Dorothy Langley, in 1985 alone, for instance, the Department of Defense spent $50 million testing for drugs.

Another concern is that the tests are not foolproof. Many legal substances, including poppy seeds, cold medicine, and prescription drugs such as Tylenol Plus 3 (with codeine) can test positive. As an example, athlete Linford Christie almost lost his silver medal in the 1988 Seoul Olympics when his drug test registered positive because of the ginseng tea he had consumed.

According to Andrew Kupfer in a 1988 article in *Fortune*, up to 10 percent of samples will register false positives. Even though a person may be asked to list medications taken prior to submitting to a drug test, they may forget having taken medication several weeks before.

A confirmatory test can be done. However, these second tests are expensive, and a number of companies do not retest if a positive result occurs, particularly when screening new job applicants. Many employees do not tell job applicants the reasons

Many people find drug testing intrusive, humiliating, and an invasion of employee rights.

they have been rejected, nor do they often give job applicants a chance to explain a positive result.

Opponents also criticize the statistics used to justify drug testing. Some of these claims, according to John Horgan in *Scientific American,* do not accurately reflect the research on which they are based. In addition, some of the studies may contain flaws and distortions, causing the figures they produce to be in question.

Finally, opponents point out that drug tests do not measure the impairment present, nor do they reveal when the substance was consumed. Positive results can be obtained days after the drug has been used. Detection times vary depending on the drug taken, the frequency of use, and the amount of drug ingested.

Figure 15.3 summarizes approximate detection time limits of commonly abused drugs. Substances that are used by employees or prospective employees on their days off may yield positive results in later screening tests.

The laws in the area of drug testing change rapidly as new court cases are decided. Presently employees in private industry are not protected from drug searches on company property or from being required to take drug tests. Because of the importance that the nation has placed on the war on drugs, it appears that testing, for the time being, will remain legal.

FIGURE 15.3   Approximate time limits within which drugs can be detected through testing.

Drug test results can be positive long after the substance was used.

Drug	Approximate Dose and Administration Route	Detection Time
Amphetamines	30 mg PO	1–120 hr
	15 mg PO	1–72 hr
	5 mg PO	3.5–30.0 hr
Barbiturates		
Short-acting	100 mg PO	4.5 days
Phenobarbital	400 mg PO	7 days
Benzodiazepines	25 mg PO	48 hr minimum
Diazepam	10 mg PO	None detected
	10 mg, 5 times daily	3–7 days
Cocaine	250 mg PO	8–48 hr
Opioids		
Heroin	10 mg IV	1–4 days
Meperidine	100 mg PO	4–24 hr
Methadone	38 mg PO	7.5–56.0 hr
Morphine	10 mg IV	84 hr minimum
Methaqualone	150 mg PO	Up to 60 hr
	250 mg PO	Up to 72 hr
	300 mg PO	Up to 90 hr
Marijuana	1 per week	7–34 days
	Daily	6–81 days

Abbreviations: PO = *per os* (oral); IV = intravenous.

Drug Testing in the Workplace *(Washington, DC: Bureau of National Affairs, 1989). Reprinted with permission of the American Society of Clinical Pathology Press*

WHAT SUBSTANCES ARE MOST ABUSED?

Commonly
abused sub-
stances can be
legal or illegal.

Understanding the short-term and long-term effects of substance abuse is important for several reasons. First, if you are abusing substances, or plan to, you should be aware of what you are doing to your body and how these chemicals will alter your ability to perform on the job. Then, too, knowing substance effects will help you detect substance abuse in those around you and will help you deal with them.

Commonly abused substances include alcohol, cocaine, and marijuana. Also abused are sedatives, tranquilizers, hallucinogens, and narcotics.

Alcohol is the most abused drug in the United States. A depressant, it slows down the activity of the brain and spinal cord and knocks out the control centers one by one. Although it may produce feelings of well-being, it can lead to sedation, intoxication, blackouts, unconsciousness, and death.

Heavy consumption of alcohol may cause immediate physical problems, such as inefficiency, low energy, weight loss, lethargy, sleeplessness, accidents, and memory loss. Emotionally, it can cause a person to feel jealous, sexually aroused, impotent, moody, easily angered, guilty, depressed, worthless, despondent, and suicidal.

Over a period of years, the effects of heavy drinking include malnutrition, brain damage, cancer, heart disease, liver damage, ulcers, gastritis, and birth defects in children whose mothers abused alcohol during pregnancy.

Cocaine is a stimulant derived from the coca leaf. It has been used in the United States for years and, prior to 1900, was an active ingredient in many soft drinks and patent medicines. Common feelings experienced by the person who has taken cocaine are hyperalertness, euphoria, and power. These feelings are short-lived, not over 30 minutes. For these reasons, cocaine is highly psychologically addictive, and individuals begin to want more and more the sensations they receive from cocaine.

Heavy use of cocaine can lead to weight loss, insomnia, and anxiety reactions. Paranoid thinking may also develop, as well as severe anxiety and depression when the effects of the drug wear off. Because of its temporary effects, cocaine has become popular among professionals who are achievement-oriented and feel an obligation to be "up" constantly.

Crack, the street name for a new and more powerful form of cocaine, is smoked rather than sniffed through the nose or injected. Crack creates the same side effects as cocaine but is even more addictive.

Another commonly abused substance is **marijuana**. Researchers are discovering that marijuana, the dried leaves and flowering tops of the pistillate hemp plant, is a much more dangerous drug than was originally thought. Because of modern agriculture, *The Marijuana Research Update* states that the THC (active ingredient) content in marijuana today is 10 to 20 times that of marijuana grown ten years ago.

Marijuana produces relaxation, spontaneity (because of loss of inhibition), disorientation of spatial relationships, heightened (though not always accurate) sensory awareness, and hunger. It also causes immediate memory loss, impairment in thinking, and a loss of motivation. These effects can be particularly disruptive in the workplace. The heavy smoker is detached, cannot judge or concentrate, and is not motivated. Psychologically, heavy usage can cause "flashbacks" (viewing scenes from the past) and acute adverse reactions.

The physical effects of heavy marijuana usage are cause for concern. Regular marijuana use appears to cause lung and other types of cancer and respiratory diseases more rapidly than does cigarette smoking. In addition, it has an adverse effect on both the male and female hormonal balance and reproductive functions. THC also possibly suppresses the immune system, leading to lower resistance to disease.

Sedatives (barbiturates) and **tranquilizers** include Seconal, Tuinal, Nembutal, Phenobarbital, Quaaludes, Glutethimide, Doriden, and Valium. Street names may be downers, ludes, 714s, yellow jackets, reds, blues, or rainbows. Some of them are legal drugs that can be obtained with a prescription.

Sedatives and tranquilizers are depressants and can cause drowsiness, agitation, intellectual confusion, and physical impairment. Abusers may have slurred or emotional speech as well as poor body coordination. Overdoses can be characterized by difficulties in walking and speaking, constant uncontrolled eye movements, lethargy, and coma.

Amphetamines are synthetic nervous system stimulants. They have a number of street names, such as speed, ice, bennies, dexies, uppers, copilots, and pep pills. They are used to lose weight, stay awake, increase energy, and "get high." The physical effects are dilated pupils, rapid heartbeat, loss of appetite, anxiety, irritability, rapid speech, tremors, and destructive mood elevation.

Some drugs, called designer drugs, have been derived from amphetamines. Known by names such as ecstasy, eve, and rhapsody, they temporarily make people feel more alive and sensitive to people around them. However, research shows that these drugs destroy cells in the brain that produce dopamine, a vital nerve transmitter.

Inhalants are another category of abused substances. The practice of sniffing hydrocarbons contained in substances such as airplane glue, gasoline, cleaning fluid, and aerosols is prevalent among children 11 to 15 years old. Symptoms include restlessness, excitement, lack of coordination, confusion, and coma.

Long-term use of inhalants can cause damage to the brain, nerves, liver, and kidneys. Fatalities have occurred from suffocation caused when the abuser used a plastic bag to inhale the substance and lost consciousness.

Hallucinogens produce chemically induced hallucinations. The list of hallucinogens includes LSD, mescaline, MDA, PCP (or angel dust), and acid. The fact that these hallucinogens can create immediate emotional disturbances or cause flashbacks years later makes them particularly dangerous in the workplace. Symptoms include euphoria, loss of inhibition, agitation, confusion, stupor, and paranoia. Violent or bizarre reactions are not uncommon, and extreme doses can lead to convulsions, coma, or death.

Narcotics include heroin, opium, morphine, dilaudid, and codeine. All are derivatives of the opium poppy. They can cause euphoria, sedation, nausea, vomiting, insensitivity to pain, watery eyes, and skin problems and infections. These drugs are physically addictive, and withdrawal causes painful physical symptoms.

Many prescription and over-the-counter medications, such as cold remedies, can cause drowsiness, impairing an employee's ability to drive or operate machinery on the job. These drugs can also be abused. Employees operating equipment and taking medication should consult their supervisors.

We can readily see that abusing substances takes a toll on people's ability to perform as well as their physical and mental health. Those who are abusing substances need to seek help immediately.

WHAT IF YOU ARE AN ABUSER?

If you are abusing substances, you need to take action before their use interferes with your current job, prevents you from obtaining a job, disrupts other major areas of your life, or destroys your health. See Figure 15.4 for ways in which your life may be affected.

FIGURE 15.4   Substance abuse affects many life areas.

Relationships	Individuals who abuse substances have difficulty maintaining healthy family relationships. Friends who do not abuse substances may avoid contact with the substance abuser, particularly at social functions, because the abuser, many times, behaves in a fashion that causes embarrassment. Many substance abusers drop nonusing friends in favor of those who also abuse substances.
Finances	Abusing substances is expensive, and abusers may spend more than they earn to support the habit. In addition, the abuser may not pay attention to finances and may become careless with money.
Work performance	Performance may deteriorate, resulting in disciplinary action or termination. Friction with coworkers may become a problem as coworkers become irritated at the abuser for not doing a fair share of the work.
Health	Abusers develop health problems such as high blood pressure, deterioration of brain cells, depression, malnutrition, and cirrhosis of the liver.

Adapted from Robert B. Maddux and Lynda Voorhees, Job Performance and Chemical Dependency *(Los Altos: Crisp Publication, 1987)*

Check the telephone book or community resources for treatment and counseling centers. If you are currently employed and your company has an employee assistance program, use it. This program is designed to help employees with substance abuse and other personal problems. It is confidential and almost always free of charge.

Substance
abusers need
to seek help.

Many individuals are reluctant to use an employee assistance program for fear that their employer will learn they have a problem. Most plans ensure confidentiality and do not reveal to the employer which employees have used the services. Employers will eventually find out about substance abuse problems left untreated when performance declines.

FIGURE 15.5   Seeking help is the first step in controlling a substance abuse problem.

Photo by Richard Younker

Many individuals are able to use alcohol in moderation without any interference with their performance. If you drink socially, you can take several steps to ensure that your alcohol intake is under control and to keep it within responsible boundaries. Harriet B. Braiker, in an article in *Working Woman*, suggests the following precautions:

> Limit drinking to under one ounce of ethanol, the intoxicating ingredient in
> alcoholic beverages, on any day that you drink. (One-half ounce of ethanol

equates to 12 ounces of beer, five ounces of wine, or one ounce of hard liquor.)

Abstain completely from alcoholic beverages for at least two consecutive days each week.

Measure your alcohol when making your own drinks. A standard single drink of hard liquor should contain no more than one ounce of alcohol. A standard serving of wine is five ounces.

Drink slowly and intersperse alcoholic drinks with nonalcoholic drinks while at parties.

Don't drink on an empty stomach.

Don't medicate yourself with alcohol. It will only make you feel more depressed.

Avoid social patterns that revolve around alcohol, and associate with responsible drinkers.

Some individuals, however, should not drink at all. Abstinence may be the only way that recovering alcoholics and individuals from alcoholic families are able to prevent abusing substances. More information can be obtained from the National Council on Alcoholism, Alcoholics Anonymous, or other organizations that deal with alcohol abuse. (People who consume alcohol can check for problem drinking by answering the questions in Figure 15.6.)

If you do not take action to correct your substance abuse problem, most likely your supervisor will. Most organizations that operate drug testing programs have

FIGURE 15.6 Do you have a problem with alcohol?

1. Do you drink to relieve stress and escape problems?
2. Is it difficult to stop drinking once you start?
3. Are you, at times, unable to remember what was said or done while drinking?
4. Do you drink alone?
5. Do you find it necessary to drink larger quantities to obtain the same effect?
6. Is your drinking becoming a worry or concern to your family?
7. Is it necessary to have a drink to get over a hangover?
8. Is drinking interfering with your ability to perform your job?
9. Do you find yourself craving a drink at certain times of the day?
10. Does your personality change, causing you to become more moody, irritable, and harder to get along with while drinking?
11. Is your social life centered around activities that involve alcohol?
12. Has drinking become a daily necessity?

Yes answers to several of these questions may indicate a problem with alcohol.

FIGURE 15.7 How a "troubled employee" behaves.

EFFICIENCY	CRISIS POINTS DURING DETERIORATION	BEHAVIOR

(Chart content as depicted in figure)

CRISIS POINTS DURING DETERIORATION labels:

- CRITICISM FROM BOSS
- FAMILY PROBLEMS
- LOSS OF JOB ADVANCEMENT
- FINANCIAL PROBLEMS WAGE GARNISHMENT
- WARNING FROM BOSS
- IN TROUBLE WITH LAW
- TYPICAL CRISIS
- PUNITIVE DISCIPLINARY ACTION
- SERIOUS FAMILY PROBLEMS-SEPARATION
- SERIOUS FINANCIAL PROBLEMS
- FINAL WARNING FROM BOSS
- AREA OF GREATEST COVER-UP
- TERMINATION
- HOSPITALIZATION
- SUPERVISOR'S EVALUATION
- ACTUAL JOB DETERIORATION

Efficiency axis: 90%, 75%, 50%, 25%

BEHAVIOR

EARLY PHASE
ATTENDANCE
  Late (after lunch)
  Leaves work early
  Absent from office
GENERAL BEHAVIOR
  Fellow workers complain
  Overreacts to real or imagined criticism
  Complains of not feeling well
  Lies
JOB PERFORMANCE
  Misses deadlines
  Mistakes through inattention or
    poor judgement
  Decreased efficiency

MIDDLE PHASE
ATTENDANCE
  Frequent days off for vague ailments
    or implausible reasons
GENERAL BEHAVIOR
  Statements become undependable
  Begins to avoid associates
  Borrows money from coworkers
  Exaggerates work accomplishments
  Hospitalized more than average
  Repeated minor injuries on and off the job
  Unreasonable resentment
JOB PERFORMANCE
  General deterioration
  Spasmodic work pace
  Attention wanders-Lack of concentration

LATE MIDDLE PHASE
ATTENDANCE
  Frequent time off-Sometimes for several
    days
  Fails to return from lunch
GENERAL BEHAVIOR
  Grandiose, aggressive, or belligerent
  Apparent loss of ethical value
  Money problems, garnishment of salary
  Hospitalization increases
  Refuses to discuss problems
  Trouble with the law
JOB PERFORMANCE
  Far below expected level

LATE PHASE
ATTENDANCE
  Prolonged unpredictable absences
GENERAL BEHAVIOR
  Totally undependable
  Repeated hospitalization
  Visible physical deterioration
  Money problems are worse
  Serious family problems and/or divorce
JOB PERFORMANCE
  Uneven and generally incompetent

trained their supervisors to recognize behavior that signals substance abuse. These signs are listed in Figure 15.7.

Many substance abusers deny having a problem and fail to realize that the problem is interfering with their work. Because of employee denial, organizations usually instruct their supervisors to do the following about suspected instances of substance abuse:

Judge on performance only and do not accuse the employee of having a substance abuse problem.

Do not accept excuses for prolonged poor work performance or absenteeism.

Document all poor performance.

Assist employees in obtaining treatment if asked.

Do not preach or moralize.

Begin action up to and including discharge if the employee does not satisfactorily perform the job.

Employees with substance abuse problems should recognize that supervisors have higher management support in taking these actions. Abusers should address their problem if they wish to remain employed.

WHAT IF YOU KNOW AN ABUSER?

Becoming aware that a coworker or supervisor is exhibiting the warning signs in Figure 15.7 presents a dilemma. If you allow such people to operate machinery or perform any activity that might injure them or others or destroy equipment or property and something actually happens, living with yourself will be difficult. If you report the individual to management, resentment will most likely result, causing future difficulties in working with this individual. Others in your work group may feel uncomfortable around you, feeling that you will report their activities to management.

Covering up for coworkers or supervisors by doing their work or making excuses for their tardiness or absence is called **enabling**. This behavior allows substance abusers to continue this conduct and to avoid confronting the problem. Enabling will keep peace in your work group. However, you will continue to perform extra work while the abuser carries on the pattern of missed hours and substandard performance. Resentment on your part will soon build.

Additionally, you may wish to assist the individual in trouble. You may give advice, preach, or moralize. This action generally does not help, because substance abusers typically deny that they have a problem. The more you attempt to help, the more resentful the substance abuser will become, frustrating both of you.

Dealing with substance-abusing coworkers and supervisors, then, requires human relations skills. Use tact and diplomacy, involving only those with a need to know. Tell abusers that their behavior is making your working with them difficult. Point out a specific behavior, such as absence, that is causing you difficulty. Offer support by showing concern that they do not appear to be their old selves and asking what you can do to help. Be supportive if they decide to enter treatment.

Take action when a co-worker abuses substances.

Not allowing impaired employees to operate equipment, refusing to "enable" by covering for them, and not preaching or moralizing are the best ways to help yourself and your fellow employees. Doing so will force the abuser into treatment quicker and not leave you feeling used or taken advantage of.

SUMMARY

Organizations are concerned about substance abuse because abusers cost them money in the form of lost productivity, industrial accidents, and excessive use of benefits. Many companies are beginning to take action to control substance abuse by testing both prospective and current employees and by offering employee assistance programs and substance abuse education. A variety of testing schedules of current employees, such as expected interval testing, random testing, or "for cause" testing, are used to detect substance abuse.

Critics of drug testing point out that it is humiliating, intrusive, and an invasion of privacy. False positives on tests are possible, and tests do not reveal when the drug was taken or the level of impairment. Opponents also criticize the statistics used to justify testing, saying the tests are misinterpreted or flawed.

Knowledge of the commonly abused substances can help you understand how, if you abuse or intend to abuse substances, you decrease your own productivity and threaten your health. Also, you can better recognize abuse in others and react appropriately. Commonly abused substances include alcohol, cocaine, marijuana, sedatives, tranquilizers, amphetamines, inhalants, hallucinogens, heroin, and prescription drugs. Individuals who are abusing substances need to take action to control their problem. If they do not, their supervisors may take action. Any employee confronted with a coworker who is abusing substances needs to take positive steps to handle the problem.

KEY TERMS

substance abuse
Executive Order 12564
Federal Drug-Free Workplace Act
expected interval testing
random interval testing
"for cause" testing
alcohol
cocaine
marijuana
sedatives
tranquilizers
amphetamines
inhalants
hallucinogens
narcotics
enabling

REVIEW QUESTIONS

1. List the costs of substance abuse to organizations.
2. What are companies doing to combat substance abuse?
3. What three types of drug testing schedules do companies use?
4. What is the downside of drug testing?
5. What substances are commonly abused? What are their effects?
6. How does the substance abuser behave in the early, middle, and late phase of abuse?
7. What actions can an abuser of substances expect from a supervisor who has been trained to deal with substance abusers?
8. How can you handle a coworker who is abusing substances?

DISCUSSION QUESTIONS

1. Review the effects of each of the major types of substances. Give examples of accidents or mistakes that the misuse of substances can cause on the job.
2. What difficulty would you have in handling a coworker and good friend who is abusing substances? What might happen to the coworker if you "enable"? To you? To others? To the company?
3. Should employers have the right to administer drug tests to employees? Why or why not?
4. What resources are available in your community to assist individuals in controlling substance abuse?
5. Study the information in Figure 15.7 carefully. Have you ever been around individuals exhibiting some of these behaviors at work or at home? What happened to them? How did their behavior affect you? Others?

CASE STUDY 15.1

OPPORTUNITIES UP IN SMOKE

Jane was excited. She was scheduled to start her new job Monday. It was a good feeling, after having worked so hard—two years in junior college and ten weeks of intensive searching for the perfect job. As she sat on the couch daydreaming about the new car she was going to buy, the phone rang. Suzette, the personnel officer who had interviewed her for the position, was on the telephone.

"I'm sorry, Jane," Suzette said, "but your drug test was positive. We can't hire you for the position."

Jane hung up and frantically called her boyfriend, Carl.

"It's not fair," she sobbed. "I only smoked one joint at the party last week. I never dreamed it would show up on my test. That's just not fair!"

1. Was Jane's test fair? Should Jane have the right not to be tested? Should employers have the right to test her?
2. What could Jane's drug use cost the company in the future?
3. What did Jane's drug use cost her? What should Jane do in the future?

**CASE STUDY
15.2**

LIQUID LUNCHES?

"Where is Harry? He was supposed to have returned from lunch an hour ago. He was going to give me the figures for the mid-year report. The report is due at 5 P.M. today," grumbled Albert.

"You know," said Yuki, "he's had many problems lately. He and his wife have separated. Give him a break."

"Yuki, it's more than that," replied Albert. "His lunches have gotten longer, and last week he didn't even come back after lunch. His work has gotten so bad that I don't know if I can cover for him any longer. If the boss finds out about this, he'll hit the ceiling."

1. What do you think may be happening to Harry?
2. What should Albert and Yuki do?
3. Are they helping Harry by covering for him?

BIBLIOGRAPHY

"Alcohol at Work." Weymouth, MA: Life Skills Education, Inc., 1986.

Baird, Jane. "To Test or Not to Test." *The Houston Post* (September 4, 1989): E1, E8.

Barbou, John A. "Cracking Down: What You Must Know about Dangerous Drugs." Series in *The Houston Post,* 1986.

Bechner, George, and Alfred Freedman. *Teen Drug Use.* Lexington, MA: Lexington Books, 1986.

Berger, Gilda, and Franklin Watts. *Crack—The New Drug Epidemic.* New York: Impact, 1987.

"Body Invaders." *The Nation* (January 8/15, 1990): 39–40.

Braiker, Harriet B. "What All Career Women Need to Know about Drinking." *Working Woman* (August 1989): 72.

Cohn, Sidney. *The Substance Abuse Problem.* New York: Haworth Press, 1981.

Decrese, Robert P., et al. *Drug Testing in the Workplace.* Washington, DC: Bureau of National Affairs, 1989.

Deming, Janet. "Drug-Free Workplace Is Good Business." *HRMagazine* (April 1990): 61–62.

Fear Itself: A Legal and Personal Analysis of Drug Testing, AIDS, Secondary Smoke, VDTs. Alexandria, VA: ASPA Foundation, 1987.

Haverland, Larry R. *Drug Information Guide.* Brooklyn, NY: Promotional Slide Guide Corporation, 1980.

Horgan, John. "Test Negative." *Scientific American* (March, 1990): 18, 22.

Hyde, Margaret O. *Addictions: Gambling, Smoking, Cocaine Use and Others.* New York: McGraw-Hill, 1978.

Kupfer, Andrew. "Is Drug Testing Good or Bad?" *Fortune* (December 19, 1988): 133–139.

Langley, Dorothy A. *Drug Testing: The Right to Privacy vs. the Right to Test.* Dayton: Pamphlet Publications, Inc., 1988.

Maddux, Robert B., and Lynda Voorhees. ***Job Performance and Chemical Dependency.*** Los Altos, CA: Crisp Publications, 1987.

Marijuana Research Update. Salt Lake City: University of Utah School of Drug and Alcohol Abuse, 1985.

CHAPTER SIXTEEN
ETHICS

THE MAN IN THE GLASS

When you get what you want in your
    struggle for self
And the world makes you king for a
    day,
Go to the mirror and look at yourself
And see what THAT man has to say.

For it isn't your father or mother or
    wife
Whose judgment upon you must
    pass;
The fellow whose verdict counts
    most in life
Is the one staring back from the
    glass.

Some people may think you a
    straight-shootin' chum
And call you a wonderful guy,
But the man in the glass says you're
    only a bum
If you can't look him straight in the
    eye.

He's the fellow to please, never
    mind all the rest,
For he's with you clear up to the
    end.
And you've passed your most dan-
    gerous, difficult test
If the man in the glass is your friend.

You may fool the whole world down
    the pathway of life
And get pats on your back as you
    pass,
But your final reward will be heart-
    aches and tears
If you have cheated the man in the
    glass.

Dale Wimbrow, in Blanchard and
Peale's *The Power of Ethical
Management*

OBJECTIVES

After studying this chapter, you should be able to:
1. Explain the differences among ethics, values, integrity, and social responsibility.
2. Identify events that have resulted in the current emphasis on ethics.
3. Describe some of the methods of determining ethical standards.
4. Explain what is meant by an ethical dilemma.
5. Describe some of the methods used to resolve ethical dilemmas.
6. Discuss when and how ethics might be introduced to potential workers.

WHAT IS ETHICS?

We are faced with decisions every day that require drawing on our sense of what is right or wrong, good or bad, ethical or not. We make the ultimate choice from a set of values instilled early in life. The process of choosing can be complicated by many factors, so that we often find ourselves facing difficult situations with questions not easily answered. We must remember the man or woman in the glass.

Ethics, as defined by the *American Heritage Dictionary*, is "the study of the general nature of morals and of the specific moral choices to be made by individuals in their relationships with others; a set of moral principles or values." More simply stated, ethics is the basis for moral choices we make. Making ethical choices means not only choosing what is legal, but also what is right based on our values. To understand ethics, we must explore a few related terms.

One term frequently linked with ethics is **integrity**, which is the strict adherence to a code of behavior. The lack of integrity has become a critical issue in individual and business behaviors today, causing some of the very incidents discussed later in this chapter. Another term closely related to ethics is values. **Values** are principles, standards, or qualities you consider worthwhile or desirable. More specifically, your values are your beliefs about what is right or wrong, good or bad, and acceptable or unacceptable. These beliefs developed during your formative years and are heavily influenced by your family, friends, religion, schools, and the media.

Integrity is strict adherence to a code of behavior.

These values, or beliefs, form the basis of our value systems that lock in at about age 20 and remain relatively stable throughout our adult lives. We demonstrate our values by how we interact with others and make decisions in our daily lives. Ethics brings our value systems into play.

Ethics is not only an individual issue but an organizational issue. We cannot avoid ethical issues in business any more than we can in other areas of our lives. The corporate culture influences decisions that affect not only the organization's employees, but its customers and the general public.

Both individuals and corporations must deal with ethical issues on a day-to-day basis. James Stoner and R. Edward Freeman in their book *Management* describe four levels of ethical issues, which are mutually exclusive:

1. *Societal issues.* At the societal level questions deal with the basic institutions in a society. For example, is apartheid in South Africa ethically correct when the majority of people is systematically denied basic rights? Is capitalism satisfactory if gross inequalities of wealth, status, and power occur?

2. *Stakeholders' issues.* Stakeholders' issues pertain to appropriate treatment of and relationships with employees, suppliers, customers, shareholders, bondholders, and others. They deal with business policy, such as how much obligation a company has to notify its customers about the potential dangers of its products.

3. *Internal policy issues.* Questions of internal policy pertain to the relationship between a company and its employees at all levels. Examples are policies

dealing with employee rights, due process, free speech, employee participation, and others.

4. *Personal issues.* Personal issues are the day-to-day questions that occur in
every organization. They revolve around two basic questions: Do we have
the right to treat other people as means to our ends? Can we avoid doing
so?

At work ethics concerns the ground rules on all four of these levels. Because
most of our ground rules are already in place, making ethical decisions requires us to
be critical of our own ground rules and to improve them. Occasionally situations in
business result in applying a set of ground rules different from personal life. Consider
the following situation:

William: Clarence, I appreciate your recommendation of my company to
            head the study project. I consider that a real bonus to the growth
            and expansion of my business. Such a favor should be rewarded,
            and I want you to have these box seat tickets to the big upcoming
            basketball game. Thanks, buddy.

Clarence: That is very thoughtful of you, William, but my company code of
            ethics prohibits my accepting gifts from contractors with whom we
            do business. These rules protect both my personal and profes-
            sional integrity. Besides, I made the recommendation because I
            genuinely felt that you were the most qualified bidder on the job.

Clarence made the decision to refuse the gift based on his belief in the code of
ethics established by his company. Figure 16.1 describes possible unethical behaviors in personal and business settings.

Unethical behaviors may lead people to financial gain or other benefits, but the
consequences may range from a guilty conscience to a fine or prison term. Corporations may gain sizable market shares and higher profits but, if exposed, may be faced
with fines and penalties as well as decreased sales and a loss of confidence from

FIGURE 16.1 Some unethical behaviors.

Personal	Business
• Cheating on exams/tests. • Accepting credit for favors not per-formed. • Cheating on income tax reports. • Betraying personal confidences. • Keeping unauthorized materials/mon-ies. • Violating minor traffic rules.	• Copying computer software. • Accepting gifts from subordinates. • Falsifying time/expense reports. • Doing personal business on company time. • Taking company materials/supplies for personal use. • Polluting the environment with toxic waste.

customers and the general public. For these reasons ethics is a concern for both individuals and organizations.

WHAT IS SOCIAL RESPONSIBILITY?

Social responsibility plays a key role in decisions about pollution, discrimination, welfare, and the well-being of society.

Social responsibility is the obligation we have to make choices or decisions that are beneficial to the whole of society. These types of decisions most commonly involve issues such as environmental pollution, welfare, inflation, discrimination, and homeless and hungry people. Corporate social responsibility may be viewed from one of three perspectives—classical, accountability, and public.

The **classical perspective** holds that businesses need not feel responsible for social issues and should concentrate on being profitable, as an economy based on strong businesses best serves society overall. This view suggests that ethics should

FIGURE 16.2   Social responsibility is the obligation to make choices or decisions that are mutually beneficial to the whole of society.

Barbara Alper/STOCK, BOSTON

have little influence on decisions and that profit is the bottom line. We need only consider the effects this approach could have on our environment if no concern were shown for air quality or water pollution.

The **accountability perspective** holds businesses accountable for their actions, with a responsibility to be fair and considerate in their business practices. This view requires sensitivity to environmental and social issues and prevents unethical decisions in such matters as toxic waste disposal and discrimination against minorities, women, aged, or handicapped workers.

Three different perspectives may affect our views on social responsibility.

The **public perspective** links businesses with the government and other groups to actively solve social and environmental problems. This view requires involvement by all parties in improving the general quality of life. Decisions are made with the goal of profit for the business but also with consideration of impact on pollution or unemployment.

From any of these perspectives, ethics plays a critical role in the decisions to be made. Should a company pollute the air or water because control devices are expensive to install and would reduce profits? Should the company install expensive pollution devices that may negatively impact the budget and cause employee layoffs, affecting local unemployment problems? Considering these questions makes more obvious the relationships of the terms mentioned in the chapter's beginning. Values, integrity, and ethics must all be exercised in situations involving social responsibility.

WHY IS ETHICS IN THE SPOTLIGHT?

Unethical behavior has been with us since the beginning of time. From all appearances, however, the United States is currently suffering a crisis in ethics. Television news broadcasts and newspapers (beginning in the 1960s and mushrooming in the late 1980s) have been filled with reports of unethical business practices and unethical

Recent events suggest a need for more ethical decision making.

personal behaviors. Few professions or occupations are left unscathed. Corporate CEOs, bankers, doctors, lawyers, government officials, defense contractors, investment counselors, food and medicine manufacturers, and military employees are being indicted in unprecedented numbers for a variety of unethical activities. Figure 16.3 describes some of the well-known events that have brought national attention to questionable ethics in recent years.

With the obvious escalation in numbers of events in recent years, we are left wondering whether we are living in a mindless, valueless society on a path of destruction or whether we are victims of media hype. Were these kinds of events happening in previous years but unnoticed because the ethical culture of those times was "It's okay, just don't get caught"? With the media now probing all areas of society, government, and business activities and focusing on negative ethics, individuals and organizations have a greater need to improve current ethical practices.

Aside from the media keeping the subject in the forefront, the public seems to have reached the full span of the pendulum swing. Public opinion now reflects the sentiment, "We are fed up. Let's all play by the rules." During the last decade, the Reagan administration witnessed approximately one hundred government officials facing charges of unethical misconduct of some nature. The presidential campaigns saw Senators Hart and Biden face political destruction in the wake of personal ethical blunders. House Speaker Jim Wright and Senator John Tower were investigated by ethics committees, dashing their aspirations.

Prominent names in other fields faced similar charges. In the sports arena, Pete Rose was found guilty of gambling activities and an Olympic champion admitted illegal use of steroids. Religious leaders Jimmy Swaggart and Jim Baker violated

FIGURE 16.3   Events that have focused attention on ethical issues.

The Homeless and Hungry • Greenhouse Effect •
ILLITERACY • *Civil Rights* • **ILLEGAL ALIENS** •
Child Abuse • **Explosion of the Space Shuttle**
• *Nuclear Power Safety* • ENVIRONMENTAL POLLUTION
AND DESTRUCTION • *U.S. Involvement in Foreign Wars* • **AIDS** •
Insider Trading Scandals • *SAVINGS AND LOAN SCANDALS* •
SCANDALS OF RELIGIOUS LEADERS • Payments to
Japanese Interns from World War II • **Investigations of Cabinet and**
Supreme Court Nominees • Illegal Drug Use by Athletes • SELLING
MILITARY SECRETS • *Iran-Contra Affair* • *HUD scandals*
1960s to 1990s

moral codes. Business tycoons stole the headlines for what seemed an eternity. Ivan Boesky was indicted on charges of insider trading, paid $100 million in penalties, and served a three-year jail sentence. T. Boone Pickens, Carl Icahn, and Ron Perelman raised billions of dollars for corporate takeovers that put businesses on the alert for signs of unethical activities. Michael Milken of Drexel Burnham Lambert gained fabulous wealth with illegal money market manipulations.

Unethical practices cut across all occupations.

At the base of all these activities are human beings placed in positions of making ethical decisions. All bring their own set of standards, traditions, rules, and values, and all must struggle with deciding what is ethical.

HOW DO YOU SET ETHICAL STANDARDS?

Methods have been developed to assist us in evaluating whether a decision is ethical. Five of these methods are described below.

1. *Legality.* Is your decision within the legal limits? Laws governing situations usually correct some previous misjudgment or define the boundaries of an activity. Some people believe that if a decision complies with current laws, it will by definition be ethically sound. Other people suggest that the demonstration of ethics begins where the law ends.

2. *Personal morality.* Abiding by personal commitment to uphold human rights and dignity will most always assure ethical choices. This method reflects personal integrity and moral sensitivity.

3. *Enlightened self-interest.* Some people argue that organizations should promote socially responsible behavior because it is good business. This idea, termed **enlightened self-interest,** suggests that organizations' and people's best interests are served by being genuinely concerned for others. The internal payoff for being socially responsible may be self-esteem. External payoffs may be higher profits and other measurable consequences.

4. *Corporate or professional codes of ethics.* Many organizations attempt to institutionalize ethical policies and decision making in a number of ways, such as ethics committees and training in ethics. One popular approach is adoption of a **code of ethics** that requires and prohibits specific practices. Although few companies actually display their codes, most will dismiss, demote, or reprimand employees who intentionally violate the codes. Codes may not actually change people's behaviors, but proponents argue that they do communicate to employees that the company is committed to its standards and is asking employees to adopt them. Codes of ethics are sometimes categorized in two ways: corporate if they are for business organizations and professional if they are for a specific professional group. Figure 16.4 outlines the National Management Association's Code of Ethics. Following these types of standards when making your decisions will influence your choices in a positive manner.

FIGURE 16.4   The National Management Association's Code of Ethics.

NMA Code of Ethics for Management

I will recognize that all individuals inherently desire to practice their occupations to the best of their ability. I will assume that all individuals want to do their best.

I will maintain a broad and balanced outlook and will recognize value in the ideas and opinions of others.

I will be guided in all my activities by truth, accuracy, fair dealing and good taste.

I will keep informed on the latest developments in techniques, equipment and processes. I will recommend or initiate methods to increase productivity and efficiency.

I will support efforts to strengthen the management profession through training and education.

I will help my associates reach personal and professional fulfillment.

I will earn and carefully guard my reputation for good moral character and good citizenship.

I will promote the principles of our American Enterprise System to others, by highlighting its accomplishments and displaying confidence in its future.

I will recognize that leadership is a call to service.

The National Management Association

By permission of the National Management Association

Legality, personal morality, enlightened self-interest, codes of ethics, and common practices may help you make ethical decisions.

5. *Common practices.* The last means of ethical decision making, known as common practices, relies on the belief that "everyone else does it this way." This method is least likely to assure ethical choices. If others accept gifts from contract bidders, following their example does not make you right. You will suffer the consequences if caught in this unethical act.

Relying on our value system to guide us in our decision making will most often result in ethically sound judgments. We may, however, experience conflicts with this method when we operate in an environment that does not share similar values. Operating in certain other ethnic cultures, for example, may create difficulties. What may be considered unethical in our culture may be perfectly acceptable in another. **The Foreign Corrupt Policy Act of 1977** was passed to guard against such conflicts. This law requires United States companies to operate ethically in their worldwide business dealings, and the U. S. Justice Department polices activities of U.S. companies overseas to prevent unethical actions.

HOW DO YOU SOLVE ETHICAL DILEMMAS?

Ethical dilemmas, or conflicts in values, arise when our sense of values or social responsibility is questioned internally or challenged externally. Figure 16.5 provides examples of situations that may be considered ethical dilemmas. These dilemmas are separated into those facing us in personal and business situations. See if you recognize any of these situations. Think how you handled them or what ethical decision you might make.

The heart of ethical dilemmas is not whether you know what is right or wrong, but whether you will choose the right behavior. Individuals must decide whether they are willing to risk making a decision that challenges wrongdoing:

Lydia worked for a private employment agency and was paid strictly on commission. She had worked hard to attract the business of the Alpha Corporation, a large company in her city. Finally the human resources director of Alpha called her, asking her to fill an order for three clerical employees.

"I want the all-American types," the human resources director said. "I want blond-haired, blue-eyed women who are attractive. I don't want any minorities sent over to be interviewed."

After considerable thought, Lydia declined to do business with Alpha, because she knew that the failure to refer minorities to job openings was illegal.

Several weeks later her coworker, Lorenzo, came in with an expensive new suit. "Do you like it?" he asked. "I landed a big catch, the Alpha Corporation. They've sent me lots of business lately. I have placed ten people there in the last two weeks alone. With their business I'll be able to buy that new car that I want and, if I continue with this sales streak, I may even be able to open my own business and earn even more!"

Ethical dilemmas challenge us to make the right choice.

Values in conflict here are Lydia's respect for the law and her desire to succeed financially at work. Responses to value conflicts are different for each individual. Some people may respond physically with ulcers, alcoholism, or mental disturbance.

FIGURE 16.5 Examples of personal and business ethical dilemmas.

Personal	Business
• Should I pay at the checkout counter for the candy bar I ate while grocery shopping? • Should I tell the salesclerk that the item I am purchasing is mismarked with a lower price or consider it a lucky bargain and buy two? • Should I call in sick today and enjoy the time off? • Should I turn in the billfold I found in the ladies lounge to the lost and found? • Should I cheat on my income tax? They will never know. • Should I tell the bank they have credited my account with extra amounts of money? • Should I admit I got the exam answers from another student? • Should I take this book from the library without properly checking it out with the desk clerk? • Should I completely stop at the red light even though there is no one around for miles? • Should I take credit for this presentation even though I borrowed most of the materials from my neighbor?	• Should I turn in 8 hours time worked today even though I took 2 hours for Dave's retirement luncheon? • Should I accept these rodeo tickets from my contractor? • Should I pad my trip expense report to pick up a few extra dollars? • Should I copy this new computer software to load onto my PC at home? • Should I run copies of the recipe of the cake Jane brought in this morning for the office staff? • Should I type my term paper on the company's word processor during duty hours because it is more convenient? • Should I pay my quarter for the coffee or just enjoy a free cup? • Should I select my old basketball team member for the job opening or the most technically qualified applicant? • Should I pressure my new employee for a date this weekend? • Should I authorize the dumping of this waste material directly into the remote landfill site without proper hazardous waste handling and labeling?

Others will show no symptoms and easily adjust their value to the new accepted norm.

If your boss asked you to bend the rules, how would you react? An article by Pat Amend in the December 1988 issue of *Working Woman* suggests the following steps:

1. *Validate the conflict.* It may not be real. You may not have all the facts. Play dumb and ask questions in a nonthreatening way: "Are we allowed to do that in our work agreement?"

2. *Assess the risks involved.* How much are you personally willing to risk? Amend quotes Barbara Ley Toffler, author of *Tough Choices: Managers Talk Ethics*, as saying, "Everyone has to decide where the line is. You have to pick your cause." Doing a cost-benefit analysis to assess the possible harm versus the probable benefits of your choice may clearly guide your decision.

3. *Act on your decision.* Decide, and then proceed with tact. If you are willing to take the risk, you might mention that you are uncomfortable with what

you have been asked to do. Rather than making accusations, give your boss a chance to save face or reverse the request.

4. *Get help in a troubled situation.* If the talk with your boss does not resolve the situation, seek help from a slightly senior-level manager you know and trust. Opposing decisions, policies, or practices within the organization if we consider them to be detrimental or illegal is known as **whistle-blowing.** It also can include publicizing such behavior to people outside the organization, a sensitive matter. Correcting detrimental or illegal situations may involve replanning, redesigning, and reworking and, hence, much time and money. For this reason, many managers choose to ignore these situations. Toffler, according to Amend, suggests that if you go to someone above you, you should be subtle and not name names or point fingers. Approach this advisor with a general question, such as "Does the company usually do this?"

5. *Consider a change in jobs.* If your boss's ethics are in conflict with yours, you may choose to transfer or leave the company. In a survey conducted by McFeely Wackerle Jett and reported in the Amend article, 77 percent of the 1,000 executives agreed that in order to be ethical, you must have the support of an ethical boss. Although individuals can behave ethically on their own, they may be "frozen out" by the boss. You may, therefore, adjust your ethics in order to survive professionally in this particular organization. Then, at age 50, you may not like the "man in the glass" but be reluctant to leave because you are locked into a high salary and comfortable benefits. You have become the organization.

These steps may be useful in ethical decision making.

Authors Kenneth Blanchard and Norman Vincent Peale offer a simple three-step approach to resolving ethical dilemmas. In their book, *The Power of Ethical Management,* they propose the following questions to be used in an ethics check of behavior:

1. Is it legal? Will you be violating any laws or company policies?
2. Is it balanced? Will your decision be fair to all parties concerned, and will it promote a win-win situation?
3. How will my decision make me feel about myself? Will I be proud of my choice? Will I feel good when my family reads about my decision in the local newspaper?

Blanchard and Peale think that ethical behavior is strongly related to self-esteem and that people who feel good about themselves are more able to make ethical decisions and withstand the pressures against those choices.

One other approach to ethical decision making, suggested by Stoner and Freeman, is a questioning process using common morality. Common morality is a set of ground rules covering ordinary ethical problems. These questions may help you when faced with ethical dilemmas:

Promise keeping. Am I keeping promises that I have made?

Nonmalevolence. Am I refraining from harming other human beings?

Mutual aid. Am I helping someone else if the cost is not too great for me to bear?

Respect for persons. Am I treating people as ends in themselves, rather than as mere means to my own ends? Am I taking them seriously, accepting their interests as legitimate, and regarding their desires as important?

Respect for property. Do I have the consent of others before using their property?

HOW ARE COMPANIES IMPROVING THEIR BUSINESS ETHICS?

In a poll sponsored by *The Wall Street Journal* in the fall of 1988, Roger Riclefs asked 1,558 general citizens and approximately 400 business executives what they felt was happening to ethics in business. He found those surveyed believed that behavior in the United States had declined ethically in the last ten years and that most business people engage in unethical business practices such as padding expense accounts.

Companies are working to improve their tarnished ethics.

Major corporations to small businesses are scrambling to improve this tarnished image. They are adopting codes of ethics, conducting in-house seminars on ethical behavior expectations, and hiring outside consultants to help put integrity back into their corporate cultures.

Specifically, companies are facing ethics problems by providing guidelines to their employees for dealing with vendors, competitors, and customers. In August 1987 The Boeing Company published and distributed to all employees a handbook entitled *Corporate Policies* that provides guidelines on ethical business conduct. Topics covered in the policy handbook include proper marketing practices, proper relationships with suppliers, proper use of company resources, conflicts of interest, offering business courtesies, and acceptance of business courtesies. An Ethics and Business Conduct Committee was established to set company-wide standards of conduct required of all Boeing employees, agents, and consultants. Each operating company is required to establish an education and training program designed to ensure that all employees are made aware of the standards of ethical business conduct required by the company. A business ethics advisor was appointed to provide decision-making guidance and counsel to managers and employees. President and CEO Frank Shrontz gave his support to the effort and emphasized the organization's commitment to ethical conduct.

This approach to improving ethical conduct illustrates the seriousness of the subject to The Boeing Company. Other corporations are following suit. Nearly 80 percent of United States companies have issued codes of ethics. IBM has a "Speak Up!" program that provides a discreet method for employees to appeal supervisory actions. Many other companies have established ethics review committees and conduct training programs to acquaint employees with expected codes of conduct. Violators of ethical standards receive immediate discipline and, depending on the severity of the violation, can quickly lose their jobs. Companies have heard the message from the public and are acting responsibly.

Noted author George S. Odiorne, in an article for *Manage*, a National Management Association publication, suggests that if we are looking for a model for the new ethical behavior standards in businesses, we should read the autobiography of

FIGURE 16.6   Companies today try to prevent unethical behavior, such as stealing software.

Benjamin Franklin. Odiorne's article, entitled "Ethics for the Nineties," describes some 13 virtues suggested by Franklin to be the qualities of moral perfection and ethical excellence. They include temperance, order, sincerity, justice, moderation, and humility.

Commitment, communication, and mutual trust are the keys to a successful ethics program.

A successful ethics program must embody commitment, communication, and mutual trust, with the tone set by top management. The key is the CEO. A strong code of ethics, written rules, and corporate procedures are important, but without strong commitment and enforcement from senior management they are merely words on paper. Communicating expectations through continuous training programs may serve to build the mutual trust required in an effective ethics program.

WHEN SHOULD BUSINESS ETHICS BE TAUGHT?

Changing adults' ethics is difficult, but we can train young people.

As businesses scramble to register employees for ethics classes, the question remains whether business ethics should be introduced at the college level, in business schools, in high schools, or in the work world. The overwhelming response is to begin introducing ethics at the high school level, continue it through college or business school, then strengthen the groundwork with continuous training specific to a particular ethical culture. Peter Drucker, in *Managing in Turbulent Times*, says that changing adults' ethical systems is difficult. He believes that ethics are an expression of personal standards and that those standards are established during youthful, formative years. Most scholars agree with Drucker's assessment. Rather than trying to change adults' ethical systems, efforts should focus on preparing young people to face ethical dilemmas in the workplace.

One successful program that supports this idea is bringing the topics of ethics into high schools across the state of Missouri with backing and support from the school districts and the local chambers of commerce. Leaders from the business community affiliated with the chamber of commerce hold workshops at the school, exploring how ethical decisions are made in the workplace. The crash course introduces potential business recruits to tough ethical choices faced daily by those already in the business world. Using a case study method with open discussion of the ethical issues, students get first-hand exposure to tough decisions and appropriate responses or alternative choices. The business professional mediates between conflicting values and then facilitates reaching an ethical consensus.

William Kanaga, chairman of the advisory board of Arthur Young & Co. and immediate past chairman of the board of the U.S. Chamber of Commerce, strongly supports this program and hopes to see this model spread across the country. A *Nation's Business* article in July 1989 quotes him: "We have failed our young people if we do not give them the right foundation to make tough decisions."

Other educational institutions are responding also. Harvard Business School now requires incoming students to take a three-week mini-course on ethics. As in the Missouri high school program, students work in small business groups, making decisions on complex problems concerning plant relocations, hazardous waste disposal, conflicting cultural values in multinational corporations, and other issues that test honesty and integrity. Once a supposed ethical decision is made, the students are asked to reflect on their decision and consider the impact it may have in a ripple effect. Harvard scholars echo Drucker's belief that ethics cannot be taught, because students bring lifetime values with them at this stage. The intent of the course is to subject individuals to the situation, familiarize them with the process, and have them realize the responsibility inherent in their decisions.

The University of Pennsylvania's Wharton School of Business is requiring attendance at two ethics sessions during orientation. Their international business students are also required to take a cross-cultural ethics course. Columbia University, University of Virginia, and Stanford all have ethics or social responsibility courses in their curricula.

In 1989 Columbia Business School students invited Dennis B. Levine as a guest speaker to trace his methods of turning $40,000 into $12.6 million in only five years on Wall Street. Levine is best known for telling authorities about Ivan Boesky's and Michael Milken's activities in illegal takeovers and information trading. Levine pointed out the dangers of getting caught up and lost in the competitive whirlwinds of Wall Street and how easy losing sight of an ethical base is. Levine served two years in prison, paid $362,000 in fines, and returned $11.6 million in illegal profits as payment for his part in securities fraud, tax evasion, and perjury. Lessons learned from Levine may have a profound impact on students about to enter the work world and face similar ethical dilemmas.

WILL ETHICS PROGRAMS SUCCEED?

A former professor at Washington State University, Marilyn Cash Mathews, surveyed over 350 leading corporations about their ethical policies and programs. She was surprised by the disturbing conclusion that companies with written ethics policies were charged more often with illegal and unethical wrongdoing than those companies without prescribed codes of ethics. Her survey findings were reported by Todd Barrett in *Newsweek* in May 1988.

Some critics claim that if programs are less than successful, employers are to blame. Such programs may lack the commitment of top management, which is vital. They may not keep employees involved in continuing education on ethical behaviors. They may even discourage participation through a corporate culture that punishes whistleblowers, looks the other way during shady deals, and is lax in administering punishments for violators of ethical guidelines. These actions send a clear message to employees and deliver the kiss of death to any formal program.

Citicorp uses a board game to teach employees corporate ethics codes.

On the other hand, some programs have been extremely successful, with proven results that employees are making better decisions. Some companies are trying innovative methods for getting the message across. For example, Citicorp has devised a board game used at employee orientations and department retreats to illustrate ethical dilemmas, encourage discussion about the issues, and promote the company's ethics credo. The game has been played by over 40,000 employees ranging from clerk to top executive in over 45 countries. The program's success is attributed to its use of an interactive and participative approach rather than simply an ethics lecture or sermon from management.

So far the success of ethics programs is questionable. However, the resurgence of public interest in high ethical standards in business bodes well. A show of strong ethical principles may keep the United States healthy and growing as we compete in the global marketplace. For now, ethics has taken its rightful place high on the corporate priority list. It must be a top concern in our personal and professional lives.

SUMMARY

Ethics is the application in decision making of values learned in early years. These values are heavily influenced by our environment. Individuals and organizations may gain temporary benefits from unethical behavior, but in the long run, they reap problems. Personal ethics involves decisions outside work, whereas business ethics applies to work-related decisions. Beginning in the 1960s, unethical practices began to escalate, resulting in today's ethics crisis. Unethical practices have penetrated political, environmental, religious, military, business, and sports fields, affecting all of us. The topic of ethics is now receiving attention in hopes of reversing this trend. The five most common methods for determining appropriate ethical standards are following common practices, checking the legality of the action, considering enlightened self-interest, abiding by codes of ethics, and relying on personal morality.

Each person is faced with ethical dilemmas in everyday life situations. These dilemmas involve making decisions on issues that question our value system. Several steps guide ethical decision making: validate the conflict, assess risk, decide, get help, and, if necessary, change jobs.

To improve business practices, companies are issuing codes of ethics and ethical standards handbooks. Training programs are being used to reinforce company positions on ethical issues. Top management participates in these programs to emphasize their importance. Some programs are being introduced into high school curricula, and many prominent colleges are requiring their students to take ethics courses. The high school level is believed to be the best place to begin exposing students to ethical dilemmas to prepare them for situations that they may well face when entering the work world. The long-term effects of these training programs remain to be seen. In the short term, the United States is experiencing a return to more honest and ethical business practices.

KEY TERMS

ethics
integrity
values
social responsibility
classical perspective
accountability perspective
public perspective
enlightened self-interest
code of ethics
Foreign Corrupt Policy Act
ethical dilemmas
whistleblowing

REVIEW QUESTIONS

1. Explain the differences among ethics, values, integrity, and social responsibility.
2. Identify two events that have fostered the current emphasis on ethics.
3. What are some of the methods used in determining ethical standards?
4. What is meant by ethical dilemmas?
5. What methods can you use in dealing with ethical dilemmas?
6. When and how should ethics be introduced to potential workers?

DISCUSSION QUESTIONS

1. From Figure 16.2 select the three events that you think have had the most profound effect on ethics in business. Why did you pick those three events?
2. Which of the dilemmas in Figure 16.4 have you faced?
3. Do you agree with the scholars that ethics cannot be taught? How would you bring ethics into the education process, and at what age would you begin the education?
4. Does the company for which you work have a code of ethics or some other form of ethics program? Discuss that program and its effectiveness.

CASE STUDY 16.1

ALL MONEY IS GREEN

Guy Walters is the chief executive officer of a major engineering firm. He has been appointed committee chairman for the High Speed Transportation System (HSTS). This group is expected to develop a viable method of transporting mass quantities of products safely and quickly to major distribution points around the world. Funding for this project has come from many companies interested in rapidly moving their products into global marketplaces. Guy feels strongly about making a success of this project and believes that it will greatly benefit the transportation industry, his company, and his personal career.

In a meeting with Annette Hall, his chief financial officer, Guy discovers that his budget is too limited to complete the project. Annette explains that they are confined by the company's policies to using the HSTS funds and that getting approval for additional funding will be difficult.

"We'll just have to bring the matter before the executive board and request additional funds before we can go on," explained Annette.

Guy responded to the news with, "I don't want to do that! You know how they feel about budget overruns. Why can't we just divert some of the leftover funds from other study programs to wrap this thing up? What's the big deal anyway? All money is green! We are all working toward the same end—profits for the company. We're so near completion on this job that I don't want to slow the progress by begging for dollars. Go do some of that 'creative financing' for which you budget people are famous. They'll never know the difference!"

1. What is the ethical issue in this situation?
2. What does Guy mean by "all money is green"? Is he correct?
3. How should Annette respond to Guy's instructions?
4. How would you resolve the ethical dilemma Annette faces?

CASE STUDY 16.2

THE FLOPPY COPY

John was to report to the office on Monday as the new supervisor. Alan was eager to make a good impression on his new boss and had heard John was fond of using his PC. As a special treat, Alan decided to load John's PC with all the bootlegged software that he had acquired over the last few years. He knew some of the applications would be needed by John as soon as he hit the door. Getting orders through the regular channels took as much as six months and then only if you knew someone to pull strings for you. He felt that John would appreciate his outfitting the PC and he could make some points.

When John arrived on Monday and discovered that his PC was loaded with software that was not authorized, he immediately called his staff together for a meeting. He told them that he felt very strongly about the ethical issues in question in copying software and that he had asked the software specialists to unload the bootlegged copies from his machine. "I have also asked them to remove all illegal copies from your machines. We should be able to order whatever we need. That may take a while, but at least we'll be legal."

1. Why did Alan think that John would appreciate the added software?
2. Could Alan have handled this situation so that John would have felt more comfortable? How?
3. Do you think that John acted responsibly by ordering all machines stripped, possibly limiting the working capability and quick response time to problems answered by his staff?
4. How might you have handled this dilemma?

BIBLIOGRAPHY

Amend, Pat. "The Right Way to Deal with Ethical Dilemmas." *Working Woman* (December 1988): 19.

Barrett, Todd. "Business Ethics for Sale." *Newsweek* (May 9, 1988): 56.

Berenbeim, Ronald. *Corporate Ethics*. New York: The Conference Board, 1987, 13.

Blanchard, Kenneth, and Norman Vincent Peale. *The Power of Ethical Management*. New York: William Morrow and Company, Inc., 1988.

Business Conduct Guidelines. The Boeing Company. August 1987.

Broadwell, Martin M. "A New Look at Ethics in Supervision." *Training* (September 1988): 40–42.

Byrne, John A. "Businesses Are Signing Up for Ethics 101." *Business Week* (February 15, 1988): 56–57.

Center for Business Ethics, Bentley College. "Are Corporations Institutionalizing Ethics?" *Journal of Business Ethics* 5, (May 1986): 86.

Drucker, Peter. *Managing in Turbulent Times*. New York: Harper & Row, 1980.

Gray, Robert T. "Making Ethics Come Alive." *Nation's Business* (June 1988): 17–18.

Grove, Andrew S. "What's the Right Thing? Everyday Ethical Dilemmas." *Working Woman* (June 1990): 16–21.

Leo, John. "An Apology to Japanese Americans." *Time* (May 2, 1988): 70.

Morris, William, Ed. *The American Heritage Dictionary*. Boston: Houghton-Mifflin Company, 1975.

Odiorne, George S. "Ethics for the Nineties." *Manage* (April 1988): 8–33.

Perry, James M. "Report Reflects a Shift in Attitude on Ethics." *The Wall Street Journal* (April 18, 1989): A17.

Powell, Bill, and Carolyn Friday. "The Feds Finger the King of Junk." *Newsweek* (September 19, 1988): 42–44.

Riclefs, Roger. "Ethics in America." *The Wall Street Journal* (October 31–November 3, 1988).

Sandroff, Ronni. "How Ethical Is American Business?" *Working Woman* (September 1990): 113–116. (Questionnaire in February 1990 issue, pages 61–62.)

Silk, Leonard. "Does Morality Have a Place in the Boardroom?" *Business Month* (October 1989): 11–13.

Solomon, Jolie. "How You Play the Game Says Whether You Win." *The Wall Street Journal* (April 18, 1989): B1.

Stoner, James A. F., and R. Edward Freeman. *Management*. Englewood Cliffs, NJ: Prentice-Hall, 1989.

Thompson, Roger. "No Easy Answers." *Nation's Business* (July 1989): 19–39.

Toffler, Barbara Ley. *Tough Choices: Managers Talk Ethics*. New York: John Wiley & Sons, 1988.

SUGGESTED READING

Madsen, Peter, and Jay M. Shafritz, eds. *Essentials of Business Ethics (A Collection of Articles by Top Social Thinkers)*. New York: Meridian (Penguin Books USA Inc.), 1990.

Naisbitt, John, and Patricia Aburdene. *Megatrends 2000*. New York: William Morrow and Company, Inc., 1990.

PART FIVE

YOUR GROWTH AND FUTURE

CHAPTER SEVENTEEN
BUSINESS ETIQUETTE

With the popularity of telephone answering machines, fax machines, portable telephones, beepers, home computers, and call-waiting devices, the Machine Age has arrived—and along with it a whole new set of etiquette problems, as demonstrated by the following incidents:

A man sitting alone in a restaurant carried on a loud conversation over his portable telephone, annoying diners around him.

When a portable pager went off in a business conference, the executive did not excuse himself to answer. Instead, he carried on his conversation with the caller in the presence of the other conference participants.

The head of an executive recruiting firm accidentally faxed a resume of a promising executive to the firm where he was currently working instead of the one trying to hire him.

A newspaper columnist received a 12-page fax that contained only about two lines of information useful to her.

Clifford Pugh, "High Tech Etiquette," *The Houston Post* (1989)

In June 1979 after graduating with her MBA from Harvard, Mary Cunningham began work at Bendix as executive assistant to the chairman, Bill Agee. Ms. Cunningham became Mr. Agee's trusted confidant. He soon promoted her to two high positions in the corporation. Rumors began to swirl, however, that the two were romantically involved. Finally the unrest became so great that Ms. Cunningham was forced to resign. The two later married, after which Mr. Agee was eased out in 1983 during a corporate takeover.

Mary Cunningham, *Power Play* (1984)

OBJECTIVES

After studying this chapter, you should be able to:
1. Define etiquette and protocol.
2. List five reasons a knowledge of etiquette is more important than ever today.
3. Maintain habits in dress, hygiene, and appearance that enhance your professional and social image and convey respect for others.
4. Use basic table manners in socially acceptable ways.
5. Introduce and meet people with confidence.

6. Use good judgment in face-to-face interactions, including male/female situations, office romances, and work involving people from other cultures.
7. Use socially appropriate behavior to develop effective customer relations.
8. Write correspondence and use the telephone in a way that reflects well on you and your organization.
9. State general guidelines of etiquette for correct use of communication technology.
10. Use networking, mentoring, and office politics sensibly.
11. Differentiate among passive, aggressive, and assertive behaviors and use appropriate behavior.

WHAT IS ETIQUETTE?

Etiquette is acting appropriately in social and business situations.

Practically every week another article appears in the newspaper or in a popular journal about the growing importance of business etiquette. **Etiquette,** according to Webster's, is "the forms required by good breeding or prescribed by authority to be observed in social or official life." In simple words, when we use correct etiquette, we act appropriately in social and business situations.

The articles report that people are signing up for etiquette classes in record numbers, that businesses are sending their employees to etiquette classes, and that business schools are incorporating etiquette lectures and classes into their programs. Such a contemporary emphasis seems odd when we remember that in the recent past, specifically the 1960s and 1970s, etiquette was considered almost old-fashioned and outdated.

Companies see business etiquette, often called corporate etiquette, as a way of giving them a competitive edge in winning and retaining clients. Knowledge of the finer points of good manners can help build long-term relationships among employees and with customers and clients. Chip Ricketts, in an article in the *Dallas Business Journal,* reports that people skills account for about 85 percent of a person's success and technical skills only 15 percent. Therefore, social skills are increasingly important. In the same article Valerie Sokolosky and Robert Rasbery point out that ability to engage in small talk over dinner or in small groups, listen effectively, and make introductions—all in a natural and sincere way—are a part of corporate protocol and a company's marketing strategy.

Etiquette provides us with a code of behavior in different settings, much as rulebooks provide us with a set of directions for playing golf, tennis, bridge, and other games. If we know the rules, we can play the game better and enjoy it more. When we walk into a situation and are sure that we know how to handle ourselves, our self-confidence will be obvious to others.

Protocol involves rules for business, diplomatic, or military etiquette.

Protocol is that part of etiquette dealing with behavior in business, diplomatic, or military situations. It is used in determining matters such as displaying the flag of this country, seating people at formal dinners, determining the sequence for introducing people, and using formal titles correctly. Protocol is designed to simplify meetings. It answers questions and everybody accepts it. Mike Dorning, in an article in *The Houston Post* while the 1990 Economic Summit was underway, pointed out that protocol took the guesswork out of diplomacy. The summit began with a 21-gun salute, a ritual dating back to at least the sixteenth century. That is the salute diplomatic protocol requires for two of the attendees at the summit (the presidents of the United States and France). Protocol rules unambiguously answered questions about the order in which dignitaries arrived, how flags were flown, and how the leaders were saluted.

Rules, then, are an important component of etiquette, but they are not the only one. Knowledge of etiquette rules alone will not strengthen your human relations skills. You must use two other components: courtesy and good taste. When you act with courtesy, you are combining kindness and politeness. An unkind act is never a courteous one, no matter how correct it may be, and impolite acts are neither courteous nor correct. Several etiquette experts point out that being courteous involves the following behaviors:

> Considering others, even in little ways.
> Respecting and encouraging accomplishments in other people.
> Being thoughtful of others.
> Being democratic in our relations with others.
> Saying "thank you" with sincerity.
> Using a friendly voice.

Good taste is concerned with the suitability or fitness of actions, objects, and other things. An important part of good taste is the ability to recognize good proportions, orderliness, symmetry, quality, and beauty.

WHY IS ETIQUETTE IMPORTANT TODAY?

Marilyn Pincus, author of *Mastering Business Etiquette and Protocol,* points out that mastering the social graces is important to any person who wants to attain and maintain success in today's rapidly changing, fast-paced business world. Lack of knowledge of protocol can cause embarrassment and misunderstanding. Pincus and other writers on etiquette emphasize that etiquette is more important than ever today and give several reasons:

1. The development of high technology all too often results in our being treated impersonally and our treating others that way. This situation leaves us desiring human sensitivity, a need that can be at least partially met through socially correct interpersonal behaviors.
2. The growth of the global economy and our own diverse population requires that we interact with people of all cultures. If we are to be successful in our dealings, we must be careful not to offend people of other cultures by violating their communication or behavioral norms.
3. Because of the influx of women, minorities, and the handicapped into the workplace, old behavioral rules are having to be reexamined and new ones created. Some of these behaviors are being determined legally; others fall outside of the legal domain and are less specific.

4. During the 1960s and early 1970s "doing your own thing" became the norm and children were not taught etiquette, resulting in a generation of business people who may feel awkward and ill at ease in social and official situations.

5. Because work is being increasingly restructured to include teams and group decision making, people must get along with each other. Studying etiquette can improve our ability to do that.

Knowledge of etiquette, then, is a key ingredient in human relations and in business and personal success. Such knowledge can help you feel comfortable because you know what to do and can do it with grace, style, and ease. Work situations that call for effective etiquette include relationships with coworkers, with managers above you, with people below you in the hierarchy, with customers and clients, and with the general public where you are seen as representing your organization. Away from work you will enhance your chances for satisfactory relationships with people if your behavior says that you respect them.

Appropriate behavior depends on where you are, when, and with whom.

An important point needs to be recognized about etiquette: what is appropriate will depend to a certain extent on where, when, and with whom the interaction occurs. Behavior considered appropriate with one group or individual may be considered offensive with someone else. Think, for example, about the different perceptions of the handshake around the world, as discussed in Chapter 3. Another example is the use of the title Ms. This abbreviation is generally used when a woman's marital status is unknown or is considered not relevant to the situation. Although some women prefer it, other women become hostile when addressed that way. Therefore, a woman's preference should be respected. Because etiquette depends on timing and setting, you must develop good judgment and a sensitivity to people around you. This awareness will give you the best chance of success in your relationships, in business situations such as negotiations and sales, in leadership positions, and in any situation requiring cooperation and teamwork.

The remainder of this chapter will discuss etiquette as a typical worker might use it on a normal workday. Etiquette starts with dressing for work in the morning and carries through work activities such as writing and using the telephone and other forms of communication technology. It also applies to meeting people, introducing people, having lunch, networking, mentoring, and participating in office politics. Imagine yourself in these situations and apply the suggestions to your own life.

WHY IS APPEARANCE A FORM OF ETIQUETTE?

Experts point out that we form our impressions of people in the first few seconds we see them and that initial impressions can be difficult to change. If that is the case, consider what you wore to work or class today and your overall appearance, which includes hygiene. When dressing this morning, did you consider whether the statement your clothes would make would be the one you want to make? Did you ask yourself whether your appearance would indicate that you fit in with the environment in which you function?

Appropriate dress, hygiene, and appearance show respect for situations and people.

If etiquette pertains to appropriate behaviors, certainly it must be extended to include appropriate dress, hygiene, and grooming. Inappropriate dress suggests a lack of respect for the situation and the people involved. People who take their careers seriously know that image is important. You will be a poor representative for your company if your appearance is making a statement that does not agree with the image of the company.

Additionally, our clothing and accessories can help us feel better about ourselves, which can in turn make us feel more comfortable interacting with others. If we can forget about our appearance because we are satisfied with it, we are free to concentrate on the other person.

This, then, is the most important rule of dress for work: dress appropriately for your organization. Some organizations are conservative in nature and expect their employees to dress accordingly, such as insurance companies. Other organizations, stressing creativity, such as advertising firms, expect that their employees will reflect that value and will tolerate less conservatism in dress if coupled with good taste. Sexy clothes in most kinds of jobs are never considered to be in good taste. Neither are strong colognes, flashy jewelry, dirty or messy hair, or extreme hairdos and makeup. Earrings and ponytails on men may also be inappropriate. Many experts still suggest following the adage "Dress for the position to which you aspire." Also important is consistency in dress. People will not be viewed as stable employees who know where they are going if they dress professionally one day and messily or inappropriately the next.

Clothes do not have to be expensive, but they should fit well, be made of natural-looking fabrics, and include well-polished leather shoes. Tasks such as freshening your makeup, combing your hair, or adjusting your shirt and tie should be done in private, not at your desk.

WHAT TABLE MANNERS SHOULD YOU USE?

Practically everyone shares meals with others at some time as a part of the workday. Whether you are eating in the company cafeteria with coworkers or attending a business luncheon outside the company, you can make these times more relaxed and enjoyable by understanding certain basic rules of etiquette. In general, these rules are to be used in any setting:

1. To keep people from bumping into each other, sit down from the left side of the chair when possible.
2. In general, wait until all people at the table are seated and have their food before beginning to eat. The company cafeteria, where people are on different schedules, may be an exception. Another exception may be when you are served a dish that will lose its flavor if cooled or warmed.
3. Place your napkin in your lap as soon as you are seated, and sit with both feet on the floor.
4. Avoid playing with your silverware or food.
5. Keep the hand not holding the fork in your lap. Do not place your elbows on the table while eating or lean on the table to eat. Remember to sit straight but not rigid throughout the meal.

FIGURE 17.1   Correct table manners make business luncheons more relaxed and enjoyable.

6. Never reach for food or condiments across the table. Ask the person nearest the item you want to "please pass the . . . ." Bowls are passed to the right.

7. Do not smack or slurp while eating or talk with your mouth full.

8. Do not groom at the table. If women need to add lipstick or men or women need to smooth wind-blown hair, they should go elsewhere to do so.

9. When finished eating, lay your silver in your plate and your napkin on the table. Do not shove your plate away from you or comment about how full you are.

10. Although most restaurants have sections reserved for smoking, always ask your table mates before lighting up, avoid smoking during the meal, and make sure that your smoke does not go into others' faces.

11. Cocktails before or after dinner may be appropriate in a social setting, but alcohol is best avoided at work-related meals.

FIGURE 17.2   Mealtimes need not be stressful if you understand basic table etiquette.

BORN LOSER® by Art Sansom

Reprinted by permission of NEA, INC.

HOW SHOULD YOU HANDLE INTRODUCTIONS?

Introductions
should put
people at ease
and show them
respect.

We are constantly meeting new people in our jobs and at times must introduce
people to each other. The latter situation is more likely to create anxiety. You can
reduce your anxiety, be more comfortable, and create a gracious atmosphere if you
remember the overriding goals of putting people at ease and showing them proper
respect.

General rules for making introductions are the following:

1. Introduce younger people or people lower on the organizational hierarchy
   to older people (those appearing to be 15 years older) and superiors. We
   address the older person or person higher on the hierarchy first: "Dr.
   Rutherford, I would like you to meet Rhonda Elliott, the new secretary in
   our office."
2. Introduce a man to a woman if they are about the same age and on the same
   level of the hierarchy: "Ms. Solerno, I would like you to meet Mr. Freedman."
3. If you forget the name of someone you are introducing, as we all do occasionally, be honest and ask people to introduce themselves to each other,
   as follows, "My mind is not giving me names today. Will you please introduce yourselves."

If you are the one being introduced and your name is mispronounced, you may
give the correct pronunciation when acknowledging the person to whom you are
introduced. For example, if your name is Dalton and you are introduced as Dawson,
you may correct this mistake simply by saying, "Sam Dalton. I'm glad to meet you."
If no one introduces you in a group, you may handle the situation graciously by
smiling and saying something like, "I'm Danielle Muster from accounting."

The handshake, a common part of introductions, should be firm but not hand-
breaking. It may include one or two gentle pumps and should be accompanied with a
smile, eye contact, slight forward lean, and a short phrase such as, "I am happy to
meet you." When you shake hands with someone, make it brief by releasing the hand
after the pumps.

Although in some social situations people routinely kiss or hug when meeting
each other, such behavior is totally out of place in a United States business setting.
We should not put an arm around coworkers of either sex, place a hand on their
shoulder, or touch them in any way.

When a new person or boss comes into your work group, exercise your best
etiquette by extending a sincere, warm welcome. You may offer to help show the
new group member around, if appropriate.

WHAT IS MALE–FEMALE ETIQUETTE AT WORK?

The women's movement and the influx of women into the work world have created
confusion and uncertainly for many men and women. If you are male, you may
wonder whether you should open doors for women at work, help them take off their
coats, or automatically pay for business lunches shared with a woman. If you are

female, you may wonder whether you are insulting men if you open the door yourself or acting improperly if you let men help you remove your coat. Marilyn Pincus suggests the "offer and refusal technique" and the "understanding strategy" as simple ways of eliminating this dilemma. The **"understanding strategy"** suggests that once you know someone's preferences regarding business protocol, you should comply with them. The **"offer and refusal technique"** suggests that men continue to offer the kind of manners they were taught and that women accept those gestures they consider proper in the setting and graciously decline those they would rather not have. Courtesy is courtesy! People can help men *or* women with doors and coats.

Men should offer manners they were taught, and women should feel free to refuse.

Pincus cites these examples:

> When approaching a door, the woman can slow her pace and let the man open it. If she reaches the door first, she can open it for him. If a man reaches around her to open it, she can, if she prefers, say, "Thank you. I have it."

FIGURE 17.3   Today's woman may choose to open doors for men.

Once people know someone's preferences in business protocol, they should comply with them.

> If a man tries to help a woman when she is removing her coat, she can either accept his assistance or simply say, "Thank you. I can handle it myself."

Business lunches involving men and women are special cases. The person who is hosting the meeting should simply reach for the bill without comment. Waiters and waitresses still sometimes give the bill to males without asking. This mistake can be avoided by calling the restaurant ahead of time or telling the maitre d' discreetly on arrival to whom the check is to be presented.

Business travel involving men and women is becoming more common but still poses some potentially awkward situations. Meetings should probably be held in public rooms or only in suites with a sitting room.

Terms such as "Honey," "Dear," and "Sweetheart" should never be used at work.

An additional guideline that should not have to be pointed out pertains to the use of words like "Honey," "Dear," or "Sweetheart." Although these terms have been more commonly used by men when talking to women, their use is inappropriate and demeaning to either sex in the workplace.

In an article in *Fortune,* Judith Martin, known as Miss Manners, offers further advice on male-female interactions at work. She suggests that comments such as "Gee, you look adorable," to a woman about to make a business presentation are inappropriate because they imply the woman is a social creature and not a serious worker. She advises that men err on the side of caution lest such comments be interpreted as sexual harassment.

Be wary of developing personal or social relationships off the job with your supervisors or subordinates of either sex. Such relationships can prove to be harmful to you, your subordinate, or your supervisor for two reasons. First, they may convey inappropriate appearances if the employee and the supervisor are of different sexes. Additionally, problems may develop because of the potential resentment that other employees may feel.

WHAT ABOUT OFFICE ROMANCES?

Currently 45 percent of the work force is female, and this percentage is expected to increase to 47 percent by the year 2000. Women are also beginning to enter fields that were traditionally held only by males. Additionally, a growing proportion of our population is single and feels that the office or work site is a good and safe place to meet members of the opposite sex. Romances, then, are inevitable. Also inevitable is that other people in the organization will learn of the relationship. Office romances carry with them a number of pitfalls, and any employee contemplating a relationship with someone else in the same organization should consider the potential for trouble.

A romantic relationship at work has pitfalls.

The situation of a boss and subordinate dating is a particularly difficult one. If you are the boss and are initiating the moves, be cautious. Your subordinate may not be interested in becoming romantically involved and may complain of sexual harassment. Even if your subordinate is willing, the relationship could cause havoc in the organization:

John, the accounting supervisor, is attracted to Olivia, the new accountant who works for him. After working with her for several months, he asks her for a date. She accepts and within weeks their romance is flourishing.

Everything is not heavenly, however. The other members of his group—Sylvia, Marshall, Willis, and Ann—are unhappy about the relationship. They wonder what will happen when perfor-

mance appraisals are due. Will Olivia receive a higher rating because she is dating the boss? What about that promotion that will be opening soon in payroll? Will Olivia be recommended?

What about confidential information? Will John tell Olivia that Marshall has a substance abuse problem and is going for counseling? Will he tell Olivia that Sylvia has not been performing up to par?

Even if the boss acts appropriately, subordinates may not take the same view of the situation. Morale may suffer and productivity decline.

Dating among coworkers takes on some of the same risks. Unwilling persons may view the romantic activity as sexual harassment.

If the relationship breaks up, other problems may develop. For the boss, the danger exists that the other party may now allege sexual harassment as a motive for revenge. For the subordinate, the danger is that the boss may retaliate through poor performance appraisals and less favorable job assignments. Additionally, former lovers may not be able to function productively when they see each other daily. Communication and cooperation may be hampered, causing office productivity to decline.

If you are contemplating a romance at work, you may find the advice by Harriet B. Braiker in *Working Woman* helpful. She suggests that you be discreet to avoid becoming a source of gossip, not leave cute messages or notes, and not touch each other in the office. Keeping job performance high, not bringing personal matters into the office (and vice versa), and not indicating that you have special "inside" information, which can threaten others, are important. You should not feel that you must continue the relationship simply because you have begun. Additionally, in situations where romances between coworkers may be acceptable, they should be conducted on private time, not at work.

Some companies have policies stating that no fraternization may take place among employees. Others have rules stating that relatives or spouses cannot work under the same supervisor or supervise one another. Be aware of the policies where you work before considering a relationship.

If you are a supervisor and one of your subordinates is involved in an office romance, your best approach is to ignore it unless the romance causes problems or decreases productivity of the parties involved. If the relationship is causing performance difficulties, the participants should be counseled. The counseling should be done in an objective fashion, with an emphasis on productivity. Moral judgments concerning the relationship should not enter into the conversation. If one of your male employees makes plays for practically every female employee (or vice versa), you should tell the employee to keep such behavior out of the office.

Most companies take a dim view of supervisor-subordinate relationships because of the conflict of interest. If you are a supervisor, you should refrain from romantic associations with subordinates.

WHAT IS CROSS-CULTURAL ETIQUETTE?

With the growing global economy, European Economic Community trade reforms, and the increased investment of foreign companies in the United States, business people are recognizing the need to learn how to work effectively both abroad and at home with foreigners. John Petty, writing in *The Houston Post*, reports that failures of U.S. managers sent abroad cost their firms about $2 billion a year—and this figure does not include indirect costs, like damaged reputations or lost business opportunities. Short courses on cross-cultural work relationships are springing up all over, but so are stereotypes about such relationships.

Some common stereotypes concern Japanese business practices: American managers in Japanese firms have no real power, the Japanese punish initiative, the Japanese insist that management be by consensus or else, and the Japanese do not respect women employees. Americans experienced in working with the Japanese suggest that the stereotypes are not valid. Numerous authorities point out that experience with other cultures, even if only through travel, is helpful in working with foreign business people. Such experience is likely to give a person greater tolerance—even admiration—for ways unlike those at home.

Tolerance is necessary when working with people of other cultures.

If you are called upon to work with people from another country, as you probably will be, certain guidelines may help you:

1. Learn as much as you can about the nonverbal communication of the other culture. Numerous organizations offer such classes, books and articles are available, and people familiar with the culture can be helpful. This aspect of communication is a ripe area for misunderstandings. For example, the Japanese almost always bow when exchanging their business cards. In Arab nations, a man will hold another man's hand a long time when they meet. Additionally, business transactions almost always take longer outside the United States. Knowing these cultural differences, you will not be caught off guard.

2. Learn some of the other language. Even a little knowledge will demonstrate that you are trying to meet people of other countries half way rather than insisting that everyone know your native language. The French, for example, are usually more helpful if requests for directions are first preceded with, *"Pardonnez-moi, s'il vous plaît. Parlez-vous Anglais?"* (Pardon me, please. Do you speak English?) By using a beginning like this, you are communicating that you do not necessarily expect them to know English.

3. Talk to someone knowledgeable about the culture before offering gifts, inquiring about family members, or beginning business discussions. Norms for these behaviors vary from culture to culture, and the pace at which discussions flow from personal to business differs. The Japanese, for example, frequently give gifts, whereas western European business people generally do not.

4. Conform to foreign norms more when you are abroad than when you are in the United States.

5. Being courteous and sincere can help you over the rough spots.

HOW SHOULD YOU TREAT THE PUBLIC?

How employees treat customers and clients is a crucial factor in the success of a business. Chapter 1 pointed out that many customers never return to a business because of unkind treatment that they received. Although they seldom tell the company about the treatment, they do tell their friends and others. Effective customer relations, then, are an important part of an organization's marketing strategy.

If you come in contact with customers in person, by mail, or over the telephone, the most important guideline that you can remember is, "Do unto others as you would have them do unto you."

The best rule for customer relations is the Golden Rule.

The ways that employees should treat customers seem so obvious that mistreatment seems almost unthinkable; yet it occurs every day and drives customers away by the dozens. One rude employee can do untold damage to a business, whereas one helpful employee is worth thousands in marketing dollars:

> *Incident 1—Poor treatment.* **About five minutes before Arnold was to leave for the day to start a two-week vacation, a customer, Helen Williams, came in wanting to submit an application for credit. When Arnold was told that the customer was in the outer office, his loud response was, "Well, she had better hurry. I have things to do." When the supervisor said, "Shhhh," with a finger to her lips, Arnold replied, again loudly, "Oh, she didn't hear me."**

> *Incident 1—Correct treatment.* **Arnold should have either handled the application or have politely asked someone else to help her. No comments about his leaving should have been made in front of the customer.**

> *Incident 2—Poor treatment.* **Wanda has been taken off the telephone to free her for handling customers. However, when all of the other clerks are on the telephone or busy, the calls will roll over to her station. This chore displeases her so much that when she answers the phone, she is abrupt with her "Hello" and snaps out answers to the callers' questions.**

> *Incident 2—Correct treatment.* **Because callers do not know what a situation is in an office and have every right to expect the person answering to be ready to deal with their business, Wanda should treat each call with patience, respect, and consideration.**

> *Incident 3—Poor treatment.* **Ronald is busy waiting on a customer in the eyeglass shop when Angie walks in. He continues to help the customer with whom he was working, assuming that Angie can look around while she is waiting. After about five minutes of standing nearby and waiting for his attention without even getting a glance from the salesclerk, Angie leaves the shop.**

> *Incident 3—Correct treatment.* **Ronald should have acknowledged Angie as soon as she walked into the store. This he could have done with a friendly, "Hello. I'll be with you shortly. Would you like to look around in the meantime?"**

In reviewing these incidents, think how you would have felt if you had been the customer. If you are like most people, you would have been somewhat hurt or angered by the treatment. More than likely, you would have been reluctant to return. These three situations could have been improved if the employees had remembered these basic guidelines pertaining to customer relations:

1. Never say anything *about* a customer that you would not say *to* the customer.
2. When serving a customer by phone or in person, give that person your full attention. Do not shuffle papers or try to do other work at the same time.
3. Every customer who walks into your place of business should be acknowledged immediately. Your manner should be pleasant and helpful. The customer should not be left unattended long.
4. Consider the role you play in your company's marketing strategy by dressing appropriately each day. Remember to exercise good hygiene by having clean clothes, hair, and teeth. Do not chew gum or eat in front of customers. Your demeanor should be professional. A ready smile, eye contact, correct posture, and smooth voice are helpful in client relations.
5. Remember to use "please," "thank you," "thank you for your interest in our company," and "please come again." Calling people by name is an easy way to make them feel important.
6. Never conduct personal telephone calls or carry on personal conversations in front of clients or customers.
7. If you must answer a phone while working with a customer who is with you, ask that person, "Will you excuse me please while I catch this call?" Remember to take care of the first customer first by asking the second whether he or she can hold or would like you to call back. Use the telephone guidelines presented in the next section.

Manners in Correspondence and on the Telephone

Manners are as important in correspondence and on the phone as in person.

As an employee of a company, you portray the image of that company each time you write someone or use the telephone for a business purpose. Effective human relations are just as important in correspondence and on the telephone as in person.

In writing, the tone of a message is important. Polite requests, such as "Please return both copies" sound much more pleasant than "Return both copies." Including a person's name on all correspondence rather than just a company or department name can help to make the receivers feel that they are dealing with real people, not just an impersonal organization. Additionally, because everyone's time is at a premium, unnecessarily long messages are a form of waste and poor manners. To improve your writing, review the suggestions given in Chapter 3.

When you answer the phone, you represent the company. Therefore, your voice and manner should present a friendly and professional image. Right and wrong ways to handle telephone communications exist—ways that are tactful, courteous, and efficient, and ways that are abrupt and rude.

The following are suggestions from Southwestern Bell Telephone's *Telephone Manners*. They can help you present the best possible impression for your company and do an efficient job at the same time:

FIGURE 17.4 You represent the company each time you answer the telephone at work. Your voice and manner should present a friendly and professional image.

1. *Answer promptly*. Answer calls on the first ring, if possible, in a friendly, enthusiastic way.
2. *Answer correctly*. Speaking clearly and enthusiastically, say, "Good morning (or good afternoon)," and on an outside line, give your company name. On an inside line, use your first and last names in answering instead of the company name. Adding "May I help you?" is a courteous way of letting the caller know that you are immediately available and interested.
3. *If you are answering for someone else*. First identify the department, office, or area, and then identify yourself as a substitute for the expected person and add "May I help you?"
4. *Transfer calls only when necessary*. People become irritated when their calls are switched from one person to another. Instead, put the caller on hold, get the information, and return to the line. If you cannot get the information, explain to the caller who can help and ask if you may transfer them to that number. Always ask first. Then indicate that you are transferring by saying, "I'll transfer your call now. One moment, please."
5. *When the caller asks for someone you do not know*. Use a courteous, gracious manner and a tactful reply, such as, "May I have that name again, please?" or "I'm sorry. I don't find that name on our list. Could you tell me in which department she works?"
6. *Calls on hold*. If you are going to be delayed in continuing a call, tell callers

that you are going to put them on hold for a moment and then, before placing the instrument down, put it on hold.

7. *If you are delayed.* Do not leave callers on hold more than 30 seconds without returning to say that you have not forgotten them. If you must leave the telephone for more than a minute, offer to call back and state the approximate time when you will do so.

8. *If the requested party is busy.* Explain in a courteous manner that the person is unavailable and offer the caller the option of waiting on the line or being called back.

9. *If the party is out.* Project your company's image by stating that "Ms. McWright is out of the office until . . . ." Ask callers whether someone else can help or would they like to leave their names and numbers.

10. *Taking messages.* Keep a message pad and pencil by your telephone. Request the information courteously, using a phrase such as, "May I have your name, please?" Correct spelling of names is important. Ask if you are unsure. Repeat the number to the caller to make sure that you have it right.

11. *Saying goodbye.* Continue your professional demeanor by thanking the party for calling and saying goodbye.

Another suggestion offered by Southwestern Bell is to cultivate a good telephone personality. Be alert, keep a smile in your voice, speak clearly and distinctly, and greet the caller pleasantly. Other ways to project a good telephone personality include using the caller's name, treating every call as important, being tactful, apologizing for errors or delays, taking time to be helpful, and saying "please," "thank you," and "you're welcome."

Rules for Other Communication Technology

The increased use of communication technology has brought with it a whole new set of etiquette problems, as shown in the chapter opening anecdotes. Employees act inappropriately when they send personal messages over the company fax (no love notes or carry out orders, please!), leave one caller hanging to talk with the second one, spend excessive time on personal telephone calls, or violate confidentiality of information they receive through computer usage. Clifford Pugh offers these guidelines:

1. *Fax etiquette.* Be careful, be considerate, and be brief. Pugh points out that perhaps no other electronic device has caused more etiquette problems in a short period of time than the facsimile machine. He suggests that faxes over five pages should probably be delivered to avoid tying up the machine. He also advises that you know your fax recipient. To prevent problems, call ahead to check for any ground rules and to notify your recipient that a fax is on its way. Sending unwanted or long correspondence can tie up the machine unnecessarily.

2. *Car phone etiquette.* Because the owner of a car phone pays for every call, that person may choose to limit the people to whom the number is given

and to tell callers politely that the call will be returned later. Callers should refrain from calling unless absolutely necessary.

3. *Call waiting etiquette.* The call waiting feature on telephones signals us while we are on the line that another call is coming in. Except in emergencies, the first caller should receive our complete attention. Many etiquette writers consider call waiting to be a rude interruption and suggest that the accounting method of first in, first out be used. That is, do not ask the person with whom you are speaking to wait while you handle a second caller. Instead, once you have determined that no emergency exists, politely ask the second caller to call back or offer to return the call yourself, stating when you will be free.

4. *Answering machine etiquette.* Messages on answering machines should be clear and precise. Jokes and blaring music are distasteful in any setting and totally inappropriate on office telephones.

5. *Voice mail etiquette.* Stating that voice mail "may be the most infuriating of the new electronic devices" because callers receive instructions from a computer, Pugh points out that it is, nevertheless, much more accurate than written messages, which have been found to have at least one error 90 percent of the time. His advice on using voice mail is to leave a straightforward message about your reason for calling and the information you desire.

6. *Beeper etiquette.* Pugh suggests treating beepers in public like babies: when they make a noise, remove them immediately to another room. Noisy users of beepers can be politely asked to be quiet.

HOW SHOULD YOU TREAT ASSOCIATES?

Having "a friend in the business" can be helpful when you face a problem or need advice. **Networking**, according to *Women in Business*, is a process whereby you can get moral support, career guidance, and important information in areas outside your expertise by developing contacts with people in your place of employment and in professional organizations. Networks can be used by members to exchange information, ideas, and occasional favors, thus enhancing their careers.

Networking contacts should not be abused.

To be effective, you must use your networks appropriately. Members of a network will come to resent anyone who abuses the process, for example, by trying to solicit free advice from professionals such as doctors, lawyers, and accountants. You must also assist others in the network in turn. Needless to say, confidentiality is important, as it is in any relationship.

Respect your mentor's time and position.

A **mentor** is an experienced person who will give you objective career advice. Such a person can give you pointers and help you avoid mistakes. A mentor can be someone inside your organization, outside your organization but in your profession, or recently retired from your profession. Your choice of a mentor should be someone you respect. Therefore you should act in such a way that your mentor will admire both the way you behave and the way you handle your job. Do not abuse your mentor's time or position.

Office politics are impossible to avoid but can be extremely sensitive. Discretion and courtesy should be your guidelines in participating in office politics. Participating in or even listening to gossip is not only ill-mannered, but it can also kill your career. When confronted with gossip, one way that you can avoid the discussion is by simply saying, "Oh, I never pay attention to things like that."

If you are unsure of what to do in a sensitive situation at work, discuss it with your mentor. Being in the same profession, this person has probably encountered similar situations.

Should conflict develop between you and another person at work, kindness and graciousness may restore your relationship. If you did something that offended the other person, you need to apologize. If you do not know why the person is upset or is making nasty comments about you, ask in a kind, concerned manner. Refrain from making critical comments of your own. Your goal, after all, is a win-win resolution of the conflict.

Etiquette can help coworkers resolve conflicts.

WHAT ARE THE THREE BEHAVIOR TYPES?

How well you put etiquette into practice depends on your usual behavior. Three basic behaviors can be found in the workplace—passive, aggressive, and assertive. Understanding the different behaviors can assist you in becoming more effective on the job. Edward Charlesworth and Ronald Nathan, in *Stress Management*, define these behaviors.

Passive Behavior

Individuals who consistently engage in **passive behavior** value themselves below others, do not appear self-confident when they speak, want to be liked and try to please others, and avoid unpleasant situations and confrontation. Their passivity shows, in part, through their nonverbal communication. Passive people may look down or to the side in order to avoid eye contact. They will also mumble and hesitate when speaking. Slumped shoulders and poor posture may round out this person's passive demeanor.

Failure to communicate wants and needs is also part of passive behavior. Others may become angry, especially when they sincerely want to know the passive person's desires or preferences. A common example is the group questioning passive persons about their choice of restaurants. Frequently, even after repeated questioning, the only response from the passive person is, "I don't care. You decide."

Others often become irritated at passive individuals' manner and begin to view them as "pushovers," "nerds," or "wimps." This loss of respect may lead some persons to attempt to take advantage of passive individuals by burdening them with excessive work or responsibilities:

Jane asks Juan to finish a report for her because she wants to take an extra 30 minutes for lunch. She knows that he will not refuse because he has never objected the numerous other times

she has asked for a favor. She also knows that when she wants to leave work early next week, she can count on him to answer the telephones and cover for her absence.

Passive individuals will say nothing, but inside them anger is building and eventually that anger must be confronted. Juan may, for example, explode at Jane one day, or even worse, at someone who is not even involved in the incidents, such as a coworker or a family member.

Aggressive Behavior

People who consistently engage in **aggressive behavior** value themselves above others and say what they feel or think at the expense of others in an attempt to get anger off their chests. They may attempt to dominate or humiliate, use threats and accusations, or try to show up others. They also frequently choose for others and speak with an air of superiority and in a voice that is demanding or rude. Their aggressive behavior includes nonverbal communication intended to intimidate or put down other persons. It consists of glaring at others with an angry facial expression or using a voice that is sharp and curt, demanding, and rude. Aggressive individuals' stance makes them appear to be ready to fight, and, in fact, their fists may be clenched.

Others, of course, are offended by this type of behavior. They may feel angry, defensive, or humiliated and may possibly want to strike back at the aggressor.

Often aggressors get what they want but, by offending others, have trouble working with coworkers later:

Millie is trying to train another employee to work the cash register, and Len keeps interrupting and giving unwanted advice. She turns to face Len with a nasty scowl and harshly says, "Shut up!"

This treatment may stop Len's behavior, but he will not be happy about it. He will probably watch for an opportunity to obtain revenge at a later date.

Both of these behaviors—passive and aggressive—can damage your career. For instance, suppose that you are working on an important project for your supervisor and discover that your supervisor has made a huge mistake that will cost the company thousands of dollars unless corrected. If you are a passive person, you will not want to tell your supervisor about the mistake. You will be afraid of causing offense. What do you think will happen later, when your supervisor learns that you did not report the error? Is this the kind of person supervisors like to have on their teams?

If you are aggressive, you will not fare much better. You will tell your supervisor but will probably say something like, "Well, you really blew it this time." Such behavior will immediately make your supervisor defensive and unwilling to listen, even though you are right. The supervisor will most likely look for something for which to reprimand you in the future as a form of revenge.

Assertive Behavior

The situations above are better handled with **assertive behavior**. Assertive individuals are comfortable in using correct etiquette, feel that they are equal to others, and make their own choices. They also use "I" phrases and other effective communication techniques, appear calm and confident, and want to communicate and be respected. They have self-esteem and are respected by others.

Assertiveness requires that you speak clearly, calmly, and firmly. Maintain eye contact without staring. Have a relaxed facial expression with no evidence of tenseness in your body. Keep your shoulders back and your posture erect. This type of nonverbal communication is not intimidating but shows that you have confidence.

Assertive persons are respected and valued by others and, therefore, often obtain what they want. Others do not feel offended or violated, and everyone's rights are respected:

> **Alex was trying to explain to his supervisor the reasons that his project was not finished. Linda kept interrupting him and trying to give her version. Alex finally turned to Linda and said, "Please, I would like to explain this myself."**

Sometimes you will need to repeat your message because the other person does not pay attention to your first efforts. When repeating your message, do it with firmness and respect.

An assertive person would approach the supervisor about the serious mistake and say, "I am concerned about this part of the work that you have asked me to do. Could we sit down and go over it together?" The supervisor will not feel inferior, and the employee will have exposed an important problem and gained respect as a competent and concerned member of the work group.

HOW CAN YOU BECOME ASSERTIVE?

Learning to behave assertively takes patience and practice. Try the following steps to build assertive behavior:

1. Monitor your own behavior. Pay particular attention to your own responses—eye contact, gestures, body posture, facial expression, and voice tone and volume. Decide which behavior you usually exhibit.
2. Imagine situations at work and at home. What would have been the outcome if you had behaved differently? Practice how you would handle the situations assertively by saying the appropriate words aloud when you are alone. Practice nonverbal communication in front of a mirror.
3. Begin communication with "I" phrases. Opening a conversation with "I think" or "I feel" is particularly effective. Practice this phrasing and other communication techniques presented in Chapter 3.
4. Enlist a friend to help you practice assertive behavior. Role playing assertiveness with someone whose advice you trust and respect can be effective.

5. After you have practiced and are confident, try the new behavior on those around you.
6. If you need more help, consider enrolling in an assertiveness training short course. Your local community college and other groups no doubt offer one. Many people have benefited from such instruction.
7. If your lack of assertiveness results from negative feelings about yourself, professional counseling may help. Your school counselor is a good starting point in seeking assistance.

Remember that it will take some time for everyone (including you) to become comfortable with your behavior. If you are a passive person, those around you may be uncomfortable when you become assertive. Also, you may go overboard and become aggressive while trying to become comfortable with your new behavior. However, continued practice will help you become skilled and confident in dealing with other people.

SUMMARY

Etiquette, acting appropriately in social and business situations, is becoming ever more important in business. It gives companies a competitive edge in winning and retaining clients. Etiquette involves following rules, using courtesy, and showing good taste. What is appropriate will depend to a certain extent on where, when, and with whom the interaction occurs.

Appearance is a form of etiquette because it communicates respect for the situation and the people involved. Dress should be appropriate for the situation. Almost all people share meals with others at some time as a part of their workday. Following basic rules of table etiquette can make these times more relaxed and enjoyable. Etiquette is used when making introductions to put people at ease and to show them proper respect.

Male/female interactions at work are changing because of the women's movement and the influx of women into the work world. Following the "offer and refusal technique" and the "understanding strategy" can simplify uncertain business protocol that involves men and women. Awkward situations can be avoided when men and women travel for business if meetings are held in public rooms or in suites with a sitting room. Terms such as "Honey," "Dear," and "Sweetheart" are inappropriate at work. Comments that could be construed as sexual harassment are also inappropriate. Personal and social relationships with supervisors and subordinates off the job are best avoided to eliminate potential harm to both parties.

Office romances may be inevitable, but anyone contemplating one should be aware of the pitfalls. Dating between supervisors and subordinates is especially delicate. Some companies prohibit fraternization of employees or relatives and spouses working under the same supervisor or supervising each other. If no policy exists, supervisors should ignore office romances unless they hurt productivity or cause problems. If counseling is necessary, it should focus on productivity, not moral judgments.

Today's business person must be able to work effectively with people of other cultures. Through experience and travel, we can develop greater tolerance for ways unlike those at home. Studying the nonverbal communication of the other culture, knowing a little of the language, being sensitive to the norms of that culture, and using courtesy with sincerity will help.

Effective customer relations can make or break a business. The best rule to follow in working with clients in person, through correspondence, or on the telephone is the Golden Rule. Remember that to customers you are the company. Cultivating a good telephone personality is important.

The increased use of communication technology has brought with it a whole new set of etiquette problems. Exercise common sense in using faxes, car phones, call waiting, voice mail, and beepers.

Networking and mentoring can help your professional development if you use your network appropriately and treat your mentor with respect. Discretion and courtesy should be your guidelines in participating in office politics. Kindness and graciousness can help you overcome conflict at work.

Three types of behavior found in the workplace are passive, aggressive, and assertive. Assertive behavior will bring you the best results. You should, therefore, try to develop your assertive behavior skills by following the steps recommended in this chapter.

KEY TERMS

etiquette
protocol
"offer and refusal technique"
"understanding strategy"
networking
mentor
passive behavior
aggressive behavior
assertive behavior

REVIEW QUESTIONS

1. Define etiquette and protocol. What is the relationship between the two?
2. Why do many business experts believe that knowledge of etiquette is more important than ever today?
3. List three guidelines for dress, hygiene, and appearance that will enhance your professional and social image and communicate respect for others.

4. List three basic guidelines for table manners.
5. Name two points to be remembered in making introductions.
6. What are some ways to handle male-female situations in the workplace today? Office romances? Work with foreign business people?
7. Describe ways in which employee behavior can help or hinder customer relations.
8. What can you do to make your correspondence and use of the telephone reflect well on your organization?
9. List at least one etiquette guideline for correct use of each communication technology discussed in this chapter.
10. How can you use networking, mentoring, and office politics to help, not hurt, your career?
11. Differentiate among aggressive, passive, and assertive behaviors and explain which is appropriate.

DISCUSSION QUESTIONS

1. Think of times when someone showed poor manners. What part of etiquette was violated? How did the violation make you feel? How did you respond to it?
2. Name some examples of protocol in your daily life or work.
3. Assume that a friend has developed a crush on a coworker. What advice would you give your friend? Suppose the person with the crush is above or below the other in the hierarchy. Would your advice change?
4. If you are female, how do you prefer to handle situations at work such as opening doors or removing your coat when a man is with you? How do you communicate your preference?
5. Think of times when you encountered rudeness on the telephone. Describe the action and your feeling. How could the situation have been handled better?
6. Name some instances of communication technology abuse of which you are aware through experience, the media, or friends. What are the correct behaviors?
7. Do you have a mentor? If so, describe your relationship. How does this person help you? How and when do you interact? What rules of etiquette do you follow?
8. Are you a member of a professional network? If so, describe it. How do you use it? How do you contribute to it?

HOT TIMES IN HAMBURGER HEAVEN

"Yeah, what do you want?" Gary said gruffly to the lady on the other side of the counter at Hamburger Heaven.

"Well, I'm not sure yet," Ms. Quigly said, as she looked at her two small children, who were trying to make up their minds.

Gary rolled his eyes and frowned. He stamped around in a circle and said, "You ready now?" When Ms. Quigly shook her head, Gary slammed down the tray and went to check the french fries.

"What's wrong with him?" Ms. Quigly's son asked. "Did I do something wrong?"

"No, son," she said. "I'll tell you one thing. I don't like his attitude. You can bet our next meal will be down the street at Bea's Burgers. He has just spoiled my appetite."

1. Was Gary displaying passive, aggressive, or assertive behavior?
2. How should Gary have behaved?
3. What has Gary cost his company?

CASE STUDY 17.2

TELEPHONE TALES

Tom had just had a wonderful date, and he was busy telling his buddy, Ernest, about it on the phone. Things were slow in the plant, and Tom was bored with his book-keeping job. Just as Tom was getting to the good part, the other line blinked. He picked up the phone and mumbled quickly, "Ashton Enterprises. May I help you?"

The caller on the other end of the line did not speak at first, and Tom said, "Hello, hello?" in an irritated fashion.

Mr. Zanigo said, "Oh, is this Ashton Enterprises?"

"Yeah, what do you need?" Tom said impatiently.

"Is Ms. Tate in?" said Mr. Zanigo.

"Yeah, hang on," Tom replied. Tom then switched back to his friend. "Sorry about that, Ernie. I had to catch the other line. Let me tell you what a fine dancer she is . . . ." When he went back to the caller's line ten minutes later, it was dead.

About two hours later Mr. Ashton, the president of Ashton Enterprises, called Tom into his office. "Tom," he said, "I'm going to have to let you go. My best client was trying to reach Ms. Tate and finally gave up in frustration. If we lose that contract, our business is ruined."

1. What telephone etiquette rules did Tom violate?
2. How should Tom have handled the telephone call?
3. What might Tom's behavior cost the business?

BIBLIOGRAPHY

"ABWA Chapters Form Basis for Local and National Networking." *Women in Business* (May–June 1985).

Alberti, Robert E., and Michael L. Emmons. *Stand Up, Speak Out, Talk Back!* New York: Pocket Books, 1975.

Braiker, Harriet. "The Etiquette of Love." *Working Woman* (November 1988): 148–153.

Charlesworth, Edward A., and Ronald G. Nathan. *Stress Management*. New York: Atheneum, 1984.

Cunningham, Mary. *Power Play*. New York: Linden Press, 1984.

Dorning, Mike. "When World Leaders Gather, Protocol Takes the Guesswork Out of Diplomacy." *The Houston Post* (July 9, 1990): S4.

Flax, Ellen. "Should You Outlaw Romance in the Office?" *Working Woman* (August 1989): 16.

Martin, Judith. "Miss Manners on Office Etiquette." *Fortune* (November 6, 1989): 155, 158.

Petty, John Ira. "When in Rome, and Tokyo, and . . . ." *The Houston Post* (July 9, 1990): E1, E8–E9.

Pincus, Marilyn. *Mastering Business Etiquette and Protocol*. New York: National Institute of Business Management, Inc., 1987.

Pugh, Clifford. "High Tech Etiquette." *The Houston Post* (July 9, 1989): F1, F4.

Ricketts, Chip. "Please, Thank You Key Words to Manners-Minded Sokolosky." *Dallas Business Journal* (January 2, 1990): 12.

UPDATE: Telephone Manners—A Guide for Using the Telephone. Southwestern Bell Telephone Company, n.d.

Webster's New Collegiate Dictionary. Springfield, MA: G. & C. Merriam Company, 1976.

Zastrow, Charles. "How to Become Assertive." *Understanding Human Behavior and the Social Environment*. Chicago: Nelson Hall, 1987.

SUGGESTED READINGS

Baldrige, Letitia. *Letitia Baldrige's Complete Guide to Executive Manners*. New York: Rawson Associates, 1985.

Baldrige, Letitia. *Letitia Baldrige's Complete Guide to the New Manners for the '90s*. New York: Rawson Associates, 1985.

Draves, William A. *Marketing Techniques for Office Staff*. Manhattan, KS: Learning Resources Network, 1986.

Martin, Judith (Miss Manners). *Guide for the Turn-of-the-Millennium*. New York: Pharos Books, 1989.

CHAPTER EIGHTEEN
JOB-SEEKING SKILLS

A typical job hunt:
NO NO NO NO NO NO NO NO NO NO NO NO NO NO
NO NO NO NO NO NO NO NO NO NO NO NO NO NO
NO NO NO NO NO NO NO NO NO NO NO NO NO YES

Tom Jackson,
Guerrilla Tactics in the Job Market

OBJECTIVES

After studying this chapter, you should be able to:
1. Explain the importance of strong job-seeking skills.
2. Define an ideal job for yourself based on your skills and abilities.
3. Identify potential obstacles to job hunting and how to overcome them.
4. Describe resources for information concerning organizations and careers.
5. Write a solid resume.
6. Identify methods of locating a job opening.
7. Explain the appropriate behavior for a job interview.
8. Identify ways to handle the stress of the job search.
9. Identify early warning signs of termination.
10. Explain how to cope with the termination process.

WHY ARE JOB-SEEKING SKILLS NECESSARY?

Job seeking is one of the most difficult tasks we ever face.

Job-seeking skills are those skills that assist us in finding employment. They include the ability to determine the type of position that will satisfy our needs, to locate available positions, to obtain interviews for those positions, and to land the job.

Everyone who wants to work searches for a job at least once. However, the first job search is usually not the only one. Some individuals lose jobs because of layoffs or terminations. Others simply want to find another position that is more suitable to them in working conditions, location, wages, or job duties.

Strong job-seeking skills are necessary because finding a job is one of the most difficult tasks we ever face in our lives. It is full of frustration and rejection. A job search is something you must do on your own and for yourself:

Lorenzo went to see the job placement counselor at school.
He had graduated two months ago and still had not found a job.
The counselor, Jana, asked him to explain all the job-hunting

actions he had taken in the past week. Lorenzo thought for a minute and said, "Well, I looked in the Sunday paper."

"Is that all?" Jana asked. "Did you expect a company to just pick your telephone number at random and call to offer you a $100,000 a year job complete with a 20-hour work week, three secretaries, and a designer office? Just let me know if that happens, so I can see about a job with that company! While you're waiting for that magic call, let's see if we can set up a job search program that will work."

For these reasons a carefully organized, well-executed job search is vital to obtain the best possible job in the shortest amount of time. To begin the search, develop a profile of the type of position you would like to have.

FIGURE 18.1   Job seeking is full of rejection.

WHAT TYPE OF JOB WOULD YOU LIKE?

The first step in determining the perfect job for you is to review your previous activities—paid work, volunteer work, professional organizations joined, and educational courses taken. What things did you do well? What courses did you enjoy? Which activities did you like best? The form in Figure 18.2 will help you develop this list. After developing an idea of what you like to do and do well, analyze these activities to determine the skills you used. Richard Bolles, in his book *What Color Is Your Parachute?*, says skills will be in the following areas:

FIGURE 18.2   Transferable skills.

Skills I Have	How and Where I Used These Skills	How I Can Use These Skills on the Job
People	Organized a 10 K race open to all runners in the city for a charitable organization	Can organize, coordinate, + direct — can delegate responsibility. Follow up to see that everything is in order
Data	Prepared weekly sales report when I worked for X, Y, Z Corporation	Collect, analyze, + prepare data in usable format
Things	Responsible for maintenance on photocopy machine — adding paper, clearing paper jams, + replacing toner for the church	Understand office equipment + can perform routine maintenance duties

People. Do you communicate effectively orally and in writing, and do you get along with others? Do you know how to handle, motivate, organize, direct, persuade, and coach others? Are these activities enjoyable to you?

Data. Are you able to gather, compile, interpret, analyze, and problem solve around data (mathematical or other)? Do you enjoy these types of activities?

Things. Do you competently operate machines, equipment, or tools? Do you like these activities?

Analyzing your skills shows the types of jobs you would like and the skills you can market.

After identifying those skills, determine how you might use them on the job. This process will assist you in identifying the type of job for which you are best suited as well as recognizing what skills you can market to your prospective employers.

Values are another important area to explore. What is important to you? Respect? Helping others? Freedom of expression? Caring for the environment? Someone who values helping others, for instance, may be happier in a position of social worker or teacher than as an accountant.

Environmental preference is another factor to consider. Would you rather work inside or outside? Alone or with others? In a structured or unstructured environment? In a large or small organization? Pay requirements are an additional consideration. How much do you actually need to earn? Also, do you have any physical or mental handicaps that would prevent you from performing certain jobs?

Answering these questions will help determine the types of jobs for which you will be ideally suited. This activity is particularly helpful for the individual beginning a first career or seeking a career change. Complete your self analysis by becoming aware of your personal strengths and potential obstacles to overcome.

WHAT ARE YOUR STRENGTHS AND OBSTACLES?

Analyzing your strengths and potential obstacles shows your realistic prospects.

Become aware of the strengths you do have. Intelligence, punctuality, trustworthiness, sense of humor, patience, and loyalty are but a few of the personal characteristics that are valued by a company. Figure 18.3 shows you a way to chart both these strengths and potential obstacles to employment.

FIGURE 18.3 Personal strengths and potential obstacles analysis.

Personal strengths	How these strengths can be valuable to an employer
Type 65 words/minute, completed computer courses + know Word Perfect and Lotus 1, 2, 3.	I can use my skills + knowledge to turn out work quickly with a minimum of training time for the company.
Potential obstacles	**How potential obstacles can be turned into an asset**
Have been out of job market for 4 years. Have 3 young children.	I'm mature, know what I want, performed volunteer work while being out of the job market. I am a responsible adult.

Many applicants have obstacles to overcome. However, with careful thought and preparation, these liabilities can be turned into assets. Review the following list and determine whether you have special concerns:

You have been convicted of a crime.
You are older.
You are unable to relocate.
You have been away from the job market for a long time.
You are young and have no work experience.
You were fired from your previous job.
You were not born in the United States.
You have a physical disability.
You have a mental disability.
You are a minority.
You are a woman.
You have too much education.
You have too little education.
You have no experience in the industry for which you have applied.

Being older, for instance, can be turned into an asset. You have maturity and poise and understand the nature of work. Develop a positive attitude and work on presenting your obstacles to employers in a positive light. Once you have realistically evaluated yourself, you are ready to identify occupations that interest you.

HOW CAN YOU LEARN ABOUT OCCUPATIONS?

Information on careers may be obtained through the library or interviews.

The local library and your school career counseling center are the two best places to start learning about careers. Many books, magazines, and journals concerning careers describe what different occupations entail. The librarian or career counselor can direct you to this information.

Several references, in particular, are extremely helpful. The *Occupational Outlook Handbook, Occupational Outlook Handbook for College Graduates, Occupational Outlook Quarterly,* and *The Job Outlook in Brief* from the U.S. Bureau of Labor Statistics are a good starting place for your search. The *Occupational Outlook Handbook,* for instance, lists major occupations and explains what the future of those careers looks like, the nature of the work, earnings, working conditions, and usual training required.

If you are still unsure, try an informational interview. Start with your teachers. If you know that they are familiar with a profession in which you are interested, ask to discuss it with them. Perhaps they know people currently employed in this profession who would be willing to talk with you about what their jobs are like.

Friends and neighbors are another source of informational interviews. Ask if they know someone who does the type of work in which you are interested. Also, you can call a company and ask for an informational interview. Ask the receptionist for the name of an individual who holds a position in the area in which you are interested. For instance, if you are curious about jobs in accounting, you may ask the name and correct title of the accounting manager. Then, armed with that information, either call or write that individual and ask for an appointment.

When calling, explain that you are interested in learning more about the individual's occupation and ask for an appointment at a time that would be convenient. If you were referred by someone else, mention that individual's name as your referral source. Be prepared with some questions to ask, such as what tasks are performed, what entry-level positions lead to the individual's position, and what salary you could expect. Do not stay too long. Be sure to thank the individual speaking with you. Then, when you have decided on a career area, you are ready to develop a resume.

WHAT GOES INTO YOUR RESUME?

A resume's sole function is to get a job interview.

A **resume** is a sales tool designed to assist you in obtaining an interview. It provides a prospective employer with a brief summary of your skills, education, and job experience. The resume does not get you a job. However, a poorly written resume that does not identify your skills and abilities, contains typographical errors, and is unattractive will not get you an interview.

Formats

Endless formats exist for resumes. The two basic forms are chronological and functional. The **chronological resume**, which is illustrated in Figure 18.4, is the most common resume style. It lists experience in reverse chronological order, identifying the most recent employment first. This format is good when an individual has a continuous work history with progressively more responsible positions. However, it may not be helpful for those who have gaps in their employment or are attempting to return to the job market after a prolonged absence such as caring for a family.

The **functional resume** emphasizes special skills that can be transferred to other areas, making it useful for individuals reentering the job market or who want to change careers. Also those with little work experience and extensive volunteer experience can benefit from this format. The functional resume is shown in Figure 18.5.

Resumes can also be developed that incorporate both chronological and functional forms. Figure 18.6 demonstrates this **hybrid resume**.

Keep these tips in mind while developing a resume:

Limit the resume to one page if possible, two at the most.

Target your resume to specific employers. If you have access to word processing equipment, you can develop resumes that fit the job or company for which you are applying.

Do not enclose a photograph or list your marital status, number of children, height, weight, race, or religion. This information may disqualify you from the interview.

List extracurricular activities if they are relevant to the position for which you are applying or highlight skills that could be useful in that position.

Use action verbs such as earned, planned, wrote, achieved, and completed when describing your accomplishments.

Avoid the use of "I."

Expect to complete several rough drafts. Ask someone else to read your draft critically, reviewing for clarity, spelling errors, and format.

Be sure that your resume is pleasing to the eye. A well laid out resume with white areas will be easier to read.

A resume that has been printed on a laser printer and then photocopied on a higher grade paper is a relatively inexpensive alternative to a professional resume.

Avoid off-size or strange-colored paper when printing your resume.

Honesty in your resume is the best policy. According to Margot Gibb-Clark, a newspaper writer, experts estimate that from 10 to 30 percent of job applicants lie on resumes. This practice, however, is not wise. Many applicants who appear the best qualified will not be hired when their credentials and references are checked and are not verifiable. Persons who passed the initial check may be terminated later when the information on the application is found to be incorrect, even though job performance is acceptable.

FIGURE 18.4   Sample of a chronological resume.

James W. Adams
278 Maple Street
Cowpens, SC 29682
803-555-1234

JOB OBJECTIVE
Entry-level sales position leading to opportunities for advancement to supervisory position and
broad opportunities for utilizing communications
skills.

EDUCATION
Associate degree, Spartanburg Junior College,
1992
Specialized in marketing and communications.
Grade point average: 3.2 (A=4.0)

Diploma, Spartanburg County High School, 1990
(Upper third of class)

EXPERIENCE
1990-1992   Sales clerk in Montgomery Crawford
            Hardware Store after school. Respon-
            sible for entire store when owner
            was away.

1990-1992   Summers; counselor and lifeguard at
            Camp Sequoia for boys

1987-1990   Miller's Grocery Store; clerk, de-
            livery and stock boy on Saturdays
            and during summer.

ACTIVITIES
High school varsity letters in football,
basketball, and track.

President, Methodist Youth Fellowship, Grace
Methodist Church, Cowpens, SC

Member of the Debating Club and French Club,
Spartanburg County High School

REFERENCES
References are available upon request.

FIGURE 18.5 Sample of a functional resume.

```
                    Kelly D. Watson
                  114 West 23d Street
                  Nashville, TN 46302
                     615-555-1708


JOB OBJECTIVE
     Secretarial or data-entry position.


EDUCATION
     Candidate for word processing certificate,
     Nashville Business School, Sept. 1992. GPA: 3.7
     (A=4.0)

     Diploma, West End High School, Nashville,
     TN, 1991.


SPECIAL SKILLS
     Developed high capabilities in operating word
     processing equipment and utilizing several word
     processing software packages, including WordStar
     and WordPerfect.

     Capable of utilizing spreadsheet software pack-
     ages, i.e., Lotus 1-2-3.

     Trained in office procedures, including tele-
     phone etiquette and reception techniques.


EXPERIENCE
     Prepare, edit, and publish weekly business
     school newsletter.

     Assistant editor of high school newspaper, The
     Scribbler, at West End High School.

     Typed theses, themes, and other papers for Van-
     derbilt students during the summer.


REFERENCES
     References are available upon request.
```

FIGURE 18.6   Sample of a hybrid resume.

```
                    Pauline R. Smith
                10 New England Ridge Road
                  Washington, WV 26181
                     304-555-1234


JOB OBJECTIVE
     Laboratory technician in hospital, doctor's of-
     fice, or medical laboratory

EDUCATION
     West Virginia University
     B.S. degree, General Science, 1975.

     West Virginia University Parkersburg campus
     Laboratory techniques course, 1992.


ACCOMPLISHMENTS
     Performed x-rays, various laboratory tests, as-
     sisted patients, and aided the physician in mi-
     nor in-office surgical procedures.

     Processed blood and other advanced laboratory
     tests in state medical laboratory.

EMPLOYMENT HISTORY
     Office Assistant
     Dr. Mortimer Smith, Charleston, WV
     1980-1985

     Laboratory Technician
     West Virginia State Laboratory, Charleston, VW
     1978-1979

     Office Assistant
     Dr. Cynthia Raddock, Morgantown, WV
     1975-1977

REFERENCES
     References available upon request.
```

References

References are individuals who can vouch for your work performance and your character. They include former bosses, coworkers, teachers, and fellow professionals or neighbors who know you socially. Family members are not considered good references, as most employers do not view them as unbiased. Offer references such as former employers and teachers who can attest to your performance first. Only if you are asked for character references should you provide the names of others.

Never use individuals' names for a reference without obtaining permission. Tell them about your job search plans and the type of work you are seeking. Be sure that you have their complete mailing address, a daytime telephone number, and the correct spelling of their name. Between three and five references is the usual number.

Be sure to express appreciation to references for being willing to assist you in your job search. Calling them after an interview to let them know that they can expect a telephone call from your prospective employer is a good idea.

You are now ready to begin actively seeking a job. The first step is to identify organizations that can use your skills.

WHAT COMPANIES ARE OUT THERE?

Before deciding which organizations will be the focus of your job search, you must make some decisions concerning the locations in which you are willing to work. In what area of the country do you want to work? Are you willing to relocate? How far are you willing to drive to a job? What areas of town are inaccessible to you because of distance or unreliable public transportation?

Organizations in your area can be identified through library resources. Some of the available resources are:

> Local business directories, such as the Chamber of Commerce directory
> Company reports, such as annual reports and *10K* reports
> *Encyclopedia of Associations*
> *Standard and Poor's Register*
> *Dun and Bradstreet Million Dollar Directory*
> *Thomas Register of American Manufacturers*
> *Value Line*

Library resources can help target specific companies for your job search.

Local libraries contain information specific to your community. Ask the librarian for assistance in locating this information.

These resources can tell you where organizations are located and other information about them. This information will be useful during the interviewing phase. At this point a realistic look at the job market is in order.

WHAT CAN YOU REALISTICALLY EXPECT?

After reviewing what you would like in a job, what skills you have, and what types of companies exist, you can realistically evaluate what type of job you will be able to

FIGURE 18.7 Assessing the difference between what you want and what is available is an important part of the job search.

JOB PARAMETERS

	Ideal	Realistic
Salary	$ 22,000 a year	$18,000 a year
Location	Los Angeles	LA, Sacramento San Francisco
Hours	9 – 5	7Am – 7Pm any time between these hours
People (Groups) Young, Old, Individual	work by self	groups near my age
Outdoors/Indoors	outdoors	in + out
Size of Company	below 50	any size
Dress Code/Supervision	no dress code minimal supervision	willing to conform to moderate dress code + more close supervision

Evaluation of the companies and the economic realities of your region gives you realistic expectations.

obtain. Figure 18.7 will assist you in this exercise. Take into consideration your local economy. If the unemployment rate is high and layoffs are occurring, you may have to accept a position that is not quite what you want in terms of job duties and pay. With these realities in mind, locating the jobs can actually begin.

WHERE ARE THE JOBS?

You must take a number of approaches to find an open position. Networking, the direct approach, newspaper want ads, hot lines, private employment agencies, public employment agencies, temporary agencies, summer jobs and internships, and school placement centers are all ways in which individuals find jobs.

Networking

Networking is one of the most effective methods of looking for a job opening. It involves telling people you know that you are looking for a job and asking them to contact you if they hear of any openings. These people include teachers, former employers, friends, parents of friends, former coworkers, and contacts in professional organizations. Ask these acquaintances to inquire in your behalf. Having a friend within the organization you are targeting deliver your resume and recommend you for a position will dramatically increase the odds of receiving an interview.

The informational interview mentioned previously can also be used in networking. Ask individuals with whom you speak to refer you to others who may know about jobs and to call you if they have any openings at their firm.

Direct Approach

The direct approach to a company is another extremely effective method of locating an opening. Many large organizations have human resources departments that post all job openings and accept applications for employment on a regular basis. Before going to the company, call human resources to determine when the company takes applications and where jobs are posted. Going to a company unannounced is not suggested.

Another approach is to call the company, asking for the name of the individual who supervises the department in which you wish to work. For instance, you can call and ask for the name of the data processing manager and the correct company address, explaining that you are developing a mailing list. Then, send a target letter to that individual, giving your qualifications and asking for an interview. Figure 18.8 is a sample of a target letter. This letter should be modified to fit the qualities you have that may interest this particular employer. Follow up by telephone and ask for an interview. If you are told that the company has no openings, ask if you can call back later or if the official knows of any other job openings. Express thanks (and remember that a sense of humor is refreshing). Always be polite and professional.

Newspaper Want Ads

The want ads of the newspaper contain many positions. However, the newspaper is probably the least effective way to find a job. The competition is fierce for the positions advertised. Scan the ads and answer only those advertisements for which you are qualified. Never depend totally on the newspaper to identify positions.

Many large employers, such as hospitals, universities, corporations, and governmental entities, have telephone hot lines that run a recording of open positions. These lines can be checked at your convenience, and many run 24 hours a day. Develop a list of these numbers and check them weekly.

Private Employment Agencies

Private employment agencies have jobs for those with skills and a proven track record. However, carefully check to see what your financial obligations to the agency may be. Some require you to pay a fee for the job you obtain through them. Other jobs are fee paid. This term means that the employer, rather than the employee, will pay the fee.

FIGURE 18.8   Sample target letter.

489 Longren Circle
Rancho Palos Verdes, CA 90274
714-555-2645
August 28, 1991

Ms. Darnelle Johnson, Data Processing Manager
Springboard Products, Inc.
836 Spring Oaks Avenue
Los Angeles, CA 90047

Dear Ms. Johnson:

I recently obtained an associate degree in data processing. My willingness to work hard and my ability to cooperate with others, along with this degree, will make me a valuable member of your data processing staff. To further highlight my accomplishments, I have attached a copy of my resume.

I would appreciate an opportunity to discuss my skills and abilities with you. I will call in a few days to schedule a mutually convenient time for us to meet.

Sincerely,

Lucinda Colton

Lucinda Colton

Public Employment Agencies

Public employment agencies operate in each state. Visit your state employment commission and find out how its services operate and what positions are available. Many organizations with government contracts are required to place job openings with the state employment commissions, and federal and other government openings can be obtained through them as well.

Temporary Agencies

Individuals working with temporary agencies frequently find permanent employment through a long-term temporary job assignment. Finding a job in this manner can be beneficial because you have a chance to learn about the company and the individuals in it prior to accepting permanent employment. If you do not wish to stay there, you simply ask for a new assignment.

Summer Jobs and Internships

Summer jobs and internships are an excellent way to find a full-time position. After seeing the individual's skills and capabilities, companies will often offer full-time employment.

School Placement Office

Do not overlook your school placement office. Assistance in interviewing, job leads, and moral support can be obtained through the center. Recruiters frequently come to campus and interview students through the placement office.

Using only one of these sources is not the most efficient way to obtain a job interview. Taking advantage of as many job search methods as possible will allow you to quickly locate more positions and generate more interviews. These interviews must happen before hiring occurs.

HOW DO YOU HANDLE AN INTERVIEW?

The interview, which obtains the job, requires practice and planning.

An **interview** is a process by which the prospective employer learns more about you and evaluates whether you are the best qualified candidate for the position. As the interviewee, you have the responsibility to sell yourself, allowing the interviewer to see exactly what you are capable of doing for the company. In addition, the interview is a time when you can evaluate the company and learn more about the position that is available.

FIGURE 18.9   At an interview you learn about the company, and the company learns about you.

Preparing Yourself

A number of steps can be taken to prepare for the interview. The first is to be prepared to answer questions that the interviewer might pose. Possible questions are shown in Figure 18.10. Extensive time should be spent in developing honest, thoughtful answers. Prepare a two-minute summary of yourself in response to the "tell me about yourself" question. Study potential weaknesses and learn how to

FIGURE 18.10   Questions an interviewer might ask.

Tell me about yourself.
What are your strengths?
What are your weaknesses?
Why should I hire you?
What are you looking for in a job?
Why did you leave (or why do you want to leave) your current job?
Why do you want to work for this company?
What are your long-term career objectives?
What are your short-term career objectives?
How long would you stay with us?
What do you know about this organization?
What do you find most appealing in a job? Least appealing?
How would you describe your personality?
What interests you most about this job? Least?
What don't you do well?
What did you think of your last boss?
What would be an ideal job for you?

present them in a positive light. For instance, if you are younger and have little work experience, present yourself as eager, energetic, and willing to work hard. Remember, interviewers will not believe that individuals have no weaknesses and appreciate frank answers to their questions. In addition, study the questions in Figure 18.11. These are samples of the kinds of questions you will want answered about the position.

When an offer to interview is extended, be sure that you verify the correct time, date, location, and the name of the person with whom you will be speaking. Then research as much information about the company as possible. You might go to the library, call a friend who is employed there, or read the annual report or *10K* report. Be sure that you know how to get to the location; if necessary, make a trial run on the day before the interview.

FIGURE 18.11   Possible questions to ask the interviewer.

What are the job duties of the position?

What types of skills are you looking for?

What type of training program do you have?

What will be expected of me within 3 months, 6 months, a year?

If I perform well, what are the opportunities for promotion?

What hours would I be working?

What is the salary range for this position?

What benefits are available/provided?

Be prepared for the interview to take one of several forms—directed, non-directed, group interview, board interview, or stress interview. A directed interview has specific predetermined questions, whereas a nondirected interview is less structured, involving more frank and open discussion. At a group interview several candidates are interviewed at one time by one or more interviewers. At a board interview one candidate is interviewed by more than one individual at the same time.

The stress interview may take place in any of these formats. This type of interview is designed to test an individual's reactions to uncomfortable situations. The candidate may be subjected to verbal attacks, silence, or rapid questioning. Not allowing yourself to become flustered and remaining calm will earn you passing marks in this type of interview.

Sometimes you can expect a series of interviews. A representative from the human resources department may perform a screening interview to be sure that you meet the general job qualifications and then refer you to the department with the opening. The supervisor will then interview you. Sometimes you may interview with several individuals in management with whom you would be working.

Presenting Yourself

The following suggestions will help you make the most of your interview:

Be on your best behavior from the time you drive onto company property. Many a job applicant has unknowingly run into the interviewer in the hallway, parking lot, or rest room.

Arrive a few minutes early.

Dress appropriately for the position, as if you were working there. Clothes that are revealing are unacceptable. If you feel you can wear the outfit to a party or a picnic, it is unsatisfactory for the interview. Be sure that your clothing is clean and wrinkle-free. Polish your shoes. Do not wear too much jewelry, perfume, or makeup. A watch, small to medium earrings for women only (men should not wear earrings), and one ring is considered appropriate. Do not wear large chains, ankle bracelets, or other heavy jewelry. Dressing conservatively is a good idea.

Be physically clean, with combed hair, clean nails, fresh breath, and deodorant.

Do not smoke or chew gum.

Smile and be pleasant. If offered a hand, make sure your handshake is firm.

Use eye contact but do not stare. Review the oral communication skills presented in Chapter 3 and make extensive use of them.

Remember that the first few minutes of the interview develop the all important first impression. Small talk can be expected.

Explain how your qualifications make you the best candidate for the position. Use the knowledge you developed earlier about your skills to explain how you have used them in the past and how you will use them to the benefit of the company.

Never speak badly about a previous employer. Interviewers fear you will one day speak badly about their organization.

If you must, explain any negative work experiences in an unemotional manner, emphasizing how this experience makes you a better employee.

Remain enthusiastic even if you feel that this position may not be for you. Ask for the position. Ask the interviewer when the decision will be made and whether you may call to inquire about the decision.

Be prepared to take pre-employment tests, such as a typing test.

Ask several questions about the job or the company.

Salary Questions

Know ahead of time the least amount of money you require. This amount will most likely be quite different from what you would like. Knowing what the local market generally pays for that position is also important. This information can be found through library research or by asking individuals in similar positions or counselors at your school placement center. With a bottom line in mind, you can decide whether a particular job is worth a lower salary because it offers a chance for rapid advancement or is in an industry that you are eager to enter.

Do not bring up salary first. If the interviewer asks what salary you had in mind, you may try something such as, "I'm fairly open. Do you have a salary range for this position?" Once you know the range, you can better handle negotiations.

Sometimes, if the salary is lower than you can comfortably handle and is on the low side for your skills, abilities, and the market, you may want to decline the position. Refusing is particularly important if you feel you would not be happy with yourself if you accepted the position.

Inappropriate Questions

At times you may be interviewed by an inexperienced interviewer and asked questions that are inappropriate. Some of the improper questions and the ways in which they can be asked are shown in Figure 18.12.

FIGURE 18.12 Inappropriate interview questions.

Topic	Inappropriate	Appropriate
Age	How old are you?	Are you at least 18?
Marital status	Are you married? Divorced? Single?	The job requires frequent over-time. Are you able to meet this requirement?
Children	Do you have children? If so, how many?	(Same as above)
Criminal record	Have you ever been arrested?	Have you ever been convicted?
National origin	Where were you born? Are you a citizen?	Not appropriate. New hires must provide proof of ability to work in the United States within three days of hire
Religion	What religion are you?	Not appropriate
Disability	What is your handicap?	This job requires lifting and walking. Are you able to per-form these tasks?

These questions may indicate discrimination and are illegal in some states. If these questions were used during an employment interview and you feel that they are the basis for failing to hire you, contact your state fair employment commission or the Equal Employment Opportunity Commission. Remember, however, that most interviewers are not professional interviewers, are likely to be unaware of the law, and probably do not intend to discriminate.

Being faced with one of these questions poses a dilemma. If you refuse to answer or if you tell the interviewer that the question is illegal, you may diminish your chances for employment because the interviewer may feel you have something to hide. Also, you may embarrass the interviewer or cause discomfort. On the other hand, answering it may decrease your chances for employment. An employer who learns that you are a single parent with four preschool children may not hire you for fear that you will be absent frequently.

Be prepared with an answer in the event you are asked any of these questions. For instance, a good response when faced with the question of how many children you have would be, "You need not worry about my family. I have made arrangements, and I do not let my personal obligations interfere with my work."

H. Anthony Medley, in his book *Sweaty Palms: The Neglected Art of Being Interviewed*, suggests that if the response will not hurt you, give an answer. Examples of replies that are safe would be "no" if you have never been arrested or "Catholic" if you are interviewing for a position at a Catholic school. However, he says that if the reply will hurt you, try to avoid answering it in a joking manner. If the interviewer persists, say that you thought he was joking because that question is not a permitted pre-employment inquiry. You could also explain that you would be happy to answer the question if the interviewer will tell you how the question pertains to your ability to perform the job.

Following Up

Immediately after the interview, write a thank you letter to the individual with whom you interviewed. Express your appreciation for the interview, discuss your interest in the job, add any facts or points you may have omitted from the interview, and ask for the job. A sample thank you letter is in Figure 18.13.

FIGURE 18.13   Sample thank you letter to an interviewer.

128 Daisy Trail Lane
Edmond, Oklahoma 73013
405-555-5432
September 20, 1992

Mr. Sam Hathaway, Accounting Manager
Von Rheen Enterprises
611 Cutler Lane
Edmond, OK 73018

Dear Mr. Hathaway:

Thank you for the opportunity to interview for the accounts payable position. Attention to detail and ability to follow instructions will allow me to do an excellent job for you as accounts payable clerk. I look forward to hearing from you on September 26.

Sincerely,

Michael Ottero

Michael Ottero

Keeping progress charts will help you measure your job search progress. Count the applications placed, resumes mailed, and followup telephone calls made each week. Also, develop an interview chart that will help you keep track of interviews and followups. Samples of these charts are in Figures 18.14 and 18.15.

HOW DO YOU HANDLE THE JOB SEARCH STRESS?

Seeking employment is one of the most stressful activities ever. Rejection abounds, and we hear more "no's" than "yes's." Picking up the telephone or writing a letter or going out to fill out an application that may lead to rejection takes an unusual amount of self-confidence when we are feeling good about ourselves. Having lost a job or being unsure of our ability to do a first job plays on our self-doubt, making even more difficult the task of facing the rejection that will occur during the job search.

FIGURE 18.14   Sample interview chart.

Company/ Official Name	Date Interviewed	Thank You Note Sent	Followup Date	Analysis	Offer/ No Offer
1. SPIDEX INC. Frank Turner President	3/26	yes	4/4	good company would like to work there	no offer
2. ART INC. Lois Frazier	4/8	yes	4/10	salary not what A want	no offer
3. The Roy Company Lou Smith Vice President	4/4	yes	4/12	good company, liked you and people	offer $18,000/yr
4.					
5.					
6.					
7.					
8.					
9.					
10.					

FIGURE 18.15   Sample progress chart.

	Applications	Resumes Mailed	Followups/ Phone Calls	Interviews	Thank You Notes
Week 1	⊬⊬	|||	||||	||	||
Week 2	⊬⊬ |||	⊬⊬	⊬⊬ ||				
Week 3					
Week 4					
Week 5					
Week 6					
Week 7					
Week 8					
Week 9					
Week 10					

The rejection itself is not the only part of the job search that is stressful. Driving to new locations for interviews, meeting with unfamiliar people, waiting for telephone calls or letters, and worrying about finances all increase the tension. Learning how to cope with these strains is of the utmost importance for a smooth job search.

To ease job-seeking anxiety, construct a less stressful environment.

Arranging your environment is a first step in coping with job stress. Statistics show that individuals who join a job search club or group find jobs quicker than those who work alone. You can share your distress concerning rejection and receive support from others in the job search group. Ask your school counselor or inquire at your state employment commission concerning job groups. If an established group is not available, start one with another friend who is also searching for a job. Meet regularly and discuss what you have tried, what happened, and how you are feeling about the search. Use each other to practice interviewing.

Discuss job search problems with your family. Explain to them how rejection feels. Solicit their cooperation in taking telephone calls. Be sure that children are trained how to answer the telephone and take messages. Let them know how important accurate telephone messages are. If you do not have a telephone answering machine, add an alternate number of someone who has a machine or who is usually home to take messages for you.

Approach job seeking as a job. Work at least six hours a day on your job search—doing research, writing letters, making telephone calls, and completing applications. Spend some time each day exercising and doing pleasurable activities such as a hobby or volunteer work with others less fortunate. These types of activities will help you manage the stress of job rejection. (Refer to Chapter 19 for tips on managing stress.)

The fear of rejection is the main reason job searches are unsuccessful. This fear can be countered by concentrating on the adage "Nothing ventured, nothing gained." Keep this attitude in mind when picking up the telephone, writing a letter, or filling out an application.

HOW DO YOU HANDLE JOB OFFERS?

Job offers can be made by telephone, letter, or in person. If the job, the organization, the location, and the salary are right, accept the job immediately. Be sure to inquire when you are to start, where and to whom you should report, and what time you should arrive.

Many times, however, you may want to think about a job offer. You may have another offer that you expect to materialize, or you may need to discuss the offer with your family or friends before accepting. Asking for 24 to 48 hours to allow for a decision is acceptable, with a maximum of 72 hours. Be sure that you have asked the company representative if a decision-making period is permissible and set a time when you will get back with the representative.

If you decide to reject a job offer, do so professionally. Practice your reasons for refusing the job ahead of time. Avoid reasons such as a personality conflict with the new boss or an offer of more money from your old company. According to Eleanor Raynolds, a partner in a New York executive-search firm quoted by Anne Russell in *Working Woman,* acceptable excuses are:

> I want very much to work for the company but feel the position offered does not fit with my career objectives.
>
> At present, I am unable to relocate, but I expect to be able to do so in several years.
>
> Your offer is excellent, but the opportunity for promotion does not seem to be as great as I need to meet my career objectives.

Raynolds suggests that after declining a job offer, you should write a thank you letter. You may want, at a later date, to work for this company and should leave the door open for future employment.

HOW IS THE FIRST WEEK ON THE JOB?

The first week on a new job is both exciting and stress-filled.

The first week on the job can be a frightening affair. Although we are excited to have the position, we have much to learn, everything from people's names to where the restroom is. These adjustments can be stressful even though we looked forward to beginning the new job:

FIGURE 18.16   The first day on the job can be an exciting and stressful experience.

"What a day!" Adrian thought, as she sank onto the couch. She had never expected it to be like this. She had ridden the bus and, being unsure where the stop was, ended up getting off four blocks from the office. She had had to run so that she would not be late. Then, after being introduced to her new supervisor, she had called him Bob instead of Bill. To top it all off, she had worn a pair of nice slacks. All the other women had on dresses.

"I hope it's better tomorrow," she sighed, as she turned on the TV. "I can't handle many more days like this."

Be patient with yourself and with the job. Give yourself time to get adjusted before you make any judgments concerning your new position.

ARE JOBS FOREVER?

Jobs do not last forever, and knowing when and how to leave is a must.

Jobs are not forever. Individuals may become bored and find no opportunity for growth. Companies lay off workers because of economic conditions, mergers, or buyouts. Sometimes people are terminated because of ethical misconduct, poor work performance, or personal chemistry that is not right. Whatever the cause, almost everyone leaves a job for one reason or another.

Warning signs of impending termination abound. If you begin to recognize some of them, it may be time to take action. The signs are:

1. You hate your job and spend more time thinking about what you will do after work than at work. You find getting out of bed in the morning difficult. These attitudes tend to show at work, and others on the job realize how you feel about your job.

2. You lose your voice. Your ideas and opinions are not listened to and others around you pull back and quit communicating with you, perhaps because they realize your job is in danger. You see others being promoted around you as you stay in the same position.

3. The economy is working against you. You begin to hear about layoffs because of a recession or a potential takeover.

4. You're not personally productive, which appears in the form of missed objectives, poorly managed time, or confused priorities.

5. You fail to change. You feel unwilling to adapt and learn new skills and ways of doing things.

If you see the handwriting on the wall and feel you will soon be terminated, or if you are bored and ready for a job change, decisions must be made. Just how bad is the job? Can you hang in there until you find another position? If you do not have another job offer, how will you support yourself if you resign? Can you draw unemployment if you resign? Will the company pay severance pay if you resign?

Finding another job is usually easier while you still have one. In fact, approximately one-third of all job seekers are looking for another position while employed. Never use company time to conduct your job search. Do research in the evenings or on weekends and schedule telephone calls on breaks and interviews during your lunch period. Many times prospective employers will agree to see you late in the evening or even on Saturdays.

If you decide to resign, even if you have a new job, give two weeks' notice of your resignation. This length of notice is standard and proper. Your new employer usually will allow you time to give notice. Sometimes a company may ask you to leave immediately once your resignation is submitted, especially if you deal with trade or strategy secrets or if they feel that your immediate removal is in the best interests of the other employees.

No one is ever totally prepared for termination from a job. However, if you have been reading the warning signs and suspect it is a possibility, start preparing yourself. Expect to feel anger, shame, fear, sadness, and self-pity. Try to control these emotions during the termination interview and remain as professional as possible. When you have left the job site, these emotions can be unleashed and dealt with.

During the termination interview, find out what benefits, if any, the company may give you. Ask, if you think you will need it, for a reference that is positive or at least neutral. If you feel too out of control to discuss benefits and any termination package, ask if you can return the next day to do so.

Be aware of the unemployment laws in your state. Some states will not pay unemployment if you resign but will if you are terminated. If you are asked to resign rather than be terminated, this factor may be important in your decision.

Never burn your bridges. Throwing a tantrum while being terminated, threatening to kill someone, destroying computer files, tearing up documents, or smashing furniture may make you feel better temporarily but will hurt you in the long run. You may need a reference or want to return to the company under different circumstances.

Do not be surprised if your supervisor or a member of security escorts you to your work area to remove articles. This procedure is standard practice in a number of companies because of terminated employees who have destroyed company property.

Many employees, after being terminated, react with disbelief. Some are relieved to be out of an uncomfortable situation, whereas others turn to violence or drinking. Many experience a combination of these reactions. Whatever your reaction, you can expect to grieve because of the loss of a job and experience the grieving process that is discussed in Chapter 2.

SUMMARY

Job-seeking skills, which help us in finding employment, are important. Finding a job is one of the most difficult tasks we face. The job search is often filled with frustration and rejection.

Before we can begin a job search, we must determine the type of position that interests us and identify which skills we have to offer an employer. The library is a good source of information about different organizations that can use our talents and skills.

The resume is a device that enables us to obtain an interview; however, it does not land us a job. A poorly done resume, with typographical errors, can prevent us from being interviewed. Various formats of the resume are available, including chronological, functional, and hybrid resumes. Each has its advantages and disadvantages. Above all, a resume should be factual.

Many approaches are necessary to land an interview. These approaches include networking, the direct approach, newspaper want ads, private employment agencies, public employment agencies, temporary agencies, summer jobs and internships, and the school placement office. A variety of strategies must be utilized in order to secure interviews.

Interviewing is an art in itself, and preparation is the key to a successful interview. The interview can come in several forms—directed, nondirected, group interview, board interview, or stress interview.

The job search can be stressful. We hear many more "no's" than "yes's." Discussing the situation with our family, joining others who are job seeking, getting regular exercise, and working at the job search at least six hours a day will help manage stress.

Once a job is obtained, we can expect a stressful first week. We should give ourselves time for transition to the new position. Leaving a job can be just as stressful. We should learn the warning signs of impending termination and be prepared to leave our jobs gracefully, without burning bridges.

KEY TERMS

job-seeking skills
resume
chronological resume
functional resume
hybrid resume
reference
networking
interview

REVIEW QUESTIONS

1. Why are strong job-seeking skills important?
2. How can you figure out an ideal job for your skills and abilities?
3. What are the potential obstacles to job hunting, and how can you overcome them.
4. What resources for information concerning organizations and careers are available?
5. What goes into a solid resume?
6. Where can you locate job openings?
7. What behavior is appropriate for a job interview?
8. How can you handle the stress of the job search?
9. What are the early warning signs of impending termination?
10. How can you cope with the termination process?

DISCUSSION QUESTIONS

1. Have you ever looked for a job? Describe your job search and discuss the feelings associated with it.
2. Have you ever been terminated from a job? What happened? Could you have better handled the termination interview?
3. What is the economic situation in your community? Are jobs plentiful or scarce? What adjustments will you need to make in your search because of the economy?
4. What are your strengths? How can you market these strengths to potential employers?
5. What are your potential obstacles? How will you overcome them?

GRADUATION BLUES

"I've had it," Joshua's father, Alex, remarked to his wife, Selma. "That boy has just been sitting around the house since he graduated. I don't even think he's picked up the newspaper to look for a job. At this rate we'll be supporting him until he's 40. I wonder, what can we do to get him interested in looking for a job?"

"You know," Selma said thoughtfully, "at first he really tried. He did look in the want ads and applied for a few jobs. I remember he even had one interview. He was upset when he returned from the interview, but he never said what happened. After that he seemed to lose interest in looking for work."

"Well, I don't care. If he doesn't take some action soon, I will," muttered Alex.

1. What do you think happened that caused Joshua to stop looking for a job?
2. What do you think he could do to get his job search back on track?
3. What other methods of job search should he employ?
4. What types of environmental controls does Joshua need to establish?

CASE STUDY 18.2

NINE O'CLOCK NIGHTMARE

Cindy breezed in for her 9 A.M. interview five minutes late. She always liked to attract attention and keep the men waiting. As she told Darin, Mr. Grump's secretary, that she was here for the interview, she began to pull out her hairbrush and lipstick to freshen up a bit. Just as she was tucking everything away in her purse, Mr. Grump walked out. He did a double take as he stared at Cindy. She had on a low-cut spaghetti strap dress that was bright red and yellow.

Mr. Grump escorted Cindy into his office. She dropped into the chair and exclaimed, "The traffic was awful! It really got my nerves jangled. I've just gotta have a cigarette." She opened her purse and lit up. "Want one?" she asked.

Mr. Grump proceeded to interview Cindy. She told him how good a typist she was and how much she wanted to work for the company.

Mr. Grump walked her to the door and, as she left, turned to Darin and said, "Well, what do you think?"

"Seems like a real flake to me, Mr. Grump. I wouldn't hire her if I were you. I see nothing but trouble."

"Darin, I think you are right. She does type 90 words a minute and has mastered Lotus 1-2-3, but I don't think she would fit in here. Call that young lady, Martha, I interviewed yesterday and offer her the job."

1. What interview rules did Cindy break?
2. What should Cindy have done during the interview?
3. Are skills always the most important factor?
4. What do you think would have happened if Cindy had been hired?

BIBLIOGRAPHY

Birsner, E. Patricia. *Job Hunting for the 40+ Executive*. New York: Facts on File Publications, 1985.

Bolles, Richard Nelson. *What Color Is Your Parachute?* Berkeley, CA: Ten Speed Press, 1989.

Gibb-Clark, Margot. "Applicants Often Inflate Resumes, Say Experts." *Houston Chronicle* (April 10, 1988), section 5, 4.

Graves, Morris, ed. *University of Houston Placement Manual 1989–1990*. Santa Ana, CA: Career Research Systems, Inc., 1989.

Jackson, Tom. *Guerrilla Tactics in the Job Market*. New York: Bantam Books, 1978.

Levitt, Julie Griffin. *Your Career and How to Make It Happen*. Cincinnati: South-Western Publishing Company, 1990.

McIntosh, George. *Hawks Do, Buzzards Don't: The Complete Job-Finding Guide*. Plano, TX: Wordware Publishing, 1990.

Medley, H. Anthony. *Sweaty Palms—The Neglected Art of Being Interviewed*. Berkeley, CA: Ten Speed Press, 1984.

Morin, William J., and James C. Cabrera. *Parting Company*. New York: Hartcourt Brace Jovanovich Publishing Company, 1982.

Russell, Anne M. "How to Say No to a Job Offer and Still Stay a Hot Prospect." *Working Woman* (April 1989): 118.

Sandroff, Ronni. "You Like Your Job, But Should You Leave It?" *Working Woman* (May 1990): 81–85.

Silver, Sheryl. "The Library Can Assist in Your Job Search." *The Houston Post* (January 29, 1989): M1.

Truitt, John. *Telesearch*. New York: Facts on File Publications, 1983.

SUGGESTED READINGS

Bureau of Labor Statistics. *The Occupational Outlook Handbook.* Washington, D.C.: Supt. of Documents, U.S. Government Printing Office.

Holland, John L. *Making Vocational Choices*. Englewood Cliffs, NJ: Prentice-Hall, Inc., 1985.

Irish, Richard K. *Go Hire Yourself*. New York: Doubleday, 1987.

Kocher, Eric. *International Jobs: Where They Are, How to Get Them*. Reading, MA: Addison-Wesley Publishing Company, Inc., 1989.

Krannich, Ronald L., and Caryl Rae Kannich. *The Complete Guide to Public Employment*. Woodbridge, VA: Impact Publications, 1990.

Rosenberg, Arthur D., and David V. Hizer. *The Resume Handbook: How to Write Resumes and Cover Letters for Every Situation*. Holbrook, MA: Bob Adams, Inc., 1990.

Smith, Carol Cox. *How to Break into Glamorous Careers*. New York: Monarch Press, 1985.

Smith, Michael Holley. *The Resume Writers Handbook*. New York: Barnes and Noble Books, 1987.

Wegmann, Robert, Robert Chapman, and Miriam Johnson. *Work in the New Economy: Careers and Job Seeking into the 21st Century*. Indianapolis: JIST Works, 1989.

CHAPTER NINETEEN

WELLNESS

.

In 1981 Adolph Coors Company of Golden, Colorado, opened a 25,000-square-foot wellness center because Chairman and CEO William Coors was committed to the concept that people can prevent illness by developing healthy life-styles. Today the exercise program includes an indoor running track, aerobics, and strength training, as well as cardiovascular equipment. Courses are offered in nutrition, stress management, smoking cessation, and weight loss. Employees can have mammography and blood pressure screenings on location as well as attend pre- and postnatal education classes.

This commitment to wellness has paid off. The company currently estimates that it saves $1.9 million annually in decreased medical costs, reduced use of sick leave, and increased productivity. A return of $6.15 is realized for every dollar spent on wellness.

Shari Caudron, *Personnel Journal* (July 1990): 55-60

OBJECTIVES

After studying this chapter, you should be able to:
1. Define a wellness program and describe the benefits to both employer and employee.
2. Identify some of the physical and mental results of a stress overload.
3. Describe several methods of effective time management.
4. Discuss the importance of proper diet in minimizing stress effects.
5. Discuss the methods and positive results of exercise and relaxation in achieving wellness.
6. Identify methods of changing stressful thoughts, attitudes, and behaviors.
7. Describe what companies are doing to encourage wellness.

WHAT IS A WELLNESS PROGRAM?

Wellness programs develop happier, more productive employees while reducing corporate costs.

A **wellness program** is a total approach to employee health care and well-being that addresses the emotional and physical health of individuals or groups. Individuals who are healthy are happier, more productive, suffer less illness, and are less at risk for disease.

Organizations are becoming increasingly interested in the wellness of their employees, not only because it increases productivity but also because it reduces insurance costs. An article published in *Personnel Administrator* by Leonard Abramson reported the results of a survey by the Health Research Institute done in 1987. Organizations that conducted wellness programs had only a 2.8 percent increase per employee in health care costs in 1987 over 1986, whereas organizations with no wellness programs had a 9.9 percent increase.

For these reasons both individuals and organizations are interested in programs that address total health. A complete wellness plan includes an understanding of stress. Estimates are that as many as 75 percent of all medical complaints are stress-related. An understanding of stress and a knowledge of skills to cope with it are essential for reducing stress-related illnesses.

WHAT IS STRESS?

Stress is the physical state of the body in response to environmental pressures that produce emotional discomfort. The mind actually prepares the body for some activity in response to external stimuli. In the rapid pace of daily living you encounter many pressures and feel anxieties that will affect your body and ultimately your behavior.

Origins of Stress

Stress is not a new phenomenon. It was first recognized on the battlefield in the Civil War. Nervous and anxious reactions in the form of heart palpitations were so common among fearful soldiers that they became known as "soldier's heart." Stress was called "shell shock" during World War I and "battle fatigue" during World War II.

These reactions, in fact, existed in prehistoric times. When faced with possible danger, the autonomic nervous system responded by preparing cave people to face the situation with additional strength, energy, and endurance. Stored sugar and fat poured into the bloodstream to provide fuel for quick energy, breathing speeded up to provide more oxygen, and blood-clotting mechanisms were activated to protect against injury. Muscles tensed for action, digestion slowed to allow blood to be directed to the muscles and brain, pupils dilated to allow more light to enter the eye, and hormone production increased to prepare the cave people either to fight or to run for safety. This response to anxiety is commonly known as the "fight or flight response."

Modern humans respond similarly to the pressures and demands of daily events. For example, you may worry or feel anxiety about inflation and soaring energy costs, an international crisis, a career-limiting mistake you made at work, or a wreck you nearly had on the freeway. In each of these instances, your body may react in the same way the cave people reacted to expected danger. A series of biochemical changes occurs, and the body's system is thrown out of balance.

Physiological reactions occur in stressful situations.

In today's society, however, you can seldom fight or flee in these situations. The physiological responses get turned on without being used for the intended purpose. The body is unable to release its stored energy, because aggressive behavior would not be appropriate in most social situations. Repeated or chronic preparation for action without the action following can lead to stress-related diseases and disorders.

Stress Overloads

Stress can be caused by either good or bad events. Holidays, weddings, births, and moving into a new house are examples of pleasant events for most people that may be stressful as well. The death of a loved one, divorce, being fired from work, or just experiencing trouble on the job are negative events that can also cause stress. Even simple daily stressors have an effect on your body. Fights with the kids, a missed bus, a flat tire, traffic, a rush job at work—all these small stressors add up.

Some experiences are obviously more stressful than others. Often, the same type of experience will be more stressful to one person than to another. Regardless of the varying intensities of the experience, each person has a limit, or a stress threshold, to the amount of stress that can be handled physically and psychologically.

Stress overload may cause various physical symptoms.

As stress builds up, people will experience an overload, which results in negative symptoms or behaviors. Overeating, loss of appetite, overindulging in alcohol, ulcers, temper tantrums, headaches, hypertension, and heart disease are common results of stress overloads. Additionally, a decrease in the ability to concentrate, memory problems, insomnia, anxiety, depression, and other personality changes may accompany stress overloads.

Learning to deal with stress, then, can literally be a matter of life or death. A total wellness program can help you deal with stress and other health-related matters. It should include effective time management, proper diet, no smoking, exercise, relaxation, and other leisure activities. It also involves changing stressful thoughts, attitudes, and behaviors.

HOW CAN YOU MANAGE TIME?

Time is a precious commodity. Every individual is given the same amount of time each day to be wasted or well spent. How we choose to use our time makes the difference in whether or not we achieve our goals. Effective **time management** is simply maximizing the time that we have to our greatest advantage. When we are in control of our time, we perform better, feel better about ourselves, and suffer fewer stress-related illnesses. We can develop better time management by assessing how we use time, identifying how we waste it, and planning to use it better.

Assessing How You Spend Time

The first step in assessing whether you are managing your time wisely is to determine if you are suffering any of the negative symptoms of poor time management. These negative symptoms are:

1. *Indecision.* You have so much to do that you cannot decide what to do first. You end up doing nothing and getting nowhere.
2. *White rabbit habit.* "I'm late, I'm late, for a very important date" accurately describes your life. Like the rabbit in Lewis Carroll's *Alice's Adventures in Wonderland,* you are always in a hurry, running late, and missing appointments and deadlines.

3. *Stress illnesses.* Responses to the pressures of poor time management include headaches, backaches, insomnia, and hives.
4. *Irritability and anger.* You stay angry and upset and have a tendency to take your frustration out on others.

Assess the effects of poor time management and then correct it.

Negative symptoms may make you look "out of control" and keep you from getting results. Good time management tends to be reflected in a confident and controlled approach to activities.

FIGURE 19.1   The white rabbit habit is a symptom of poor time management.

Another valuable step in assessing your time usage is to keep a time log. Figure 19.2 provides a sample time log. Use a log for at least a one-week period. Logging your daily activities for this length of time will allow you to identify your major time-wasters. You may be surprised at the amount of time you spend on innocent activities that rob you of using your precious commodity more productively.

Identifying Time-Wasters

Time-wasters include lack of planning, drop-in visitors, telephone games, and procrastination.

Lack of planning, drop-in visitors, telephone games, procrastination, meetings, over-commitment, fighting brush fires, personal disorganization, the inability to say "no," and television are among the most frequent time-wasters. You may recognize some of them as being at the top of your list. Methods of handling some of the biggest time-wasters are described below.

FIGURE 19.2 Sample time log.

Time	Planned Work	Telephone	Interruption	Meeting	Unplanned/New	Reports	Other	Subject	Originator (Person)	Priority A	B	C	Other	Comments
7:30														
7:45														
8:00														
8:15														
8:30														
8:45														
9:00														
9:15														
9:30														
9:45														
10:00														
10:15														
10:30														
10:45														
11:00														
11:15														
11:30														
11:45														
12:00														
12:15														
12:30														
12:45														
1:00														
1:15														
1:30														
1:45														
2:00														
2:15														
2:30														
2:45														
3:00														
3:15														
3:30														
3:45														
4:00														
4:15														
4:30														
4:45														
5:00														

Priority Definitions:
A-Very important; high priority item
B-Important; have more time to complete
C-Less important; could be delegated or rescheduled for later time
Other-Could "not do;" wasted time

Planning your time and tasks will produce effective results.

Lack of Planning

An old adage appropriate to this situation states, "If you fail to plan, you plan to fail." Planning a course of action is crucial in accomplishing your goals. One of the easiest methods of planning is to make a list of tasks to be accomplished. Ideally, you will have a daily list of five to ten major actions in order of importance. Limiting your list to five to ten items enables you to add unexpected or forgotten items while keeping the list manageable. The important point is to stick to your list and not overcommit. Carry over any unfinished tasks to the next day and integrate them into that day's priority list. An effective way of handling your priority list is to keep it on a calendar throughout the year. This practice also provides you with an excellent record of your activities.

Another useful method of planning is to use your "peak times" for tough tasks. You may be a morning person or a night person. Our body clocks, or biological rhythms, do tick strongest at different times of the day for each person. Recognizing your peak performance time may assist you in planning your more difficult tasks for that time to maximize your effectiveness. For instance, if you are a morning person, you will want to complete a difficult report early in the morning rather than waiting until late afternoon when you are not as alert.

Another time-saving tip is to plan certain activities for their nonpeak times. For example, banking on Friday afternoons will most certainly cost you more time than a midweek visit. Attempting postal business during your lunch break will find you in long lines with other individuals who had the same idea. A mid-morning or afternoon visit to the post office will probably save you time.

Drop-in or Casual Visitors

Friends and colleagues may unwittingly rob you of precious time needed to meet personal or professional commitments. That drop-in visit from the coworker down the hall to discuss the Monday night football game may disrupt your concentration on an important report due by noon to your boss or throw your daily schedule completely off track. To control such intrusions, close your office door if you have one. If this signal is not successful, use your body language to show that you are busy or stand up and start toward the door. Additionally, the following phrases can be useful in controlling the length of visits:

> "I appreciate your stopping by, but. . ."
> "I have a tight schedule; could we talk about this on. . ." (and set a time and date)
> "I have about 10 minutes before I have to go. . ."
> "How can I help you today?"

Telephone Games

You may have been involved in a game of "telephone tag" or applied evasive tactics with "Gabby Gerty." The game of telephone tag—two people calling numerous times but never reaching each other—can take hours of unproductive time. This contest can be avoided in several ways. Leave a message specifying what you want or leave instructions concerning required actions. If someone you need does not return your call, you might try leaving a message such as, "Unless I hear from you by close of business today, I plan . . . " This warning will normally prompt action by the other party. If all else fails, try to get your information elsewhere.

FIGURE 19.3   Telephone tag can waste valuable time.

Reprinted with special permission of North America Syndicate.

An encounter with "Gabby Gerty" involves receiving a call from someone who wants to discuss everything but the important purpose of the call. The following phrases may help control the length of time you spend on these calls:

"I appreciate your call, but. . ."

"I'm working on a term paper due this week. Can we visit later when I am not so pressed for time?"

"Could you call back when we might have more time?"

Procrastination   One of the most difficult time-wasters to control is your own procrastination. **Procrastination** is defined as putting off or intentionally delaying activities that need to be done. Once you understand the problem, you can develop methods of overcoming it. Chapter 7 and Figure 19.4 present some of the major causes of procrastination and describe when delaying is appropriate or inappropriate.

We occasionally find ourselves saying and meaning two different things:

> We often have hidden mean-ings in what we say.

Saying:	I really should . . .	Meaning:	I don't really want to . . .
	I can't do . . .		I won't do . . .
	I might . . .		I won't . . .
	I'll try to . . .		I won't . . .
	Could we discuss this some other time?		I really don't *ever* want to talk about it.

Each of these phrases illustrates our attempt to avoid committing to action. If procrastination is a problem for you, the following methods may help:

1. Tackle tough problems at your body's peak performance times.
2. Break large tasks into smaller segments, so they will not seem over-whelming.
3. Use daily "to do" lists and set specific goals.
4. Fight perfectionism.
5. Seek help if needed.
6. Let go of low priority tasks in order to focus and concentrate on high priority ones.

FIGURE 19.4 Major causes of procrastination.

Inappropriate Causes	
• Perfectionism	You put off tasks until you can do them *exactly* right, the very best you can. You fear they won't be right or good enough.
• Abdication	You wait for things to "happen" rather than *make* them happen; you make panic decisions; you let someone else make the decision; you do nothing at all.
• Overwhelmed	Job/task appears too big to handle. It seems threatening.
• Uncertainty	You are unsure how to do the task.
Appropriate causes	
• Stressed/exhausted	You are too tired to think through the problem effectively. You might make a poor or wrong decision. You tend to use bad judgment and may wind up doing it over again.
• Impulsive/emotional	You might make snap judgments or might do things in a fit of anger and regret them.
• Lack of Information	You need more facts to make a good decision.
• Don't Want to	You heed a subconscious message that you should not do that activity.

7. Schedule appropriate blocks of times to do specific tasks.
8. Establish a reward system for positive reinforcement.

Managing Time at Meetings

Methods of managing meetings to save time depend on whether you are attending the meeting or leading the meeting. If you are asked to attend a meeting, consider whether you actually "need" to attend the entire meeting or only some portion of it. Reviewing the meeting agenda can help you make that decision.

If you are leading the meeting, you are responsible for using time well. The following guidelines may help you:

1. Provide advance agendas reflecting timed subjects.
2. Invite only those people who are needed.
3. Start on time.
4. Set clear goals/purposes for the meeting.
5. Set time limits on the meeting and discussion topics.
6. Strictly adhere to your agenda.
7. Record and assign action items during the meeting.
8. Distribute meeting minutes within 48 hours.
9. Schedule an action-item followup.

A **planned agenda** is an outline or list of what is to be discussed or accomplished during the meeting. The agenda is a valuable tool for controlling your meeting. Ideally, an agenda should be distributed a week to ten days prior to the meeting time. People will be able to schedule their time to support the meeting and prepare information that may be needed. The agenda will serve as your guideline for a smooth transition from topic to topic and prevent the introduction of hidden agendas. A **hidden agenda** consists of topics that attendees wish to discuss that have no relevance to the purpose of your meeting. A hidden agenda can be disruptive:

> **Sam called a very important meeting of the office staff to discuss the new corporate policies effective the following week. There was little time to get the word out, and some policies were fairly complicated to understand. Early in the meeting, Linda from payroll began to ask questions that seemed completely off the subject but of great interest to all in attendance. "Will the new policies do away with our having the annual holiday party here in the office? You know, that party is coming soon, and we need to start planning the events now."**
>
> **Terry's eyes lit up with excitement at the mention of the party, and he responded, "I'll head the planning committee this year, but what should the theme for the party be, and what date do you want to set?"**
>
> **Sam realized that his meeting about new policies had the potential of becoming the first planning session for the annual party unless he took control now and got back on the real subject.**

As the meeting leader, you have the responsibility for adhering to the planned agenda. A successful meeting should move quickly, sufficiently cover all scheduled topics in the shortest possible time, and accomplish the planned meeting objectives.

To manage time outside of meetings, you may want to develop some definite action plans. Figure 19.5 provides you with a format and brief example of an action plan.

FIGURE 19.5   Sample time management action plan.

Change Required:	*Quit watching excessive TV*
Desired Result:	*Be more productive; read more, watch less*
Target Date:	*Within a week*
Actions Required:	*Unplug TV*
Key People Involved:	*Family – they won't like it*
Evaluate/modify:	*Did I achieve desired results? If not, try another approach*

WHAT IS PROPER DIET?

The second component of an effective wellness program is proper diet. *The Surgeon General's Report on Nutrition and Health* in 1988 states that diseases caused by dietary excess and imbalance rank among the leading causes of illness and death in

Your eating
patterns affect
your mental
and physical
condition.

the United States and generate substantial health care costs. Coronary heart disease, some types of cancer, strokes, diabetes and atherosclerosis (hardening of the arteries) have all been associated with improper diet. Cirrhosis of the liver, accidents, and suicides have been associated with excessive alcohol intake. These eight conditions alone accounted for nearly 1.5 million of the 2.1 million total deaths in 1987. Additionally, dietary excesses or imbalances contribute to problems such as high blood pressure, obesity, dental diseases, osteoporosis, and gastrointestinal diseases.

The United States Department of Agriculture (USDA) recommends that we eat a balanced variety of foods and avoid excess salt, saturated fat, and cholesterol. The USDA also suggests that people eat foods with adequate starch and fiber, avoid excessive sugar and sodium, and, if they drink alcohol, do so in moderation. Suggested food groups and appropriate serving sizes are listed in Figure 19.6.

FIGURE 19.6   Food groups and suggested servings.

Food Group	Suggested Daily Servings
Breads, Cereals, and Other Grain Products • Whole grain • Enriched	6 to 11 (Include several servings a day of whole grain products.)
Fruits • Citrus, melon, berries • Other fruits	2 to 4
Vegetables • Dark green leafy • Deep yellow • Dry beans and peas (legumes) • Starchy • Other vegetables	3 to 5 servings (Include all types regularly; use dark-green leafy vegetables and dry beans and peas several times a week.)
Meat, Poultry, Fish, and Alternates (Eggs, dry beans and peas, nuts and seeds)	2 to 3 servings—total 5 to 7 ounces lean
Milk, Cheese, and Yogurt	2 servings (3 servings for teens and women who are pregnant or breastfeeding; 4 servings for teens who are pregnant or breastfeeding)
Fats, Sweets, and Alcoholic Beverages	Avoid too many fats and sweets. If you drink alcoholic beverages, do so in moderation.

NOTE: Vegetarians and others may not eat one or more of these types of foods. These people may wish to contact a nutritionist in their community for help in planning food choices.

United States Department of Agriculture, Human Nutrition Information Service, Home and Garden Bulletin #232-2 *(April 1986).*

Obesity affects approximately 34 million adults and is a risk factor in a number of other diseases. In deciding whether you need to lose weight, consult the chart entitled "Desirable Body Weight Ranges" shown in Figure 19.7. In addition, you may want to consider the following USDA guidelines:

FIGURE 19.7   Desirable body weight ranges.

Height without shoes	Weight without clothes	
	Men (pounds)	Women (pounds)
Desirable Body Weight Ranges		
4'10"		92–121
4'11"		95–124
5'0"		98–127
5'1"	105–134	101–130
5'2"	108–137	104–134
5'3"	111–141	107–138
5'4"	104–145	110–142
5'5"	117–149	114–146
5'6"	121–154	118–150
5'7"	125–159	122–154
5'8"	129–163	126–159
5'9"	133–167	130–164
5'10"	137–172	134–169
5'11"	141–177	
6'0"	146–182	
6'1"	149–187	
6'2"	153–192	
6'3"	157–197	

Note: For women 18–25 years old, subtract one pound for each year under 25.

United States Department of Agriculture, Human Nutrition Information Service, Home and Garden Bulletin #232-2 (April 1986).

1. Are you wider at the waist than at your chest?
2. Does your middle interfere with sight of your toes?
3. Pinch a fold of skin from the back of your upper arm. Is it more than an inch thick? If so, diet and exercise are in order. Before beginning a diet or strenuous exercise program, you should consult a physician.

Alcohol abuse leads to health risks such as suicide and alcohol-related fatalities and accidents, fetal alcohol syndrome, and other physical impairments. These health risks were more fully detailed in Chapter 15. Elimination of or at least moderation in the consumption of alcohol is an important part of any wellness program.

WHAT ARE THE HAZARDS OF SMOKING?

Cigarette smoking is the most important single preventable cause of death in our society. Cancers of the lung, larynx, oral cavity, esophagus, pancreas, and bladder; heart and blood vessel disease; chronic bronchitis; and emphysema have been linked to smoking. Additionally, involuntary or passive inhalation of cigarette smoke can cause or worsen symptoms of asthma, cardiovascular and respiratory diseases, pneumonia, and bronchitis. Smoking during pregnancy has been associated with premature births, small or underweight babies, and respiratory and cardiovascular problems in infants. Besides these physical implications, smoking is also a major contributor to death and injury from fires and other accidents.

In 1986 the U.S. Department of Health and Human Services reported that the number of individuals who smoke had declined from 42 percent in 1965 to 30.5 percent in 1985. Despite the fact that fewer people are smoking, those who do smoke appear to be smoking more.

Smoking is no longer considered glamorous.

In an effort to curb smoking-related problems, most states have passed legislation limiting or restricting smoking in enclosed public places. Smoking has been banned on domestic air flights, and more nonsmokers today are demanding a smoke-free environment at work and in public areas. Asking someone not to smoke around you should be done tactfully.

Giving up the smoking habit takes determination. Smoking often serves as an outlet for nervousness. The habit of smoking can become psychologically addictive. Nicotine, a key ingredient in cigarette smoke, is physiologically addictive, making it even more difficult to stop. Many programs designed to help people stop smoking are available. They are often provided in total wellness programs.

WHY IS EXERCISE IMPORTANT?

Exercise is one of the most effective methods known for reducing stress. Although it is not a cure-all, exercise releases the stored energies of the "fight or flight" response. Moderate running, swimming, biking, racquetball, and basketball are all good forms of exercise for reducing stress. Regardless of which exercise form you choose, fitness experts recommend a minimum of 20 minutes of continuous exercise, three or four times a week.

Exercise can play a key role in relieving stress and controlling weight.

However, lighter forms of exercise can be equally effective stress reducers. Working in the garden, mowing the yard, playing ping pong or pool, or taking a brisk walk can disengage you from the sources of stress. These exercises provide a "mental break."

Exercise need not be dull or seem like a chore. Its benefits, such as relieving tension, helping control weight, and lowering cholesterol, can be obtained through small changes in your personal routine. You do not have to be an accomplished athlete or a physical fitness expert to achieve desired results through exercise. In addition to establishing a regular exercise program at home or at a gym, you might consider changing simple daily habits. The following small changes in your life-style can increase your physical activity:

1. Use the stairs rather than the elevator.
2. Park your car at the back of the parking lot and walk to the store.
3. Put more vigor into everyday activities.
4. Take a walk each day at lunchtime or after work, and keep walking shoes in your car for these occasions.
5. Go dancing or join a square dance club.
6. Use the restroom on a different floor at work and take the stairs.

Before starting any exercise program, however, you should consult a physician to determine what is appropriate for your age and physical condition.

HOW DO YOU RELAX?

Learning the art of relaxation is crucial to controlling stress. Headaches, backaches, and nervousness can be reduced or eliminated by using progressive relaxation techniques. Nervousness wastes energy, making us more fatigued and less alert.

To relax, spend 20 to 30 minutes twice a day applying some of the various relaxation techniques. All that is necessary is a quiet place where you will not be disturbed. Mini-relaxation breaks of five minutes each throughout the day can also be invaluable in reducing stress. Only a comfortable chair or sofa is necessary. One of these techniques is described below:

> **Loosen any tight clothing. Close your eyes and concentrate on breathing slowly and deeply into the lower part of your chest. As you exhale, imagine the tenseness leaving you. Begin to concentrate on your toes and feet, telling yourself that they are relaxing. Think slowly and deliberately. Concentrate on relaxing and breathing until your toes and feet feel thoroughly relaxed. Gradually progress to other parts of your body until you are completely relaxed.**

After you are fully relaxed, you may wish to practice visual imagery:

> **Marcia lay back in her chair, totally relaxed. She pictured herself lying on the beach, with the warm sun beating down on her body. She could hear the gentle roaring of the surf and the faraway cry of the seagulls. As she lay there, completely at ease, she imagined the clouds lazily drifting overhead and recalled the salty tang of sea air. She felt all stress and tension leaving her body as she became a part of her visual imagery scene.**

Your local library or bookstore can provide you with further exercises on relaxation. Additionally, audio and visual relaxation tapes and recordings of peaceful sounds are available.

Spend time during the day scanning your body. Are your muscles tense? Is your stomach in knots? Do you have a tension headache or a case of indigestion? If so, you may choose to spend a few minutes breathing deeply, concentrating on relaxation, and applying some of the stress and tension-relieving exercises. With practice, you can quickly bring yourself into a peaceful state.

HOW CAN YOU ENJOY LEISURE?

Despite the constant quest for more leisure time, statistics show that the average person in the United States enjoys only 18 hours of actual leisure time per week. The results of a poll conducted by Louis Harris and reported by the *Houston Chronicle* in November 1989 indicate that our average leisure time had shrunk by 37 percent since 1973, while the average workweek had increased from 41 to 47 hours.

Enjoying leisure time is an essential part of reducing stress.

Leisure time is important. It allows us a chance to relax and get away from daily stresses, permitting us to return refreshed and ready to work. Unfortunately, obtaining that time seems to be difficult at best. Although we live in what is often called the "short-cut society," we still have less time to enjoy stress-free activities. With the advent of fast foods, fax machines, car phones, lap-top computers, microwaves, satellites, and robotics designed to make our lives easier, the pace of life has simply increased, and we are part of the frenzy.

This inability to make time for leisure activity is part of the pattern of workaholism, considered the disease of the 1990s. This malady affects one out of every twenty people in this country and is not limited to the corporate executive. **Workaholics** are persons who are consumed by their jobs and derive little pleasure from other activities. These people are certain candidates for heart attacks, depression, hypertension, insomnia, and other physical ailments. They often view their lives as one long, continuous workday reaching well into the night and are rarely able to enjoy even the thought of leisure time. They are known to carry a briefcase full of work along anywhere they go and phone into the office frequently for messages that often add pressures. For workaholics, even vacations are seldom restful because they take thoughts and worries of their jobs with them, compounding the stress.

Personality traits can also contribute to stress conditions. Two well-known personality types have been identified by extensive psychological research on behavior patterns. **Type A personalities** tend to be highly competitive, aggressive, achievement-oriented, and impatient. They typically appear pressured, rushed or hurried, and volatile, and dislike waiting in lines or for traffic lights to turn green. **Type B personalities** exhibit an opposite behavior pattern. They appear more relaxed, easy-going, and even-paced in their approach to life in general. The Type B individual seldom overcommits, can say no without feeling guilty, and takes time to smell the roses along the way.

Type A individuals are more likely to experience high stress levels and exhibit stress symptoms than Type B individuals. Type A personalities are twice as prone to cardiovascular heart diseases such as heart attacks and clogged arteries as Type B personalities. An important step in your personal wellness program may be to identify these patterns in your personality and strive to reduce any Type A tendencies you may have.

Learning how to enjoy leisure time can help make the most of the small amount of time we have. Leslie Jay, in an article in *The Houston Post*, offers several suggestions for leaving stress at the office rather than bringing it home:

1. Try to end the day as smoothly as possible. Start unwinding about one-half hour before you leave. Save easier jobs for last to assist you in unwinding.

2. To cut down worry about unfinished items, make a list of what needs to be done, imagine successfully completing these items, and leave them until the next morning.

3. Maintain a perspective. Remember that today's disasters are not the end of the world and will be of little importance in the future.

4. Use your commute to unwind. Listen to soothing music, read a good book, or enjoy a picturesque magazine if you are not driving.

5. Arrange with your family to be allowed a small bit of quiet time. This will help ease the transition between work and home.

6. Do not make dinner an ordeal with fancy meals. Turn off the television and limit interruptions. Limit work-related conversations at meal time.

7. Do not overschedule your leisure hours. Do not bring work home on a routine basis, and discourage colleagues from calling in the evenings with work-related questions.

In addition to making the most of our leisure time, we should choose activities carefully. Competitive sports, such as softball and tennis, can be as stressful as work.

HOW CAN YOU CHANGE STRESSFUL THOUGHTS, ATTITUDES, AND BEHAVIORS?

Changing stressful thoughts, attitudes, and behaviors takes time and practice.

Setting realistic goals, learning to take risks, raising self-esteem, practicing positive self-talk, using communication skills, understanding the grieving process, and developing assertive behavior have been discussed in Chapters 2, 3, and 17. All of these skills can assist you in changing stressful thoughts, attitudes, and behaviors.

Another important skill that reduces stress is the ability to be self-focused. Harriet Goldhor Lerner in her book, *The Dance of Intimacy*, states that individuals who are not self-focused see others as the problem and believe the solution is for the other person to change. These individuals are unable to achieve intimacy with those around them, which increases stress. The best idea is to focus on our own problems and work on resolving them rather than changing the behavior of others.

Lerner also suggests avoiding what she calls "triangles." A triangle occurs when one person brings you into a problem that he or she is having with a third:

> **"Julio, I really need your help. David is always taking advantage of others. Yesterday he borrowed money from Francisco and then asked to use Gracie's car during lunch. Can you talk to him about it?" asked Sally.**
>
> **Julio thought for a minute. He did not like the way David was always asking for things. He had, in fact, clarified his position with David when David wanted to use his stereo. He made it plain to David that he did not want to loan his belongings because David did not take care of them. However, he did not want to be caught in a triangle between David and Sally.**
>
> **"Sally," Julio replied, "I understand how you feel about David. However, I think the best approach is for you to discuss your feelings directly with him."**

In this example, Julio has detached himself and placed the responsibility for action with Sally. She has the problem with David's behavior and should let him know how she feels. There is no need for Julio to become a part of the triangle.

You can cultivate other healthy attitudes and behaviors:

1. Do not try to change others; accept them as they are.
2. Do not expect actions from others. Thoughts such as "they should" and "they must" can cause anger and frustration.
3. Clarify what you want and firmly state your wants in an assertive manner.
4. Recognize situations in which you have no control. A traffic jam will unclog at the same time whether you remain angry at the inconvenience or attempt to relax and spend the time productively.
5. View situations realistically. What will failure in this situation mean next month, next year, in ten years?
6. Recognize that you do have options and control of many situations. Review Chapter 6 on how to seek alternative ways of meeting wants and needs.
7. Develop a support system of friends and relatives with whom you can discuss stressful events and situations.
8. When choosing a relationship, ask whether it will be good for you or whether it will increase your stress.
9. Take coffee and lunch breaks away from the office.
10. Schedule some quiet time to be alone, during which you may dream, relax, or think.

Accepting and applying some of these attitudes and behaviors will ease feelings of stress that complicate your daily routine.

HOW DO COMPANIES ENCOURAGE WELLNESS?

Companies encourage wellness through health education, employee assistance plans, early disease detection, and fitness programs.

Companies operate a variety of programs to encourage wellness. These programs fall into the broad categories of health education, employee assistance (discussed in detail in Chapter 8), early disease detection programs, and fitness programs.

Health education programs are designed to educate employees about various health issues such as smoking, nutrition, diet, cancer, diabetes, seatbelt safety, and exercise. For instance, Sunseeds Genetics, Inc., conducts lunchtime seminars for employees on how to maintain a pain-free back. Other companies spread information through seminars or printed materials such as newsletters or brochures.

Early disease detection programs provide employees with free or reduced-cost screening for health problems such as breast cancer, diabetes, high blood pressure, and high cholesterol. Many times companies bring these tests to the job site in order to increase employee participation. Bell of Pennsylvania and Diamond State Telephone, for instance, use a mobile van to provide female employees and the spouses of male employees with mammography testing.

Companies are beginning to develop fitness centers offering a wide range of physical activities. Offering reduced price memberships to community fitness cen-

FIGURE 19.8   Exercise is encouraged in corporate wellness programs.

ters is another method to encourage physical activity. In addition, many companies sponsor employee bowling, golf, or softball leagues and walking clubs.

SUMMARY

A wellness program addresses emotional and physical health. Organizations show interest in these programs because they result in higher productivity and decreased medical and insurance costs. A good wellness plan will include an understanding of stress and of skills to control it.

Stress is the physical state of the body in response to environmental pressures that produce emotional discomfort. Stress can result from good or bad causes. When the body reaches its stress threshold, certain physical and mental reactions occur. Overindulging, hypertension, insomnia, anxiety, depression, heart attacks, and mental disorders are only a few of the symptoms of stress illnesses. A well-rounded wellness program helps people learn to manage stress and prevent other diseases through time management, proper diet, nonsmoking, exercise, relaxation, other leisure activities, and changing stressful thoughts, attitudes, and behaviors.

Today, many companies are encouraging wellness by health education, employee assistance plans, early disease detection programs, and fitness programs.

KEY TERMS

wellness program
stress
time management
procrastination
planned agenda
hidden agenda
workaholics
Type A personalities
Type B personalities

REVIEW QUESTIONS

1. What is a wellness program? Why is it good for both employer and employee?
2. What are the physical and mental results of stress overload?
3. What are the most effective methods of time management?
4. What is the importance of proper diet in minimizing stress effects?
5. How do exercise and relaxation help in achieving wellness?
6. How can you change stressful thoughts, attitudes, and behaviors?
7. What are companies doing to promote employee wellness?

DISCUSSION QUESTIONS

1. Does your organization have a wellness program for employees? If so, what are the obvious benefits of the program?
2. What symptoms of stress do you feel? What do you believe are the major causes? What do you do to reduce the stress?
3. What method of time management do you use? What benefits do you realize from your method? How might you improve your method?
4. Do you procrastinate? Why? How might you overcome your procrastination?
5. Do you have a problem finding leisure time in your daily schedule? Do you exhibit symptoms of being a workaholic? How might you better plan for leisure time?
6. Which of your thoughts, beliefs, or behaviors contribute to your feelings of stress? How might you reduce these sources of stress?

**CASE STUDY
19.1**

ALICE IN WONDERFUL LAND

Alice had just been awarded a contract to provide a training seminar on supervisory skills to a group of new first-line supervisors at a major oil company in Dallas. This opportunity could establish her as a leader in the training field, and with the right exposure she could receive more contracts with other companies. She already had a comfortable amount of business that pushed her busy schedule, but this job could really boost her practice into high gear. Alice smiled with satisfaction at the prospects.

The only problem was the amount of time and effort required in putting a new seminar together. "How can I crowd all this new preparation into my schedule?" she wondered out loud. "I already work 14, 16, . . . sometimes even 20 hours a day just keeping up with my current contract load." The day did not seem to have enough hours to do all that needed to be done. She was also teaching a class two nights a week at the local college and had just agreed to collaborate on a project for her community that was a full year's commitment of time and effort. Her work with the youth group at the church might have to be cut back if this wonderful opportunity really got off the ground.

"With a little luck, I'll be able to pull this off and get over the hump this time. If only I don't get those awful headaches I had last week. They certainly put a damper on my productivity."

1. What symptoms of stress is Alice exhibiting?
2. Do you believe that Alice is an effective time manager? How might she solve her problem?
3. Should Alice accept the new contract? Why or why not?

**CASE STUDY
19.2**

WATCH OUT FROM BEHIND!

Carey had planned for weeks in advance to make this meeting successful. He had carefully selected the attendees, reserved the conference room well in advance, and prepared his briefing materials in plenty of time to go over them and make the necessary changes for clarity. He had even sent a well-organized agenda a week ago to all attendees so that they could be prepared to discuss the topics outlined. Everything would go smoothly, and they would be finished before noon.

Carey started the meeting promptly at 10:00 A.M. and moved swiftly through the first several items with good decisions made and all action items appropriately assigned. The next topic generated a great deal of conversation. Almost everyone was commenting on the plans he had outlined in his briefing. Suddenly Frank from the engineering division put a new proposal on the table for discussion. Everyone was surprised that Frank had thought out this approach so thoroughly, but they were clearly interested. Some people began adding their ideas to Frank's, and before Carey knew it, they were completely off the primary subjects of his meeting. Somehow he had lost control of his meeting and wasn't sure how he would meet the noon deadline for getting the decisions and results he needed from this fiasco.

1. What caused Carey's meeting to get off track?
2. How might Carey have prevented this problem?
3. How would you have handled Frank's action?

BIBLIOGRAPHY

Abramson, Leonard. "Boost to Bottom Line." *Personnel Administrator* (July 1988): 36–39.

Carroll, Lewis. *Alice's Adventures in Wonderland*. New York: Simon and Shuster, 1986.

Caudron, Shari, and Michael Rozek. "The Wellness Payoff." *Personnel Journal* (July 1990): 55–62.

Cavanagh, Michael E. "What You Don't Know about Stress." *Personnel Journal* (July 1988): 53–59.

Charlesworth, Edward A., and Ronald G. Nathan. *Stress Management: A Comprehensive Guide to Wellness*. New York: Atheneum, 1984.

Hallett, Jeffrey. "The Value of Wellness: It's All in the Mind." *Personnel Administrator* (July 1988): 28–30.

Jay, Leslie. "Fax Yourself This Message: You Can Leave Stress at Work." *The Houston Post* (April 9, 1989): F1, F12.

Kolson, Ann. "Leisure Time: Is There Really Less of It?" *Houston Chronicle*, (November 5, 1989): H6.

Lerner, Harriet Goldhor. *The Dance of Intimacy*. New York: Harper & Row, 1989.

Public Health Service, U.S. Department of Health and Human Services. *The 1990 Health Objectives for the Nation: A Midcourse Review*. Washington, DC: U.S. Government Printing Office, 1986.

Stokes, Stewart L., Jr. *It's About Time*. Boston: CBI Publishing Co., Inc., 1982.

The Surgeon General's Report on Nutrition and Health—Summary and Recommendations. Washington, D.C.: U.S. Government Printing Office, 1988.

United States Department of Agriculture, Human Nutrition Information Service. "Dietary Guidelines for Americans Maintain Desirable Weight." *Home and Garden Bulletins* 232-1–232-3. Washington, DC: U.S. Government Printing Office, 1986.

Wallis, Claudia. "Stress: Can We Cope?" *Time* (June 6, 1983): 48–54.

CHAPTER TWENTY

TRANSITION TO THE FUTURE

America in the future will consist of:
> a rapidly aging white population
> a large but stable black population
> a rapidly increasing, diverse, and youthful Asian and Hispanic population
> a new blend of service and "high tech" jobs
> rapid immigration from many nations
> a declining base of middle-class people of working age
> transiency and crime
> environmental vulnerability
> contrasts in wealth
> social systems that cannot keep up with growth
> exciting new social and political innovations
> the agony of unfulfilled expectations

Harold L. Hodgkinson in *Community College Week* (April 2, 1990)

OBJECTIVES

After studying this chapter, you should be able to:
1. Summarize the emerging demographics of this country.
2. Discuss the major forces shaping our economy.
3. Explain what the country must do to meet the challenges of a changing work force and new economic realities.
5. Explain what skills will be in demand in the twenty-first century.
6. Discuss what you can do to prepare yourself to enter the work force of 2000.

HOW WILL SOCIETY CHANGE

What will life be like in 100 years? Will we lead a life of leisure, with computers and robotics performing all of our work? Will we commute to jobs in outer space? Will we live in the aftermath of a nuclear holocaust, protecting our belongings from roving gangs bent on destruction?

All of these scenarios have been predicted by various groups and individuals, but no one knows the answer. However, experts can tell us what to expect as we enter the twenty-first century. Changes sweeping our economic landscape are so vast that they will forever change the way we work and live. Innovations in technology have made our world smaller, ushering in a fast-paced, global economy that calls for drastic changes in the manner in which companies do business. In addition, the changing nature of our work force will require more changes in the way companies operate if they wish to remain competitive. Understanding this quiet revolution in the makeup of our society is important if you are to succeed at work.

Demographics are statistics showing population characteristics about a region or group, such as education, income, age, marital status, ethnic makeup, and other factors. Such information is necessary in preparing for the future. For example, the milestone publication by the Hudson Institute, *Workforce 2000—Work and Workers for the Twenty-First Century*, forecasts who will be working in the year 2000, what they will be doing, which occupations will grow most rapidly, which groups of workers will increase in the work force, and which will decline.

Demographics in the United States are shifting.

According to a 1989 article in *Business Week* ("The New America"), our society is experiencing four major shifts in its demographic makeup. They are an aging population, more Hispanics and Asians, a widening gap between the haves and have-nots, and new immigrants. *Workforce 2000* also cites the increased number of women in the work force as a shift. Let us discuss each shift and its probable impact. Unless otherwise noted, the statistical and demographic information in the remainder of this chapter is derived from *Workforce 2000*.

FIGURE 20.1   The work force of the future will be more diverse than ever before.

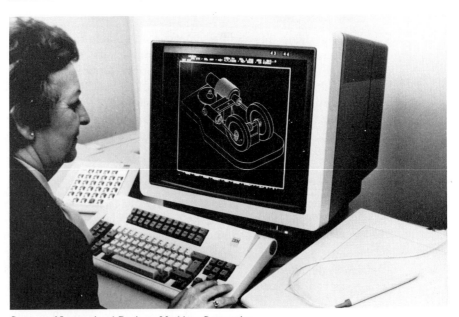

Courtesy of International Business Machines Corporation.

Aging Population

The median age by 2000 will be six years older than ever before.

During the decade of the 1990s the average age of both the population and the work force will rise, and the pool of young workers entering the labor market will shrink. The median age of the population is expected to be 36 years by the year 2000 and the median age of the work force 39—six years older than at any other time in the history of this country.

The greatest increase will be in middle-aged people, a jump of 38 percent in the 35–47-year-old group and 67 percent in the 48–53-year-old group. People aged 20–29 will make up only 13 percent of the population. According to a 1989 article in *Business Week* ("Plotting the Gray Lines"), one in eight people today is over 65; that figure will probably rise to one in six by 2020.

The aging of the population and the work force is expected to have dramatic impact, both positive and negative. One concern, for example, is whether the nation will be able to afford the rising costs of pensions. As more individuals live longer, more pensions will have to be paid for an extended period of time. The positive impacts of this trend are:

1. The work force will be more experienced, stable, reliable, and generally healthy. Additionally, workers' education and training will be largely completed.
2. The proportion of people not in the work force will continue to drop, meaning that fewer people will be dependent on workers. In the year 2000 we will have less than one dependent per worker.
3. Because younger people generally have greater expenses for cars, homes, and other items, as our population ages, we should see a rise in savings rate. The results of this trend are expected to be lower real interest rates, greater investment, and improved productivity.
4. The reduction in the pool of younger workers will cause employers to pay higher salaries, hire less qualified workers, invest in labor-saving technology, or all three.

Negative effects of the aging of the work force are:

1. Our economy may become more rigid, because older people are more reluctant to leave homes and children's schools, to be retrained, or to move between occupations.
2. The ability of companies to grow rapidly or to respond to economic changes may be hampered. Workers between the ages of 16 and 34, who have traditionally been the pool of labor for new corporate divisions, will not only be scarce, but they will also be more expensive.
3. Costs of older workers may make companies uncompetitive. Older workers have higher salaries in general, and the expense of their vested pensions and higher health care may put companies at a competitive disadvantage.
4. As middle-aged workers increase, they will compete for fewer middle-management jobs. Additionally, if they lose their jobs, they will have difficulty finding jobs that pay as well. Therefore, many workers, unlike their

parents and grandparents before them, will no longer continue to increase earnings until retirement.

5. Many industries that depend on young people for their income will suffer because of the aging population. They include not only companies that build and own rental housing and manufacturers and sellers of household furnishings, but also colleges and universities.

Older people make good workers.

A study of perceptions of employees about workers age 50 and up, reported by Cyril Brickfield in *Manage*, found that management has a strongly positive view of that age group. Managers interviewed in the study believed that older workers' strengths are experience, skills, and knowledge, and that they have a strong commitment to quality, emotional stability, and dependability in a crisis. Management perceived the weaknesses to include resistance to new techniques, physical limitations, low ambition, and less capability to learn new skills quickly.

However, 83 percent of the survey participants believed that older workers have special problem-solving skills based on knowledge and experience. Brickfield concludes that productivity does not decline with age, older managers make capable decision makers, and older workers change jobs less frequently and have a greater commitment to the job, with attendance as good as or better than other age groups. He adds that perceived weaknesses of older workers can be overcome by training, job redesign, and effective management.

An Increasing Income Gap

A 1989 article in *Business Week* ("A U-Turn in the Road to Riches") points out that in the past rising incomes and standards of living have decreased the gap between those people who have enough money to live satisfactorily and those who do not. In the early 1970s, however, the trend stopped, and the gap between rich and poor people began once again widening.

The gap between the haves and the have-nots has been widening.

Several factors led to this reversal. One cause is the stagnation of our economic productivity and decrease in higher paying manufacturing jobs. Another is the increase in the number of single-parent families. Other factors include discrimination, poor education and housing, and the movement of jobs to the suburbs. The result is an increase in the number of children living in poverty and a widening gap between people living in the city and those living in the suburbs.

The impact of this widening gap is expected to be felt in a number of ways. One, of course, will be in the additional cost to taxpayers for public support. Another is the increased frustration of those without, which may make itself felt in ways from how they vote to an increase in crime.

More Women in the Work Force

By 2000 women will comprise approximately 47 percent of the work force.

Women will make up approximately 47 percent of the work force by the year 2000, and 61 percent of women will work in paid jobs. Their entrance is expected to peak at that time. *Business Week* in an article entitled "For American Business, A New World of Workers," reported that 73 percent of all working women are of childbearing age, 60 percent of all school-age children have mothers in the work force (up from 39 percent in 1970), and women with children under six are the fastest growing segment of the work force.

According to a Gallup poll summarized in *Workforce 2000*, only half of all women believe that they can fulfill their responsibilities to their children satisfactorily while working full time. Many corporations now desire to train, retain, and accommodate women. They are beginning to respond to the expectations women have of employers.

Demographic changes that are reducing the pool of educated men and bringing talented women into the workplace are enabling women today to be in stronger bargaining positions. The increased number of women in the work force is expected to have a number of important impacts. It will affect policies on child-rearing, taxation, pensions, hiring, compensation, and industrial structure. The February 9, 1990, *Wall Street Journal*, for example, reports that the number of days that parents of preschool children miss from work because of youngster illness appears directly related to the type of day care the children receive. Additionally, work force flexibility may be affected, with two-career families reluctant to move. Part-time, flexible, and work-at-home arrangements are expected to increase. Total work hours per employee may be reduced to accommodate working mothers. The distinctions between male and female jobs will lessen, and the differences in male and female pay will decline. Today, according to the March 27, 1989, issue of *The Wall Street Journal*, the median income of college-educated women is about the same as that of high-school-educated men. Women's wages, while increasing, will still lag behind men's in 2000. A Rand study cited in *Workforce 2000* projected that women's wages will still equal only 74 percent of men's at the end of this decade.

The *National Institute of Business Management* suggests that pregnant women and new mothers do the following to be taken seriously by their managers and colleagues and to avoid being perceived as dropping their commitment or performance:

1. Be the first to tell your boss that you are pregnant. Unless you are ill or believe that your boss already suspects, wait until the end of the first trimester. Make this communication a business negotiation rather than a social occasion.
2. Reassure your boss that you are committed by making suggestions about how your work can be coordinated. Indicate how much you want to be on call during your leave and how often you are willing to come to the office. Think through the political ramifications of your recommendations.
3. Be willing to reconsider and renegotiate if necessary.
4. During your pregnancy, limit discussions of your pregnancy and expected baby.
5. If you plan to adjust your work schedule after you return to work, discuss this change before your leave, explaining how you will complete your work. Be sure that colleagues know you will be putting in the same amount of effort.
6. When you must be away from work because of family-related matters, explain that you are taking a day of personal business leave.

7. Even when you are tired because of lack of sleep or the strain of managing a career and a family, maintain your professional image.

New Ethnic Mix

Minorities will make up a larger proportion of new workers in the labor force, comprising 15 percent in the year 2000. Additionally, the labor market is expected to be increasingly comprised of disadvantaged minorities. White males will make up only 15 percent of the net additions to the labor force between 1985 and 2000. The total work force in 2000 will be about 39 percent white men, down from about 45 percent in 1986, according to Jolie Solomon in *The Wall Street Journal.*

The Occupational Outlook Handbook reports that Blacks will make up 12 percent of the work force in the year 2000, Hispanics 10 percent, and Asians and others, 4 percent. Hispanic and Asian populations are predicted to double, to 30 million and 10 million, by 2000. Figure 20.2 summarizes diversities expected in the workplace in 2000. The result of these shifts will be that companies previously hiring mostly young white men will have to look elsewhere. This change will enhance job opportunities for well-qualified minorities and women.

FIGURE 20.2   Native white females will account for the greatest growth of the work force through 2000.

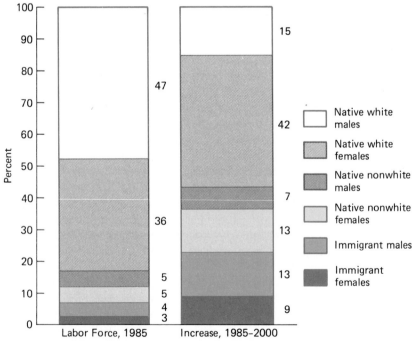

Workforce 2000, Work and Workers for the 21st Century: Executive Summary. (Washington, D.C.: U.S. Government Printing Office, 1987).

Workforce 2000 and an article in *Business Week* ("The Changing Face of a Restless Nation") report that immigrants will be a growing share of the population and the labor force, representing the largest share of the increase since World War I. They now account for more than 14 percent of our annual population growth. Between 1970 and 1980 (latest figures available), the foreign-born population of this country grew by about 4.5 million. This amount was about one-fifth of the population gain during that period. At least 450,000 immigrants are expected to enter the United States each year until 2000. Since 1970, 78 percent of the immigrants have come from Latin America and Asia. According to the *Monthly Labor Report*, although Asians and others will account for 11 percent of the projected growth in the labor force during the 1990s, this growth rate is actually slower than in 1979–1986. Entry of Asian refugees in connection with the Vietnam War has virtually stopped.

During this decade we expect 450,000 immigrants annually, most from Latin America and Asia.

Contrary to many people's fears, the increased influx of immigrants is expected to help those areas where they settle, particularly the south and west. Their presence provides a pool of young workers who attract new jobs and, thereby, increase economic growth.

"A Nation within a Nation" (*Business Week*, September 25, 1989) points out that about 20 million people of Latin American background now live in the United States. Most of them are from Mexico. Others come from Cuba, the Dominican Republic, Puerto Rico, and elsewhere. Hispanics now make up 8 percent of the population and may become the largest ethnic minority by 2015. Their growth will have a marked impact on this country socially, economically, and politically.

This new wave of immigration is bringing new values and languages to the culture. For example, Spencer Rich in the *Houston Chronicle* points out that Asian Americans generally equal or outstrip native-born Whites in family income. Their relatively high income levels can be explained in part by the stress placed on education. *Business Week* in an article entitled, "How the Next Decade Will Differ," (September 25, 1989) reports that Asians are enrolling in universities at unprecedented rates.

Literacy and Education Level

According to Rick Gladstone in *The Houston Post,* the Department of Education estimates that more than 27 million people older than the age of 17 cannot read or write well enough to function in everyday life. Another 45 million are barely competent in these basic skills. This figure means that one out of every three adults may not have the necessary skills to perform jobs that require reading and writing. This trend is particularly alarming when you consider that most materials written for business are geared to a twelfth-grade level.

Federal officials report that this number is growing by 2 million people annually. Ronni Sandroff in *Working Woman* reports that one out of eight 17-year-olds in the United States leaves school functionally illiterate.

Our larger Hispanic work force will bring its own set of unique literacy problems as a result of a school dropout rate of 50 percent, the highest in this country. Several factors have been blamed for this rate, such as difficulty with English, less cultural emphasis on education, low expectations from teachers, and close family ties that encourage young people to drop out and contribute earnings.

Employers are also experiencing difficulties in finding job applicants with skills necessary to perform the available jobs. Karen DeVenuta reports in *The Wall Street Journal* that 20 to 40 percent of job applicants who take an entry-level examination requiring seventh- to ninth-grade English and fifth- to seventh-grade math fail.

In addition, recent studies reveal that students in the United States lag behind those of other nations in math and science achievement. *The Wall Street Journal* in "Education Openers" reports the findings of an international study of 13-year-olds. United States students ranked last in math proficiency. South Korean students ranked first. We also lag behind other countries in the study of foreign languages. For example, the same article reports that 100 percent of Japanese high school students have had at least six years of English, and only two-tenths of 1 percent of U.S. students have studied Japanese. This foreign language deficit will increasingly detract from our ability to compete in the international marketplace.

The growing illiteracy of the work force threatens our economy.

This trend, unless reversed, will cause even more difficulties in our economy. Horror stories already abound about costly errors caused by illiteracy. A steelworker misordered $1 million in parts because he could not read well. An assembly line worker nearly killed several of his coworkers because he did not properly assemble a heavy piece of equipment. He was unable to read the assembly instructions. These costly errors will become even more numerous as we move into the twenty-first century.

This changing work force will bring with it new wants and needs (Chapter 6). Their priorities will be different. To assure that these individuals remain productive, organizations will be required to address new issues. These issues, combined with forces that are shaping the economy, will revolutionize the work force of the future.

WHAT FORCES WILL SHAPE THE ECONOMY?

Six forces are shaping our economy.

Six trends will reshape jobs and industries in the United States during the 1990s. These include a shift from goods to services, advanced technology, renewed productivity in services, deflation, increased competition, and globalization.

Shift from Goods to Services

Service industries create economic value without creating a tangible product, unlike manufacturing, agriculture, and other goods-producing industries. Services such as transportation and retailing add value to manufactured goods by making them more available or useful to consumers. Services such as education and health care create value without being directly related to goods. This shift in production will affect the rate of growth of our economy, the distribution of income, the location and organization of work, and the balance of trade.

With this shift, the typical workplace will become smaller. Most new jobs will be in small businesses. Wages may become less equally distributed, with some professional groups commanding much higher pay than other service workers. Part-time work will increase, cycles of recession will be reduced, the nature of world trade will change because services are seldom traded internationally, and economic growth will be sluggish.

Advanced Technologies

Five technologies have been identified as apt to have the greatest impact between now and the year 2000. They are information storage and processing, communications, advanced materials, biotechnologies, and superconductivity. The impact of these technologies is expected in a variety of ways. Workers will be able to choose more freely where and when they will work. Products will become lighter, more intensively processed, and more durable, and their per capita demand will decline, thus preserving our natural resources. Changing technology will result in the necessity for constant learning and adaptation by workers.

The leading technological influence in our lives will be the computer. Continued job losses will occur in fields ripe for computerization. The computerized secretary, or robotic secretary, will take and edit dictation, decreasing the numbers of clerical and secretarial workers. Office management systems will continue to convert to computer-based operations for billing, mailing, and telemarketing.

Industrial robots will replace the assembly-line worker in greater numbers. Michael Kiernan predicts in *U.S. News & World Report* in 1989 that within ten years, 250,000 robots will displace 4 million workers. This change comes on the heels of automation already eliminating two-thirds of the assembly-line workers in the auto industry.

An area not usually associated with corporate productivity woes, the agricultural industry, will also be affected. "Agribots" will gather fruit from orchards at harvest time and eliminate the requirement for human fruit pickers and crop harvesters.

Computers, increasingly complex, are being programmed to mimic human intelligence. This process is called **artificial intelligence**. The B-2 Stealth bomber, which is one of the most complex mechanical systems ever conceived, was engineered and produced totally on the computer. Not a shred of paper was used.

These technological innovations will displace millions of employees but provide a better product at lower prices. Overall, the numbers of jobs will not diminish. As some occupations disappear, new ones will be created.

Renewed Productivity in Services

Poor and deteriorating performance of services has been blamed for dragging down output, wage gains, and national growth during the 1970s and 1980s. However, service industries such as health care, education, government, and retailing may be about to dramatically increase productivity. This increase will be fueled by the use of new and existing technologies combined with the declining numbers of new workers entering the job market.

Deflation

The high inflation rates seen between 1965 and 1982 are not expected to recur during the 1990s. Rather, deflation may pose a problem. **Inflation**, according to *The MBA's Dictionary*, is a rise in the costs of goods and services and a fall in the value of currency. **Deflation** is the opposite: a fall in costs and a rise in the value of money. Deflation is expected from an excess of oil, food, natural resources, and manufactured goods, and from the failure of international governments to stimulate demand along with production.

Increased Competition

The recent competition among world economies is expected to continue into and beyond 2000. Several factors contribute to this trend. They include the integration of global markets, excess production capacity, the rapidly growing world labor force, the decline of labor unions, and the general deregulation of industry by western nations. To compete internationally, nations will need to continue innovating, adapting, and growing. Industries and individuals within nations, therefore, must value these behaviors.

Globalization

Container ships, jet airplanes, and satellite and fiber optic communications have created an international market. Additionally, workers now move around the world with increasing ease. The resulting integrated economy means that all nations progressively lose control of their own economic destiny, as we have recently seen happen in this country. No nation can expect to continue growing unless the world economy also grows.

This trend toward making goods and services worldwide in scope with no national boundaries or trade barriers on where they are sold or where they are produced is called **globalization**. This phenomenon is responsible, in part, for the new concern about productivity. Globalization is a crucial piece of the changes we face as we enter the twenty-first century.

WHAT MUST OUR COUNTRY DO?

To remain economically viable, we must change the way we do business.

All these changes challenge us to do business in new ways. Already some innovative organizations are moving to meet these challenges. However, much more must be done by private and public sectors as well as by individuals to ensure that the United States remains a force in the world economy.

Joining the Global Economy

As a nation we must pay less attention to the United States share of world trade and more to the growth of economies throughout the world, including our competitors.

Our advanced technologies, for example, will enable us to prosper more in a world with proliferating knowledge, technology, and markets than in a slowly growing world economy.

Other nations are beginning to focus on globalization. The 12 European Common Market nations are scheduled to eliminate their internal barriers after 1992. A **common market** is a group of countries that share trade policies on agricultural product limitations, the transportation of goods, taxes, and import/export quotas. Economically they act like a single country. The merged European Market will boast approximately 350 million consumers with buying patterns similar to other major economic forces in the world.

The Japan-centered Pacific Rim area of the globe will also emerge as a strong part of our single international market. The Pacific Rim countries include Japan, Taiwan, Korea, Hong Kong, Singapore, Australia, and their neighbors. Japan, the leader in this group, has risen over the last 40 years to be a respected force in several world markets. As more nations begin to compete in the world economy, national lines will become increasingly blurred.

Many corporations now operate globally.

Companies are becoming multinational in scope. These companies, known as **multinational corporations (MNCs),** have goods and services based in several countries and require business planning and marketing strategies to fit global operations rather than narrow domestic ones. Current examples of MNCs that you may recognize are IBM, Exxon, Ford, Mobil, and General Motors.

FIGURE 20.3   Many U.S. companies are multinational organizations. This McDonald's is in the Soviet Union.

Courtesy of McDonald's Restaurants of Canada Limited.

These organizations use a planning process called **rationalization**: they buy supplies from countries that produce them at the lowest prices and then sell the finished product wherever the highest price can be obtained. Electronic components may be bought from Japan, assembled in Mexico, and sold in the United States.

With this diverse unification, gone will be the days of "Made in Japan" or "Made in the U.S." as identifiers of product origin. Figure 20.4 illustrates the multinational

FIGURE 20.4   Companies use the process of rationalization to remain competitive.

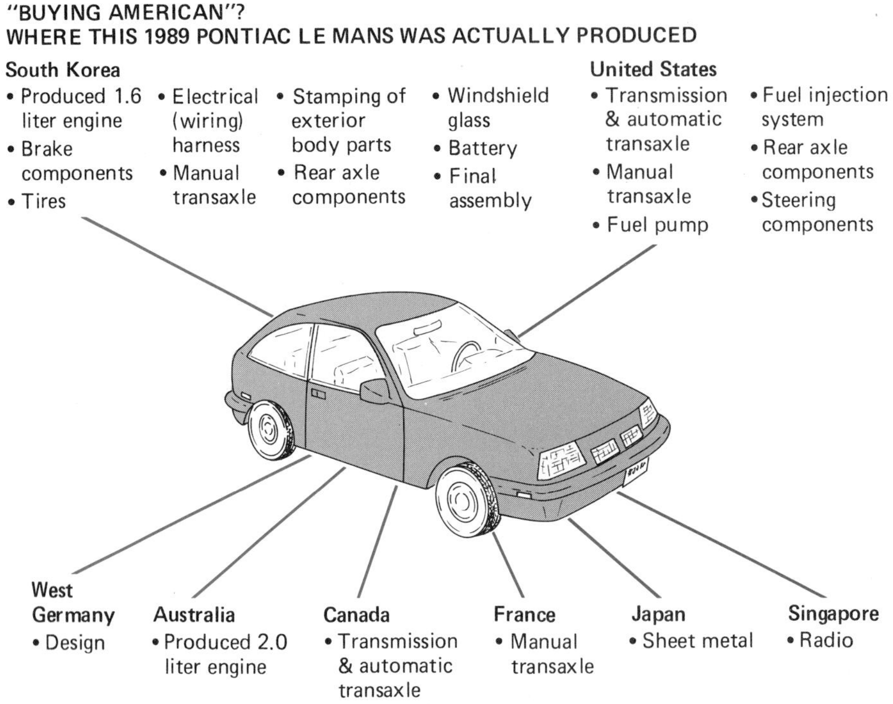

"BUYING AMERICAN"?
WHERE THIS 1989 PONTIAC LE MANS WAS ACTUALLY PRODUCED

South Korea				United States	
• Produced 1.6 liter engine	• Electrical (wiring) harness	• Stamping of exterior body parts	• Windshield glass	• Transmission & automatic transaxle	• Fuel injection system
• Brake components	• Manual transaxle	• Rear axle components	• Battery	• Manual transaxle	• Rear axle components
• Tires			• Final assembly	• Fuel pump	• Steering components

West Germany	Australia	Canada	France	Japan	Singapore
• Design	• Produced 2.0 liter engine	• Transmission & automatic transaxle	• Manual transaxle	• Sheet metal	• Radio

The Plain Truth *(January 1990)*

involvement in the production of the 1989 Pontiac Le Mans, believed by most consumers to be an "American" product.

Other examples of globalization abound in the car industry, according to Neil Gross in *Business Week* (November 1989). General Motors owns 50 percent of Saab, 38 percent of Isuzu and 100 percent of Lotus; Ford owns 100 percent of Jaguar and 25 percent of Mazda; and Chrysler owns 12 percent of Mitsubishi and 100 percent of Lamborghini. Recently, U.S. car manufacturers closed eight plants in the United States and moved the operations to Mexico, whereas Japan opened eight plants here.

Lastly, to integrate into the global economy, our businesses will need to convert to the metric system of measurements for global compatibility. Although the Metric Conversion Act was passed in 1975, little has been done about enforcing the conversion. Plans for the change must be introduced and implemented during this decade.

Increasing Productivity and Quality

To remain competitive, our corporations must increase quality and productivity.

As the economy becomes service-oriented, we must increase worker output in health care, education, retailing, government, and other services. To stimulate the economy, the government needs to privatize many of its services and invest in technologies that enhance productivity in services, particularly education and health care.

The quality of products and services must become the concern of all people involved, from the CEO to the shop floor employee, because firms involved in the process of rationalization will increasingly buy from those who offer high quality, low cost products.

Productivity is also a concern. Although we lead the world in innovative ideas, we take too long to get the product into the marketplace, according to Ronni Sandroff in *Working Woman*. For example, Japan takes only 40 months to move a new car from design concept through manufacturing into the market. Our system requires approximately 60 months. The United Kingdom produces new drug products in approximately 2 months, but we take 5 months. Those firms involved in rationalization will buy from sources that have the product in the market first.

These types of problems require restructuring our management approaches. We must reshape worker attitudes and use new technology in manufacturing to increase productivity and reduce costs. Many companies are now using progressive leadership and motivational techniques to help improve quality and productivity. These techniques are discussed in detail in Chapters 6, 9, and 12.

Educating and Training Our Work Force

Continuing education is a key to economic success.

We must make sure that our work force does not lose its adaptability and willingness to learn, a danger of an aging work force. National policies that promote corporate and personal willingness to retrain must be developed. We must support them with changes in the tax code to encourage lifelong learning.

As technology outpaces skill levels and skill requirements change rapidly, more companies are offering continuing education to their employees as a means to remain productive. Computer literacy heads the list of types of training offered to employees, followed closely by basic math skills. Continuing education has become a fixture in corporations.

A February 1990 article by Karen DeVenuta in *The Wall Street Journal* estimates that annual spending by employers on formal and informal training of employees amounts to $210 billion. Employers provide training not only in occupational skills but also in basic skills such as reading, arithmetic, and logical reasoning.

The same article describes two examples of employer training. Springs Industries of Fort Mill, South Carolina, offers on-site facilities for classes before and after work in basic literacy and basic skills needed in a technical setting. Travelers Insurance company has two programs: MOST (Modern Office Skills Training), begun in 1967, which prepares disadvantaged persons for jobs at Travelers; and BEST (Business English for Spanish-Speaking Trainees). Other languages have since been added. Most candidates for these programs are referred by community and state agencies. The MOST/BEST program teaches English, typing, filing, word processing, human relations, problem solving, and decision making. Counseling is provided, and graduates are hired in office positions as telephone dispatchers, filers, and word processors.

Most community colleges in the country have partnerships with businesses and industries to help train local employees, either at the company site or on campus. The training covers a variety of topics, including updated technical skills, such as new computer software; human relations and supervisory training for new supervisors; and training in new processes and procedures for employees ranging from secretaries to chemical process operators.

Meeting the Needs of the Changing Work Force

We must address the new needs of workers.

The conflicting demands of work and family must be addressed to accommodate the increased number of women in the work force. Because everyone is now expected to work, including women with young children, practices and policies must be changed to provide time off for parents and more high quality day care. Welfare reform should require all able-bodied mothers without infants to work and should provide training, day care, and job counseling.

Companies are beginning to respond to this challenge in a number of ways. Some are opening on-site or near-site day care centers that operate during company business hours. Some of these centers offer reduced or sliding fee scales as a fringe benefit. Sometimes companies band together to start a child care center.

Other companies offer a research and referral system to help families locate adequate child care. Still others use a voucher system, which reimburses an employee for child care expenses, or the vendor system, which involves purchasing slots in a child care center and reselling them to employees.

Offering liberal parental leave, job sharing, and flexible work schedules are other ways in which needs are being accommodated. American Express is experimenting with a job-sharing program for managers, and Steelcase Inc., a major office furniture manufacturer in Michigan, is realizing excellent results from an employee job-sharing program. Employees feel that selecting their own work hours as long as they put in 40 hours per week gives them the flexibility to meet the demands of home and work.

Working out of the home is another way in which companies are addressing the needs of working parents. By the year 2000, according to a *Business Week* article, "How the Next Decade Will Differ" (September 1989), predictions are that some 30 million people in the United States will operate service- or information-based businesses from electronically equipped homes. Working at home helps avoid commutes, gives individuals more control over their work schedules, and allows them to care for children. However, the drawbacks, such as not having a regular routine or contact with colleagues, being distracted by chores and family, and not having the necessary equipment, may restrict the use of this alternative.

Today's workers bring a new set of expectations into the work force. Greater responsibility and increased involvement in decision making, recognition and appreciation for a job well done, interesting and challenging work, and more leisure time are priorities. Chapter 6 addresses ways in which corporations are changing management styles to satisfy these needs.

The desire for **entrepreneurship**—organizing, managing, and assuming the risks of a business enterprise—is stronger in today's worker. Michael Kiernan points out that 70 percent of recent graduates from the Harvard Business School want to own and manage their own businesses within the next five to ten years. They desire to be the masters of their own fates.

Companies are responding to this challenge by developing what is called intrapreneurship. **Intrapreneurship** is the conscious effort of organizations to identify and support employees who wish to pursue an entrepreneurial idea for a new service or product. IBM used this process successfully to develop the personal computer.

Some companies are experimenting with motivating employees through profit-sharing, which allows employees to take home in bonuses what they help earn in profits for the company. Piecework or incentive pay arrangements are also being explored, with minimal hourly rates set and additional dollars earned for extra work performed.

Companies are also offering "cafeteria-style" benefit packages. Employees can select from a variety of options for medical and dental plans, short- and long-term insurance plans, and other programs for retirement benefits or child care options. This approach is more appealing to workers than being limited to a single plan that was selected with an economic advantage for the company.

Valuing Diversity

Minority workers must be fully utilized, as they represent our primary solution during the 1990s to the problems of a shrinking pool of young people, the rapid pace of industrial change, and rising skill requirements of the economy. Prejudices and social institutions must change. Jobs being created require much higher levels of skills, and an emphasis on education, training, and employment assistance for minorities is crucial. If minorities miss the opportunities now present, problems of minority unemployment, crime, and dependency are expected to be much worse by 2000.

Companies are making efforts to integrate minorities and women into the work force by training employees to value diversity. Du Pont, for instance, runs programs such as "Women and Men as Colleagues," designed to promote understanding of the differences in male and female work styles. Other programs at Du Pont focus on career management for minorities, professional development for women, and management of work force diversity.

Increasing the Educational Level of Workers

The education and skills of all workers must be improved. If we are to compete and grow as a nation, we must have capable human capital with knowledge, skills,

FIGURE 20.5   A high rate of job growth is expected in health-related occupations, the sciences, and legal professions—fields that require postsecondary training.

THE CHANGING OCCUPATIONAL STRUCTURE, 1984–2000

Occupation	Current Jobs	New Jobs	Rate of Growth
	(000s)	(000s)	(Percentage)
Total	105,008	25,952	25
Service Occupations	16,059	5,957	37
Managerial and Management-Related	10,893	4,280	39
Marketing and Sales	10,656	4,150	39
Administrative Support	18,483	3,620	20
Technicians	3,146	1,389	44
Health Diagnosing and Treating Occupations	2,478	1,384	53
Teachers, Librarians, and Counselors	4,437	1,381	31
Mechanics, Installers, and Repairers	4,264	966	23
Transportation and Heavy Equipment Operators	4,604	752	16
Engineers, Architects, and Surveyors	1,447	600	41
Construction Trades	3,127	595	19
Natural, Computer, and Mathematical Scientists	647	442	68
Writers, Artists, Entertainers, and Athletes	1,092	425	39
Other Professionals and Paraprofessionals	825	355	43
Lawyers and Judges	457	326	71
Social, Recreational, and Religious Workers	759	235	31
Helpers and Laborers	4,168	205	5
Social Scientists	173	70	40
Precision Production Workers	2,790	61	2
Plant and System Workers	275	36	13
Blue Collar Supervisors	1,442	−6	0
Miners	175	−28	−16
Hand Workers, Assemblers, and Fabricators	2,604	−179	−7
Machine Setters, Operators, and Tenders	5,527	−448	−8
Agriculture, Forestry, and Fisheries	4,480	−538	−12

Workforce 2000, Work and Workers for the 21st Century: Executive Summary. (Washington, D.C.: U.S. Government Printing Office, 1987).

organization, and leadership abilities. Many companies are beginning to interface with schools and colleges to ensure this pool of skilled individuals.

In *Working Woman* Sandroff reports that during the 1987–88 school year, 73 percent of the nation's 83,000 public schools had a working relationship with businesses. Some programs recruit volunteers from the business community to mentor students and prepare them for mainstreaming into the work world.

Workforce 2000 emphasizes, "If every child who reaches the age of 17 between now and the year 2000 could read sophisticated materials, write clearly, speak articulately, and solve complex problems requiring algebra and statistics, . . . U.S.-based companies would reassert historic American leadership in old and new industries. . . ."

Jobs of the future will require more education.

Employers will be looking for better-educated workers. A number of the jobs in the least-skilled job classes are expected to disappear, while high-skilled professions will grow rapidly, as reflected in Figure 20.5. Of all new jobs created from 1984 to 2000, more than half will require some kind of education beyond high school, and almost one-third of those jobs will be filled by college graduates. Currently only 22 percent of all occupations require a college degree. DeVenuta in *The Wall Street Journal* (February 9, 1990) states that within approximately five years job classifications will require postsecondary training for entry-level jobs. The fastest-growing jobs will require more language, math, and reasoning skills.

The biggest job creation categories, in absolute numbers, are expected to be service occupations, administrative support, and marketing and sales. The last two require more than the median level of education.

WHAT SHOULD YOU DO?

Continuing education, communication skills, valuing diversity, and adaptability will help you succeed in the twenty-first century.

You need a personal strategy to navigate the exciting and turbulent times ahead. Education, communication skills, valuing diversity, and adapting to change will become crucial to your success in the twenty-first century.

In a competitive and rapidly changing economy, old skills become outdated and new skills are needed. Because most people after the age of 25 change occupations three times and jobs six times, you must be prepared to learn new skills.

Do not wait for your employer to train you. Take advantage of courses at your community college. Get a degree or certificate. Learn a foreign language. Sign up for any optional training offered by your employer. Become a master of computers—these technological marvels are here to stay, and many future jobs will be tied into their use.

Educate yourself by reading and watching educational television programs. The more you understand about how business operates and what is going on in the world, the more effective you will be as an employee.

Acquire and practice the effective communication skills presented in Chapter 3. As the workplace becomes more complex and fast-paced, these skills will become even more important.

Because our work force will become more diverse, you must learn how to appreciate the cultural diversity it will bring. In the October 1988 issue of *Manage*, Sondra Thiederman suggests tips for managing a multicultural work force. These

FIGURE 20.6 Technological advances have become a part of everyday life.

"Somehow I can't take seriously an anti-technology
diatribe written on a word processor."

Copyright © 1989. Reprinted courtesy of Hoechst and Parade.

recommendations are good for all of us in our personal and professional interactions
with people from other cultures:

1. Accept the fact that diversity exists.
2. Avoid thinking in stereotypes.
3. Show that you respect the culture of others.
4. Avoid projecting your own culture onto others.
5. Expose workers to the mainstream culture.
6. Be yourself.
7. Trust your instincts.
8. Expect the best of all people.

The final and perhaps most important skill is learning to be flexible and to adapt
to change. A thorough discussion of change can be found in Chapter 8. If you have
the ability to change, your options in the twenty-first century will be unlimited.

SUMMARY

The composition of the work force and the dynamics of the economy will
dramatically change in the next century. The work force will diversify, with
women, minorities, and older individuals entering in record numbers throughout this last decade of the twentieth century. In addition, illiteracy is a tremendous problem. Concerns are that future workers will not have the educational
levels necessary to perform the jobs available.

The economy faces several challenges, among them a switch from manufacturing to service, advanced technology, faster gains in productivity, deflation, increased competition, and globalization. To meet these challenges, companies must begin to make changes to address the needs of the diverse work

force, increase quality and productivity, educate and train the work force, and promote diversity.

The new jobs of the twenty-first century will require more skills. To meet the challenges that the future holds, you must obtain all the education possible, practice good communication skills, learn to value diversity, and become adaptable.

KEY TERMS

demographics

service industries

artificial intelligence

inflation

deflation

globalization

common market

multinational corporation

rationalization

entrepreneurship

intrapreneurship

REVIEW QUESTIONS

1. What are the emerging demographics of this country?
2. What are the major forces shaping our economy? Explain their effects.
3. What must this country do to meet the challenges of a changing work force and new economic realities?
4. Which skills will be in demand in the twenty-first century?
5. What can you do to prepare yourself to enter the work force of 2000?

DISCUSSION QUESTIONS

1. Imagine yourself in the year 2001. What job do you expect to be performing? From what age and ethnic groups do you expect your coworkers to be? What types of equipment do you expect to be using?
2. What do you think will happen to the economy if the literacy level of the work force continues to drop?
3. What skills do you need to develop to be a part of the work force of 2000?
4. Are you fluent in another language? Why or why not? What would be the advantages of learning another language?
5. Which of the major forces shaping the economy do you think is the most important? Why?
6. What do you think will happen if the gap between the haves and the have-nots continues to widen?

CASE STUDY 20.1

R.I.P. MANUFACTURING

John, the production manager, wandered down the silent hall of the R.I.P. Manufacturing Company. He and Wilma, the personnel manager, were the last employees left. Everyone else had been laid off, and they would be leaving and locking the doors for the final time this afternoon. He stopped by Wilma's office one last time.

"I just don't understand what happened, Wilma." John said thoughtfully. "I thought those new precision machines would help us improve our quality. We just couldn't compete with the Germans, though. I could never get the product cost down as low as they could. And the quality just wasn't there. You know, I can't blame our customers for buying foreign."

"I know, John," Wilma sighed. "I just couldn't find employees who care about quality. You know, some of those folks simply had no skills. Then, when we finally got them up to speed on the equipment, they would leave. That made keeping the plant running at peak capacity impossible."

1. To what forces did R.I.P. fall victim?
2. What changes would have been necessary to save the company? Is the company responsible? Society? Both?
3. Do you foresee this same fate for other U.S. businesses today? Why or why not?

CASE STUDY 20.2

DIVERSITY DOES IT!

John Johnson, the head research scientist at Alchemy Laboratories, drummed his fingers on the desk impatiently. "Well, I still like Jasper best for the job. I think he'll make a top-flight researcher for our team."

"Oh, come off it, John," replied Phil, the human resources manager. "You just don't want to consider Mai because she's a woman and she's Vietnamese. You know that she has more education and experience than Jasper. She's the best qualified candidate."

"Well, Phil, I just have this thing about Vietnamese," John replied. "You know I served in Viet Nam during the war. I still have nightmares about the whole affair."

"It's your decision, John, but just remember this," Phil said curtly as he rose to leave. "Your department is in real trouble. You haven't come up with a new idea in two years. Jasper won't help you get there. He's not capable. Besides, if you fail to hire Mai, you'll have the EEOC on your back."

1. Why does John not want to hire Mai?
2. What are the possible financial outcomes for Alchemy Laboratories if John fails to hire Mai?
3. What types of problems might occur at the lab if she is hired?
4. What can the company do to make cultural diversity a workable reality?

BIBLIOGRAPHY

"A Nation within a Nation." *Business Week* (September 25, 1989): 144–145.

"A U-Turn in the Road to Riches." *Business Week* (September 25, 1989): 94–95.

"Boomers at Fortysomething." *Business Week* (September 25, 1989): 142–143.

Brickfield, Cyril F. "Managing an Older Work Force." *Manage* (February 1988): 7–9.

Castelli, Jim. "Education Forms Common Bond." *HRMagazine* (June 1990): 46–49.

DeVenuta, Karen. "The Education Gap." *The Wall Street Journal* (February 9, 1990): 5.

"Education Openers." *The Wall Street Journal* (February 9, 1990): R5.

Fix, Janet L. "Corporations See Changes in Women's Expectations." *Houston Chronicle* (March 16, 1990): E8.

"For American Business, a New World of Workers." *Business Week* (September 19, 1988): 112–120.

Fullerton, Howard N., Jr. "Labor Force Projections: 1986 to 2000." *Monthly Labor Review* (September 1987): 19–29.

Gladstone, Rick. "Illiteracy—An Economic Time Bomb." *The Houston Post* (February 21, 1988): D1.

Goddard, Robert W. "The Crisis in Workplace Literacy." *Personnel Journal* (December 1987): 73–81.

Gross, Neil. "Taking on Japan." *Business Week* (November 13, 1989): 111–118.

"How the Next Decade Will Differ." *Business Week* (September 25, 1989): 142–43.

"It's Time to Put Our Money Where Our Future Is." *Business Week* (September 19, 1988): 140–141.

Johnston, William B., and Arnold E. Packer (Project Directors). *Workforce 2000—Work and Workers for the Twenty-First Century*. Indianapolis: Hudson Institute, June 1987.

"Keeping Off the Mommy Track." *Personal Report for the Executive*. New York: National Institute of Business Management, May 16, 1989, 2–3.

Kiernan, Michael, "Best Jobs for the Future." *U.S. News and World Report* (September 25, 1989): 60–62.

King, Thomas R. "Working at Home Has Yet to Work Out." *The Wall Street Journal* (December 22, 1989): B1.

McGee, Lynne F. "Teaching Basic Skills to Workers." *Personnel Journal* (August 1989): 42–47.

Nazario, Sonia L. "Bearing the Brunt." *The Wall Street Journal* (February 9, 1990): R20–21.

Occupational Outlook Handbook, 1988–1989 Edition (Bulletin 2300). Washington, DC: U.S. Department of Labor, Bureau of Labor Statistics, April 1988.

Oran, Daniel, and Jay M. Shafritz. *The MBA's Dictionary*. Reston, VA: Reston Publishing Company, Inc., 1983.

"People Patterns." *The Wall Street Journal* (March 27, 1989): B1.

"Plotting the Gray Lines." *Business Week* (September 25, 1989): 98.

Rich, Spencer. "U.S. Family Income Data Show Asian Americans Outpace Whites." ***Houston Chronicle*** (July 17, 1988): A23.

Sandroff, Ronni. "Why It Won't Be Business as Usual." ***Working Woman*** (January 1990): 58–62.

Sher, Margery Leveen, and Gary Brown. "What to Do with Jenny." ***Personnel Administrator*** (April 1989): 31–41.

"Smart Factories: America's Turn." ***Business Week*** (May 8, 1989): 142–148.

Solomon, Jolie. "Firms Address Workers' Cultural Variety." ***The Wall Street Journal*** (February 10, 1989): B1.

Solomon, Jolie. "Managing." ***The Wall Street Journal*** (September 22, 1989): B1.

Spence, Charles. "Growth Management: Lead, Follow, or Get Out of the Way." ***Community College Week*** (April 2, 1990): 5.

Thiederman, Sondra. "Managing the Foreign-Born Work Force: Keys to Effective Cross-Cultural Motivation." ***Manage*** (October 1988): 26–29.

"The Changing Face of a Restless Nation." ***Business Week*** (September 25, 1989): 92–99.

"The New America." ***Business Week*** (September 25, 1989): 91.

"The Password Is Flexible." ***Business Week*** (November 25, 1989): 152–154.

"Where Did the Cleavers Go?" ***Business Week*** (September 25, 1989): 102.

SUGGESTED READINGS

Davis, Stanley M. ***Future Perfect***. Reading, MA: Addison-Wesley Publishing, Inc., 1987.

GLOSSARY

ABC analysis concentration of decisions where the potential for payoff is greater

Accountability perspective view that businesses are accountable for their actions, with a responsibility to individuals and the general public to be fair and considerate

Accounting function sector of the company that keeps track of the money coming in and leaving the organization

Active listening a conscious effort to listen to both the verbal and nonverbal components of what someone is saying, without prejudging

Ad hoc committee a committee that has a limited life and serves only a one-time purpose

Affirmative action an active effort to improve the employment or educational opportunities of members of minority groups and women. (*Webster's*)

AFL-CIO a combined union of members from the AFL craft unions and the CIO industrial unions that merged in 1955 as a show of strength to improve union bargaining power

Age Discrimination in Employment Act federal legislation that prohibits discrimination against individuals age 40 and over in the workplace

Agency shop an agreement that requires workers to pay union membership dues whether or not they choose to join the union

Aggressive behavior valuing ourselves above others and saying what we feel or think but at the expense of others; attempting to dominate or humiliate; using threats and accusations or trying to show up others; choosing for others; speaking with an air of superiority and in a voice that is demanding and rude

AIDS acquired immunodeficiency syndrome. Rights on the job have been extended to those with AIDS.

Alcohol the most commonly abused drug in the country. Alcohol is a depressant that slows the activity of the brain and spinal cord.

American Federation of Labor (AFL) a craft union formed in 1886, led by Samuel L. Gompers

Amphetamines synthetic nervous system stimulants

Anthropology academic discipline that focuses on the origins and development of various cultures

Arbitration a method used to reach a final decision or ruling in labor-management disputes that enlists the services of an arbitrator whose decision is legally binding to both parties

Arbitrator a professional person whose services are requested by both the union and management to conduct a formal hearing and develop a final decision in a dispute over contract interpretation; the decision is considered legally binding to both parties

Artificial intelligence a process whereby computers are programmed to mimic human intelligence

Assertive behavior using correct etiquette; feeling equal to others; making our own choices; using "I" phrases and other effective communication techniques; appearing calm and confident; having positive self-esteem and being respected by others

Autocratic leadership leadership style that is task-oriented and highly directive and involves close supervision and little delegation

Avoidance conflict resolution by totally refraining from confronting the conflict

Bargaining unit the group of employees whom the union may represent in collective bargaining with management

Behavioral school of management study of management that focused on techniques to motivate workers

Behavioral science approach part of the behavioral school of management that began in the late 1950s and used controlled experiments and other scientific methods to view human behavior in the workplace

Blacklist a list that identified persons whom management perceived as potential troublemakers and that was exchanged among company managers to assure that union organizers were denied employment. Names of labor agitators and any other persons known to be sympathetic to unionizing efforts were placed on this list.

Bona fide occupational qualification (BFOQ) a legitimate defense for an employer to eliminate certain groups of individuals from a job. Employers must show a legitimate business necessity for their action.

Brainstorming group problem-solving technique that involves the spontaneous contribution of ideas from all members of the group

Business agent a union official who helps run the affairs of the union, such as negotiating and administering the agreement, collecting dues, and recruiting new members

Centralized management distribution of power so all major decisions are made by those high up in the organization

Chain of command the direction in which authority is exercised and policies and other information are communicated to lower levels

Change agent person who diagnoses problems, provides feedback, assists in developing strategies, or recommends interventions to benefit the organization as a whole. Also known as an Organization Development practitioner or an OD consultant.

Checkoff a union agreement provision that allows unions to receive dues directly from a worker's paycheck if authorized by the employee's signature on a routinely used form

Chronological resume resume that lists experience in reverse chronological order, listing the most recent employment first. This format is beneficial when an individual has a continuous work history with progressively responsible positions.

Classical organization theory approach begun by Fayol that focuses on management of the organization as a whole. It is part of the classical school of management.

Classical perspective holds that businesses need not feel responsible for social issues and should concentrate on being profitable

Classical school of management study of management that focused on the technical efficiency of work as a way to maximize production

Closed shop a method used by unions to assure union membership that required persons to belong to a bargaining unit prior to being hired and to lose their jobs if they were expelled from the union; abolished by the Taft-Hartley Act

Coaching a method of employee development that closely resembles on-the-job training where a senior experienced and skilled employee helps develop or train a junior employee

Cocaine stimulant derived from the coca leaf or synthesized

Code of ethics list that requires or prohibits specific practices by employees in a particular organization or by all members of a professional group

Coercive power power based on fear and punishment

Cohesiveness degree to which group members are of one mind and act as one body

Collective bargaining a process of negotiations between union representatives and company management representatives to establish a mutual agreement on hours, wages, and working conditions. Both parties are expected to bargain in good faith to reach a mutually acceptable agreement.

Committee type of task group

Common market a group of countries that share trade policies that affect agricultural product limitations, the transportation of goods, tax laws, and import/export quotas

Communication process by which we exchange information through a common system of symbols, signs, or behavior

Communication breakdown the result when a situation exceeds a person's capacity to receive and transmit messages and communication deteriorates or fails

Comparable worth the issue that concerns the differences in salaries paid in traditionally female occupations versus traditionally male occupations

Compensation a defense mechanism by which individuals attempt to relieve feelings of inadequacy or frustration by excelling in other areas

Competition a healthy struggle toward goal accomplishment without interference, even when the goals are incompatible

Compromising a method of conflict resolution that addresses the issue but seldom resolves it to the complete satisfaction of both parties

Conceptual skills administrative or big picture skills; ability to think abstractly and to analyze problems

Conflict disagreement between individuals or groups about goal accomplishment

Conflict resolution the active management of conflict through defining and solving issues between individuals, groups, or organizations

Confrontation conflict resolution by openly exchanging information and actively working through the differences to reach agreement

Congress of Industrial Organizations (CIO) an industrial union formed in 1936, led by John L. Lewis

Consensus a solution that all members of the group involved can support

Context conditions in which something occurs, which can throw light on its meaning

Contract a mutually acceptable written agreement signed by both the union and company representatives that is legally binding and outlines the various terms and conditions of employment agreed upon through collective bargaining

Cooperative counseling method a mutual problem-solving effort involving both parties in exploring and solving issues

Cost-benefit analysis examination of the pros and cons of each proposed solution

Counseling a discussion technique used to assist employees with problems affecting performance on the job

Counselor a person, usually a trained professional or a supervisor, capable of dealing with a wide variety of employee problems

Craft union a union representing skilled workers primarily concerned with training apprentices to be masters of their craft

Creativity thinking process that solves a problem or achieves a goal in an original and useful way; the ability to come up with new and unique solutions to problems

Critical incident technique an appraisal technique in which supervisors record in writing actual incidents of behavior that they observe in employees

Critical norms norms considered essential to the survival and effectiveness of the group as a whole

Critical Path Method (CPM) the critical path is the sequence of activities requiring the longest time for completion. It will show the minimum time to complete the project.

Decentralized management distribution of power so that important decisions are made at a lower level

Decision tree graphic depiction of how alternative solutions lead to various possibilities

Defamation open publication of a false statement tending to harm the reputation of a person

Deflation a fall in costs and a rise in the value of money

Delegated method giving employees the responsibility and authority to effect change

Delegation assigning tasks to subordinates and following up to ensure proper and timely completion

Democratic leadership leadership style, also described as participative, that is usually preferred by modern management and involves showing concern for followers, sharing authority with them, and involving them in decision making and organizational planning

Demographics statistics showing population characteristics about a region or group, such as education, income, age, marital status, or ethnic makeup

Denial a defense mechanism by which a person refuses to believe something that creates anxiety or frustration

Derivative power power obtained from close association with a powerful person

Deviance not conforming to group norms

Directive counseling a method of counseling that involves the counselor's listening to the employee's problem, allowing emotional release, determining an action plan, and advising the employee on what needs to be done

Discrimination a difference in treatment based on a factor other than individual merit

Displacement a defense mechanism by which an individual acts out anger toward a person who does not deserve it but who is a "safe" target

Downward communication communication that begins at higher levels of the organization and flows downward

Emergent leader an informal leader who emerges without formal appointment and can exert as much or more power than the formal leader

Employee assistance program (EAP) a formal company program designed to aid employees with personal problems, such as substance abuse or psychological problems, that affect their job performance

Employee association a group or association of workers from the white-collar and professional sectors of the work force, such as teachers, nurses, public sector employees, business professionals, doctors, lawyers, and clerical workers; seldom engage in collective bargaining activities; historically denied the right to strike

Employment at will a philosophy that states the employee serves at the discretion of an employer and can be terminated at any time and for any reason, even if the employee is performing well

Enabling covering up for or making excuses for the behavior and performance of individuals who are abusing substances, allowing them to continue their disruptive conduct

Entrepreneurship organizing, managing, and assuming the risks of a business enterprise

Equal Employment Opportunity Commission federal agency that regulates employment discrimination in the workplace

Equal Pay Act federal law that requires males and females be paid the same salary provided they perform the same job and have the same experience and education

Essay appraisal an appraisal instrument on which the supervisor writes a paragraph or more concerning employee performance

Esteem needs level of Maslow's hierarchy that includes the need for respect from self and others and that can be met by increased responsibility, recognition for work well done, and merit increases and awards

Ethical dilemmas conflicts of values that arise when our sense of values or social responsibility is questioned internally or challenged externally

Ethics "the study of the general nature of morals and of the specific moral choices to be made by individuals in their relationships with others; a set of moral principles or values" *(American Heritage Dictionary)*

Etiquette "the forms required by good breeding or prescribed by authority to be observed in social or official life" *(Webster's)*; i.e., acting appropriately in social and business situations

Executive Order 12564 executive order that establishes a drug-free federal workplace and a drug testing program for federal employees

Expected interval testing the process of giving drug tests at specific, preannounced times

Expert power power based on having specialized skills, knowledge, or expertise

Fair Labor Standards Act federal legislation that sets the minimum wage, equal pay, overtime, and child labor standards

Federal Drug-Free Workplace Act act that requires federal contractors and grantees who receive more than $25,000 in government business to certify that they will maintain a drug-free workplace

Federal Mediation and Conciliation Service a federal agency that maintains a list of mediators to assist in resolving labor-management disputes

Feedback information given back to a sender that evaluates a message and states what the receiver understood

Finance function sector of the company that helps make decisions about how businesses should be financed

Follower-readiness a worker's desire to achieve, willingness to accept responsibility, ability and experience with the task, and confidence

"For cause" testing drug testing of employees only when they are suspected of being under the influence of drugs or alcohol

Force field analysis a technique used to analyze the complexities of a change and identify the forces that must be altered

Forcing results when two persons or groups reach an impasse and allow an authoritative figure to choose one preference rather than work toward a mutually agreeable solution

Foreign Corrupt Policy Act law requiring companies to operate ethically in their business dealings in other cultures

Formal communication communication that flows up or down the formal organizational structure along the chain of command

Formal group a group designated by the organization to fulfill specific tasks or accomplish certain organizational objectives

Formal leader an individual who is officially given certain rights or authority over other group members and who has a degree of legitimacy granted by the formal group or organization

4 C's of communication reminders to improve writing: complete, concise, correct, conversational/clear

Free rein leadership leadership style, also called laissez-faire or integrative, that allows followers to lead themselves, provides advice or information only when requested, and makes little or no effort to increase productivity or nurture or develop followers

Free rider a person who does not pay union dues but is afforded the same benefits afforded dues-paying members because he or she is a part of the bargaining unit represented by the union

Functional authority authority given to staff personnel to make decisions in their area of expertise and to overrule line decisions

Functional group groups made up of managers and subordinates assigned to certain positions in the organizational hierarchy

Functional resume resume that emphasizes special skills that can be transferred to other areas. This resume is useful for individuals reentering the job market or wanting to change careers.

Globalization making goods and services available worldwide with no national boundaries or trade barriers on where they are sold or where they are produced

Goal objective, target, or end result expected from the completion of tasks, activities, or programs

Grapevine an informal person-to-person means of circulating information or gossip

Graphic rating scale an appraisal instrument that outlines categories on which the employee is rated; the scale for each category can range from unacceptable to superior

Great man theory a theory of leadership based on the belief that certain people are born to become leaders and will emerge in that role when their time comes

Grievance a dispute between labor and management over contract interpretation

Grievance procedure a specifically defined procedure written into the contract outlining the formal steps for resolving contract disputes

Group two or more persons who are aware of one another, interact with one another, and perceive themselves to be a group

Group norms shared values about the kinds of behaviors that are acceptable or unacceptable to the group

Groupthink process of deriving negative results from group decision-making efforts as a result of in-group pressures

Hallucinogens drugs that produce chemically induced hallucinations

Halo effect a process by which an individual assumes that another's traits are all positive because one trait is positive

Hawthorne effect the idea that the human element is more important to productivity than the technical or physical aspects of the job. The effect was identified through experiments conducted by Mayo.

Health the role of the working environment in the development of diseases such as cancer and black lung

Hear to perceive sound with our ears

Herzberg's two-factor theory of motivation a popular theory of motivation that says two sets of factors or conditions influence the behavior of individuals at work: one set to satisfy and the other to motivate

Hidden agenda topics that meeting attendees wish to discuss that have no relevance to the purpose of the current meeting

Horizontal communication communication that occurs between individuals at the same level in an organization

Human relations study of relationships among people

Human relations approach part of the behavioral school of management that emphasized the human effect of productivity

Human relations skills ability to deal effectively with people through communicating, listening, being empathetic, inspiring and motivating, being perceptive, and using fair judgment

Human resources function sector of the company responsible for hiring, training, setting salaries and benefits, and monitoring employees in the organization

Hybrid resume resume that combines the format of functional and chronological resumes

Hygiene factors factors identified by Herzberg that are necessary to maintain a reasonable level of satisfaction, such as working conditions, job security, quality of supervision, and interpersonal relationships on the job

Incubation stage of the creative process that is mysterious and below the surface and involves reviewing ideas and information

Industrial union a union representing primarily unskilled or semiskilled industrial workers

Inflation a rise in the costs of goods and services with a fall in the value of a country's currency

Influence ability to change the attitude or behavior of an individual or group

Informal communication communication that does not follow the chain of command

Informal group a group created to satisfy the needs of individual members that are not satisfied by formal groups

Informal leader a person within the group who is able to influence other group members because of age, knowledge, technical skills, social skills, personality, or physical strength

Information Age the current economic era, characterized by increasingly large and complex organizations, advanced technology, and the computer

Information overload an inability to continue processing and remembering information because of the great amount coming at us at one time

Inhalants hydrocarbon-containing substances that are inhaled for their intoxicating effects

Innovation the end product of creative activity

Inspiration the "aha" stage of the creative process; when solutions break through to conscious thought

Integrity strict adherence to a code of behavior

Interview process by which the prospective employer learns more about you and evaluates whether you are the best qualified candidate for the position

Intrapreneurship the conscious effort of organizations to identify and support employees who wish to pursue an entrepreneurial idea for a new product or service

Job design/redesign a method of bringing about change within the organization aimed directly at the tasks performed by individuals

Job enlargement increasing the complexity of a job by adding similar tasks to those already being performed

Job enrichment building greater responsibility and interest into task assignments

Job rotation shifting employees from one job to another in hopes of reducing boredom and stimulating renewed interest in job performance

Job-seeking skills skills that assist us in finding employment

Johari Window model that helps us understand our relationships with others; panes represent parts of us known or not known to ourselves and others

Labor agitator influential person capable of rallying workers toward unionizing

Laissez-faire leadership leadership style, also called free rein or integrative, that allows followers to lead themselves, provides advice or information only when requested, and makes little or no effort to increase productivity or nurture or develop followers

Landrum-Griffin Act a federal law enacted in 1959 that requires unions to disclose the sources and disbursements of their funds, hold regularly scheduled elections by secret ballot, and restricts union officials from using union funds for personal means; intended as a means of control over possible corruption in union activities and misuse of union funds

Leadership the process of influencing the activities of individuals or organized groups so that they follow and do willingly what the leader wants them to do

Leadership style pattern of behavior exhibited by a leader

Legitimate power power derived from formal rank or position within an organizational hierarchy

Life cycles stages of a business, consisting of start-up, expansion and growth, stability, decline, and phase-out or revitalization

Line and staff structure a complex organization structure in which the line (production employees) are given support by staff in such areas as law and safety

Listen to make a conscious effort to hear something and to interpret it using reason and understanding

Lockout an anti-union technique used by company management whereby the company locks the doors and shut down factory operations to avoid worker demands for improved conditions

Management use of resources to accomplish a goal; may be nonbehavioral

Management by Objectives (MBO) a method and philosophy of management that emphasizes self-determination and allows employees to participate in setting their own goals

Management science school of management branch of management that began after World War II and was used to solve complex management problems. The computer has played an important part in this school.

Managerial Grid® leadership theory developed by Blake and Mouton that uses a grid to plot the degree to which leaders show concern for people and concern for production

Marijuana drug derived from the dried leaves and flowering tops of the pistillate hemp plant

Marketing and sales function sector of the company responsible for determining consumer needs and selling the company's products or services to the consumer

Maslow's hierarchy of needs motivation theory that recognizes five levels of needs. Individuals are motivated by the needs within each specific level. When these needs are met, individuals are no longer motivated by that level and move upward.

Matrix structure a complex organization structure that uses groups of people with expertise in their individual areas who are temporarily assigned full or part time to a project from other parts of the organization

McClelland's acquired needs theory a motivational theory that states that through upbringing individuals acquire a strong desire for one of three primary needs—achievement, affiliation, and power

Mediation a method of resolving a deadlocked dispute that enlists the services of a mediator

Mediator a person viewed as an unbiased third party whose services are requested to assist in resolving difficult or deadlocked labor-management disputes

Medium the form in which a message is communicated

Mentor an experienced person who will give you objective career advice. A senior-level manager or retired professional with political savvy and an interest in helping employees achieve both career goals and the objectives of the organization.

Mentoring a popular form of coaching on a personal level with the emphasis on help-

ing employees develop to their fullest potential

Message the content of the communication sent or received; may be verbal, nonverbal, or written

Motivation needs or drives within individuals that energize behaviors

Motivational factors factors identified by Herzberg that build high levels of motivation, such as achievement, advancement, recognition, responsibility, and the work itself

Motivational source fields forces that motivate; can be outside, inside, or early

Multinational corporation a company that has goods and services based in several countries and requires business planning and marketing strategies to fit global operations rather than narrow domestic ones

Narcotics drugs that are derivatives of the opium poppy

National Labor Relations Board (NLRB) a government agency responsible for enforcing the provisions of the Wagner Act, established in 1935

Negotiation discussion that leads to a decision acceptable to all involved

Networking (1) process whereby you give and receive moral support, career guidance and important information by developing contacts with people in your place of employment and in professional organizations. (2) Method of finding employment that involves telling all individuals you know that you are seeking a job and asking them to contact you if they hear of any openings.

Nondirective counseling a method of counseling viewed as a mutual problem-solving effort involving both parties in exploring and solving issues

Nonverbal communication meaning conveyed through the body, the voice, or position

Norris-LaGuardia Act a federal law enacted in 1932 to abolish the use of yellow-dog contracts by companies as an anti-union technique

Occupational Safety and Health Act federal legislation that sets safety and health standards and ensures that they are observed in the workplace

Occupational Safety and Health Administration (OSHA) federal agency that regulates safety and health in the workplace

"Offer and refusal technique" suggestion that men continue to offer manners they were taught while women accept those they consider proper and decline those they would rather not have

Official goals formally stated, abstract goals that are developed by upper management

Ongoing committee a committee that is relatively permanent, addressing organizational issues on a standing or continuous basis

One-way communication communication that takes place with no feedback from the receiver

Operational goals concrete and close-ended goals that are the responsibility of first-line supervisors and employees

Operative goals goals that are developed by middle management and are more specific than official goals

Optimists persons who always look on the positive side of situations

Organizational culture a mix of the beliefs and values of society at large, the individuals who work in the organization, and the organization's leaders and founders

Organizational development a holistic approach to organizational change involving the entire organization—its people, structures, culture, policies and procedures, and purpose

Overachiever individual who takes on unattainable goals

Participative method a method of implementing organizational change that uses employee groups in the problem-solving and decision-making processes preceding the actual change

Passive behavior the valuing of ourselves below others; lack of self-confidence while speaking; wanting to be liked and trying to please others; and avoiding unpleasant situations and confrontation

Passive power power source that stems from a display of helplessness

Perception (1) way in which we interpret, or give meaning to, sensations or messages; (2) the first stage in the creative process requiring that we view objects or situations differently

Perceptual defense mechanisms mechanisms individuals use to handle anxiety

Performance appraisal a measurement of how well an employee is doing on the job

Peripheral norms norms that, if violated, are not perceived as damaging to the group and its members

PERT chart graphic technique for planning projects in which a great number of tasks must be coordinated (Program Evaluation and Review Technique)

Pessimists persons who always look on the negative side of situations

Physiological needs a level of Maslow's hierarchy of needs that includes the desire for food, sleep, water, sex, shelter, and other physiological drives

Planned agenda an outline or list of what topics are to be discussed or what is to be accomplished during a meeting

Planning an attempt to prepare for and predict the future; it involves goals, programs, policies, rules, and procedures

PODSCORB an acronym for the functional abilities required of leaders—planning, organizing, directing, staffing, coordinating, reporting, and budgeting

Power the ability to influence others to do what we want them to do even if we are not a formal leader

Power-compulsive power personality with a lust for power; seldom satisfied with the amount of power achieved

Power politics developing opportunities for success

Power positioning conscientious use of techniques designed to position an individual for maximum personal growth and gain in an effort to develop power

Power-positive power personality that genuinely enjoys responsibility and thrives on the use of power

Power-shy power personality that tends to avoid being placed in positions that require overt use of power

Power symbols physical traits, personality characteristics, and external physical factors that are associated with those who are perceived to be powerful

Pregnancy Discrimination Act federal law that prohibits discrimination against pregnant women in the workplace

Primary groups groups made up of family members and close friends

Primary needs basic needs required to sustain life comfortably, such as food, water, air, sex, sleep, and shelter

Proactive management management that is characterized by looking ahead, anticipating problems, and determining solutions to potential problems before they develop

Problem disturbance or unsettled matter that requires a solution if the organization or person is to function effectively

Problem-solving teams groups of 5 to 12 volunteers from different areas of a department who meet once or twice a week to discuss ways of improving quality, efficiency, or work conditions

Procrastination the intentional putting off or delaying of activities that need to be done

Production function the sector of an organization that actually produces goods or performs services

Program Evaluation and Review Techniques (PERT) a model used by managers to plan and control work

Projection a defense mechanism whereby individuals attribute unacceptable thoughts or feelings about themselves to others

Protocol business, diplomatic, or military etiquette

Psychology academic discipline that focuses on the behavior of individuals

Public perspective view that links businesses with the government and other groups to actively solve social and environmental problems

Pyramidal hierarchy triangular shape of an organization with the single head of the organization at the top. Smaller pyramids appear within the larger.

Quality circle committee of 6 to 15 employees who meet regularly to examine and suggest solutions to common problems of quality

Random interval testing the process of giving drug tests to employees at varying and unannounced times

Rationalization (1) a defense mechanism by which a person explains away a problem; (2) a planning process used by organizations for buying supplies from countries that produce them at the lowest prices and then selling the finished product wherever the highest price can be obtained

Reactive management management characterized by being caught off guard and moving from one crisis to the next

Realistic achiever individual who sets challenging but attainable goals

Receiver one to whom a message is transmitted; one who receives the message

Reference individual who can vouch for your performance and character

Referent power power based on respect or admiration

Regression a defense mechanism whereby a person retreats to an earlier behavior pattern

Relationship behavior leader behavior with people; the extent to which the leader is supportive of followers and engages in two-way communication with them

Repression a defense mechanism by which an individual cannot remember an unpleasant event

Resume sales tool designed to assist in obtaining an interview

Reverse halo effect a process by which an individual assumes that another's traits are all negative because one trait is negative

Reward power power based on the ability to give something of material or personal value to others

Right-to-work law a provision of the Taft-Hartley Act that allows states to prohibit both the closed and the union shop contract agreements, thereby giving the worker the choice of union membership

Role ambiguity confusion that occurs when individuals are uncertain about what role they are to fill or what is expected of them

Roles differing parts that individuals play in their lives

Safety absence of hazards that can result in a direct injury

Safety and security needs a level of Maslow's hierarchy of needs that reflects the desire for physical, economic, and emotional security, such as safe working conditions, job security, and periodic salary increases

Sanctions actions taken to force compliance with established norms

Scapegoating a defense mechanism that relieves anxiety by blaming other persons or groups for problems

Scientific management theory approach begun by Taylor and enhanced by the Gilbreths that focuses on the work itself. It is part of the classical school of management.

Secondary groups groups made up of fellow workers or social acquaintances

Secondary needs needs that include security, affiliation or love, respect, and autonomy; developed as a result of an individual's values and beliefs

Sedatives depressants that can cause drowsiness, agitation, intellectual confusion, and impairment

Self-actualization needs a level of Maslow's hierarchy that includes the need for personal growth, freedom of creative expression, and using one's abilities to the full extent

Self-disclosure revealing information to others about yourself

Self-esteem feelings about yourself that can be high or low

Self-managing teams groups of 5 to 15 employees who produce an entire product in a truly entrepreneurial sense

Self-talk making positive statements to ourselves

Semantics the study of the meanings and the changing meanings of words

Sender person who transmits, or sends, the message

Service industries industries that create economic value without creating a tangible product, as opposed to manufacturing, agriculture, and other goods-producing industries

Sexual harassment unwelcome sexual advances, requests for sexual favors, or verbal or physical conduct of a sexual nature found in the workplace

Situational leadership leadership theory developed by Hersey that says leadership style must be adapted to the situation and the readiness of subordinates

Smoothing conflict resolution by playing down strong issues, concentrating on mutual interests, and seldom discussing negative issues

Social needs a level of Maslow's hierarchy that centers around the desire for meaningful affiliation with others, such as love, affection, and acceptance

Social responsibility obligation we have to make choices or decisions that are beneficial to the whole of society; involves issues such as environmental pollution and welfare

Social Security Act federal legislation that mandates retirement, survivors', disability, and Medicare benefits

Sociology academic discipline that focuses on the interaction of two or more individuals and their relationships in group settings

Span of control number of people that an individual supervises

Special-purpose teams groups of worker and union representatives collaborating to improve quality and productivity

Statistical models mathematical models that assist managers with planning and controlling factors such as inventory, product mixes, and sales forecasts

Strategic planning the systematic setting of organizational goals, defining strategies and policies to achieve them, and developing detailed plans to ensure that the strategies are implemented

Stress the physical state of the body in response to environmental pressures that produce emotional discomfort

Strike the majority of the union membership's refusal to work under the current conditions until some agreement can be reached toward the desired improvement

Sublimation a defense mechanism by which an individual finds a socially acceptable way to act out feelings

Substance abuse the misuse of alcohol, illegal drugs, and prescription drugs

Synergism interaction of two or more independent parts, the effects of which are greater than they would attain separately

Taft-Hartley Act a series of amendments to the Wagner Act that imposes controls on unions' organizing activities and methods used in collective bargaining attempts

Task behavior the extent to which a leader directs and supervises a task

Task group a group formed for a specific reason with members drawn from various parts of an organization to accomplish a specific purpose

Team a number of persons associated together in work or activity; representatives from a variety of different disciplines, departments, or different lines of business coming together to achieve common goals and objectives

Teambuilding a series of activities designed to help work groups solve problems, accomplish work goals, and more effectively function through teamwork

Teamwork the combined effort of several disciplines for maximum effectiveness in achieving common goals

Technical skills skills required to perform a particular task

Theory X and Y two sets of assumptions that leaders hold about followers, as outlined by Douglas McGregor; Theory X is a pessimistic view and Theory Y an optimistic view

Time management using the time available to the greatest advantage

Title VII of the Civil Rights Act of 1964 federal law that prohibits discrimination based on race, color, religion, sex, or national origin in the workplace. This law also prohibits sexual harassment.

Tranquilizers depressants that can cause drowsiness, agitation, intellectual confusion, and impairment

Transactional leadership leadership in which leaders determine what followers need to achieve their own and organizational goals, classify those needs, and help followers gain confidence that they can reach their objectives

Transformational leadership leadership that motivates followers to do more than they originally expected to do by raising the perceived value of the tasks, by getting them to transcend self-interest for the sake of the group goal, and by raising their need level to self-actualization

Triangle situation in which a person having a problem with a third person places the responsibility for solving the problem on you

Two-way communication communication in which feedback is received

Type A personalities persons who tend to be highly competitive, aggressive, achievement-oriented, and impatient and typically appear pressured, hurried, and volatile

Type B personalities persons who tend to be relaxed, easygoing, and even-paced in their approach to life

"Understanding strategy" suggestion that once people know someone's preferences regarding business protocol, they will comply with them

Underachiever individual who sets goals that are lower than abilities in order to protect himself from risk and anxiety

Unemployment compensation benefits paid to those who have become unemployed involuntarily

Unilateral method a method of implementing organizational change that allows supervisors to dictate change with little or no input from the employees

Union a group or association of workers who collectively bargain with employers for improved working conditions and protection from unfair or arbitrary treatment by management

Union shop a method used by unions to assure union membership that required an employee to join the union within a specified time after being hired, usually within 60 to 90 days

Union steward a union official who represents union members' interests and protects their rights while on the job; acts as a go-between representing the union member to the company supervisor in settling disagreements

Upward communication communication that begins in the lower levels of the organization and goes to higher levels

Upward management process by which individuals manage their bosses

Values principles, standards, or qualities considered worthwhile or desirable

Verbal communication any message sent or received through the use of words, oral or written

Verification last stage of the creative process; testing, evaluating, revising, re-testing, and reevaluating an idea

Visualization a thought process by which you view yourself as being successful

Vroom's expectancy theory a theory that views motivation as a process of choices and says people behave in certain ways based on their expectation of results

Wagner Act a federal law enacted in 1935 that ordered management to stop interfering with union organizing efforts and defined what constituted unfair labor practices; established the right of employees to form unions and collectively bargain with management on employment issues; established the National Labor Relations Board

Wellness program a total approach to employee health and well-being that addresses emotional and physical health

Whistleblowing opposing decisions, policies, or practices within the organization if they are considered detrimental or illegal; can include publicizing such behavior outside the organization

Win-win situation the result when negotiation is handled in such a way that both sides of an issue feel they have won

Workaholics persons who are consumed by their jobs and derive little pleasure from other activities

Workers' compensation compensation to those who have been physically or mentally injured on the job

Yellow-dog contract contract requiring would-be employees to sign a statement that they will not join a union

INDEX

H

Hall, E. T., 62
Hallett, Jeffrey, 19
Hallucinogens, 324
Halo effect, 26
Handicapping conditions, AIDS as, 288
Happiness, It's Your Choice (Applegate), 118
Harassment, and deviance from norms, 82, *See also* Sexual harassment
Harris, Louis, 420
Hatch Act, 287
Hawthorne effect, 9, 74
Health and Human Services, U.S. Department of, 418
Health education programs, 422
Health Research Institute, 408
Health standards, 275
Hearing versus listening, 51
Hensley, Wayne, 217
Hersey, Paul, 189
Herzberg, Frederick, 121
Hidden agenda, 415
Hidden area, Johari window, 28
Hierarchy
pyramidal, structural flow in, 98
structure, and team effectiveness, 257
Hierarchy of needs theory, 118–120
Hoerr, John, 308
Horgan, John, 322
Horizontal communication, 103
Houston Chronicle, 192, 193, 309, 420, 433
Houston Post, The, 130, 217, 357, 365
Hudson Institute, 428
Human behavioral goals, and needs, 117
Human capital, 441–443
Human relations, 9, 19
defined, 3–4
skills for good, 194–195
Human Relations of Organizations, The (Berkman and Neider), 89
Human resources, 13
Human Side of Enterprise, The (McGregor), 187, 258
Humor, 67
and communication, 66

Hybrid resume, 384
Hygiene factors in motivation, 121

I

Icahn, Carl, 339
Illegal activities, sanctions for reporting, 290
Image
and appearance, 50
and communications, 67
and conformance, 33
and etiquette, 358–359
and grapevine communication, 105
professional, 29–30
Imagination and creativity, 235
Immigration Reform and Control Act (IRCA), 286–287
Improper questions in an interview, 395–396
Inc. magazine, 131
Income gap, 430
Incubation stage of creativity, 237
Individuals
behavior in groups, 80–81
power needs and responses, 210–211
Industrial Era, 6
Industrial unions, 303
Inflation, 436
Influence, 185
and leadership, 185
and power, 220
and power compared, 206
Informal communication, 104–105
Informal groups, 77–78
norms communicated in, 84
Informal leader, 78–79
Information
and communication, 45
coordination on teams, 254
for problem identification, 226
structural flow of, 98
Information Age, 6
Information overload, 51, 244
and problem solving, 240–241
Ingham, Harry, 27
Inhalants, 324